# OUTLINE OF HINDI GRAMMAR

# OUTLINE OF HINDI GRAMMAR

*with exercises*

Second Edition

BY

R. S. McGregor

DELHI
OXFORD UNIVERSITY PRESS
BOMBAY CALCUTTA MADRAS
1977

*Oxford University Press*

OXFORD LONDON GLASGOW NEW YORK
TORONTO MELBOURNE WELLINGTON CAPE TOWN
IBADAN NAIROBI DAR ES SALAAM LUSAKA ADDIS ABABA
KUALA LUMPUR SINGAPORE JAKARTA HONG KONG TOKYO
DELHI BOMBAY CALCUTTA MADRAS KARACHI



*First published 1972*
*Second edition 1977*
*published by arrangement with*
*Oxford University Press, Oxford*

Printed in India
by G. D. Makhija at India Offset Press, New Delhi 27
and published by R. Dayal, Oxford University Press
2/11 Ansari Road, Daryaganj, New Delhi 2

# PREFACE

THIS book is a revision of an *Outline of Hindi Grammar* which has been used in mimeographed form by my students over the past ten years. Many of these students, at London and Cambridge Universities, have been taking degrees in which the study of Hindi and its literature forms a major part; they required an adequate but concise presentation of the essential grammar of the language, with exercises, which would bring them as quickly as possible to the point where they could start the reading of modern Hindi prose texts with profit. Others had already worked through Hindi courses in which the chief emphasis was on conversation, but had done relatively little work with the written language. For different reasons both these types of student have found the *Outline* useful, and I have been asked for copies of it by a number of teachers at other universities. It therefore seemed desirable to publish it, keeping as close to the original, tried version as possible, and adding whatever extra material appeared necessary.

The book presupposes no knowledge of the language. The student should read through the introductory section before proceeding to the Lessons and Exercises. He should try to master the script as soon as possible. The transliteration used will allow him to work through the Lessons without being impeded by script problems, however, and will probably assist him throughout the entire period he is using the book. It is assumed that he will usually have the help of a Hindi speaker with pronunciation and the provision of phrase and sentence drills and suitable conversation material as he progresses; he should spend several hours a week if possible working with a native speaker or in the language laboratory. (It should be possible to use the book without access to a native speaker, but an effort should be made to obtain suitable tapes or records as quickly as possible.) On completing the Lessons and Exercises, the student should work through the Supplement and, as a revision of this, attempt the Reading Passages. With a good grasp of all this material he should be able to start reading modern Hindi literary prose very largely on his own, and to write the language correctly at a simple level. The Composition Passages have been added as a further exercise in control of grammar and idiom. The student could well delay attempting these until he has read two or three short stories on his own and begun to consolidate his grasp of grammar and command of simple spoken language.

It will be clear from the above that my aim has been to include most of what the student needs to know in the early stages of his study of Hindi and of what he needs to have accessible for easy reference while consolidating his grasp of the language. I hope that I shall be found to have struck a fair balance between inclusions and omissions of material. It should hardly be necessary to add that the material has been organized with the requirements of students in mind, and that its presentation inevitably differs, in varying degrees in different sections of the book, from that which might be expected in a reference grammar. I have added as an appendix a short list of some recent works on aspects of Hindi grammar which the student interested in grammatical questions may eventually wish to consult, and in which he will find references to other books and articles on the subject.

*Acknowledgements*

It is a pleasure to acknowledge my indebtedness in preparing this book to Dr. Yamuna Kachru, who commented on the text and examples of the original *Outline* in 1961 and on a draft of the third section of the Introduction in 1969, and wrote draft translations of four of the Composition Passages; to Dr. Lakshmisagar Varshneya, Professor of Hindi in the University of Allahabad, who commented on the Exercises, Key, Composition Passages, and many examples of the revised version in 1967; to Mr. A. S. Kalsi and Mr. J. N. Tiwari for comments on many points during the final revision; to Shri Upendranath Ashk for permission to use extracts from his novel *Baṛī baṛī āṁkheṁ*; to my students; and finally to my wife, for her great but unseen contribution to the production of the book.

# PREFACE TO SECOND EDITION

Collected Hindi-English and English-Hindi Vocabularies have been added for the student's convenience, and some corrections made. Otherwise the first edition is reprinted unchanged.

June 1976 R. S. M.

# CONTENTS

# ABBREVIATIONS

| | | | |
|---|---|---|---|
| adj. | adjective | m. | masculine |
| adv. | adverb | n. | note |
| Ar. | Arabic | obl. | oblique |
| conj. | conjunction | P. | Persian |
| dir. | direct | pl. | plural |
| f. | feminine | pron. | pronoun |
| H. | Hindi | sg. | singular |
| interj. | interjection | Skt. | Sanskrit |
| intr. | intransitive | trans. | transitive |

---

Square brackets are used to indicate a few common alternative forms or spellings given in vocabularies.

# INTRODUCTION

## MODERN STANDARD HINDI, AND ITS LOANWORDS

WRITTEN Hindi, based on the *Khaṛī Bolī* dialect spoken to the north and east of Delhi, is relatively standardized over the whole of the Hindi language area (the area within which Hindi is the predominant language of administration and public life). One may thus speak of a written 'modern standard Hindi'. Furthermore, educated persons throughout the Hindi language area are able to conform to a large degree in their speech to the norm of *Khaṛī Bolī* grammatical usage and pronunciation, which can to this extent be called a spoken 'modern standard Hindi' usage and pronunciation. However, considerable variations can occur, especially if the speakers' native dialects are related only rather distantly to *Khaṛī Bolī.* This is particularly true of pronunciation, and as a result there cannot really be said to be any one 'standard' pronunciation of the standard language. Uneducated persons outside the *Khaṛī Bolī* area normally have little knowledge of *Khaṛī Bolī.* The forms used in this book are all of the *Khaṛī Bolī* dialect as used by educated persons very largely throughout the Hindi language area, but especially by those brought up in the western part of it.

During the Muslim period many Arabic and Persian loanwords found their way into Hindi dialects, especially into *Khaṛī Bolī.* Those that denote common objects or ideas are usually fully acclimatized in modern standard Hindi. More formal, literary Arabic and Persian loanwords (corresponding in style roughly to the *higher* range of Latinate vocabulary in English) are usually restricted to that form of Persianized *Khaṛī Bolī* known as *Urdū*, which is used chiefly in Muslim society or by persons familiar to some extent with that society. Almost no words of the latter kind are used in this book.

In addition to its Persian and Arabic loanwords, modern Hindi has loanwords of Sanskrit origin, either borrowings direct from Sanskrit or new formations on Sanskrit words. The more literary of these are restricted very largely to the written language, but increasing use is being made of simpler loanwords of Sanskrit origin in the spoken language.

Modern Hindi usage does not generally favour the use of Persian and Arabic loanwords in more formal contexts if equivalent words of Hindi origin, or loanwords of Sanskrit origin, are also generally current and can be used instead of them. As a result, Persian and Arabic loanwords for which such equivalents are current are more closely restricted to informal use than other Persian and Arabic loanwords. Persian and Arabic loanwords whose use is restricted in this way have been marked for the student's convenience with † in the vocabularies and notes, and in some cases in the text of Lessons.[1] Loanwords of Sanskrit origin that are predominantly restricted to the written language or to more formal spoken use are similarly marked with *.

English loanwords are, of course, also frequent in Hindi, often competing with Sanskrit, Persian and Arabic loanwords, or words of Hindi origin.

## THE SOUND SYSTEM OF HINDI[2]

The following outline description of the sounds of Hindi will assist the student to articulate and to distinguish them. Continuous practice and attention to the pronunciation of a native speaker are essential.

### 1. *Vowels*

*a*

A low-mid or mid central unrounded vowel, similar to the first, de-stressed vowel in the English verb *subject*, or to the vowel in English *but*, articulated with the lips somewhat closer together than in southern standard English.

*ā*

A low central unrounded vowel, similar to the first vowel in English *father* (but in southern standard English pronunciation the vowel *ā* is articulated further back in the mouth than is the case with Hindi *ā*).

*i*

A quite high front unrounded vowel, rather like the vowel in English

[1] For instance, the word †*aurat* 'woman', of Arabic origin, which co-exists in Hindi with the common Sanskrit loanword *strī* and belongs characteristically to informal usage. A word such as *imārat* 'building', although also of Arabic origin, has no very commonly used equivalent of Sanskrit or Hindi origin and as a result is not restricted as specifically as †*aurat* to informal use, and so goes unmarked in the vocabulary.

The question of how definitely a given Persian or Arabic loanword is restricted to informal use is of course one of opinion. The mark † has been used fairly sparingly, i.e. only with words about whose restriction to informal use there can be no real question. Some users of Hindi would restrict a greater proportion of Persian and Arabic loanwords to informal use than that indicated in this book.

[2] A number of sounds of relatively rare occurrence are not mentioned in this section. Those which will concern the student particularly are mentioned at suitable places elsewhere.

*sit* in southern standard English pronunciation. (In some pronunciations of English the vowel *i* is articulated rather lower in the mouth than is the case with Hindi *i*.)

Many speakers of Hindi often employ a higher, tenser, somewhat longer pronunciation of this vowel than that indicated here (in which it is less distinct from the following vowel, *ī*).

*ī*

A high front unrounded vowel, similar to the vowel in English *seat* in southern standard English pronunciation. (In some pronunciations of English the vowel *ī* is articulated lower in the mouth and more laxly than is the case with Hindi *ī*.)

*u*

A quite high back rounded vowel, rather like the vowel in English *put* in southern standard English pronunciation, though tending to be slightly higher. (In some pronunciations of English the vowel *u* is articulated distinctly lower in the mouth than is the case with Hindi *u*.)

Many speakers of Hindi often employ a higher, tenser, somewhat longer pronunciation of this vowel than that indicated here (in which it is less distinct from the following vowel, *ū*).

*ū*

A high back rounded vowel, rather like the vowel in English *food* in southern standard English pronunciation, but with slightly less lip rounding than this vowel sometimes receives in that pronunciation. (In some pronunciations of English the vowel *ū* is articulated with much less lip rounding than is the case with Hindi *ū*.)

*e*

A high-mid front unrounded vowel, similar to the first vowel in German *geben* or French *été*. This sound does not occur as a single vowel in most pronunciations of English, but is similar to the first component of the diphthong heard in the southern standard English pronunciation of the word *play*. Most English speakers need to take special care not to pronounce a diphthong for *e*.

*o*

A high-mid back rounded vowel, similar to the vowel in German *Sohn* or French *beau*. This sound does not occur as a single vowel in most pronunciations of English, but is similar to the first component of the diphthong heard in Scottish or American pronunciations of the word *go*. Most English speakers need to take special care not to pronounce a diphthong for *o*.

*ai*

The sound represented by the digraph *ai* is frequently a low to low-mid front unrounded vowel, rather like the vowel in English *had* in southern standard English pronunciation, but tending often to be pronounced with a slightly higher point of articulation (as in many other pronunciations of the word *had*). The student is recommended to adopt this monophthongal type of pronunciation, which is fairly normal in the western part of the Hindi language area. Elsewhere a diphthongal pronunciation of the sound is common (Hindi *a* + short *e* usually; sometimes *a* + *i*).

*au*

The sound represented by the digraph *au* is frequently a low-mid to mid back rounded vowel, somewhat like the vowel in English *nod* in southern standard English pronunciation, but rather longer, and tending usually to be pronounced with a slightly higher point of articulation. The student is recommended to adopt this monophthongal type of pronunciation, which is fairly normal in the western part of the Hindi language area. Elsewhere a diphthongal pronunciation of the sound is common (Hindi *a* + short *o* usually; sometimes *a* + *u*).

*Vowel nasality*

All vowels may be pronounced with or without nasality. The articulation of a vowel generally does not change when it is nasalized; note particularly that nasalized *ā̃* does not have the value of French nasalized [ã] in *enfant*, which shows low back, not low central, vowels. The point of articulation of *e* and *o*, however, tends to be slightly lowered when these vowels are nasalized.

2. *Consonants*

(*a*) *The voiceless unaspirated plosives k, ṭ, t, p; affricate c*

*k*

Velar plosive, similar to unaspirated *k* in English *skin* (but not to *k* in most English speakers' pronunciation of *kin*, *king*, etc., which is aspirated).

*ṭ*

Retroflex plosive; the closest English equivalent is the unaspirated *t* in *steam*, *stop*, etc. The tongue tip is retroflexed so that its underside touches the roof of the mouth, usually further back than in the case of English *t* (in which the tip touches the alveolum or ridge behind the teeth). Note that *t* in most English speakers' pronunciation of *team*, *top*, etc., is aspirated, and is not a good model for the articulation of Hindi *ṭ*.

*t*

Dental plosive, in which the tongue tip touches the teeth, not the ridge behind the teeth. This articulation of *t* is common in English before a word beginning with a dental fricative, e.g. in the sequence *at the* . . . It is most important that the student should master the pronunciation of *t* and other dental sounds in Hindi and distinguish them from the corresponding retroflexes.

*p*

Bilabial plosive, similar to unaspirated *p* in English *spin* (but not to *p* in most English speakers' pronunciation of *pin*, *pat*, etc., which is aspirated).

*c*

Pre-palatal affricate; the closest English equivalent is *ch* in *church*, etc., but Hindi *c* has minimum aspiration, and is more tense in articulation than English *ch*. The student will be helped to avoid aspiration by keeping the tongue tip down in the mouth, behind the bottom teeth, and trying to say *ty* rather than *ch*.

(*b*) *The voiceless aspirated plosives kh, ṭh, th, ph; affricate ch*

These aspirated consonants correspond to the above five unaspirated consonants. Their pronunciation will give no difficulty to most English speakers, except that *ṭh* and *th* must be carefully distinguished. The bilabial plosive *ph* is very frequently replaced by a bilabial fricative (in which the lips are very slightly parted from the beginning of articulation of the sound).

(*c*) *The voiced unaspirated plosives g, ḍ, d, b; affricate j*

*g*

Velar plosive; as English *g* in the word *go*.

*ḍ, d*

Retroflex and dental plosives, distinguished like *ṭ* and *t*, above.

*b*

Bilabial plosive; as English *b*.

*j*

Pre-palatal affricate; similar to English *j*, but with a more tense articulation than that which is often shown by this sound. The student may produce a more Indian *j* by keeping the tongue tip down in the mouth and trying to say *dy* rather than *j*.

(*d*) *The voiced aspirated plosives gh, ḍh, dh, bh; affricate jh*

These sounds are difficult for non-Indian (and some Indian) learners of Hindi. The difficulty is to keep both plosive and aspiration voiced, (accompanied by vibration of the vocal chords), and at the same time to avoid allowing a vowel to intervene between them, i.e. to avoid saying either *khar* or *gahar* for *ghar*, etc. Constant practice of these sounds is necessary. It may be helpful at first to try repeating the sound-group *hāg-hāg-hāg* as quickly as possible, when *h* will probably coalesce with preceding *g* as voiced rather than voiceless aspiration (similarly with *hāj*, *hāḍ*, etc.).

Voiced aspirates before consonants and at the end of words tend to show reduced aspiration; thus *ghar* has more aspiration than *samajhnā*, *bāgh*.

(*e*) *The nasals ṅ, ñ, ṇ, n, m*

*ṅ*

Velar nasal; as the final consonant in southern standard English *sing*. Occurs chiefly before velar *k*, *g*, *kh*, *gh*, and glottal *h*.

*ñ*

Pre-palatal nasal; rather like the consonant in French *ognon*. Occurs only before *c*, *ch*, *j*, *jh*, and *ś*.

*ṇ*

Retroflex nasal. Occurs before retroflex *ṭ*, *ṭh*, *ḍ*, *ḍh*, and in Sanskrit loanwords (where it is often replaced by dental *n* or, where an effort is made to distinguish it from *n*, by a nasalized retroflex flap *r̤̃*; for the flap *ṛ* in Hindi see below).

*n*

Dental nasal, distinguished from *ṇ* as *t* from *ṭ*, etc., above.

*m*

Bilabial nasal; as English *m*.

Nasal consonants induce marked nasality in following vowels. There is thus a clear difference between the quality of the first and second vowels of such words as *ānā*, *khānā*, etc.

(*f*) *The semivowels y, v and the voiced alveolars r, l*

*y*

Palatal semivowel; somewhat like English *y* in the word *yard*, but more laxly articulated and vocalic in quality, especially when non-initial.

*v*

Labio-dental semivowel; upper teeth just touch lower lip, always with loose contact, and lips are unrounded. The effect is very different from that of English *v*, even when contact between teeth and lip is at its firmest (when the sound produced might be termed a fricative rather than a semivowel). Sometimes, especially following consonants, a bilabial rather than a labio-dental sound may be heard.

*r*

Voiced alveolar or post-dental with weak roll, or tap; usually like Scottish rolled *r* except that the roll is not so prolonged. In some pronunciations the tongue tip merely taps the alveolar ridge once.

*l*

Voiced alveolar or post-dental lateral, similar to 'clear' *l* in English *lick* (not *l* in English *kill*, which has a 'dark' or even vocalic quality).

(*g*) *The sibilants ś, ṣ, s*

*ś*

Voiceless pre-palatal fricative; similar to English *sh*, but often more tense in articulation.

*ṣ*

Voiceless retroflex fricative. Can be practised by placing the tongue in the position to pronounce *ṭ*, then withdrawing it to allow the passage of breath. This sound only occurs in Sanskrit loanwords and is often replaced by *ś*.

*s*

Voiceless alveolar or post-dental fricative; similar to English *s*.

(*h*) *Other sounds*

*ṛ*

Retroflex flap. The tongue is retroflexed as for pronouncing *ḍ*, but the tip, instead of making firm contact with the roof of the mouth, is flapped quickly forward, touching the roof of the mouth only lightly or not at all, and finishes behind the lower teeth. This sound does not occur initially in words. For nasalized *r̃* see p. xvi, under *ṇ*.

*ṛh*

Aspirated retroflex flap.

*h*

Voiced glottal fricative. English *h* is not regularly voiced, and effort will usually be required by the student to make the vocal chords vibrate throughout the articulation of the Hindi sound. The expiration of air which accompanies the voice often gives an effect of breathiness in the pronunciation of a word containing *h*.

*h* is often followed by an unstressed vocalic sound not of full syllabic value, as an echo of a preceding vowel. This tends to happen wherever *h* is otherwise final in a word or precedes a consonant, e.g. in words which may be transcribed phonologically as /kah/, /śahr/, /bahn/, /mahl/, /sihr/, /pahntā/, etc. The prominence of such vocalic sounds varies in the speech of different individuals and is affected by their phonetic environment in words. For many speakers they are noticeably prominent before consonants, whether single consonants or consonant groups, in some cases sufficiently so to be analysed as having full syllabic value; this would produce phonological transcriptions such as /śahar/, /bahan/, /mahal/, /sihar/, /pahantā/, etc., instead of those given above. The student is recommended to adopt a pronunciation in which they are not given full syllabic value. In the transliteration of Devanāgarī script forms used in this book the sounds in question in this paragraph are not represented, except in a few cases where they occur with nasality.

*h*, if not followed by a vowel of full syllabic value, exercises a fronting effect on a preceding *a*, which is then pronounced as short [ɛ], i.e. rather like *e* in English *bet*, by very many Hindi speakers, more particularly if it is stressed; e.g. in *rahnā*, *kahtā*, *kah*, *śahr*, etc., much less commonly in *vajah*, *tarah*, etc.

*h* where followed by *u* in a few words exercises a retracting effect on a preceding *a*, which is then pronounced as short [ɔ], i.e. rather like southern standard English *o* in *nod*, but shorter; e.g. in *bahut*, *pahuṁcnā*.[1]

Where *h* is preceded by unstressed *a* and is final, its articulation often weakens. This is so especially in speech of normal to fast tempo. Hence words which for Hindi in general are best transcribed phonologically as /vajah/, /tarah/, etc., might be transcribed on the basis of many utterances as /vaja/, /tara/, etc. A further variant pronunciation of such words is common, however, in which the breathiness of *h* is retained and is audible before the *a*, so that for some pronunciations the above words might be transcribed as /vajha/, /tarha/, etc.[2]

*f*

Voiceless labio-dental fricative; as English *f*. Occurs in loanwords from Persian, Arabic, and English, and chiefly in the speech of persons with some acquaintance with Urdu or English; but even in the speech of such persons *ph* tends to replace it.

*z*

Voiced alveolar or post-dental fricative; as English *z*. Occurs in the same circumstances as *f*; tends to be replaced with *j*.

*k̲h̲*

Voiceless velar fricative; as *ch* in Scottish *loch*, German *Bach*. Only in Persian and Arabic loanwords; tends to be replaced with *kh*. Can be practised by placing the tongue in the position to pronounce *k*, then withdrawing it to allow passage of breath.

[1] *ṁ* in transliterated forms indicates nasality of a preceding vowel, as is explained in the following section.

[2] *a* is sometimes lengthened in these cases, giving /vajhā/, /tarhā/, etc. (A similar lengthening is common in variant pronunciations of some numerals, but here *h* is usually lost, see p. 61, n. 1.) The articulation of *h* described in the second part of the above paragraph is also sometimes found in a few words where *h* is not final, notably *bahut* (/bahut/, /bhaut/).

*g*

Voiced velar or post-velar fricative; similar to *g* in Dutch *negen*. The voiced correlate of *kh*, occurring in the same circumstances; more usually than not it is replaced with *g*. Can be practised in the same way as *kh*, but using *g* as starting-point.

*q*

Voiceless post-velar plosive, i.e. a *k* made as far back in the mouth as possible. Occurs in the same circumstances as *kh*, *g*; much more usually than not it is replaced with *k*.

*Lengthening of consonants*

Lengthened consonants, in which the articulation of a consonant is prolonged, are common, and must always be distinguished from unlengthened consonants; *usse* is pronounced very differently from *use*, *pattā* from *patā*. (Cf. in English similar lengthened *n*, *b*, *k* in *unknown*, *lab-book*, *book-case*.)

### 3. *Syllable division, stress, and intonation*

Syllable boundaries in Hindi words fall as follows:

(*a*) Between adjacent vowels, e.g. /pā-ī/; /ā-i-e/; /ga-ī/;
(*b*) Between vowels and following single consonants, e.g. /ā-nā/; /sa-kā/; /a-pạ-ri-cit/;
(*c*) Between consonants, e.g. /sak-tā/; /vid-yā/; /hin-dū/; /gad-dī/; /abh-yās/; /kah-nā/; /niś-cay/; /sans-thā/; /tum-hā-rā/.

In general Hindi words have a more level syllabic stress than English. Certain tendencies to the stressing or de-stressing of syllables operate, however, and some brief general guidance on these may be useful for reference. Syllables may be classified as of one of three grades of weight, as follows[1]:

(*a*) Light: syllables ending in a short vowel.[2]

[1] In this classification I follow a recent detailed analysis of word stress by A. R. Kelkar (see Appendix). The apportionment of syllable types to the grades that is made here and the interpretation of stress placement tendencies in individual words differs from his in some particulars.

[2] *a i u*.

(*b*) Medium: syllables ending in a long vowel,[1] or a short vowel followed by a single consonant (these latter may also rank as light, however, especially when not preceding a consonant).

(*c*) Heavy: other syllables.

The tendency for syllables ending in short vowel + single consonant to rank as light is implied by certain variations in stress placement which occur, especially in disyllabic words.

Where one syllable in a word is of greater weight than any other, it bears the main stress. Where more than one syllable is of maximum weight in a word, the last but one bears the main stress, e.g.

/u'cit/ or /'ucit/; /sa'majh/ or /'samajh/; /sa'ṛak/ or /'saṛak/; /ki'dhar/ or /'kidhar/; /'amal/ 'action'; /a'mal/ 'pure'; /'bartan/; /'bandar/; /'baccā/; /'hindī/; /san'dūq/; /pan'jāb/; /inti'zār/; /'muskarāhaṭ/ or /muska'rāhaṭ/.

Inflexional endings, some other final syllables with long vowels, and prefixes sometimes do not influence stress placement[2]; e.g.

/ba'ṛā/ or /'baṛā/; /ṭa'kā/ or /'ṭakā/; /ni'kalnā/ or /'nikalnā/; /ka'hā/, but /'diyā/, /'liyā/; /pi'tā/ or /'pitā/; /'sansthā/ or /san'sthā/ (*sam* + *sthā*); /'sankaṭ/ or /san'kaṭ/ (*sam* + *kaṭ*); /niś'cay/; /a'mal/ 'pure'.

Words which can show more than one stress placement when pronounced in isolation tend, on the whole, to be stressed on an earlier rather than a later syllable in connected utterances. Some other words also show this tendency, e.g. /pari'cit/ or /'paricit/; /pra'gati/ or /'pragati/. In connected utterances word stress is also influenced by other factors than those discussed above, such as speech tempo, and the style and emphasis of a given utterance.

It is less important that the beginner should try to stress isolated Hindi words in a particular way than that he should acquire good habits of intonation and distribution of stress in complete Hindi sentences. The best way of doing this is by listening to native speakers, or recordings of Hindi, and trying carefully to copy the stresses and intonation which one hears. Note especially the characteristic rising-falling intonation of

[1] *ā, ī, ū, e, ai, o, au.*

[2] This is especially so of prefixes. Of inflexional endings, perfective verb endings attract stress more strongly than others.

many sentences. Possible intonations for the following sentences, with chief sentence stresses, are:

*aurteṁ apne baccoṁ ko pyār se pāltī haiṁ*

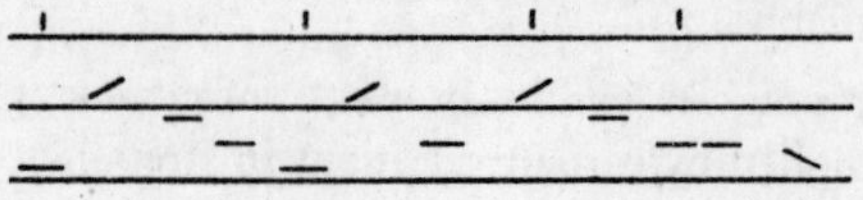

*yah tasvīr ilāhābād kā ek bahut acchā nazārā*

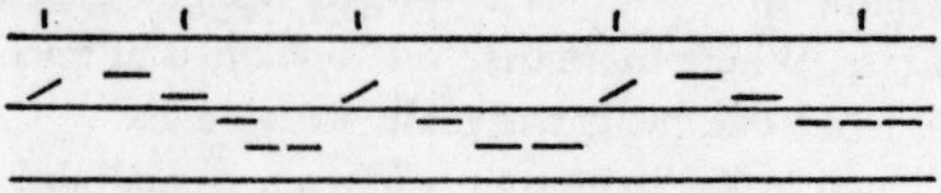

*peś kartī hai*

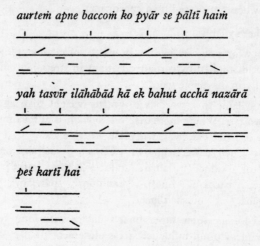

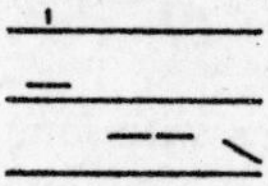

## THE SCRIPT

Hindi is written in the Devanāgarī script as used for Sanskrit, with some minor modifications. The script is syllabic in that vowels are represented differently according as they comprise entire syllables or occur within syllables (i.e. immediately preceded by consonants). The script is written from left to right. The characters of the script are given below in their traditional order, accompanied by roman characters used to transliterate them in this book; these roman characters will be found on the whole to give a close indication of the sound values (phonemic values) which they represent.

1. *Vowels*

| *Syllabic forms.* | | *Intra-syllabic forms.* |
|---|---|---|
| ऄ अ [1] | *a* | |
| ऄा आ[1] | *ā* | ा |
| इ | *i* | ि |
| ई | *ī* | ी |

[1] Alternative forms.

| *Syllabic forms.* | | *Intra-syllabic forms.* |
|---|---|---|
| उ | *u* | ◌ु |
| ऊ | *ū* | ◌ू |
| ऋ | *ṛ* | ◌ृ |
| ए | *e* | ◌े |
| ऐ | *ai* | ◌ै |
| ओ ओ[1] | *o* | ◌ो |
| औ औ[1] | *au* | ◌ौ |

[1] Alternative forms.

(*a*) The character ऋ *ṛ* does not represent a single vocalic sound in Hindi, but is vocalic in terms of the script, having separate syllabic and intra-syllabic forms. It is pronounced [ri], and found only in Sanskrit loanwords.

(*b*) For the combining of the intra-syllabic vowel forms with preceding consonant characters see below.

2. *Consonants*

| | *Voiceless unaspirated plosives.*[1] | *Voiceless aspirated plosives.*[1] | *Voiced unaspirated plosives.*[1] | *Voiced aspirated plosives.*[1] | *Nasals.* |
|---|---|---|---|---|---|
| Velars | क *ka* | ख *kha* | ग *ga* | घ *gha* | ङ *ṅa* |
| Pre-palatals | च *ca* | छ *cha* | ज *ja* | झ झ[2] *jha* | ञ *ña* |
| Retroflexes | ट *ṭa* | ठ *ṭha* | ड *ḍa* | ढ *ḍha* | ण ण[2] *ṇa* |
| Dentals | त *ta* | थ *tha* | द *da* | ध *dha* | न *na* |
| Labials | प *pa* | फ *pha* | ब *ba* | भ *bha* | म *ma* |

| | | | | |
|---|---|---|---|---|
| Semivowels, etc. | य *ya* | र *ra* | ल, ल[2] *la* | व *va* |
| Sibilants | श *śa* | ष *ṣa* | स *sa* | |
| Glottal | | ह *ha* | | |
| Flaps | | ड़ *ṛa*[3] | ढ़ *ṛha*[3] | |

[1] The consonants in the second horizontal row are affricates rather than plosives, but their behaviour as a class can be described in the same terms as that of plosives. Later references to plosives in this book apply equally to affricates unless the contrary is stated.

[2] Alternative forms.

[3] These characters are most conveniently placed last in setting out the syllabary, though in terms of dictionary order they follow ड and ढ, of which they are modifications.

(*a*) Intra-syllabic vowel forms are combined with preceding consonant characters as follows:

ा ी ो ौ follow the consonant character.

ि precedes it.

ु ू ृ are subscripts.

े ै are superscripts.

E.g.

का *kā*; की *kī*; को *ko*; कौ *kau*; कि *ki*;

कु *ku*; कू *kū*; कृ *kṛ*; के *ke*; कै *kai*.

(*b*) The vowel subscripts ु ू ृ are written below the vertical stroke of a character if it has one running throughout its height, otherwise usually under the centre of the character. Thus बु *bu*; कू *kū*; तु *tu*; सृ *sṛ*; फु *phu*; णु *ṇu*; ढू *ḍhū*, etc.

Note: रु *ru*; रू *rū*.

(*c*) Vowel superscripts are positioned in the same way as subscripts. Thus खे *khe*; से *se*; णे *ṇe*; टे *ṭe*, etc.

(*d*) Note that there is no intra-syllabic form for the vowel *a*. The value of this vowel was taken to be inherent in a consonant character in the writing of Sanskrit, and this convention still obtains for the writing of Hindi (hence the characters are transliterated *ka*, *kha*, etc., not *k*, *kh*, etc., above). However, since *a* has become or tended to become mute finally, and in some phonetic contexts medially also in the modern language, the consonant characters have come to have not only syllabic but also purely consonantal values.

Finally:

अब *ab*; सब *sab*; तालाब *tālāb*; मिलन *milan*; अतुल *atul*; लगन *lagan*; कपट *kapaṭ*, etc.

Medially:

लगना *lagnā*; समझा *samjhā*; मतलब *matlab*, etc.

The transliteration indicates whether a given 'inherent' *a* in a script form represents a normally pronounced vowel or not. Note particularly that where a word is written as three, or four, script syllables, an *a* in the penultimate script syllable is not pronounced in non-poetic style, or is only minimally pronounced,[1] where the final script syllable contains a

[1] Minimal realization of many such *a*'s will often occur, especially in more easterly parts of the Hindi language area.

vowel other than *a*; thus चलना *calnā*; समझा *samjhā*; समझी *samjhī*; समझना *samajhnā*, etc. Where the final script syllable contains *a* this will not be realized in pronunciation; the penultimate *a* will then represent a pronounced vowel, and if the word is of four script syllables the antepenultimate *a* will normally not do so. Thus कमल *kamal*; सरपत *sarpat*; मतलब *matlab*, etc. These general principles do not apply fully in the case of words containing medial *h* (see p. xviii), nor always in the case of loanwords, compounded and derivative words, and variant grammatical forms of words. Note especially that Sanskrit loanwords such as अपवाद *apavād*, अवकाश *avakāś* often retain medial *a* (though they need not do so), and that a medial *a* is represented in transliterated forms of such loanwords wherever it is frequently pronounced in normal usage.

Component parts of script syllables are best written, at least at first, in the following order: first, those parts beneath the horizontal headstroke, working from left to right; next, any subscripts or superscripts; finally, the headstroke to the entire syllable. On a ruled page headstrokes are written on the ruled lines.

### 3. *Conjunct consonants*

The device of conjoining consonant characters was used in writing Sanskrit to indicate the pronunciation of consonants without an intervening 'inherent' *a*. Conjunct consonant characters are accordingly very common in Sanskrit loanwords, and are also used commonly (though there is some variation in practice) in writing successive consonants in most Persian and Arabic loanwords, as well as in English loanwords. In words of Hindi origin they are used chiefly to indicate lengthened consonants, and sequences of nasal and plosive consonants.

The commonest conjuncts are listed below in dictionary order.[1]

क्क *kka*, क्ख *kkha*, क्त *kta*, क्म *kma*, क्य *kya*, क्र *kra*, क्ल *kla*, क्व *kva*, क्ष *kṣa*, क्स *ksa*, ख्य *khya*, ग्द *gda*, ग्ध *gdha*, ग्न *gna*, ग्म *gma*, ग्य *gya*, ग्र *gra*, ग्ल *gla*, ग्व *gva*, घ्न *ghna*, घ्य *ghya*, घ्र *ghra*, ङ्क *ṅka*, ङ्ख *ṅkha*, ङ्ग *ṅga*, ङ्घ *ṅgha*.

च्च *cca*, च्छ *ccha*, च्य *cya*, ज्ज *jja*, ज्ञ *jña*, ज्य *jya*, ज्र *jra*, ज्व *jva*, ञ्च *ñca*, ञ्ज *ñja*.

[1] For some, more than one form is current. Variant forms are not given in the table.

ट्ट *ṭṭa*, ट्ठ *ṭṭha*, ट्य *ṭya*, ट्र *ṭra*, ड्ड *ḍḍa*, ड्य *ḍya*, ड्र *ḍra*, ढ्य *ḍhya*,
ण्ट *ṇṭa*, ण्ठ *ṇṭha*, ण्ड *ṇḍa*, ण्ढ *ṇḍha*, ण्ण *ṇṇa*, ण्य *ṇya*.

त्क *tka*, त्त *tta*, त्त्व *ttva*, त्थ *ttha*, त्न *tna*, त्प *tpa*, त्म *tma*,
त्य *tya*, त्र *tra*, त्व *tva*, त्स *tsa*, त्स्न *tsna*, त्स्य *tsya*, थ्य *thya*,
थ्व *thva*, द्द *dda*, द्ध *ddha*, द्भ *dbha*, द्य *dya*, द्र *dra*, द्व *dva*,
ध्य *dhya*, ध्व *dhva*, न्त *nta*, न्थ *ntha*, न्द *nda*, न्द्र *ndra*, न्ध *ndha*,
न्ध्य *ndhya*, न्न *nna*, न्म *nma*, न्य *nya*, न्व *nva*, न्स *nśa*, न्ह *nha*.

प्त *pta*, प्न *pna*, प्प *ppa*, प्फ *ppha*, प्य *pya*, प्र *pra*, प्ल *pla*,
प्स *psa*, फ्र *phra*, ब्ज *bja*, ब्त *bta*, ब्द *bda*, ब्ध *bdha*, ब्ब *bba*,
ब्भ *bbha*, ब्य *bya*, ब्र *bra*, भ्य *bhya*, भ्र *bhra*, म्न *mna*,
म्प *mpa*, म्ब *mba*, म्भ *mbha*, म्म *mma*, म्य *mya*, म्र *mra*,
म्ल *mla*, म्ह *mha*.

य्य *yya*, ल्क *lka*, ल्द *lda*, ल्प *lpa*, ल्म *lma*, ल्य *lya*, ल्ल *lla*,
ल्ह *lha*, व्य *vya*, व्र *vra*, व्व *vva*.

श्क *śka*, श्च *śca*, श्य *śya*, श्र *śra*, श्ल *śla*, श्व *śva*, ष्क *ṣka*
ष्ट *ṣṭa*, ष्ट्र *ṣṭra*, ष्ठ *ṣṭha*, ष्ण *ṣṇa*, ष्प *ṣpa*, ष्म *ṣma*, ष्य *ṣya*,
ष्व *ṣva*, स्क *ska*, स्ख *skha*, स्ट *sṭa*, स्त *sta*, स्त्र *stra*, स्थ *stha*,
स्थ्य *sthya*, स्न *sna*, स्प *spa*, स्फ *spha*, स्म *sma*, स्य *sya*,
स्र *sra*, स्व *sva*, स्स *ssa*.

ह्न *hna*, ह्म *hma*, ह्य *hya*, ह्र *hra*, ह्ल *hla*, ह्व *hva*.

(*a*) The existence of conjunct characters in Devanāgarī script forms is not marked in the transliteration, since in this book transliterated forms are accompanied by the Devanāgarī forms themselves.

(*b*) Conjuncts involving initial *r* are written with a special superscript form for *r*: र्. Thus र्क *rka*; र्म *rma*; र्ष *rṣa*, etc. र् is written at the end of its syllable, thus र्थी *rthī*; र्सि *rsi*, etc.

(*c*) The student will see that the learning of the conjuncts poses no new difficulty, the usual principle of composition being that where feasible the second character in the conjunct is combined with a truncated form of the first. The forms where this does not apply need special attention; note especially the form of conjuncts with *r* as final component.

Note also that the conjunct ज्ञ, which represents a value /gy(ə)/ in Hindi but /jñə/ in Sanskrit, is transliterated *jña*, to avoid any confusion with the conjunct ग्य *gya*. Its original value is reflected in the fact that vowels following /gy(ə)/ of this origin are often somewhat nasalized.

(*d*) The use of conjuncts, especially clumsy ones, is sometimes avoided by the use with the first character, written complete, of a subscript sign called *virāma*, ्, whose function is to indicate absence of an 'inherent' vowel; e.g. चिट्‌ठी = चिट्ठी *ciṭṭhī*. (This sign is sometimes also written finally with single consonants in some Sanskrit and other loanwords.)

(*e*) Note that the degree to which *a* is pronounced after consonant groups varies according to the phonetic form of the group (and according to the speech of different individuals and to different styles of speech). After the group /nd/ finally in a word, for instance, *a* will not be heard, but after /ṣṭr/ finally some trace of the vowel is often present. In the transliteration the 'inherent' vowel is not represented after conjuncts where an *a* would normally not be pronounced, e.g. in बन्द *band*; दत्त *datt*, or where, if indeed pronounced, it would most usually be extremely attenuated, e.g. in पत्र *patr*; मित्र *mitr*. Elsewhere it is written, e.g. in राष्ट्र *rāṣṭra*; उत्तरदायित्व *uttardāyitva*; साहित्य *sāhitya*; but note that even in these cases an *a* is by no means always pronounced, and does not have full syllabic value. The student should generally pronounce final *a* after consonant groups as lightly as the phonetic form of the group will allow.[1]

4. *Anusvāra*

The superscript dot *anusvāra* is used:

(*a*) Preceding velar, pre-palatal, retroflex, dental or labial plosive consonant characters (see p. xxiii) to denote a preceding nasal consonant

[1] Many speakers simplify certain final consonant groups by introducing brief epenthetic vowels before the last consonant, and sometimes lengthen the preceding consonant, thus pronouncing पत्र *patr* as [pət:ᵊr], [pət:r] rather than [pətr⁽ᵊ⁾], शुक्ल *śukl* as [ʃukᵘl] rather than [ʃukl⁽ᵊ⁾], राष्ट्र *rāṣṭra* as [raʂʈᵊr] rather than [raʂʈr⁽ᵊ⁾], etc. Pronunciations with epenthetic vowels are probably best avoided by the student. Words such as साहित्य *sāhitya*, उत्तरदायित्व *uttardāyitva* show devoicing of *y*, *v* if the final vowel is completely lost: [saɦɪtç], etc. Similar devoicing sometimes occurs in words like पत्र *patr*.

sound of the class concerned, i.e. a 'homorganic' nasal. Thus

| | | | | | | |
|---|---|---|---|---|---|---|
| अंक | is an equivalent spelling to | | | | अङ्क | *aṅk* |
| अंचल | ,, | ,, | ,, | ,, | अञ्चल | *añcal* |
| अंडा | ,, | ,, | ,, | ,, | अण्डा | *aṇḍā* |
| हिंदी | ,, | ,, | ,, | ,, | हिन्दी | *hindī* |
| लंबा | ,, | ,, | ,, | ,, | लम्बा | *lambā* |

This use of *anusvāra* is, in other words, a shorthand device enabling the writing of a word containing nasal + plosive of similar articulation to be simplified, and is accordingly extremely common, even in Sanskrit loanwords. The student should familiarize himself with it from the outset, and use it freely. It is not expressed in the transliteration used in this book, however, in order to keep the latter as clear a guide to pronunciation as possible.

Where *anusvāra* is written over long vowels before plosive consonants in Sanskrit loanwords a degree of vowel nasality will usually be clearly heard preceding the homorganic nasal consonant, e.g. in एकांकी *ekāṅkī*; आंदोलन *āndolan*, etc.

(*b*) Preceding other consonant characters (chiefly in Sanskrit loanwords):

(i) Before *ya* and usually before *va* it denotes preceding vowel nasality[1]: e.g. संयम *saṃyam*; संवरण *saṃvaraṇ*.

(ii) Before *ra*, *la*, and *sa* it denotes a preceding dental or post-dental nasal consonant *n* according to the usage of most Hindi speakers[2]: e.g. संरक्षण *saṃrakṣaṇ*; संलग्न *saṃlagn*; संसार *saṃsār*.

(iii) Before *śa* it denotes a preceding pre-palatal nasal consonant according to the usage of many Hindi speakers[3]: e.g. अंश *aṃś*.

(iv) Before *ha* it denotes a preceding velar nasal consonant *ṅ*: e.g. सिंह *siṃh*.

In all these positions *anusvāra*, however realized in pronunciation, is

[1] Often with a semivocalic nasalized glide *ỹ* to *y*, and *ṽ* to *v*. For some speakers it denotes bilabial *m* before the character *va*.

[2] For some speakers it denotes preceding vowel nasality; and in a few loanwords it does so for almost all speakers (cases mentioned on p. 195).

[3] For some speakers it denotes preceding vowel nasality, sometimes with semivocalic nasalized glide *ỹ* to *ś*; and in a few loanwords it denotes preceding vowel nasality for almost all speakers (cases mentioned on p. 195).

transliterated *ṃ*, and there are no alternative spellings with conjuncts available.

(*c*) For the sign *candrabindu*; see below.

5. *Candrabindu*

The superscript sign called *candrabindu* is used to denote vowel nasality in its syllable. (It is rarely if ever used in Sanskrit loanwords.) It is transliterated *ṁ*: e.g.

| | |
|---|---|
| हाँ | *hāṁ* |
| बाँधना | *bāṁdhnā* |
| रँगना | *raṁgnā* |
| हूँ | *hūṁ* |

(*a*) Where a syllable contains superscript vowel signs, however, *anusvāra* is almost always written instead of *candrabindu*. *Anusvāra* used in this way is transliterated *ṁ* like *candrabindu*: e.g.

| | |
|---|---|
| खिंचना | *khiṁcnā* |
| मैं | *maiṁ* |
| में | *meṁ* |
| सींग | *sīṁg* |
| लोगों | *logoṁ* |

(*b*) In printed books especially, the use of *anusvāra* instead of *candrabindu* in conditions not covered by note (*a*) above is very common: e.g.

| | | | |
|---|---|---|---|
| हां | for | हाँ | *hāṁ* |
| रंगना | for | रँगना | *raṁgnā* |
| हूं | for | हूँ | *hūṁ* |
| बांधना | for | बाँधना | *bāṁdhnā* |

The majority of careful users of Hindi do not follow this usage in writing, and the student is therefore recommended not to adopt it himself.

6. *Visarga*

The sign : called *visarga*, written lineally and transliterated *ḥ*, denotes voiced aspiration in Hindi (identical with the sound denoted by the character ह). It occurs almost exclusively in Sanskrit loanwords: e.g.

| | |
|---|---|
| प्राय: | *prāyaḥ* |
| स्वभावत: | *svabhāvataḥ* |

7. *Representation of some Persian, Arabic, and English sounds*

A subscript dot is sometimes used with certain Devanāgarī characters to denote sounds of non-Indian origin in loanwords. This usage is common, but never obligatory, the more so since the great majority of Hindi speakers tend to replace these sounds (see pp. xix and xx) with sounds of Indian origin.

| | | | | | | | | |
|---|---|---|---|---|---|---|---|---|
| The sound | *f* | may be written | फ़ | (transliteration | *f*) |
| ,, | ,, | *z* | ,, ,, ,, | ज़[1] | ( | ,, | *z*) |
| ,, | ,, | *kh* | ,, ,, ,, | ख़ | ( | ,, | *kh*) |
| ,, | ,, | *g* | ,, ,, ,, | ग़ | ( | ,, | *g*) |
| ,, | ,, | *q* | ,, ,, ,, | क़ | ( | ,, | *q*) |

In writing English words in Devanāgarī the vowel sound in the English word *top* is sometimes denoted by using the superscript sign ˘ over intra-syllabic *ā*; thus जॉन 'John'.

8. *Punctuation*

Sentences are concluded with the vertical mark । (*daṇḍa*). Other punctuation in prose is of Western origin, and apart from occasional minor deviations is used in the same way as in writing English.

9. *Numerals*

| | | | | | | | | | |
|---|---|---|---|---|---|---|---|---|---|
| 0 | 1 | 2 | 3 | 4 | 5 | 6 | 7 | 8 | 9 |
| ० | १ | २ | ३ | ४ | ५ | ६ | ७ | ८ | ९, ६ |

10. *Abbreviations*

First syllables of words are used in abbreviations, punctuated with either ॰ or full-stop. Initials of names are usually given according to their English pronunciation: e.g.

| | |
|---|---|
| उ॰ प्र॰ | Uttar Pradesh |
| म॰ प्र॰ | Madhya Pradesh |
| रा॰ कु॰ | Ram Kumar (e.g. in a signature) |
| टुंडला जं॰ | Tundla Junction |
| जी॰ पी॰ मेहरोत्रा | G. P. Mehrotra |
| डा॰ आर॰ जे॰ स्मिथ | Dr. R. J. Smith |

[1] A homorganic nasal preceding the sound *z* in Persian loanwords is represented in the script by *anusvāra*, in exactly the same way as the nasal *ñ* preceding the sound *j* in words of Indian origin; e.g. मंज़िल *manzil*. (In English loanwords, however, it is more often represented by truncated न in a conjunct with ज़ (ज) or sometimes स; e.g. वर्मा ऐण्ड सन्ज़ *varmā aiṇḍ sanz* 'Varma and Sons'; सिविल लाइन्स *sivil lāins* 'Civil Lines'.)

## SCRIPT EXERCISE

1.

| | | | | | | | | | | | | | | | |
|---|---|---|---|---|---|---|---|---|---|---|---|---|---|---|---|
| खा | गि | घी | चौ | छो | जु | झू | टे | ठा | डे | ढी | णी | तृ | तै | थे | दो |
| *khā* | *gi* | *ghī* | *cau* | *cho* | *ju* | *jhū* | *ṭe* | *ṭhā* | *ḍe* | *ḍhī* | *ṇi* | *tṛ* | *tai* | *the* | *do* |
| धू | ना | पौ | फू | बु | भा | भि | ये | रो | ला | वि | शा | षु | सि | है | |
| *dhū* | *nā* | *pau* | *phū* | *bu* | *bhā* | *bhi* | *ye* | *ro* | *lā* | *vi* | *śā* | *ṣu* | *si* | *hai* | |

2.

| | | | | | | | | | |
|---|---|---|---|---|---|---|---|---|---|
| कट | काट | खाट | गत | गात | घट | घाट | घृत | घात | चप |
| *kaṭ* | *kāṭ* | *khāṭ* | *gat* | *gāt* | *ghaṭ* | *ghāṭ* | *ghṛt* | *ghāt* | *cap* |
| चिप | छिक | जन | जान | झील | टोक | ठान | डाल | ढाक | बाण |
| *cip* | *chik* | *jan* | *jān* | *jhīl* | *ṭok* | *ṭhān* | *ḍāl* | *ḍhāk* | *bāṇ* |
| तुक | थूक | दिल | दीन | नीम | पेट | फोड़ | बोझ | भीख | मैल |
| *tuk* | *thūk* | *dil* | *dīn* | *nīm* | *peṭ* | *phoṛ* | *bojh* | *bhīkh* | *mail* |
| यार | राय | लिप | वर | शत | षट | साथ | शठ | हित | |
| *yār* | *rāy* | *lip* | *var* | *śat* | *ṣaṭ* | *sāth* | *śaṭh* | *hit* | |

3.

| | | | | | | | | | |
|---|---|---|---|---|---|---|---|---|---|
| अब | आशा | आना | इस | ईख | उन | ऊन | ऋषि | ओट | और |
| *ab* | *āśā* | *ānā* | *is* | *īkh* | *un* | *ūn* | *ṛṣi* | *oṭ* | *aur* |
| एक | ऐन | | | | | | | | |
| *ek* | *ain* | | | | | | | | |

4.

| | | | | | | | | |
|---|---|---|---|---|---|---|---|---|
| कमल | विमल | अतुल | ललित | सुबोध | राजा | बेहद | गोबर | बूढ़ा |
| *kamal* | *vimal* | *atul* | *lalit* | *subodh* | *rājā* | *behad* | *gobar* | *būṛhā* |
| बड़ा | बढ़ा | चलता | बोलता | बोलती | लगता | लगती | सपना | सपने |
| *baṛā* | *baṛhā* | *caltā* | *boltā* | *boltī* | *lagtā* | *lagtī* | *sapnā* | *sapne* |
| अपने | असली | ख़तरा | कटरा | पटरी | समझा | सकता | मतलब | समतल |
| *apne* | *aslī* | *khatrā* | *kaṭrā* | *paṭrī* | *samjhā* | *saktā* | *matlab* | *samtal* |
| बरबस | सरपट | | | | | | | |
| *barbas* | *sarpaṭ* | | | | | | | |

5.

| | | | | | | | | |
|---|---|---|---|---|---|---|---|---|
| गी | गई | गे | गए | गाए | नी | नई | नाई | नए |
| *gī* | *gaī* | *ge* | *gae* | *gāe* | *nī* | *naī* | *nāī* | *nae* |
| भी | भाई | भई | कमाऊ | उपजाऊ | बोई | सोई | बढ़ाई | बढ़ई |
| *bhī* | *bhāī* | *bhaī* | *kamāū* | *upjāū* | *boī* | *soī* | *baṛhāī* | *baṛhaī* |
| बुढ़ऊ | मकई | | | | | | | |
| *buṛhaū* | *makaī* | | | | | | | |

6.

| | | | | | | |
|---|---|---|---|---|---|---|
| मक्का | मक्खन | रक्त | हुक्म | क्या | क्रम | क्लास |
| *makkā* | *makkhan* | *rakt* | *hukm* | *kyā* | *kram* | *klās* |
| क्षण | आख्यान | मुग्ध | अग्नि | ग्राम | ग्लानि | ग्वाला |
| *kṣaṇ* | *ākhyān* | *mugdh* | *agni* | *grām* | *glāni* | *gvālā* |
| अंक | अंग | शंख | बच्चा | अच्छा | च्युत | लज्जा |
| *aṅk* | *aṅg* | *śaṅkh* | *baccā* | *acchā* | *cyut* | *lajjā* |
| ज्ञान | ग्यारह | ज्वर | मिट्टी | मुट्ठा | ट्रेन | अड्डा |
| *jñān* | *gyārah* | *jvar* | *miṭṭī* | *muṭṭhā* | *ṭren* | *aḍḍā* |
| ड्राइवर | घण्टा | कुण्ठा | अण्डा | सत्ताईस | उत्थान | रत्न |
| *ḍrāivar* | *ghaṇṭā* | *kuṇṭhā* | *aṇḍā* | *sattāīs* | *utthān* | *ratn* |
| उत्पादन | आत्मा | हत्या | पुत्र | पुरुषत्व | गद्दी | विद्या |
| *utpādan* | *ātmā* | *hatyā* | *putr* | *puruṣatva* | *gaddī* | *vidyā* |
| विद्वान | ध्यान | अन्त | हिन्दी | गन्ना | जन्म | न्यून |
| *vidvān* | *dhyān* | *ant* | *hindī* | *gannā* | *janm* | *nyūn* |
| प्राप्त | प्राप्य | शब्द | लब्ध | डिब्बा | अभ्यास | सम्पादक |
| *prāpt* | *prāpya* | *śabd* | *labdh* | *ḍibbā* | *abhyās* | *sampādak* |
| लम्बा | तुम्हारा | उर्दू | अर्थ | सर्प | जल्दी | बिल्ली |
| *lambā* | *tumhārā* | *urdū* | *arth* | *sarp* | *jaldī* | *billī* |
| अल्प | व्यय | निश्चय | श्याम | श्री | राष्ट्र | कृष्ण |
| *alp* | *vyay* | *niścay* | *śyām* | *śrī* | *rāṣṭra* | *kṛṣṇ* |
| स्थान | अस्त्र | स्नान | स्पीच | स्रव | ह्रास | |
| *sthān* | *astra* | *snān* | *spīc* | *srav* | *hrās* | |

7.

| | | | | | |
|---|---|---|---|---|---|
| अंग | पंखा | कंघी | संघ | पंकज | चंचल |
| *aṅg* | *paṅkhā* | *kaṅghī* | *saṅgh* | *paṅkaj* | *cañcal* |
| पंछी | रंज | अंटी | कंठ | बंडी | अंत |
| *pañchī* | *rañj* | *aṇṭī* | *kaṇṭh* | *baṇḍī* | *ant* |
| पंथ | हिंदी | अंधा | संपादन | संबोधन | संभ्रांत |
| *panth* | *hindī* | *andhā* | *sampādan* | *sambodhan* | *sambhrānt* |
| संयुक्त | संवरण | अंश | वंश | बंसी | |
| *saṃyukt* | *saṃvaraṇ* | *aṃś* | *vaṃś* | *baṃsī* | |

| | | | | | | |
|---|---|---|---|---|---|---|
| 8. | रँगना | सँकरा | खिड़कियाँ | लड़कियाँ | अँधेरा | आँधी |
| | *raṁgnā* | *saṁkrā* | *khiṛkiyāṁ* | *laṛkiyāṁ* | *aṁdherā* | *āṁdhī* |
| | ऊँट | सिंचना | सींचना | सूँघना | रेंगना | हैं |
| | *ūṁṭ* | *siṁcnā* | *sīṁcnā* | *sūṁghnā* | *reṁgnā* | *haiṁ* |
| | परसों | सौंफ | विद्यार्थियों | | | |
| | *parsoṁ* | *sauṁph* | *vidyārthiyoṁ* | | | |
| 9. | दुःख | स्वतः | | | | |
| | *duḥkh* | *svataḥ* | | | | |
| 10. | अफ़सोस | हफ़्ता | ज़ख़्म | ख़बर | ग़म | चाक़ू |
| | *afsos* | *haftā* | *zak̲h̲m* | *k̲h̲abar* | *gam* | *cāqū* |

# LESSON I

## NOUNS

Two cases only need be distinguished, a direct and an oblique. The direct case usually denotes sentence subjects or direct objects; the oblique occurs most commonly with postpositions, see below. Nouns are of singular or plural number, and masculine or feminine gender.

1. *Masculine inflexional patterns*

| | | | ā-finals |
|---|---|---|---|
| Sg. | Dir. | कमरा | *kamrā*, room |
| | Obl. | कमरे | *kamre* |
| Pl. | Dir. | कमरे | *kamre* |
| | Obl. | कमरों | *kamroṁ* |

| | | | Others |
|---|---|---|---|
| Sg. | Dir. | दिन | *din*, day |
| | Obl. | दिन | *din* |
| Pl. | Dir. | दिन | *din* |
| | Obl. | दिनों | *dinoṁ* |

(*a*) The few masculines in final *-āṁ* are almost all inflected as कमरा *kamrā*, but with the endings nasalised, e.g. कुआँ *kuāṁ* 'well'.

(*b*) Some masculines in final *-ā* follow the pattern of दिन *din*. These are chiefly terms of relationship showing a reduplicated syllable, e.g. चाचा *cācā* 'paternal uncle'; दादा *dādā* 'paternal grandfather' (obl. pl. चाचाओं *cācāoṁ*, etc.); or loanwords from Sanskrit, e.g. पिता *pitā* 'father'; राजा *rājā* 'rajah'; देवता *devtā* 'deity'; दाता *dātā* 'giver'; also, frequently in many persons' usage, the oblique case of some common place-names, e.g. आगरा *āgrā* 'Agra'; कलकत्ता *kalkattā* 'Calcutta'.

(*c*) Masculines in final *-ī* and *-ū* shorten these vowels before the oblique plural ending, and masculines in final *-ī* show a semivocalic glide *y* before it. Thus आदमी *ādmī* 'man' has oblique plural आदमियों *ādmiyoṁ*; हिंदू *hindū* 'Hindu' has oblique plural हिंदुओं *hinduoṁ*.

(*d*) Vocatives (forms of address) are usually expressed by use of the oblique case in the singular, and in the plural by forms in *-o*, differing from oblique case forms only in that they are not nasalised: e.g.

| | | |
|---|---|---|
| लड़के | *laṛke!* | Boy! |
| लड़को | *laṛko!* | Boys! |

2. *Feminine inflexional patterns*

| | | | |
|---|---|---|---|
| | | | *ī*-finals |
| Sg. | Dir. | लड़की | *laṛkī*, girl |
| | Obl. | लड़की | *laṛkī* |
| Pl. | Dir. | लड़कियाँ | *laṛkiyāṁ* |
| | Obl. | लड़कियों | *laṛkiyoṁ* |
| | | | *iyā*-finals |
| Sg. | Dir. | चिड़िया | *ciṛiyā*, bird |
| | Obl. | चिड़िया | *ciṛiyā* |
| Pl. | Dir. | चिड़ियाँ | *ciṛiyāṁ* |
| | Obl. | चिड़ियों | *ciṛiyoṁ* |
| | | | Others |
| Sg. | Dir. | मेज़ | *mez*, table |
| | Obl. | मेज़ | *mez* |
| Pl. | Dir. | मेज़ें | *mezeṁ* |
| | Obl. | मेज़ों | *mezoṁ* |

(*a*) A final *-ī* shows the same shortening and presence of glide *y* before an inflexional ending as was noted for masculines in *-ī*. Note that this occurs in both plural forms.

(*b*) Identical in inflexion with feminines in final *-ī* are feminine loanwords from Sanskrit in final *-i*, almost all abstract nouns, e.g. स्थिति *sthiti* 'position'.

(*c*) Feminines in *-iyā* are frequently diminutives, e.g. डिबिया *ḍibiyā* '(small) box'. Cf. डिब्बा *ḍibbā*, m.

(*d*) To be particularly noted among the 'other feminines' are loanwords in final *-ā* from Sanskrit, almost all abstract nouns. (माता *mātā* 'mother' is the only common non-abstract.) A few common Arabic and Persian loanwords in final *-ā* may also be noted, e.g. हवा *havā* 'air, wind'; दुनिया *duniyā* 'world'; दफ़ा *dafā* 'time, occasion'.

(*e*) Feminine vocatives are formed in the same way as masculines.

There are no definite or indefinite articles in Hindi. A noun acting as subject or direct object in its sentence is definite rather than indefinite; but depending on its context the word मकान *makān* 'house' may have as its translation equivalent 'a house' or 'the house' or 'houses' or 'the houses'. The word एक *ek* 'one' can be used before nouns with the force of an indefinite article where explicitness is required.

In the case of nouns denoting animate beings, grammatical gender almost always agrees with natural gender. Thus आदमी *ādmī* 'man', दर्ज़ी *darzī* 'tailor', डाकिया *ḍākiyā* 'postman' are masculines following दिन *din* and कमरा *kamrā* in inflexion, not लड़की *laṛkī* and चिड़िया *ciṛiyā*.

The gender of other nouns is harder to predict from their form. Nouns in *-ā* denoting everyday objects are predominantly masculine; abstract nouns in *-ā* are almost all feminine; nouns in *-ī*, *-iyā* are feminine in most cases unless referring to males, as in the above examples. The student is advised to note the gender of each new word that he learns.

## POSTPOSITIONS

Postpositions are expressions answering in function to prepositions or prepositional phrases in English. They may be simple (i.e. one-word units), e.g. में *meṁ* 'in, into'; पर *par* 'on', or compound in form (see in due course pp. 34 f.). Postpositions are characteristically immediately preceded by a noun or pronoun in oblique case. Thus मेज़ पर *mez par* 'on the table'; मेज़ों पर *mezoṁ par* 'on the tables', etc.

## SIMPLE SENTENCES

A simple sentence is a complete utterance consisting of a noun or pronoun (or a composite nominal phrase) and a verb (or a composite verbal phrase). Either component may be expressed or understood. The nominal component forms the subject of its sentence; the verbal component may include non-verbal elements, e.g. nouns or pronouns as direct objects or indirect objects of the verb, adverbs or adverbial phrases, or a negative.

## ORDER OF WORDS

1. In simple sentences which are neutral in style and emphasis, rather than affective (emphatic or otherwise emotive) in character, the subject, where expressed, most usually comes first[1] and the verb last, in close association with any negative, while objects and adverbial expressions occupy an intervening position, in less fixed order. Expressions of time tend to precede those of place: e.g.

लड़का आज यहाँ नहीं है। *laṛkā āj yahāṁ nahīṁ hai*, The boy isn't here today [the boy today here not is].

2. This general pattern can be widely varied according to any affective value a sentence may have (as well as according to its length and the balance of its parts). For instance, an adverb advanced to initial sentence position usually gains in emphasis at the cost of a subject which it displaces. Cf. with the sentence above

आज लड़का यहाँ नहीं है। *āj laṛkā yahāṁ nahīṁ hai*, Today the boy isn't here.

Note in this connection that the sense of introductory 'there is, are, were', etc., is expressed in Hindi by an inversion of the neutral (non-affective) order of subject and following adverbial locution (emphasis on the subject being thereby diminished).

पुस्तक मेज़ पर है। *pustak mez par hai*, The book is on the table.
मेज़ पर पुस्तक है। *mez par pustak hai*, There is a book on the table.

3. Questions: Interrogative pronouns and adverbs, e.g. क्या *kyā* 'what', कहाँ *kahāṁ* 'where', do not usually introduce questions in sentences of neutral style and emphasis, but follow the subject in second position, or later.[2]

लड़की कहाँ है? *laṛkī kahāṁ hai?* Where is the girl?
यह क्या है? *yah kyā hai?* What is this?

[1] One important type of sentence where this is not so is noted in Lesson IX, pp. 50 f., another in Lesson XIII; see also in due course Lesson XII, p. 71, n. 1.

[2] Where a subject is understood but not expressed, or where a sentence is affective in character, they can occur initially.

The pronoun क्या *kyā* in initial position in a sentence is usually a question marker, serving to introduce questions not containing an interrogative. In conversation the inflexion of the voice often makes its presence unnecessary.

(क्या) लड़कियाँ यहाँ हैं? (*kyā*) *larkiyāṁ yahāṁ haiṁ?* Are the girls here?

## VOCABULARY

मेज़ *mez*, f., table
पुस्तक *pustak*, f., book
क़लम *qalam*, f.m., pen
कमरा *kamrā* m., room
कुरसी *kursī*, f., chair
घड़ा *gharā*, m., pot, jar
पानी *pānī*, m., water
कुआँ *kuāṁ*, m., well
लड़का *larkā*, m., boy
लड़की *larkī*, f., girl
आगरा *āgrā*, m., Agra
कलकत्ता *kalkattā*, m., Calcutta
आदमी *ādmī*, m., man
औरत †*aurat*, f., woman
पत्र *patr*, m., letter
चिड़िया *ciriyā*, f., bird
पिंजरा *piñjrā*, m., cage
मकान *makān*, m., house
अख़बार †*akhbār*, m., newspaper

यह *yah*, this[1]
वह *vah*, that[1]
एक *ek*, one; a, an
दो *do*, two
तीन *tīn*, three
आज *āj*, today
यहाँ *yahāṁ*, here
वहाँ *vahāṁ*, there
कहाँ *kahāṁ*, where?
क्या *kyā*, what?; and as question marker
लेकिन †*lekin*, but
में *meṁ*, in
पर *par*, on
नहीं *nahīṁ*, no, not
है *hai*, is
हैं *haiṁ*, are
और *aur*, and

## EXERCISE 1

यह मेज़ है। पुस्तक मेज़ पर है। मेज़ पर क़लम है। कमरे में दो कुरसियाँ हैं। यह क्या है? यह घड़ा है। क्या घड़े में पानी है? नहीं, लेकिन कुएँ में पानी है। पुस्तकें मेज़ पर हैं। क्या पुस्तकें मेज़ों पर हैं? यहाँ एक कुरसी है। वहाँ दो कुरसियाँ हैं। क्या यह कुरसी है? नहीं, यह कुरसी नहीं है, मेज़ है। लड़के आगरे में हैं, लेकिन लड़कियाँ कलकत्ते में हैं। यहाँ तीन आदमी हैं। औरतें कहाँ हैं? मेज़ों पर पुस्तकें हैं।

[1] For pronunciation see p. 8.

## EXERCISE 2

What is this? This is a book. The book is here. The books are there. Where is the letter? There are two boys here. The table is in the room. The jar is on the table, and there is water in the jar. What is that? That is a table. The bird is in the cage. There are three birds in the cage. There are three rooms in the house. In one room there are tables and chairs. The newspapers are on the tables.

# LESSON II

## ADJECTIVES

ADJECTIVES whose direct singular masculine form ends in *-ā* agree with nouns in gender, number, and case:

| | | m. | | f. | |
|---|---|---|---|---|---|
| Sg. Dir. | अच्छा | *acchā*, good | | अच्छी | *acchī* |
| Obl. | अच्छे | *acche* | | अच्छी | *acchī* |
| Pl. Dir. | अच्छे | *acche* | | अच्छी | *acchī* |
| Obl. | अच्छे | *acche* | | अच्छी | *acchī* |

Adjectives ending in *-āṁ* follow the pattern of अच्छा *acchā*, with endings nasalised, e.g. बायाँ *bāyāṁ* 'left' (hand); and most ordinal numerals.

Other adjectives are invariable (except for a few loanwords, and some adjectival uses of pronouns).

अच्छा लड़का *acchā laṛkā*, a good boy
बड़े मकान में *baṛe makān meṁ*, in the big house
बड़ी दूकानों में *baṛī dūkānoṁ meṁ*, in the big shops
दो लाल किताबें *do lāl kitābeṁ*, two red books

(*a*) Adjectives are used predicatively as well as attributively (i.e. following as well as preceding nouns which they qualify): e.g.

दीवार ऊँची है । *dīvār ūṁcī hai*, The wall is high.
किताबें लाल हैं । *kitābeṁ lāl haiṁ*, The books are red.

(*b*) A few adjectives in *-ā* are invariable: some showing final *-iyā*, e.g. बढ़िया *baṛhiyā* 'good, nice'; some Persian and Arabic loanwords, e.g. ज़िंदा *zindā* 'alive', मादा *mādā* 'female'; also the numeral सवा *savā* (see p. 64).

(*c*) An adjective used predicatively with two or more nouns or pronouns of different genders, and not referring to persons, agrees with the nearest: e.g.

काग़ज़ और पेंसिलें सस्ती हैं । *kāgaz aur peṃsileṁ sastī haiṁ*, Paper and pencils are cheap.

If the nouns or pronouns refer to persons the adjective usually takes masculine plural form: e.g.

मैं श्रौर सीता बूढ़े हैं । *maiṁ aur sīta būṛhe haiṁ*, Sītā and I are old.

But a composite pronoun subject, e.g. दोनों *donoṁ* 'both', is very often added in these cases to minimise the awkwardness of the concord: e.g.

मैं श्रौर सीता दोनों बूढ़े हैं । *maiṁ aur sītā donoṁ būṛhe haiṁ.*

## DEMONSTRATIVE PRONOUNS

| | | | | | |
|---|---|---|---|---|---|
| Sg. | Dir. | यह | *yah*, this | वह | *vah*, that |
| | Obl. | इस | *is* | उस | *us* |
| | Object | इसे | *ise* | उसे | *use* |
| Pl. | Dir. | ये | *ye* | वे | *ve* |
| | Obl. | इन | *in* | उन | *un* |
| | Object | इन्हें | *inheṁ* | उन्हें | *unheṁ* |

(*a*) यह *yah* is usually pronounced with a fairly high front unrounded vowel close to that of English *spin*, and little or no final aspiration, वह *vah* most frequently with a mid back rounded vowel close to that of French *beau*, and no aspiration. Pronunciations as indicated on p. xix are also heard.

(*b*) वह *vah* and its plural वे *ve*, as well as acting as demonstratives, are the normal translation equivalents of the third person pronouns 'he, she, it, they'. See p. 11.

(*c*) The singular direct case forms यह *yah*, वह *vah* are often substituted for ये *ye*, वे *ve* in both the spoken and the written language.

(*d*) The demonstrative pronouns are also used as demonstrative adjectives, preceding and in concord with nouns: e.g.
यह लड़का *yah laṛkā*, this boy
इस कमरे में *is kamre meṁ*, in this room
उन मेज़ों पर *un mezoṁ par*, on those tables
उन छोटी मेज़ों पर *un choṭī mezoṁ par*, on those small tables

(*e*) The object forms given above function both as definite direct objects and as indirect objects; they are equivalents (which tend to be preferred by many speakers) of the forms इसको *isko*, उसको *usko*, इनको *inko*, उनको *unko*, showing the postposition को *ko*. The uses of these forms and other uses of को *ko* are discussed in due course in Lesson IX, and elsewhere.

## THE POSTPOSITION का *kā*

This postposition indicates possession; it agrees in the same way as an adjective in *-ā* with nouns: e.g.

उस स्त्री का बेटा *us strī kā beṭā*, that woman's son
उस स्त्री के बेटे *us strī ke beṭe*, that woman's sons
उस स्त्री के बेटे का मकान *us strī ke beṭe kā makān*, that woman's son's house
उस आदमी की बहनों का मकान *us ādmī kī bahnoṁ kā makān*, that man's sisters' house
उसका मकान *uskā makān*,[1] his, her house

Possessive forms and expressions can be used predicatively as well as attributively: e.g.

यह मकान उसका है । *yah makān uskā hai*, This house is his, hers.
यह मकान उस स्त्री का है । *yah makān us strī kā hai*, This house belongs to that woman.

## VOCABULARY

दीवार *dīvār*, f., wall
काग़ज़ *kāgaz*, m., paper
पेंसिल *peṁsil*, f., pencil
स्त्री *strī*, f., woman[2]
बेटा *beṭā*, m., son
बेटी *beṭī*, f., daughter
भाई *bhāī*, m., brother; छोटा भाई *choṭā bhaī*, younger brother
बहन *bahn*, f., sister; छोटी बहन *choṭī bahn*, younger sister [बहिन *bahin*][3]
घर *ghar*, m., house, home; घर पर *ghar par*, at home
दरवाज़ा *darvāzā*, m., door; दरवाज़े पर *darvāze par*, at the door
बच्चा *baccā*, m., child; baby
किताब †*kitāb*, f., book
संदूक़ *sandūq*, m., box
देश *deś*, m., country
शहर *śahr*, m., city, town
गाँव *gāṁv*, m., village

[1] Postpositions are usually written as one word with oblique case pronominal forms, especially monosyllabic forms; much less often so with nouns.

[2] Words such as this, in which initial *s* is followed by a plosive consonant, are pronounced by most Hindi speakers with a 'prosthetic' or introductory short *i* of varying clarity before the consonant group.

[3] Echoing vocalic sounds after *h* preceding consonants (p. xviii) are sometimes represented in alternative spellings of this kind in a few words. These alternative spellings are in general less preferred in present-day usage, and further examples will not be noted.

सीता *sītā*, Sītā (girl's name)
क्लास *klās*, f. m., class (school)
क़िला *qilā*, m., fort
दिल्ली *dillī*, f., Delhi
इमारत *imārat*, f., building
राजा *rājā*, m., rajah
महल *mahl*, m., palace
कपड़ा *kapṛā*, m., cloth; pl. clothes
मंदिर *mandir*, m., temple
छोटा *choṭā*, small
बड़ा *baṛā*, large
बहुत *bahut*, adj. and adv., much, many; very
मैला *mailā*, dirty
खड़ा *khaṛā*, standing
साफ़ *sāf*, clean
काला *kālā*, black
सफ़ेद *safed*, white
सुंदर *sundar*, beautiful
चार *cār*, four
पाँच *pāṁc*, five; पाँचवाँ *pāṁcvāṁ*, fifth
छह, छः, छै *chah*, *chaḥ*, *chai*, six
लाल *lāl*, red
ऊँचा *ūṁcā*, high
बढ़िया *baṛhiyā*, good, nice
सस्ता *sastā*, cheap
बूढ़ा *būṛhā*, old (of persons); m., old man
मैं *maiṁ*, I

## EXERCISE 3

वह यहाँ नहीं है, लेकिन उसकी छोटी बहनें यहाँ हैं। वह घर पर नहीं है। दो छोटे बच्चे दरवाज़े पर खड़े हैं। यह पानी बहुत मैला है। काले संदूक़ में पाँच किताबें हैं। क्या किताबें इस काले संदूक़ में हैं? उस देश में बहुत शहर ग्रौर गाँव हैं। सीता पाँचवीं क्लास में है। लाल क़िला दिल्ली में है। ये उन छोटी लड़कियों की किताबें हैं। उन इमारतों की दीवारें ऊँची हैं। राजा का महल इस शहर में है। वह बहुत सुंदर है।

## EXERCISE 4

The book is on that table. The clothes are in this box. The books are on those tables. The clothes are in these boxes. They are here. Where is he? Where is she? Sītā is her younger sister. His book is on the table. Her books are in that room. Their clothes are clean and white. What's that? That's a box. In it there are four big books. These books are his. There are two temples in that small village. Calcutta is a big city.

# LESSON III

## Personal pronouns

1. *First person pronouns*

| | | | |
|---|---|---|---|
| Sg. | Dir. | मैं | *maiṁ*, I |
| | Obl. | मुझ | *mujh* |
| | Object | मुझे | *mujhe* |
| Possessive | | मेरा | *merā* |
| Pl. | Dir. | हम | *ham*, we |
| | Obl. | हम | *ham* |
| | Object | हमें | *hameṁ* |
| Possessive | | हमारा | *hamārā* |

2. *Second person pronouns*

| | | | | | |
|---|---|---|---|---|---|
| Sg. | Dir. | तू | *tū*, you | | |
| | Obl. | तुझ | *tujh* | | |
| | Object | तुझे | *tujhe* | | |
| Possessive | | तेरा | *terā* | | |
| Pl. | Dir. | | | तुम | *tum*, you |
| | Obl. | | | तुम | *tum* |
| | Object | | | तुम्हें | *tumheṁ* |
| Possessive | | | | तुम्हारा | *tumhārā* |

3. *Third person pronouns*

| | | | | | | | |
|---|---|---|---|---|---|---|---|
| Sg. | Dir. | वह | *vah*, he, she, it | यह | *yah*, he, she, it | | |
| | Obl. | उस | *us* | इस | *is* | | |
| | Object | उसे | *use* | इसे | *ise* | | |
| Possessive | | उसका | *uskā* | इसका | *iskā* | | |
| Pl. | Dir. | वे | *ve*, they | ये | *ye*, they | आप | *āp*, you; he, she, they |
| | Obl. | उन | *un* | इन | *in* | आप | *āp* |
| | Object | उन्हें | *unheṁ* | इन्हें | *inheṁ* | | |
| Possessive | | उनका | *unkā* | इनका | *inkā* | आपका | *āpkā* |

(*a*) तुम *tum* may have singular or plural reference, but is a plural pronoun in respect of its concord with verbs. For the distinction between तुम *tum* with singular reference and तू *tū* (which has only singular reference) see below.

(*b*) यह *yah* and ये *ye* are used as third person pronouns with 'proximate' force; e.g. often in reference to a person actually present at the time of speaking, or to the latter of two possible referends in a preceding sentence or clause.

(*c*) Note that by far the commonest translation equivalent of the pronoun आप *āp* is 'you', and that it may have either singular or plural reference, but that it is a third person plural pronoun in respect of its concord with verbs; see below.

(*d*) The possessive forms of first and second person pronouns are inflected as adjectives, like third person possessive forms showing -का *-kā* (see p. 9): e.g.
मेरा भाई *merā bhāī*, my brother
तुम्हारी बहनें *tumhārī bahnem̐*, your sisters
यह किताब मेरी है *yah kitāb merī hai*, This book is mine.

(*e*) The object forms of first and second person pronouns are used in the same way as the object forms of यह *yah*, वह *vah* (see pp. 8 f.). Note that आप *āp* has no specific object form.

(*f*) Pronouns are often not expressed where the sense of a sentence is clear without their presence, e.g.
वे आज कहाँ हैं? – दिल्ली में हैं। *ve āj kahām̐ haim̐? — dillī mem̐ haim̐*, Where are they today? — In Delhi.

## HONORIFIC USAGES

1. Care must be exercised in using the pronouns आप *āp*, तुम *tum* and तू *tū*, which have different honorific values. In normal educated usage आप *āp* is the pronoun of address to one's seniors (though not usually to close female relatives), and also very generally to one's peers and others whom one addresses on equal terms. आप *āp* is used with a third person

plural verb, whether the reference is to one person or more than one[1]: e.g.

आप कैसे हैं? *āp kaise haiṁ?* How are you? (masculine reference)
आप कैसी हैं? *āp kaisī haiṁ?* How are you? (feminine reference)

A person to whom one uses आप *āp* should usually be referred to, if absent, with the plural pronominal form वे *ve*, and a plural verb[2]; but if present, either with ये *ye* or आप *āp*.

(*a*) तुम *tum* expresses moderate divergence from high honorific reference. It is used by Hindi speakers in addressing many relatives (especially those not senior to the speaker), quite often in addressing close friends, and regularly in addressing persons of lower social status than the speaker, for example servants, or rickshaw-wallahs. Foreigners will most probably find that Indians with whom they are on friendly terms will address them with आप *āp*, and, if this is so, should reciprocate.

A person to whom one uses तुम *tum* can be referred to, if absent, with the singular pronominal form वह *vah*, and a singular verb; and if present, with यह *yah*.

(*b*) तू *tū* expresses feelings of great intimacy or informality, and also of contempt, disgust, etc. (extreme divergences in different directions from high honorific reference). It will rarely be used by foreigners. Indians often use it to invoke a deity, and when speaking to small children, and foreigners may of course follow suit.

2. Most educated Hindi speakers use the three-term honorific system outlined above, but for some the use of आप *āp* is not fully natural. These persons normally use तुम *tum* in the way in which आप *āp* is used within the three-term system; तू *tū* then covers the functions of both तुम *tum* and तू *tū* in the three-term system. This usage is best not imitated.

3. Plural concord in a sentence can, as seen above, be a mark of honorific

[1] There is a means of making explicit a reference to more than one person by आप *āp* or तुम *tum*. See Supplement I, p. 165, in due course.

[2] This convention is not observed systematically in referring to persons with whom one is not acquainted.

reference, but the only ***nouns*** used honorifically in plural number are the masculines in *-ā* when in direct case: e.g.

आपके बेटे कैसे हैं? *āpke beṭe kaise haiṁ?* How is your son?[1]

Cf. आपकी बेटी कैसी हैं? *āpkī beṭī kaisī haiṁ?* How is your daughter?

4. Common uses of the honorific particle जी *jī* are as follows:

(*a*) In addressing a person (male or female) to whom one uses आप *āp*, जी *jī* may be added to the last name: e.g.

वाजपेयी जी, आप कैसे हैं? *vājpeyī jī, āp kaise haiṁ?* How are you, Mr. Vājpeyī?
Where added to a first name it denotes a certain familiarity: e.g.
कैसी हैं, राधा जी? *kaisī haiṁ, rādhā jī?* How are you, Rādhā?

(*b*) In referring to persons whom one would address with आप *āp*. जी *jī* precedes last names in this case: e.g.
उस समय राम प्रसाद जी शर्मा मंत्री थे। *us samay rām prasād jī śarmā mantrī the,* At that time Mr. Rām Prasād Śarmā was secretary.

(*c*) With the words हाँ *hāṁ* 'yes' and नहीं *nahīṁ* 'no'. These used alone sometimes seem rather crude to an Indian ear. जी हाँ *jī hāṁ* and जी नहीं *jī nahīṁ* are best restricted to आप *āp* contexts. हाँ जी *hāṁ jī*, नहीं जी *nahīṁ jī* are much less circumspect, and are usually best avoided in आप *āp* contexts. For 'yes', जी *jī* alone is often heard.

5. The forms श्री *śrī*, श्रीमती *śrīmatī*, and कुमारी *kumārī* or सुश्री *suśrī* are also used in the same way as the titles Mr., Mrs., and Miss. They may always be replaced, in addressing persons, by the more traditional जी *jī*. In referring to persons formally, they are sometimes used in conjunction with जी *jī*.

## VOCABULARY

पिता *pitā*, m., father
माता, माँ *mātā, māṁ*, f., mother
स्कूल *skūl*, m., school; स्कूल में *skūl meṁ* at school
पति *pati*, m., husband
पत्नी *patnī*, f., wife
माता-पिता *mātā-pitā*, m.pl., parents
भारत *bhārat*, m., India
राजधानी *rājdhānī*, f., capital
मंत्री *mantrī*, m., secretary

[1] Alongside this sentence the sentence आपका बेटा कैसा है? *āpkā beṭā kaisā hai?* is of course also possible (and would be a more common utterance).

ठीक *ṭhīk*, correct, all right, fine
सब *sab*, all; everything; सब किताबें *sab kitābeṁ*, all the books
काम *kām*, m., work
बैठा *baiṭhā*, seated, sitting
कैसे *kaise*, what sort of?; used adjectivally in आप कैसे हैं? *āp kaise haiṁ?* How are you? etc.
अभी *abhī*, now
हाँ *hāṁ*, yes
नहीं *nahīṁ*, no
नमस्ते *namaste*, 'greetings' (common term of address; equivalent नमस्कार *namaskār*)
हम हैं *ham haiṁ*, we are
मैं हूँ *maiṁ hūṁ*, I am
उस समय *us samay*, at that time

## EXERCISE 5

मेरा बेटा अभी दिल्ली में है। मेरे बेटे का मकान बहुत बड़ा है। आपकी किताबें उस बड़ी मेज़ पर हैं। वे मेरे बड़े भाई हैं। नमस्ते, आप कैसे हैं? कैसी हैं, सीता जी? सब ठीक है? जी हाँ, सब ठीक है। श्री प्रसाद यहाँ हैं, उस कमरे में बैठे हैं। हमारा शहर छोटा है। उनके भाई यहाँ नहीं हैं। क्या यह किताब आपकी है? । जी नहीं, मेरी नहीं है, मेरे पिता जी की है।

## EXERCISE 6

Sītā is this boy's sister. The sisters of these boys are at school. Where is your mother? How is your wife? This work is unsatisfactory. That book is mine. All the books are mine. All these books[1] are my parents'. We are sitting in their room. How are you, Mr. Prasad? I am well. In India there are many villages. Delhi is the capital of India.

[1] ये सब किताबें *ye sab kitābeṁ*; note word order.

# LESSON IV

## VERB STRUCTURE AND CONCORD

1. The basic structural units of the Hindi verb are:

(*a*) The verb stem.

(*b*) Formative suffixes, which are added to stems and of which the chief are:

(i) *-tā*, *-ā*, and their concord variants, which form imperfective and perfective participles respectively. These characterise verbal actions aspectually as not completed, or as completed. This distinction is fundamental to a large number of verbal forms.

(ii) *-nā* and its concord variants. These form verbal nouns or adjectives. Verbs are quoted in the form stem + *-nā* (infinitive form).

(iii) Certain modal suffixes which appear in subjunctive and imperative forms.

(*c*) Certain forms of the verb होना *honā*, used with the participles as auxiliaries of tense and mood.

2. Verbal expressions based on stems, participles, and infinitives and containing further verbal forms other than (or additional to) those of the verb होना *honā* are very frequent. They may be described collectively as composite verbal expressions. Various types of composite verbal expression are introduced in due course, as well as types of verbal expression based on nominal forms (nouns and adjectives).

3. Finite verbs (i.e. main verbal forms of simple or complex[1] sentences) very frequently show concord of number, person, and gender (where applicable) with sentence subjects; otherwise (in cases to be defined in due course) they show concord with direct objects, or are used impersonally (not in any concord relationship).

## PRESENT, PAST, AND FUTURE TENSE FORMS OF होना *honā* 'be, become'

*Present*: 'I am', etc.

| | | | |
|---|---|---|---|
| Sg. | 1 | मैं हूँ | *maiṁ hūṁ* |
| | 2 | तू है | *tū hai* |
| | 3 | वह है | *vah hai* |

[1] See p. 46, n. 1.

| | | | | | | |
|---|---|---|---|---|---|---|
| Pl. 1 | हम हैं | *ham haiṁ* | | | | |
| 2 | तुम हो | *tum ho* | | | | |
| 3 | वे, आप हैं | *ve, āp haiṁ* | | | | |

*Past*: 'I was', etc.

| | | | | | |
|---|---|---|---|---|---|
| Sg. 1 | मैं था | *maiṁ thā*, | m. | थी | *thī*, f. |
| 2 | तू था | *tū thā* | | थी | *thī* |
| 3 | वह था | *vah thā* | | थी | *thī* |
| Pl. 1 | हम थे | *ham the* | | थीं | *thīṁ* |
| 2 | तुम थे | *tum the* | | थीं | *thīṁ* |
| 3 | वे, आप थे | *ve, āp the* | | थीं | *thīṁ* |

*Future*: 'I shall be, become', etc.

| | | | | | |
|---|---|---|---|---|---|
| Sg. 1 | मैं हूँगा | *maiṁ hūṁgā*, | m. | हूँगी | *hūṁgī*, f. |
| 2 | तू होगा | *tū hogā* | | होगी | *hogī* |
| 3 | वह होगा | *vah hogā* | | होगी | *hogī* |
| Pl. 1 | हम होंगे | *ham hoṁge* | | होंगी | *hoṁgī* |
| 2 | तुम होगे | *tum hoge* | | होगी | *hogī* |
| 3 | वे, आप होंगे | *ve, āp hoṁge* | | होंगी | *hoṁgī* |

(*a*) Note that past tense forms show gender concord with subjects, and that feminine plural past tense forms show nasality; in this way a number distinction between feminine singulars and plurals, which would otherwise be lacking, is achieved.

(*b*) Future tense forms also show gender concord with subjects. Note that future forms of होना *honā* are often used to express presumptions: e.g.

वह आदमी दक्खिनी होगा *vah ādmī dakkhinī hogā*, That man is probably a southerner.

## REGULAR CONJUGATIONAL PATTERNS

The main regular conjugational patterns of the verb are illustrated below and in the next lesson with forms of the verb चलना *calnā* 'go, move'. Irregularities of form in verbs other than होना *honā* are few; most are cited.

1. *General present*: 'I go', etc.

| | | | | | | |
|---|---|---|---|---|---|---|
| Sg. | 1 | मैं चलता हूँ | *maiṁ caltā hūṁ*, | m. | चलती हूँ | *caltī hūṁ*, f. |
| | 2 | तू चलता है | *tū caltā hai* | | चलती है | *caltī hai* |
| | 3 | वह चलता है | *vah caltā hai* | | चलती है | *caltī hai* |
| Pl. | 1 | हम चलते हैं | *ham calte haiṁ* | | चलती हैं | *caltī haiṁ* |
| | 2 | तुम चलते हो | *tum calte ho* | | चलती हो | *caltī ho* |
| | 3 | वे, ग्राप चलते हैं | *ve, āp calte haiṁ* | | चलती हैं | *caltī haiṁ* |

(*a*) General present forms express habitual action or general state, but are also used in other cases with a certain indefinite sense, for instance when there is no explicit need felt to use a continuous present form: e.g.

मैं भारत में रहता हूँ । *maiṁ bhārat meṁ rahtā hūṁ*, I live in India.

मैं भारत में हिंदी बोलता हूँ । *maiṁ bhārat meṁ hindī boltā hūṁ*, I speak Hindi in India.

मैं चलता हूँ । *maiṁ caltā hūṁ*, I'm going.

(*b*) General present forms are negatived with नहीं *nahīṁ*, preceding the participle; the auxiliary is usually dropped unless the negation is strongly stressed. In such cases the nasality of the auxiliary in feminine plural forms, which is the only feature distinguishing them from feminine singular forms, is transferred to the final syllable of the participle.

वे ग्रौरतें ग्रक्सर हिंदी नहीं बोलतीं । *ve aurteṁ aksar hindī nahīṁ boltīṁ*, Those women usually don't speak Hindi.

(*c*) होना *honā* has its own general present form होता है *hotā hai* 'is (in general)'. Note particularly the use of होता है *hotā hai* as opposed to है *hai*:

यह गाड़ी लाल है । *yah gāṛī lāl hai*, This car is red (particular case).

गाड़ियाँ महँगी होती हैं । *gāṛiyāṁ mahaṁgī hotī haiṁ*, Cars are expensive (general case).

2. *Imperfective past*: 'I went, used to go', etc.

| | | | | | | |
|---|---|---|---|---|---|---|
| Sg. | 1 | मैं चलता था | *maiṁ caltā thā*, | m. | चलती थी | *caltī thī*, f. |
| | 2 | तू चलता था | *tū caltā thā* | | चलती थी | ,, |
| | 3 | वह चलता था | *vah caltā thā* | | चलती थी | ,, |
| Pl. | 1 | हम चलते थे | *ham calte the* | | चलती थीं | *caltī thīṁ* |
| | 2 | तुम चलते थे | *tum calte the* | | चलती थीं | ,, |
| | 3 | वे, ग्राप चलते थे | *ve, āp calte the* | | चलती थीं | ,, |

(*a*) These forms have the same usual reference to habitual action or general state as general present forms. They are also common in narration where there is no explicit need felt to use a past continuous form: e.g.

उस समय में दिल्ली में रहता था । *us samay maiṁ dillī meṁ rahtā thā*, At that time I was living in Delhi.

They are negatived with नहीं *nahīṁ*, preceding the participle: e.g.

मैं नहीं चलता था *maiṁ nahīṁ caltā thā*, I used not to go.

3. *Continuous present*: 'I am going', etc.

| | | | | | | |
|---|---|---|---|---|---|---|
| Sg. | 1 | मैं चल रहा हूँ | *maiṁ cal rahā hūṁ*, m. | चल रही हूँ | *cal rahī hūṁ*, f. |
| | 2 | तू चल रहा है | *tū cal rahā hai* | चल रही है | ,, *hai* |
| | 3 | वह चल रहा है | *vah cal rahā hai* | चल रही है | ,, *hai* |
| Pl. | 1 | हम चल रहे हैं | *ham cal rahe haiṁ* | चल रही हैं | ,, *haiṁ* |
| | 2 | तुम चल रहे हो | *tum cal rahe ho* | चल रही हो | ,, *ho* |
| | 3 | वे, आप चल रहे हैं | *ve, āp cal rahe haiṁ* | चल रही हैं | ,, *haiṁ* |

(*a*) These forms, showing the perfective participle of the verb रहना *rahnā* 'remain' following the stem, stress the continuous nature of incompleted actions.[1] The verbal unit चल रहा हूँ *cal rahā hūṁ* is pronounced with a single stress on the verb stem, the following syllables being unstressed.

(*b*) Some English expressions of present participial form refer to present state as much as to continued action, e.g. *to be sitting*, *lying*, etc. These have as Hindi translation equivalents not continuous present forms but perfective participles of verbs denoting assumption of the given state, plus present tense forms of होना *honā*: e.g.

मैं कुरसी पर बैठा हूँ । *maiṁ kursī par baiṭhā hūṁ*, I am sitting on a chair.

किताब मेज़ पर पड़ी है । *kitāb mez par paṛī hai*, The book is lying on the table.

(*c*) The continuous present may be used, as in English, of future events which are thought of as already set in train: e.g.

मैं कल जा रहा हूँ । *maiṁ kal jā rahā hūṁ*, I am going tomorrow.

(*d*) Continuous present forms can be negatived with नहीं *nahīṁ* in the same way as general present forms. They are less common when negatived

[1] The element चल रहा *cal rahā* has the general sense 'having remained in, being engaged in the action चल- *cal-*'.

than the latter, however, since it is not often necessary to describe a non-occurring action as specifically 'continuous'.

4. *Continuous past*: 'I was going', etc.

| | | | | | |
|---|---|---|---|---|---|
| Sg. 1 | मैं चल रहा था | *maiṁ cal rahā thā*, | m. | चल रही थी *cal rahī thī*, | f. |
| 2 | तू चल रहा था | *tū cal rahā thā* | | चल रही थी | ,, |
| 3 | वह चल रहा था | *vah cal rahā thā* | | चल रही थी | ,, |
| Pl. 1 | हम चल रहे थे | *ham cal rahe the* | | चल रही थीं *cal rahī thīṁ* | |
| 2 | तुम चल रहे थे | *tum cal rahe the* | | चल रही थीं | ,, |
| 3 | वे, आप चल रहे थे | *ve, āp cal rahe the* | | चल रही थीं | ,, |

(*a*) The notes to subsection 3 above apply *mutatis mutandis* to the continuous past.

## VERBAL CONCORD WITH COMPOSITE SUBJECTS

Where there are two or more subjects of different genders the verb usually agrees with the subject nearest to it, although if both subjects have personal reference it often shows a 'common' masculine gender. This is normal when first and second person subjects are involved. In these cases a composite subject pronoun (e.g. दोनों *donoṁ* 'both') is often added.

काग़ज़ और स्याही सस्ती है। *kāgaz aur syāhī sastī hai*, Paper and ink are cheap.

मेरे भाई और उनकी पत्नी दिल्ली में रहते हैं। *mere bhāī aur unkī patnī dillī meṁ rahte haiṁ*, My brother and his wife live in Delhi.

मैं और मेरी बहन (दोनों) दिल्ली में रहते हैं। *maiṁ aur merī bahn* (*donoṁ*) *dillī meṁ rahte haiṁ*, My sister and I live in Delhi.

Where there are two or more subjects of the same gender the verb is plural and of that gender if they have personal reference; otherwise it most frequently agrees with the nearest subject: e.g.

लड़की और उसकी माँ कल दिल्ली जा रही हैं। *laṛkī aur uskī māṁ kal dillī jā rahī haiṁ*, The girl and her mother are going to Delhi tomorrow.

किताब और पेंसिल मेज़ पर है। *kitāb aur peṃsil mez par hai*, The book and pencil are on the table.

## THE POSTPOSITION से *se*

This postposition is used in construction with various verbs of speaking, telling, etc. (but not all such verbs); e.g. with बोलना *bolnā* 'to speak', कहना *kahnā* 'to say', and पूछना *pūchnā* 'to ask'.

मैं उससे हमेशा हिंदी बोलता हूँ । *maiṁ usse hameśā hindī boltā hūṁ*, I always speak Hindi to him.

उससे यह सवाल पूछिए । *usse yah savāl pūchie*, Ask him this question.

## SOME EXPRESSIONS OF MOTION

Expressions describing motion to a destination denoted by a place-name usually show the noun concerned without following postposition: e.g.

मैं भारत जा रहा हूँ । *maiṁ bhārat jā rahā hūṁ*, I'm going to India.

मैं कलकत्ते (कलकत्ता) जा रहा हूँ । *maiṁ kalkatte* (*kalkattā*) *jā rahā hūṁ*, I'm going to Calcutta.

The second example with its alternative forms (see p. 1) shows that oblique case usages are involved in this type of expression. Expressions of motion are discussed further in Lesson IX.

## VOCABULARY

हिंदी *hindī*, f., Hindi
गाड़ी *gāṛī*, f., vehicle (cart, car, train)
अँग्रेज़ *aṁgrez*, m.f., Englishman, Englishwoman
अँग्रेज़ी *aṁgrezī*, adj., English; the English language (f.)
भाषा *bhāṣā*, f., language
बारिश †*bāriś*, f., rain; बारिश होना *bāriś honā*, rain (verb)
पेड़ *peṛ*, m., tree
पत्ता *pattā*, m., leaf
दोस्त †*dost*, m., friend
दफ़्तर *daftar*, m., office
विद्यार्थी *vidyārthī*, m., student
गरमियाँ *garmiyāṁ*, f.pl., hot season
दिन *din*, m., day
सिग्रेट *sigreṭ*, f.m., cigarette
स्याही *syāhī*, f., ink
डाकिया *ḍākiyā*, m., postman
सवाल †*savāl*, m., question
पड़ा *paṛā*, lying, placed flat

हरा *harā*, green
लंबा *lambā*, long; tall
महँगा *mahaṁgā*, expensive
अच्छा *acchā*, good; adv., well; interj., all right, I see, etc.
भारतीय *bhārtīy*, adj. and noun, Indian
रहना *rahnā*, stay, remain, live
बोलना *bolnā*, speak, talk
बैठना *baiṭhnā*, sit
जाना *jānā*, go
लिखना *likhnā*, write
जानना *jānnā*, know
गाना *gānā*, sing; song (m.)
सीखना *sīkhnā*, learn
पढ़ना *paṛhnā*, read; study
पड़ना *paṛnā*, fall; be found
आना *ānā*, come
सोना *sonā*, sleep
अक्सर †*aksar*, usually
कल *kal*, yesterday, tomorrow

परसों *parsoṁ*, day before yesterday,    कब *kab*, when?
   day after tomorrow           क्यों *kyoṁ*, why?
हमेशा *hameśā*, always

## EXERCISE 7

आप कैसे हैं? मैं ठीक हूँ । हम अँग्रेज़ हैं । हमारी भाषा अँग्रेज़ी है । उसकी बहनें कल आगरे में थीं । मैं कल वहाँ था । क्या आज बारिश होगी? जी नहीं, आज बारिश नहीं होगी । मैं एक पत्र लिख रहा हूँ । वह मुझसे अँग्रेज़ी बोलता है । उस पेड़ के पत्ते हरे हैं । पेड़ों के पत्ते हरे होते हैं । मैं हिंदी नहीं जानता । वे भारत में हमसे अँग्रेज़ी बोलते थे । वह मेरी कुरसी पर बैठा है । हम परसों भारत जा रहे हैं । अच्छा, मैं चलता हूँ । लड़का गाना गा रहा है । आप हिंदी क्यों सीख रहे हैं?[1] ।

## EXERCISE 8

My friend's brother was here yesterday. His sisters weren't in the room. Is he in the office? No, I expect he's at home. He always speaks Hindi to the Indian students, but doesn't speak it[2] to me. We live in the capital of India. I am learning Hindi. I don't read his books. In summer the days are long. Cigarettes aren't expensive in India. When does the postman come? The girls used to sleep in that room. We are reading a very good book.[3]

---

[1] Interrogative words such as क्यों *kyoṁ*, कब *kab* usually follow any object forms in sentences of neutral style and emphasis.

[2] The pronoun may be omitted.

[3] In speech of normal to fast tempo the verb here is phonologically/paṛh ṛahe haiṁ/, *r* in the word *rahe* being assimilated to the preceding flap *ṛh*. Assimilations of this kind are quite common.

# LESSON V

## REGULAR CONJUGATIONAL PATTERNS (contd.)

1. *Perfective*: 'I went', etc.

| | | | | | |
|---|---|---|---|---|---|
| Sg. | 1 | मैं चला | *maiṁ calā*, | m. | चली *calī*, f. |
| | 2 | तू चला | *tū calā* | | चली ,, |
| | 3 | वह चला | *vah calā* | | चली ,, |
| Pl. | 1 | हम चले | *ham cale* | | चलीं *calīṁ* |
| | 2 | तुम चले | *tum cale* | | चलीं ,, |
| | 3 | वे, आप चल | *ve, āp cale* | | चलीं ,, |

(*a*) Perfective forms denote completedness of action, without specific reference to time. They are used chiefly, but not only, of events occurring in past time.[1]

(*b*) Verbs whose stem ends in *-ī* or *-ū* shorten this vowel before perfective inflexional endings: but a shortened stem *-i* coalesces with the feminine inflexional endings, restoring the long vowel in feminine forms. The perfective forms of छूना *chūnā* 'touch' and सीना *sīnā* 'sew' are thus

| | | | | |
|---|---|---|---|---|
| छुआ *chuā* | छुई *chuī* | छुए *chue* | छुईं *chuīṁ*, | touched |
| सिया *siyā*[2] | सी *sī* | सिए *sie* | सीं *sīṁ*, | sewed |

(*c*) Verbs whose stem ends in *-ā*, *-ō*, *-e* or *-ī* show a semi-vocalic glide *y* before masculine singular endings.[3] Verbs whose stem ends in *-e* show a similar glide before masculine plural endings also.

| | | | | |
|---|---|---|---|---|
| आया *āyā* | आई *āī* | आए *āe* | आईं *āīṁ*, | came |
| सोया *soyā* | सोई *soī* | सोए *soe* | सोईं *soīṁ*, | slept |
| खेया *kheyā* | खेई *kheī* | खेये *kheye* | खेईं *kheīṁ*, | rowed |
| सिया *siyā* | सी *sī* | सिए *sie* | सीं *sīṁ*, | sewed |

[1] Some usages of perfective forms with future time reference are noted in Lesson XX.

[2] *y* in this form is explained in the following paragraph.

[3] Before other endings, where the glide is either attenuated or not present in pronunciation, it need never be expressed in written forms but is often introduced by analogy. See in due course Supplement II, p. 175.

(*d*) The perfective forms of five verbs require special note:

| | m.sg. | f.sg. | m.pl. | f.pl. |
|---|---|---|---|---|
| करना *karnā* 'do': | किया *kiyā* | की *kī* | किए *kie* | कीं *kīṁ* |
| लेना *lenā* 'take': | लिया *liyā* | ली *lī* | लिए *lie* | लीं *līṁ* |
| देना *denā* 'give': | दिया *diyā* | दी *dī* | दिए *die* | दीं *dīṁ* |
| जाना *jānā* 'go': | गया *gayā* | गई *gaī* | गए *gae* | गईं *gaīṁ* |
| होना *honā* 'be, become': | हुआ *huā* | हुई *huī* | हुए *hue* | हुईं *huīṁ* |

Note the difference between perfective हुआ *huā* 'became' and past tense था *thā* 'was':

मैं लड़ाई में जख़्मी हुआ। *maiṁ laṛāī meṁ zakhmī huā*, I was wounded in the war.
मैं लड़ाई में भारत में था। *maiṁ laṛāī meṁ bhārat meṁ thā*, I was in India during the war.

(*e*) In general, perfective forms of transitive verbs[1] are not used in subject concord constructions of the type so far considered. The types of construction into which they characteristically enter are introduced in due course in Lesson XII. Perfective forms of a few transitive verbs are, however, used in subject concord constructions: e.g.

बोलना *bolnā*, speak, talk
लाना *lānā*, bring
समझना *samajhnā*, understand

(*f*) With perfective forms the negative न *na* is common, as well as नहीं *nahīṁ*.

2. *Perfective present*: 'I have gone', etc.

| | | | | | |
|---|---|---|---|---|---|
| Sg. | 1 | मैं चला हूँ | *maiṁ calā hūṁ*, m. | चली हूँ | *calī hūṁ*, f. |
| | 2 | तू चला है | *tū calā hai* | चली है | ,, *hai* |
| | 3 | वह चला है | *vah calā hai* | चली है | ,, *hai* |
| Pl. | 1 | हम चले हैं | *ham cale haiṁ* | चली हैं | *calī haiṁ* |
| | 2 | तुम चले हो | *tum cale ho* | चली हो | ,, *ho* |
| | 3 | वे, आप चले हैं | *ve, āp cale haiṁ* | चली हैं | ,, *haiṁ* |

(*a*) Perfective present forms define actions as completed and connected in some way with present time. They may describe not only actions

[1] Verbs which can be used in construction with direct objects.

occurring in the immediate past, but also actions occurring in the more distant past whose consequences are felt as continuing to the present.

मैं अभी आया हूँ। *maiṁ abhī āyā hūṁ*, I've just come.

मैं एक बार दिल्ली गया हूँ। *maiṁ ek bār dillī gayā hūṁ*, I've been to Delhi once.[1]

मैं कुरसी पर बैठा हूँ। *maiṁ kursī par baiṭhā hūṁ*, I'm sitting on a chair.[2]

3. *Perfective past*: 'I went, had gone', etc.

| | | | | | |
|---|---|---|---|---|---|
| Sg. 1 | मैं चला था | *maiṁ calā thā*, | m. | चली थी | *calī thī*, f. |
| 2 | तू चला था | *tū calā thā* | | चली थी | ,, |
| 3 | वह चला था | *vah calā thā* | | चली थी | ,, |
| Pl. 1 | हम चले थे | *ham cale the* | | चली थीं | *calī thīṁ* |
| 2 | तुम चले थे | *tum cale the* | | चली थीं | ,, |
| 3 | वे, आप चले थे | *ve, āp cale the* | | चली थीं | ,, |

(*a*) Perfective past forms define actions as completed specifically in past time, and disconnected in some way from the present. Because they have this force, they can answer not only to English pluperfects (verb forms such as 'had come', 'had gone', etc.), but also to past tenses: e.g.

मैं कल आया था *maiṁ kal āyā thā*, I came yesterday.

The implication here is that whatever the speaker is now doing is not a direct sequel to the action of his coming. Compare

मैं कल आया हूँ। *maiṁ kal āyā hūṁ*, I got here yesterday (in order to attend today's meeting, for a much anticipated stay, etc.).

and

मैं कल आया। *maiṁ kal āyā*, I came yesterday (matter-of-fact statement, neutral with regard to time and context of action).

4. *Subjunctive*: 'I may go', etc.

| | | |
|---|---|---|
| Sg. 1 | मैं चलूँ | *maiṁ calūṁ*, m., f. |
| 2 | तू चले | *tū cale* |
| 3 | वह चले | *vah cale* |
| Pl. 1 | हम चलें | *ham caleṁ* |
| 2 | तुम चलो | *tum calo* |
| 3 | वे, आप चलें | *ve, āp caleṁ* |

[1] एक बार *ek bār* 'on one occasion'.

[2] See p. 19.

(*a*) Verbs whose stem ends in -*ī* or -*ū* shorten this vowel before subjunctive inflexional endings, e.g. वह पिए *vah pie* 'he may drink'; हम छुएँ *ham chueṁ* 'we may touch'. Sometimes, however, long vowels appear, especially in first person singular written forms of verbs in -*ī*, e.g. मैं जिऊँ/जीऊँ *maiṁ jiūṁ/jīūṁ* 'I may live'.

(*b*) Subjunctive forms characterize actions as possible, desired or desirable, hypothetical, subject to some doubt, etc., rather than as objectively realized or envisaged: e.g.

मैं चलूँ? *maiṁ calūṁ?* May I go?

मैं कल शायद दिल्ली जाऊँ । *maiṁ kal śāyad dillī jāūṁ*, I'll perhaps go to Delhi tomorrow.

(*c*) The negative used with subjunctive forms is regularly *na*: e.g.

मैं कल शायद दिल्ली न जाऊँ । *maiṁ kal śāyad dillī na jāūṁ*, I perhaps won't go to Delhi tomorrow.

(*d*) The subjunctive forms of होना *honā* 'be', देना *denā* 'give', and लेना *lenā* 'take' are

| | | | | | |
|---|---|---|---|---|---|
| होऊँ (हूँ) *h(o)ūṁ* | हो *ho* | हो *ho* | हों *hoṁ* | हो (ओ) *ho(o)* | हों *hoṁ* |
| दूँ *dūṁ* | दे *de* | दे *de* | दें *deṁ* | दो *do* | दें *deṁ* |
| लूँ *lūṁ* | ले *le* | ले *le* | लें *leṁ* | लो *lo* | लें *leṁ* |

देना *denā* is used in construction with indirect as well as direct objects. The former are marked by the postposition को *ko* (except in the case of the equivalent pronominal object forms उसे *use*, etc., noted on pp. 8 f.). More frequently than not they precede direct objects in sentences: e.g.

मैं सीता को किताब दूँगा । *maiṁ sītā ko kitāb dūṁgā*, I shall give Sītā the book.

मैं उसे किताब दूँगा । *maiṁ use kitāb dūṁgā*, I shall give her the book.

(*e*) Note that subjunctives are often used with the force of polite imperatives[1] and in making suggestions: e.g.

आप मुझे पत्र लिखें *āp mujhe patr likheṁ*, Please write me a letter.

चलें ? *caleṁ?* Shall we go?

[1] Here they are close equivalents (tending to be more circumspect in force) of imperatives in -*ie*, which are introduced in Lesson VII.

5. *Future*: 'I shall go', etc.

| | | | | | |
|---|---|---|---|---|---|
| Sg. 1 | मैं चलूँगा | *maiṁ calūṁgā*, | m. | चलूँगी | *calūṁgī*, f. |
| 2 | तू चलेगा | *tū calegā* | | चलेगी | *calegī* |
| 3 | वह चलेगा | *vah calegā* | | चलेगी | *calegī* |
| Pl. 1 | हम चलेंगे | *ham caleṁge* | | चलेंगी | *caleṁgī* |
| 2 | तुम चलोगे | *tum caloge* | | चलोगी | *calogī* |
| 3 | वे, आप चलेंगे | *ve, āp caleṁge* | | चलेंगी | *caleṁgī* |

(*a*) Verbs whose stem ends in *-ī* or *-ū* shorten this vowel before future inflexional endings: e.g.

मैं पिऊँगा *maiṁ piūṁgā*, I shall drink
हम सिएँगे *ham sieṁge*, We shall sew
वह छुएगा *vah chuegā*, He will touch

(*b*) Note that future forms are derivable from subjunctives by suffixation of the adjectivally inflected element *-gā*.

(*c*) Both नहीं *nahīṁ* and न *na* are used as negatives with future forms.

6. *Imperfective, continuous, and perfective future*

These forms consist of imperfective or perfective participles, or stems followed by रहा *rahā*, etc., in conjunction with future forms of होना *honā* as auxiliaries. They express likelihood that a given action may be occurring, or may have occurred: e.g.

अभी आते होंगे । *abhī āte hoṁge*, He's probably coming now, he'll be here directly.
अभी आ रहे होंगे । *abhī ā rahe hoṁge*, He's probably on his way now.
आप जानते होंगे । *āp jānte hoṁge*, I expect you know, you will know.
अभी आए होंगे । *abhī āe hoṁge*, He must have just come.

## THE EMPHATIC ENCLITICS ही *hī*, भी *bhī*

These forms are used freely in Hindi. Their function is to stress the importance of the word or syntactic group immediately preceding them in sentences.

(*a*) ही *hī* has restrictive force:

बनारस के लोग हिंदी ही बोलते हैं । *banāras ke log hindī hī bolte haiṁ*, The people of Banaras speak Hindi (not another language).

मैं एक ही बार वहाँ गया हूँ । *maiṁ ek hī bār vahāṁ gayā hūṁ*, I've been there just once (not more often).

Note that the form अभी *abhī* 'now' represents अब *ab* + ही *hī*, and contrasts with अब *ab* 'now' as meaning 'at this particular time' rather than 'at the present time'. Note its use in such sentences as

मैं अभी आया हूँ । *maiṁ abhī āyā hūṁ*, I've just come.

मैं अभी नहीं गया । *maiṁ abhī nahīṁ gayā*, I haven't gone yet.

(*b*) भी *bhī* has inclusive force, frequently being translatable as 'also', sometimes as 'even', especially with negatives:

मैं भी वहाँ था । *maiṁ bhī vahāṁ thā*, I was there too.

उस गाँव में कुआँ भी नहीं था । *us gāṁv meṁ kuāṁ bhī nahīṁ thā*, There wasn't even a well in that village.

(*c*) Further usages of these forms are given in Lesson XXIII, Supplement III, and elsewhere.

## VOCABULARY

लड़ाई *laṛāī*, f., war
बार *bār*, f., time, occasion; एक बार *ek bār*, once
आँगन *āṁgan*, m., courtyard
बंबई *bambaī*, f., Bombay
बनारस *banāras*, m., Banaras
रेस्टरेंट *resṭareṇṭ*, m., restaurant
काफ़ी *kāfī*, f., coffee
रुपया *rupayā*, m., rupee; money (usually pl.)
सर्दियाँ *sardiyāṁ*, f.pl., cold season
मौसम *mausam*, m., season, weather
लोग *log*, m.pl., people; सब लोग *sab log*, everyone
दूध *dūdh*, m., milk
बरसात *barsāt*, f., rainy season
ज़ख़्मी †*zakhmī*, wounded
कितना *kitnā*, how many? कितने दिन *kitne din*, how long?
सारा *sārā*, entire, all; सारा दिन *sārā din*, all day
जीना *jīnā*, live, be alive
करना *karnā*, do
लेना *lenā*, take
पीना *pīnā*, drink
लाना *lānā*, bring
समझना *samajhnā*, understand
पहुँचना *pahuṁcnā*, arrive
कहना *kahnā*, say, tell
पूछना *pūchnā*, ask, inquire
अब *ab*, now
शायद *śāyad*, perhaps (with subjunctive)
से *se*, from; with, to

## EXERCISE 9

मैं अभी दिल्ली से पहुँचा हूँ । आप उसके भाई से क्या कहेंगे? वह आती होगी । शायद मैं पत्र कल लिखूँ । लड़का आँगन में खड़ा है । मैं उससे कल क्या कहूँ? विद्यार्थी दिल्ली गए, और बंबई भी गए । चलें, रेस्टरेंट में काफ़ी पिएँ । मैं लड़के को दो ही रुपए दूंगा । मैं उसे एक भी रुपया नहीं दूंगा । आप कितने दिन भारत में रहे? रुपए मेज़ पर पड़े हैं । सर्दियों में मौसम अच्छा होता है । सब लोग मकान में गए ।

## EXERCISE 10

I shan't drink milk. Shall I read his letter? What am I to say? I shall ask him. His papers are lying on the table. He will have arrived yesterday. He will give you the letter. I stayed at home[1] all day yesterday. I came here in the rainy season. He spoke Hindi to me.

[1] घर पर *ghar par*; or, if the sense is 'I didn't go out all day', घर पर ही *ghar par hī.*

# LESSON VI

## FURTHER USES OF से *se*

APART from its use with verbs of speaking, telling, etc., some other uses of से *se* are:

1. In the senses 'from, away from', and 'since, for' (referring to passage of past time): e.g.

दिल्ली कलकत्ते से दूर है । *dillī kalkatte se dūr hai*, Delhi is far from Calcutta.
आप कब से यहाँ हैं? *āp kab se yahāṁ haiṁ?* Since when have you been here?[1]
मैं एक हफ़्ते से हिंदी सीख रहा हूँ । *maiṁ ek hafte se hindī sīkh rahā hūṁ*, I've been learning Hindi for a week.[1]

2. In expressions of manner derived from nouns: e.g.

आसानी से *āsānī se*, with ease, easily
आप हिंदी आसानी से सीख लेंगे । *āp hindī āsānī se sīkh leṁge*, You will learn Hindi easily.[2]

Similarly

इस तरह से *is tarah se*, in this way
मुश्किल से *muśkil se*, with difficulty[3]
जल्दी से *jaldī se*, quickly

3. In expressions of instrumentality, means, and cause: e.g.

मैं क़लम से पत्र लिखूंगा । *maiṁ qalam se patr likhūṁgā*, I shall write the letter with a pen.
मैं मोटर से यहाँ आया । *maiṁ moṭar se yahāṁ āyā*, I came here by car.
वह दुख से मरा । *vah dukh se marā*, He died of grief.

4. In certain constructions expressing the idea of connection in general, either literally or figuratively: e.g.

किश्ती बल्ले से बँधी है । *kiśtī balle se baṁdhī hai*, The boat is tied to the pole.

[1] Hindi uses the present tense verb हैं *haiṁ*, to express the idea that the state still obtains or the action is still in progress.

[2] Compound verb forms such as सीख लेंगे *sīkh leṁge* 'will (manage to) learn' are explained in Lesson XVII, pp. 99 f.

[3] This expression is also used in the sense 'scarcely', e.g. मैं मुश्किल से बचा *maiṁ muśkil se bacā* 'I only just escaped'.

में उससे डरता हूँ । *maiṁ usse ḍartā hūṁ*, I am afraid of him.
वह उससे प्यार करता है *vah usse pyār kartā hai*, He loves her.[1]

## FURTHER USES OF में *meṁ*

Note that the use of में *meṁ* in the general sense 'in, into' includes its use:

1. To express location in time, in both the senses 'in the course of' and 'after the period of': e.g.

आप एक साल में हिंदी सीख लेंगे । *āp ek sāl meṁ hindī sīkh leṁge*, You'll learn Hindi in (within) a year.
में एक घंटे में तैयार हूँगा । *maiṁ ek ghaṇṭe meṁ taiyār hūṁgā*, I'll be ready in an hour.

2. In expressions of cost of purchase: e.g.

कितने में लेंगे? पाँच रुपए में । *kitne meṁ leṁge? pāṁc rupae meṁ*, How much will you get (take) it for? Five rupees.[2]
यह घोड़ा कितने में बेचेंगे । *yah ghoṛā kitne meṁ beceṁge?* How much will you sell this horse for?

## FURTHER USES OF पर *par*

Apart from its use in the sense 'on, on top of' पर *par* is also frequently used in the senses 'at', 'in', 'to', most often where a somewhat precise location is denoted: e.g.

वह कल घर पर था । *vah kal ghar par thā*, He was at home yesterday.
वह दूकान पर नहीं है । *vah dūkān par nahīṁ hai*, He's not in the shop.
वह दूकान पर लौटा । *vah dūkān par lauṭā*, He went back to the shop.
मैं कल पार्टी पर जा रहा हूँ । *maiṁ kal pārṭī par jā rāhā hūṁ*, I'm going to a party tomorrow.
वह ठीक समय पर आया । *vah ṭhīk samay par āyā*, He arrived punctually, at the right time.
गरमियों में मैं पहाड़ पर जाऊँगा । *garmiyoṁ meṁ maiṁ pahāṛ par jāūṁgā*, In the hot weather I shall go to the hills.[3]

In some cases पर *par* in these senses can be replaced by the postpositions में *meṁ*, or को *ko*.

[1] प्यार *pyār*, m. 'love', used with करना *karnā* to form a transitive verbal expression; for these see in due course Lesson X.

[2] Note रुपए *rupae*; singular collective usages are common with numerals (see p. 63), and in some other cases.

[3] पहाड़ *pahāṛ*: see preceding note.

## THE POSTPOSITION तक *tak* 'up to, as far as; until; by'

तक *tak* is used with reference to both space and time: e.g.

मैं आपके गाँव तक गया, फिर यहाँ लौटा। *maiṁ āpke gāṁv tak gayā, phir yahāṁ lauṭā*, I went as far as your village, then came back.

मैं कल तक यहाँ रहूँगा। *maiṁ kal tak yahāṁ rahūṁgā*, I shall remain here till tomorrow.

Note especially the use of तक *tak* to express the point of time *before* or *by* which an action occurs: e.g.

बच्चे अक्तूबर तक स्कूल में लौटेंगे। *bacce aktūbar tak skūl meṁ lauṭeṁge*, The children will return to school by October.

## SOME ADVERBIAL EXPRESSIONS

1. Oblique case nouns are frequently, as has been seen, the basis for adverbial expressions. Most of these are self-explanatory, given a knowledge of the uses of postpositions. Some adverbial expressions based on nouns which call for special comment are:

(*a*) Expressions whose oblique case is evident from their oblique form, or the form of associated adjectives or pronouns, and in which a postposition is usually superfluous: e.g.

सवेरे *savere*, in the morning
पिछले हफ़्ते *pichle hafte*, last week
अगले महीने *agle mahīne*, next month
अगले साल *agle sāl*, next year
दाहिने हाथ *dāhine hāth*, on the right hand[1]
बाएँ हाथ *bāeṁ hāth*, on the left hand
उस समय *us samay*, at that time
उस दिन *us din*, on that day
इन दिनों *in dinoṁ*, these days
इस तरफ़ *is taraf*, in this direction

(*b*) Some expressions which often involve postpositions, but may drop them in informal usage if their force in sentences is perfectly clear: e.g.

शाम (को) *śām* (*ko*), in the evening[2]
रात (को) *rāt* (*ko*), at night

[1] An oblique form दाएँ *dāeṁ* is common colloquially alongside दाहिने *dāhine* in this and other expressions.

[2] को *ko* in adverbial expressions is discussed further in Lesson IX.

दिन (को) *din (ko)*, during the (middle part of the) day
सुबह (को) *subah (ko)*, in the morning
आज सुबह (को) *āj subah (ko)*, this morning
कल रात (को) *kal rāt (ko)*, last night
जल्दी (से), जल्द (से) *jaldī (se), jald (se)*, quickly
इस तरह (से) *is tarah (se)*, in this way

(*c*) Some expressions involving direct case forms, expressing duration of time: e.g.

सारा दिन *sārā din*, all day[1]
एक घंटा *ek ghaṇṭā*, for an hour

2. Adverbial use of adjectives is quite common, and again usually self-explanatory: e.g.

आप साफ़ लिखें *āp sāf likheṁ*, Please write clearly.

(*a*) Adjectives in final *-ā* usually show oblique case when used as adverbs, but sometimes direct case:

कैसे *kaise*, how
सीधे *sīdhe*, straight, directly
दाहिने, दाएँ *dāhine, dāeṁ*, to, on the right
बाएँ *bāeṁ*, to, on the left
नीचे *nīce*, below, underneath; downstairs
अच्छा *acchā*, well

मैं यह कैसे करूँ? *maiṁ yah kaise karūṁ?* How am I to do this?
वह सीधे चली, फिर दाहिने। *vah sīdhe calī, phir dāhine*, She went straight ahead, then to the right.
मेरे भाई का कमरा नीचे है। *mere bhāī kā kamrā nīce hai*, My brother's room is downstairs.
वह अच्छा गाती है। *vah acchā gātī hai*, She sings well.

(*b*) Note that Hindi has a frequent preference for adjectival construction, where this is possible. For instance the expressions

आप कैसे हैं? *āp kaise haiṁ?* How are you? (m.)
आप कैसी हैं? *āp kaisī haiṁ?* (f.)

[1] Also सारे दिन *sāre din*.

are adjectival in construction, as the feminine concord of the second shows. Similarly note

आप अच्छी हिंदी बोलते हैं। *āp acchī hindī bolte haiṁ*, You speak good Hindi, speak Hindi well,

and compare with the second Hindi sentence given in paragraph (*a*) above the following equivalent sentence, with adjectival construction of the word सीधा *sīdhā*:

वह सीधी चली, फिर दाहिने। *vah sīdhī calī, phir dāhine.*

## COMPOUND POSTPOSITIONS

1. As compound postpositions may conveniently be described certain types of adverbial expression, whose distinctive element is preceded by a simple postposition or an equivalent form. The first element of compound postpositions is usually the oblique case possessive form के/की *ke/kī*, as in के साथ *ke sāth* 'with', के पास *ke pās* 'near, beside', की तरफ़ *kī taraf* 'towards', etc. First and second person pronouns, whose possessive forms do not involve का *kā*, show their own possessives and not forms with का *kā* preceding the distinctive elements of compound postpositions of this type.

उसके साथ *uske sāth*, with him
मेरे साथ *mere sāth*, with me
गाँव के पास *gāṁv ke pās*, near the village
आपके पास *āpke pās*, near you; in your possession
तुम्हारे पास *tumhāre pās*, near you; in your possession
आपकी तरफ़ *āpkī taraf*, in your direction
हमारी तरफ़ *hamārī taraf*, in our direction

2. Apart from these and similar forms, a very small number of postpositions showing a first element से *se* will be found:

से बाहर *se bāhar* 'outside' and से पहले *se pahle* 'before' are common, alongside के बाहर *ke bāhar* and के पहले *ke pahle*. Members of these pairs are broadly speaking interchangeable, but careful speakers of Hindi may sometimes make a distinction between them. The following pairs of sentences exemplify a distinction which is quite commonly made between the use of से बाहर *se bāhar* and के बाहर *ke bāhar*, and a less common one between से पहले *se pahle* and के पहले *ke pahle*:

मैं कल लंदन से बाहर जा रहा हूँ। *maiṁ kal landan se bāhar jā rahā hūṁ*, I'm going out of London tomorrow. (motion involved)

वह घर के बाहर खड़ा था । *vah ghar ke bāhar khaṛā thā*, He was standing outside the house. (motion not involved)

वह उससे पहले वहाँ गया था । *vah usse pahle vahām̐ gayā thā*, He had been there before that.

मैं उसके पहले वहाँ गया था । *maim̐ uske pahle vahām̐ gayā thā*, I went there before him.

3. The second elements of many compound postpositions occur independently as adverbs: e.g.

गाँव पास है । *gām̐v pās hai*, The village is near.

वह बाहर है । *vah bāhar hai*, He's outside; he's abroad.

वह साथ आया । *vah sāth āyā*, He accompanied (us, me, etc.)

मैं पहले वहाँ रहता था । *maim̐ pahle vahām̐ rahtā thā*, I used to live there formerly.

Note the two forms बाद *bād* and बाद में *bād mem̐* 'afterwards', connected with के बाद *ke bād* 'after'; the former is common in expressions of time containing nouns, e.g. एक महीने बाद *ek mahīne bād* 'a month later'.

4. Certain compound postpositions based on feminine nouns, and therefore characteristically showing की *kī* as first element, are to be compared with expressions showing के *ke* as first element when an adjective is associated with the noun: e.g.

की तरफ़ *kī taraf*, towards

but

के दाहिनी तरफ़ *ke dāhinī taraf*, on the right-hand side of

## SOME EXPRESSIONS OF WISHING

The verb चाहना *cāhnā* 'wish' is used with a preceding infinitive in constructions expressing a person's wish to carry out an action: e.g.

मैं दिल्ली में रहना चाहता हूँ । *maim̐ dillī mem̐ rahnā cāhtā hūm̐*, I want to live in Delhi.

### VOCABULARY

हफ़्ता †*haftā*, m., week
महीना *mahīnā*, m., month
साल †*sāl*, m., year
घंटा *ghaṇṭā*, m., hour
मिनट *minaṭ*, m., minute
आसानी *āsānī*, f., ease

तरह †*tarah*, f., way, manner
मुश्किल †*muśkil*, f., difficulty; adj., difficult
जल्दी †*jaldī*, f., haste, speed; adv., जल्दी (से) *jaldī (se)*, quickly; soon
जल्द †*jald*, f., haste, speed; adv., जल्द (से) *jald (se)*, quickly; soon
मोटर *moṭar*, f., car (synonyms कार *kār*, f.; गाड़ी *gāṛī*, f.)
दुख *dukh*, m., grief
किश्ती †*kiśtī*, f., (small) boat [कश्ती *kaśtī*]
बल्ला *ballā*, m., pole
घोड़ा *ghoṛā*, m., horse
दूकान *dūkān*, f., shop [दुकान *dukān*]
समय *samay*, m., time[1]
पहाड़ *pahāṛ*, m., mountain, hill
तरफ़ †*taraf*, f., direction, side
हाथ *hāth*, m., hand
शाम *śām*, f., evening, late afternoon
रात *rāt*, f., night
सवेरा *saverā*, m., morning
सुबह †*subah*, f., morning
लंदन *landan*, m., London
खिड़की *khiṛkī*, f., window
सड़क *saṛak*, f., street, road
खाना *khānā*, m., food
काम *kām*, m., work
रेल *rel*, f., railway train; रेल से *rel se*, by train
जहाज़ *jahāz*, m., ship
हवा †*havā*, f., air; wind
हवाई जहाज़ *havāī jahāz*, m., aeroplane
हिंदुस्तान †*hindustān*, m., India
दूर *dūr*, f., distance; adj., distant; कितनी दूर *kitnī dūr*, how far?
साफ़ *sāf*, clean; clear
तैयार *taiyār*, ready
दाहिना *dāhinā*, right (hand); के दाहिनी (दाईं) तरफ़ *ke dāhinī (dāīṁ) taraf*, on the right-hand side of
बायाँ *bāyāṁ*, left (hand); के बाईं तरफ़ *ke bāīṁ taraf*, on the left-hand side of
सीधा *sīdhā*, direct, straight
नीचा *nīcā*, low
अगला *aglā*, next
पिछला *pichlā*, last
काफ़ी *kāfī*, adv., quite, fairly; adj., a fair amount of (invariable)
मरना *marnā*, die
बँधना *baṁdhnā*, be tied
डरना *ḍarnā*, fear
बचना *bacnā*, be safe, saved
बेचना *becnā*, sell
लौटना *lauṭnā*, return
चाहना *cāhnā*, wish
ठहरना *ṭhaharnā*, remain, stay, wait
के साथ *ke sāth*, with, together with
के पास *ke pās*, near, beside
की तरफ़ *kī* †*taraf*, towards; to (in certain cases, see p. 50)
के/से बाहर *ke/se bāhar*, outside
के अंदर *ke* †*andar*, inside
के/से पहले *ke/se pahle*, before (time)
के बाद *ke bād*, after
के सामने *ke sāmne*, in front of
के पीछे *ke pīche*, behind
के नीचे *ke nīce*, below, underneath
के ऊपर *ke ūpar*, above, on top of
के लिए *ke lie*, for
के बारे में *ke bāre meṁ*, about, concerning
फिर *phir*, again, then, next

[1] Final *-ay* of the script represents *ai* (pronounced either as a monophthong or a dipthong, see p. xiv).

## EXERCISE 11

काग़ज़ पुस्तकों के नीचे है। खिड़की आपके पीछे है। वह बाहर बैठी है। मैं उसके पहले यहाँ पहुँचा। पहले मैं एक गाँव में रहता था। मैं उससे इसके बारे में पूछूँगा। दिल्ली आगरे से कितनी दूर है ? क्या हम दस मिनट में चलें? एक लड़की खिड़की पर खड़ी थी। उस समय मैं एक पुस्तक पढ़ रहा था। मैं अगले साल तक हिंदी सीखना चाहता हूँ। सड़क के दाहिनी तरफ़ एक बड़ी इमारत है। इन दिनों खाना सस्ता नहीं है। मैं कल रात को मकान के अंदर ही सोया था।

## EXERCISE 12

I came with him. He came with me. He is doing this work for us. I waited for her in Delhi until yesterday. My brothers are standing in front of the house. Previously I lived in Delhi. Delhi is quite near[1] our town. Your village is also nearby. I've been here since yesterday. You are learning Hindi very quickly. I shall go by train and return by car. I want to go to London by aeroplane.

[1] के काफ़ी पास *ke kāfī pās*; note word order.

# LESSON VII

## ABSOLUTIVES

By adding the suffixes कर *kar* or के *ke* to a verb stem a form answering functionally to such English expressions as 'having done', 'having slept', but also in various cases to present participial forms such as 'doing', 'sleeping' is obtained. This absolutive form is of very frequent use, and may feature in translation equivalents of a large variety of English expressions: e.g.

हम आगरे जाकर ताज महल देखें। *ham āgre jākar tāj mahl dekheṁ*, Let's go to Agra and see the Taj Mahal.

मैं हिंदी सीखकर ही भारत जाऊँगा। *maiṁ hindī sīkhkar hī bhārat jāūṁgā*, I shall go to India only after I've learned Hindi.

वह बचकर भाग गए। *vah backar bhāg gae*, He escaped safely (he, being safe, fled).[1]

हाथी झूमकर चलता है। *hāthī jhūmkar caltā hai*, An elephant sways as it walks.

(*a*) Absolutives can be formed with either suffix for every verb except करना *karnā*, which makes only करके *karke*. The के *ke* forms are very common colloquially, but more formal Hindi (written and spoken) prefers those with कर *kar*. The suffix कर *kar* is often written and printed detached from its stem.

(*b*) In informal speech the unit करके *karke* is often found following a verb stem. Sometimes a slight difference of sense is expressed by this usage.

हम यहाँ आ करके बैठ गए। *ham yahāṁ ā karke baiṭh gae*, We made our way here, got here, and sat down.[2]

(*c*) The subject implied in an absolutive form is generally the same as that of the main verb in its sentence, but not invariably. The following sentences are both good Hindi:

हम इस रेस्टरेंट में जाकर काफ़ी पिएँ। *ham is resṭareṇṭ meṁ jākar kāfī pieṁ*, Let's go into this restaurant and have coffee.

[1] Compound verb forms such as भाग गए *bhāg gae* 'fled' are explained in Lesson XVII.

[2] बैठ गए *baiṭh gae* 'sat down'; compound verb.

वहीं बैठकर बातें होंगी । *vahīṁ baiṭhkar bāteṁ hoṁgī*, We'll sit there and have a talk.[1]

Unrelated absolutives of this kind are not normal with personal sentence subjects. They are very common in passive constructions.[2]

(*d*) The verb stem itself is often used with the force of an absolutive, particularly in conjunction with following verbal forms. Note especially the collocations ले जाना *le jānā* and ले चलना *le calnā* 'take away (having taken, go)'; and ले आना *le ānā* 'bring (having taken, come)'.

वह उठकर दूसरी कुरसी पर जा बैठा । *vah uṭhkar dūsrī kursī par jā baiṭhā*, He got up and went and sat on another chair.

हम ये सब चीज़ें ले जाएँगे । *ham ye sab cīzeṁ le jāeṁge*, We shall take away all these things.

वह अमर का हाथ पकड़ कमरे में ले गया । *vah amar kā hāth pakaṛ kamre meṁ le gayā*, Taking Amar by the hand he led (him) into the room.[3]

(*e*) Absolutives are negatived with preceding न *na*: e.g.

आप बनारस न जाकर पहले इलाहाबाद जाएँ । *āp banāras na jākar pahle ilāhābād jāeṁ*, Go to Allahabad first rather than Banaras.

(*f*) Note the use of होकर *hokar* in the special sense 'via': e.g.

मैं बनारस होकर यहाँ आया *maiṁ banāras hokar yahāṁ āyā*, I came here via Banaras.

## IMPERATIVE FORMS

Most of the different forms by means of which commands and requests are transmitted are listed here. It is convenient to call these collectively 'imperative forms', even though some of them express ideas very different from that of 'command', and can be more closely equated with subjunctives in force. The use of subjunctives in making requests and suggestions has already been noted in Lesson V.

[1] वहीं *vahīṁ* = वहाँ *vahāṁ* + ही *hī*; see Lesson XXIII, p. 144. बात *bāt*, f., essentially 'something said', as here, but also used in the sense 'matter, concern'.

[2] See in due course Lesson XIX, p. 116, and Supplement II, p. 174.

[3] Use of the stem absolutive पकड़ *pakaṛ*, rather than पकड़कर *pakaṛkar*, in this sentence is the subject of a note in Supplement II, p. 175.

1. The form used to make requests to persons whom one would address with the pronoun आप *āp*. It shows the suffix *-ie* added to the verb stem, and is usually negatived with न *na* (sometimes colloquially with मत *mat*). Stems in *-ū* shorten this vowel to *-u* before *-ie*.

आौर खाइए! *aur khāie!* Please have some more![1]
वहाँ न जाइए! *vahāṁ na jāie!* Don't go there!
उसे न छुइए! *use na chuie!* Don't touch that!

(*a*) Irregular are the *-ie* forms of

| | | | |
|---|---|---|---|
| करना | *karnā*: | कीजिए | *kījie* |
| लेना | *lenā*: | लीजिए | *lījie* |
| देना | *denā*: | दीजिए | *dījie* |
| पीना | *pīnā*: | पीजिए | *pījie* |

(*b*) There is no real lexical equivalent of the word 'please' in Hindi, though of course periphrases, such as मेहरबानी करके †*mehrbānī karke* 'by your kindness', are available for formal use and where a definite favour is involved. They need not be used otherwise.[2]

Similarly the expression 'thank you' is not fully answered to by any Hindi expression. If one is under a definite obligation, शुक्रिया *śukriyā* or the expression (आपकी) मेहरबानी (*āpkī*) †*mehrbānī* can be used. Formal Hindi has the expression धन्यवाद *dhanyavād*.

2. The form used to give directions, make requests, etc., to persons whom one would address with the pronoun तुम *tum*. It shows the suffix *-o* added to the verb stem, and is usually negatived by placing मत *mat* before or after the stem (the latter is a more affective usage than the former). Stems in *-ū*, *-ī* shorten the vowels before *-o*.

मत भूलो! *mat bhūlo*, Don't forget!
भूलो मत! *bhūlo mat*, Don't you forget!
यह पानी मत पिओ। *yah pānī mat pio*, Don't drink this water.

3. The form associated with the pronoun तू *tū*, and used commonly in addressing young children; otherwise expressive of intimacy, or condescension, anger, contempt, etc. It consists of the verb stem alone, and is usually negatived with मत *mat*.

[1] आौर *aur* is stressed.

[2] For another of these expressions see Supplement III, p. 179. The first vowel of the word मेहरबानी *mehrbānī* is usually short [ɛ].

4. The infinitive, which used as an imperative implies less of a specific, immediate request than imperatives in *-o*, and is applicable more to impending events not directly visualized, generalized situations, and precepts, etc. It is frequent in giving general directions to persons whom one would address with तुम *tum.* It is negatived with either न *na* or मत *mat*, preceding it.

तुम मुझे पत्र जल्दी लिखना। *tum mujhe patr jaldī likhnā*, Write me a letter soon (some time soon).

The infinitive is also used to express sudden or urgent command, in which honorific gradation is not considered: e.g.

बचना *bacnā!* Look out!

5. A form showing the extended suffix *-iegā* added to the verb stem. This is in frequent use in आप *āp* contexts, and also occurs in तुम *tum* contexts. Its chief functions are to emphasize that requests are not made with an air of authority, or to minimize the reality of such authority; it also often occurs where requests or commands do not require immediate compliance but relate to future time.

आप कुछ बोलिएगा? *āp kuch boliegā?* Would you (be so good as to) say something?[1]

बिल दीजिएगा। *bil dījiegā*, Would you give me the bill, please?

आप उससे यह कल पूछिएगा। *āp usse yah kal pūchiegā*, Ask him this tomorrow.

Note that although these forms can be used in तुम *tum* contexts (as in the second example) the second person pronoun तुम *tum* itself cannot be expressed with them. This is because historically they are third person, not second person, forms.

## VOCABULARY

हाथी *hāthī*, m., elephant
बात *bāt*, f., thing said; matter, concern
अलमारी *almārī*, f., cupboard
चीज़ †*cīz*, f., thing
बाज़ार *bāzār*, m., bazaar
आम *ām*, m., mango
देखना *dekhnā*, see
भागना *bhāgnā*, run away, flee
झूमना *jhūmnā*, sway
ले जाना *le jānā*, take away
ले आना *le ānā*, bring
पकड़ना *pakaṛnā*, seize
खाना *khānā*, eat; food (m.); खाना खाना *khānā khānā*, have a meal

[1] कुछ *kuch* 'something, some'; this word is discussed in Lesson VIII.

रखना *rakhnā*, put, place; keep
सुनना *sunnā*, hear
उठना *uṭhnā*, rise, get up
और *aur*, (when stressed) extra, additional; adv., additionally
दूसरा *dūsrā*, second; other
आहिस्ता †*āhistā*, आहिस्ते †*āhiste*, adv., slowly
बिल *bil*, m., bill (account)

## EXERCISE 13

मैं खाना खाकर उसे पत्र लिखूंगा। आप भारत जाकर क्या करेंगे? वह सब चीज़ें अलमारी के अंदर रखकर कमरे से बाहर गया। रामाधीन, बाज़ार जाकर चार आम ले आओ। वह पुस्तक लेकर बाहर गया। सुनिए, यह दिल्ली की गाड़ी है? आहिस्ता बोलिए!

## EXERCISE 14

You'll learn[1] Hindi quickly when you go to India. He brought this book from India. I went by plane, via Bombay. Please do this work now. Please sit in[2] this chair. Please give me some more!

[1] Use the compound verb form सीख लेंगे *sīkh leṁge*, not the simple form सीखेंगे *sīkheṁge*. This usage is explained in Lesson XVII.

[2] पर *par*.

# LESSON VIII

## THE INDEFINITE PRONOUN AND ADJECTIVE
### कुछ *kuch* 'something, some'

THIS form is invariable.

उसके बारे में मुझे कुछ बताइए । *uske bāre meṁ mujhe kuch batāie*, Please tell me something about it.

मैं कुछ हिंदी जानता हूँ । *maiṁ kuch hindī jāntā hūṁ*, I know some Hindi.

मेज़ पर कुछ पुस्तकें पड़ी हैं । *mez par kuch pustkeṁ paṛī haiṁ*, There are some books lying on the table.

तालाब में कुछ पानी नहीं है । *tālāb meṁ kuch pānī nahīṁ hai*, There is no water in the tank.

(*a*) Note especially, in comparison with the last example, the collocation कुछ नहीं *kuch nahīṁ* as translation equivalent of 'nothing': e.g.

मैं उसके बारे में कुछ नहीं जानता । *maiṁ uske bāre meṁ kuch nahīṁ jāntā*, I know nothing, don't know anything about it.

(*b*) Some other common collocations of कुछ *kuch* are:

कुछ और *kuch aur*, something further, some more; something different.[1]
और कुछ *aur kuch*, something different; something further, some more.[1]
बहुत कुछ *bahut kuch*, a large amount.
सब कुछ *sab kuch*, everything.

और कुछ खाइएगा? *aur kuch khāiegā*? Won't you have something else, some more?[1]

कुछ और लोग आते होंगे । *kuch aur log āte hoṁge*, A few more people will probably be coming.

मैं रोज़ बहुत कुछ पढ़ता हूँ । *maiṁ roz bahut kuch paṛhtā hūṁ*, I read a lot every day.

(*c*) Note that कुछ *kuch* used adjectivally may sometimes be inserted in a sentence with little or no effect on an English translation equivalent. Cf. with the example above

तालाब में पानी नहीं है । *tālāb meṁ pānī nahīṁ hai*, There is no water in the tank.

[1] और *aur* is stressed in these as in all usages where it has the sense 'extra, additional(ly)', rather than the conjunctival sense 'and'.

## THE INDEFINITE PRONOUN AND ADJECTIVE
### कोई *koī* 'someone, some'

Sg. Dir. कोई *koī*, m.f.
Obl. किसी *kisī*

*koī* is not usually used as a plural[1]; note the related invariable form कई *kaī* 'a few, several'. There also exists a somewhat uncommon oblique plural form किन्हीं *kinhīṁ*, of vaguer reference than कई *kaī*.

दफ़्तर में कोई है। *daftar meṁ koī hai*, There is someone in the office.
दफ़्तर में कोई है? *daftar meṁ koī hai?* Is there anyone in the office?
किसी शहर में एक अमीर आदमी रहता था। *kisī śahr meṁ ek amīr ādmī rahtā thā*, There was a rich man living in a certain city.
गाँव में कोई तालाब नहीं है। *gāṁv meṁ koī tālāb nahīṁ hai*, There's no tank, isn't any tank in the village.
दफ़्तर में कोई नहीं है। *daftar meṁ koī nahīṁ hai*, There is no one in the office.
कई किताबें मेज़ पर पड़ी थीं। *kaī kitābeṁ mez par paṛī thīṁ*, A few books were lying on the table.

(*a*) Note that कोई *koī* used adjectivally may sometimes be inserted in a sentence with little or no effect on an English translation equivalent. Cf. with the example above

गाँव में तालाब नहीं है। *gāṁv meṁ tālāb nahīṁ hai*, There's no tank in the village.

(*b*) Note that the essential distinction between कोई *koī* and कुछ *kuch* is not that the former refers to animate beings and the latter to inanimates, but that the former particularizes, while the latter is general and partitive in force. Hence while कोई *koī* and कुछ *kuch* used pronominally do refer typically to animate beings or inanimates respectively, as adjectives they are both usable with either reference: e.g.

वह आदमी कोई साधु होगा। *vah ādmī koī sādhu hogā*, That man is probably some (kind of) holy man.
वहाँ कुछ ही आदमी थे। *vahāṁ kuch hī ādmī the*, There were just a few men there.
गाँव में कोई तालाब नहीं है। *gāṁv meṁ koī tālāb nahīṁ hai*, There's no tank in the village.
तालाब में कुछ पानी नहीं है। *tālāb meṁ kuch pānī nahīṁ hai*, There's no water in the tank.

[1] Except as indicated on p. 45, paragraph (*c*), and in Lesson XXIV, p. 148.

(*c*) Some other common collocations of कोई *koī* are:

कोई और *koī aur*, another, a different; someone else
और कोई *aur koī*, another, a different; someone else

Preceding numerals, in the sense 'approximately':

रास्ते में कोई दस ऊँट हैं । *rāste meṁ koī das ūṁṭ haiṁ*, There are a dozen or so camels in the street.

## THE INTERROGATIVE PRONOUN AND ADJECTIVE कौन *kaun* 'who, which'

| | | | | | |
|---|---|---|---|---|---|
| Sg. | Dir. | कौन *kaun*, m.f. | Pl. | Dir. | कौन *kaun*, m.f. |
| | Obl. | किस *kis* | | Obl. | किन *kin* |
| | Object | किसे *kise* | | Object | किन्हें *kinheṁ* |

यह कौन है? *yah kaun hai?* Who is this?
वह किसका मकान है? *vah kiskā makān hai?* Whose house is that?
ये कौन किताबें हैं? किसे दे रहे हैं? *ye kaun kitābeṁ haiṁ? kise de rahe haiṁ?* Which books are these? Whom are you giving them to?

(*a*) The form कौन-सा *kaun-sā* usually somewhat emphasizes the existence of various possibilities or choices, but a distinction between कौन-सा *kaun-sā* and कौन *kaun* is not regularly maintained, especially colloquially. कौन-सा *kaun-sā* shows inflexion of the suffixed particle सा *sā* as an adjective in -*ā*.

आज कौन-सा दिन है? *āj kaun-sā din hai?* What day is today?
आप कौन-सी किताब पढ़ रहे हैं? *āp kaun-sī kitāb paṛh rahe haiṁ?* Which book are you reading? (of a syllabus, a certain author, etc.)

(*b*) कौन *kaun* and its oblique case forms are very frequently reduplicated, with a distributive connotation[1]: e.g.

आप किन किन से बोले? *āp kin kin se bole?* Who did you speak to? (with what different people—honorific)
वहाँ कौन कौन थे । *vahāṁ kaun kaun the?* Who were there?

## THE INTERROGATIVE PRONOUN AND ADJECTIVE क्या *kyā* 'what'

The pronominal usage and question-marking force of क्या *kyā* were noted in Lesson I. Note further that क्या *kyā* occurs only in direct case, singular

[1] See further Lesson XXIII, p. 139.

and plural. To express its sense in other cases the appropriate forms of कौन *kaun* are used.

यह क्या है? *yah kyā hai?* What is this?
वे किसके बारे में बोल रहे थे? *ve kiske bāre meṁ bol rahe the?* What were they talking about?

(*a*) Adjectival क्या *kyā* contrasts with कौन *kaun* in the same way as कुछ *kuch* with कोई *koī*. Compare the sentences

ये कौन किताबें हैं? *ye kaun kitābeṁ haiṁ?* Which books are these?
यह क्या चीज़ है? *yah kyā cīz hai?* What (sort of) thing is this?

(*b*) क्या *kyā* is very frequently reduplicated: e.g.

आप उनसे क्या क्या कहेंगे? *āp unse kyā kyā kaheṁge?* What will you say to them? (what various things)

## THE RELATIVE PRONOUN AND ADJECTIVE
### जो *jo* '(the one) who, which'

| | | | | | |
|---|---|---|---|---|---|
| Sg. Dir. | जो *jo*, m.f. | | Pl. Dir. | जो *jo*, m.f. | |
| Obl. | जिस *jis* | | Obl. | जिन *jin* | |
| Object | जिसे *jise* | | Object | जिन्हें *jinheṁ* | |

This pronoun and adjective occurs frequently in relative clauses of complex sentences,[1] linked syntactically with a demonstrative pronoun or other word (the 'correlative') in the principal clause. Note that where an equivalent English sentence shows the definite article 'the' with its subject, the जो *jo* clause commonly precedes in Hindi, and the correlative is a part of the pronoun वह *vah*; and where it shows the indefinite article 'a', 'an', the जो *jo* clause follows, its correlative in the first clause then being a noun.

जो कहता हूँ, वह सच है। *jo kahtā hūṁ, vah sac hai*, What I say is the truth.
जो लाल गाड़ी वहाँ खड़ी है, वह मेरी है। *jo lāl gāṛī vahāṁ khaṛī hai, vah merī hai*, The red car standing there is mine.

[1] Complex sentences are expansions of simple sentences, consisting of one or more dependent, incomplete utterances of the form of simple sentences linked to one complete utterance of that form. These utterances may be termed subordinate and principal clauses respectively. Subordinate clauses containing relative जो *jo* may be termed relative clauses; other subordinate clauses frequently contain subordinate conjunctions identifying their function. See Lessons XVI and XX, in due course.

मैं एक आदमी से बात कर रहा था जो कल भारत जाएगा । *maiṁ ek ādmī se bāt kar rahā thā jo kal bhārat jāegā*, I was talking to a man who is going to India tomorrow.

मैं जिस आदमी से बात कर रहा था, वह कल भारत जाएगा । *maiṁ jis ādmī se bāt kar rahā thā, vah kal bhārat jāegā*, The man I was talking to is going to India tomorrow.

The relative often stands first in its clause, even where it is not the subject of its clause. An initial relative and any noun attached to it gains somewhat in emphasis at the expense of a non-initial clause subject. Compare with the last example above the following sentence, with slightly altered emphasis:

जिस आदमी से मैं बात कर रहा था, वह कल भारत जाएगा । *jis ādmī se maiṁ bāt kar rahā thā, vah kal bhārat jāegā*, The man I was talking to is going to India tomorrow.

## VOCABULARY

तालाब *tālāb*, m., tank
साधु *sādhu*, m., holy man
रास्ता *rāstā*, m., road, street
ऊँट *ūṁṭ*, m., camel
ओर *or*, f., direction, side; की ओर *kī or*, towards, to; की ओर देखना *kī or dekhnā*, look at, watch
तबीयत *tabīyat*, f., state of health; disposition; तबीयत ठीक होना *tabīyat ṭhīk honā*, be well
आराम *ārām*, m., comfort
सच *sac*, m., truth
अमीर †*amīr*, rich
ग़रीब †*garīb*, poor
आरामदेह *ārāmdeh*, comfortable
हर †*har*, each, every
मज़बूत *mazbūt*, strong (of objects)
सात *sāt*, seven
आठ *āṭh*, eight
नौ *nau*, nine
दस *das*, ten
बताना *batānā*, tell, inform (used in construction with को *ko*)[1]
बात करना *bāt karnā*, बातें करना *bāteṁ karnā* (*se*), talk (to)
रोज़ †*roz*, m., day; adv., daily
सुनिए *sunie*, excuse me (in attracting a person's attention)

## EXERCISE 15

कोई है? मैं उसके बारे में कुछ नहीं कहूँगा । कोई आठ आदमी उसके साथ पहुँचे । कई पुस्तकें मेज़ के नीचे पड़ी थीं । कुछ और किताबें मेज़ पर थीं । मेरे कमरे में कोई कुरसी नहीं है । ये किताबें किस किस की हैं? आप इसके बारे में किससे कहेंगे? जो किताब मैं

[1] Bracketed forms following vocabulary entries will be used from this point onwards to indicate their construction, where this seems advisable.

पढ़ रहा हूँ, वह मेज़ पर है। मैं जिस आदमी की ओर देख रहा था, वह अभी बाहर गया है। मैं जिस कमरे में काम करूँगा, वह बहुत आरामदेह है। आप इस देश में कब से हैं और कब तक यहाँ रहेंगे? आप हिंदी क्यों नहीं बोलते?

## EXERCISE 16

I shall live in some village. No one knows Hindi here. I shall ask him something about that. Several men came here yesterday. Some people go there every year. Who are these men? Whom are you going to give these books to? The men who came here yesterday are my friends. The chair I'm sitting on is quite sturdy. The boy whose book is on the table is my son. What town does he live in? Were you unwell yesterday? Excuse me, are you Rādhā's[1] sister?

[1] The name is unchanged in oblique case; see p. 2, paragraph (*d*).

# LESSON IX

## THE POSTPOSITION को

THE general function of this postposition may be described as that of a marker or specifier of oblique case in a preceding form. Four applications of this function are considered here.

1. को *ko* occurs in association with direct objects which are individualized to some extent, and to which a degree of contextual importance is thus attached; hence usually where direct objects refer to human beings, and certain animals, and quite frequently where they refer to inanimate objects. Such words may be called definite direct objects.

औरत बच्चे को बुला रही है । *aurat bacce ko bulā rahī hai*, The woman is calling the child, a child.

हिंदी में इसको क्या कहते हैं? *hindī meṁ isko kyā kahte haiṁ?* What is this called in Hindi? (what do they say this to be)

उन पत्रों को पढ़िए । *un patroṁ ko paṛhie*, Please read those letters.

दर्ज़ी को बुलाओ । *darzī ko bulāo*, Call the tailor.

(*a*) Note that the direct case is normally used to denote direct objects not of any individual importance in a given context, unless this might lead to ambiguity. These objects may be called indefinite direct objects.

ये चिट्ठियाँ पढ़िए । *ye ciṭṭhiyāṁ paṛhie*, Please read these letters.

हम हिंदी सीख रहे हैं । *ham hindī sīkh rahe haiṁ*. We're learning Hindi.

In practice words used in the direct case in this way usually have inanimate reference, but not invariably so. Occupational names, for instance, occur quite commonly as direct objects in direct case in sentences where the individuality of their referend is not emphasized.

दरज़ी बुलाओ । *darzī bulāo*, Call a tailor.

Compare also with the first example in this section the following sentence, in which the direct object is felt as not at all individualized:

औरत बच्चा बुला रही है । *aurat baccā bulā rahī hai*, The woman is calling a child.

2. को *ko* occurs in association with indirect objects: e.g.

उस आदमी को तीन पुस्तकें दीजिए । *us ādmī ko tīn pustkeṁ dījie*, Please give that man three books.

मुझे पत्र लिखिए । *mujhe patr likhie*, Please write me a letter.

3. को *ko* occurs frequently as a marker of adverbial expressions. Additional examples to those noted in Lesson VI are

बुधवार को आओ। *budhvār ko āo*, Come on Wednesday.

वह अपने देश को लौट गया। *vah apne deś ko lauṭ gayā*, He went back to his country.[1]

(*a*) In connection with the last example, note that sometimes place to which motion occurs is best indicated by a noun in the oblique case without a following postposition: e.g.

वह हिंदुस्तान लौट गया। *vah hindustān lauṭ gayā*, He went back to India.

वह अपने घर लौट गया। *vah apne ghar lauṭ gayā*, He returned to his home.

This is so chiefly when the place concerned is a geographical locality denoted by a place-name, or is otherwise felt as a specific destination. But it is rarely wrong to use को *ko* in such locutions, though in certain cases if a postposition is used में *meṁ*, पर *par* or की ओर *kī or*, की तरफ़ *kī taraf* may be preferred: e.g.

वह दफ़्तर (में) गया। *vah daftar (meṁ) gayā*, He went to the office (if में *meṁ* is used this sentence may also mean 'he went *into* the office').

कमरे (में) जाएँगे? *kamre (meṁ) jāeṁge?* Are you going to your room?

वह दूकान पर लौट गया। *vah dūkān par lauṭ gayā*, He went back to the shop.

वह कार की ओर चला। *vah kār kī or calā*, He went (over) to the car (also 'he went towards the car').

4. को *ko* occurs in association with a noun or pronoun, to indicate a close connection in the sentence structure between it and another noun, or sometimes an adjective.[2] The sentence verb is often होना *honā*, and in this case the noun or adjective usually denotes an abstract quality or condition characterizing the referend of the word with which को *ko* occurs: e.g.

मुझे बहुत ख़ुशी है। *mujhe bahut khuśī hai*, I'm delighted, very pleased.

मुझे बड़ी प्रसन्नता है। *mujhe baṛī prasannatā hai*, I'm delighted, very pleased.[3]

[1] For अपना *apnā* 'one's own' see Lesson X; for the compound verb form लौट गया *lauṭ gayā* 'returned' see Lesson XVII.

[2] Only a few adjectives, none of which are in common use attributively (preceding nouns), are found in this construction; all are loanwords.

[3] बड़ा *baṛā* is often used (in concord) as an equivalent of adjectival or adverbial बहुत *bahut*. Note that the above sentence and the preceding one are often used in the sense 'I'm very pleased to meet you'.

मुझे बहुत बड़ी ख़ुशी है । *mujhe bahut baṛī khuśī hai*, I'm very pleased indeed.
मुझे आशा है कि . . . *mujhe āśā hai ki* . . ., I hope that . . .
मुझे अफ़सोस है कि . . . *mujhe afsos hai ki* . . ., I'm sorry that . . .
उसको मालूम है कि . . . *usko mālūm hai ki* . . ., He knows that . . .[1]
उसको मालूम होता है कि . . . *usko mālūm hotā hai ki* . . ., He thinks, it seems to him that . . .
हमें समय नहीं है । *hameṁ samay nahīṁ hai*, We haven't time.
उसे एक बेटा हुआ है । *use ek beṭā huā hai*, A son has been born to him.
मुझे हिंदी आती है । *mujhe hindī ātī hai*, I can speak, know Hindi.

## THE POSTPOSITION के पास *ke pās*

This compound postposition means basically 'beside'. Its use in the sense 'near' has been noted above[2]; by extension it is also used regularly to indicate possession of ordinary chattels which are in a sense 'with one', and also frequently in expressions which describe motion towards a person: e.g.

उसका मकान नदी के पास है । *uskā makān nadī ke pās hai*, His house is near the river.
उसके पास पैसा नहीं है । *uske pās paisā nahīṁ hai*, He has no money.
आपके पास कितनी पुस्तकें हैं? *āpke pās kitnī pustkeṁ haiṁ?* How many books have you got?
मेरे पास एक गाड़ी है । *mere pās ek gāṛī hai*, I own a car.
मैं डाक्टर के पास जाऊँगा । *maiṁ ḍāktar ke pās jāūṁgā*, I shall go to the doctor.

(*a*) Sometimes colloquially this construction will occur where the construction with को *ko* noted above would be expected: e.g. in such an expression as

मेरे पास वक़्त नहीं है । *mere pās vaqt nahīṁ hai*, I haven't time.

## THE POSTPOSITION का *kā* (contd.)

Nouns and pronouns with the postposition का *kā* (and equivalent possessive personal pronouns) are common in possessive expressions which describe ownership of such things as houses, land, etc.; and also

[1] The form मालूम †*mālūm* is in origin an Arabic passive participle meaning 'known'. Note the sense distinction in the two examples given containing it.

[2] See Lesson VI, p. 34.

are found in expressions describing relationship to other people and one's 'possession' of parts of one's body. In all these types of expression what is denoted by the use of का *kā* is a permanent, characteristic or non-fortuitous type of relationship, by contrast with the more 'contingent' possession expressed by use of के पास *ke pās*: e.g.

ज़मीनदार के दो गाँव थे । *zamīndār ke do gāṁv the*, The zamindar owned two villages.

मेरी एक बड़ी जायदाद थी । *merī ek baṛī jāydād thī*, I used to have a large estate.

मेरी एक बहन है, जो ... *merī ek bahn hai, jo ...*, I have a sister who ...

उस आदमी की सिर्फ़ एक ही आँख है । *us ādmī kī sirf ek hī āṁkh hai*, That man has only one eye.

(*a*) In the first two examples cited above, expressing ownership, के पास *ke pās* might occur rather than का *kā*, and the implication of the sentences would be slightly different accordingly.

(*b*) In English idiom possession is sometimes attributed to inanimate objects; sentences of this type often have Hindi translation equivalents showing का *kā*[1]: e.g.

उस संदूक़ का कोई ताला नहीं है । *us sandūq kā koī tālā nahīṁ hai*, That box has no lock.

(*c*) Note the use of का *kā* to form adjectival phrases in sentences such as the following:

मुझे हिंदी की एक पुस्तक दीजिए । *mujhe hindī kī ek pustak dījie*, Please give me a Hindi book.

जून में आप यहाँ के मौसम से परेशान होंगे । *jūn meṁ āp yahāṁ ke mausam se pareśān hoṁge*, In June you'll find the weather here trying.

पहले कलकत्ता भारत का सबसे बड़ा शहर था । *pahle kalkattā bhārat kā sabse baṛā śahr thā*, Formerly Calcutta was the largest city in India.[2]

[1] में *meṁ* is also common in such sentences, e.g.
आपके मकान में कितनी खिड़कियाँ हैं? *āpke makān meṁ kitnī khiṛkiyāṁ haiṁ?* How many windows has your house?
मेरे सिर में दर्द है । *mere sir meṁ dard hai*, I've got a headache.

[2] The expression सबसे बड़ा *sabse baṛā* 'biggest' is explained in Lesson XVI.

मकान के पीछे का खेत मेरे भाई का है । *makān ke pīche kā khet mere bhāī kā hai*, The field behind the house belongs to my brother.
गाँव के लोग । *gāṁv ke log*, village people

(*d*) Some usages of masculine singular oblique case possessive forms, not in concord, also occur colloquially. These are really adverbial usages. They are sometimes near equivalents to usages of का *kā* in concord, or equivalents to usages of को *ko*: e.g.

उसके एक बहन है । *uske ek bahn hai*, He's got a sister.
मेरे चोट लगी । *mere coṭ lagī*, I got hurt.[1]

Cf. the following sentences:

उसकी एक बहन है, जो ... *uskī ek bahn hai, jo* ..., He has a sister, who ...
मुझे चोट लगी । *mujhe coṭ lagī*, I got hurt.

But adverbial usages of possessive forms often differ in sense from usages of का *kā* in concord. Cf. the following two sentences:

सिर पर उसके एक दुपट्टा है । *sir par uske ek dupaṭṭā hai*, Over (her) head she has a shawl.
सिर पर उसका एक दुपट्टा है । *sir par uskā ek dupaṭṭā hai*, Over (her) head she has one of her shawls.

In expressions of relationship, adverbial construction is usual if the relationship is not specified in some way; cf. the above examples, and

उसके एक बहन है, और दुनिया में कोई और नहीं । *uske ek bahn hai, aur duniyā meṁ koī aur nahīṁ*, He's got a sister, and no one else in the (whole) world.[2]

## VOCABULARY

दर्ज़ी *darzī*, m., tailor
चिट्ठी †*ciṭṭhī*, f., letter
ख़ुशी †*khuśī*, f., happiness, pleasure
प्रसन्नता *prasannatā*, f., pleasure
आशा *āśā*, f., hope
अफ़सोस †*afsos*, m., regret
नदी *nadī*, f., river
पैसा *paisā*, m., pice (1/100 rupee); money (often pl.)
डाक्टर *ḍākṭar*, m., doctor
वक्त †*vaqt*, m., time
ज़मीनदार *zamīndār*, m., zamindar
जायदाद *jāydād*, f., estate (land)
आँख *āṁkh*, f., eye

[1] The uses of लगना *lagnā* 'to be applied' are discussed in Lesson XXI. चोट *coṭ* (f.) means 'blow'.

[2] The second और *aur* is stressed; see p. 43, n. 1.

सिर *sir*, m., head
ताला *tālā*, m., lock
दर्द *dard*, m., pain
खेत *khet*, m., field
चोट *coṭ*, f., blow, knock
दुपट्टा *dupaṭṭā*, m., shawl
दुनिया †*duniyā*, f., world
बुधवार *budhvār*, m., Wednesday
शुक्रवार *śukravār*, m., Friday
मतलब *matlab*, m., intention, purpose
भारतवर्ष *bhāratvarṣ*, m., India
परेशान †*pareśān* (*se*), troubled (by)
मालूम †*mālūm*, known; मुझे मालूम है *mujhe mālūm hai*, I know; मुझे मालूम होता है *mujhe mālūm hotā hai*, it seems to me
बुलाना *bulānā*, call
पहचानना *pahcānnā*, recognize
ढूँढ़ना *ḍhūṁṛhnā*, look for, search out (with direct object)
सिर्फ़ †*sirf*, only
कि *ki*, conj., that
किसान *kisān*, m., farmer

## EXERCISE 17

वह मुझे नहीं पहचानता । मैं उन पत्रों को लिखूँगा । मैं कल आपको किताबें दूँगा । मैं शुक्रवार को घर जा रहा हूँ । क्या आप उनको जानते हैं? उस दिन मैं किताब पढ़ रहा था । आपको उससे क्या मतलब है? क्या आपके पास काग़ज़ है? मुझे कुछ दीजिए । कलकत्ते में मेरे एक दोस्त है । उस कमरे की कितनी दीवारें हैं? मेरे पास पुस्तकें नहीं हैं ।

## EXERCISE 18

Please write us a letter. I shall tell[1] you something about this tomorrow. My friend will return to England next week. I'm very pleased about that. I hope you'll go to India. The farmer is looking for the horse. When are you going to your[2] room? He was standing beside the tree. Have you any children? I've got two sons and a daughter. My village is quite near Agra. Have you any Hindi books?

[1] कहना *kahnā*; or बताना *batānā* (with को *ko*).
[2] अपना *apnā* (see Lesson X); but the word need not be expressed here.

# LESSON X

## THE POSSESSIVE ADJECTIVE अपना *apnā* 'one's own'

1. The form अपना *apnā*, rather than any of the other pronominal possessive adjectives, is used in most cases where a second reference to a possessor is made within a simple sentence, or within one and the same clause of a complex sentence: e.g.

मैं आपको अपना पता दूंगा । *maiṁ āpko apnā patā dūṁgā*, I'll give you my address.

आप मुझे अपना पता दीजिए । *āp mujhe apnā patā dījie*, Please give me your address.

आपको अपनी चीज़ें मिली होंगी? *āpko apnī cīzeṁ milī hoṁgī?* You've found your things, I suppose?[1]

(*a*) Where the referend is in a different clause of a complex sentence अपना *apnā* is not used: e.g.

मैं उससे कहूँगा कि मेरे पिता जी कल आ रहे हैं । *maiṁ usse kahūṁgā ki mere pitā jī kal ā rahe haiṁ*, I shall tell him that my father is coming tomorrow.

(*b*) Where a subject pronoun is omitted as understood अपना *apnā* is the possessive used in reference to it: e.g.

मुझे अपना पता दीजिए । *mujhe apnā patā dījie*, Please give me your address.

(*c*) Where the second reference to the possessor is within the same syntactic unit of the sentence or clause (e.g. within a composite subject or object) अपना *apnā* is not used: e.g.

मैं और मेरी बहन घर पर होंगे । *maiṁ aur merī bahn ghar par hoṁge*, My sister and I will be at home.

मुझे और मेरी बहन को ख़ुशी है कि . . . *mujhe aur merī bahn ko khuśī hai ki . . .*, My sister and I are glad that . . .

(*d*) Note that अपना *apnā* refers to a subject noun or pronoun, if one is present or understood; only if a subject referend is not present or understood will it refer to an oblique case noun or pronoun. Hence the sense of such a sentence as the following is unambiguous:

[1] The verb मिलना *milnā* 'accrue' is introduced in Lesson XV. A word-for-word English rendering of the example is 'Your things will have accrued to you?'

आपको आपके पिता जी अपने देश का इतिहास बताएँगे। *āpko āpke pitā jī apne deś kā itihās batāeṁge*, Your father will tell you the history of his country. (not '*your* country')[1]

2. अपना *apnā* is also used as follows:

(*a*) Impersonally, where there is no referend for it in a sentence: e.g.

अपना काम अच्छी तरह करना अच्छा है। *apnā kām acchī tarah karnā acchā hai*, To do one's work well is good.[2]

(*b*) Intensively, following a possessive pronoun: e.g.

मेरी अपनी कहानी बहुत लंबी है *merī apnī kahānī bahut lambī hai*, My own story is very long.

## VERBAL EXPRESSIONS WITH करना *karnā* and होना *honā*

Many words associate with the verbs करना *karnā* and होना *honā* to form verbal expressions, transitive and intransitive respectively. Some examples of expressions based on an adjective, e.g. बंद *band* 'closed', are:

मैं नौ बजे दरवाज़ा बंद करता हूँ। *maiṁ nau baje*[3] *darvāzā band kartā hūṁ*, I close the door at nine o'clock.

दरवाज़ा नौ बजे बंद होता है। *darvāzā nau baje band hotā hai*, The door is closed at nine o'clock.

दरवाज़ा नौ बजे बंद होता था। *darvāzā nau baje band hotā thā*, The door used to be closed at nine o'clock. (a general case)

कल दरवाज़ा नौ बजे बंद हुआ था। *kal darvāzā nau baje band huā thā*, Yesterday the door was closed at nine o'clock. (a specific action)

(*a*) Compare with the above expressions usages of बंद *band* with the present and past tense forms of होना *honā*: e.g.

दरवाज़ा बंद है। *darvāzā band hai*, The door is closed.
दरवाज़ा बंद था। *darvāzā band thā*, The door was closed.

[1] There are, however, some cases, which need not be noted here, where ambiguities in the use of अपना *apnā* occur.

[2] For the use of the infinitive as a noun see Lesson XIX, pp. 119 ff.

[3] For expressions of time see Lesson XI, pp. 66 ff.

(*b*) Some similar pairs of complementary verbal expressions are given below. Note that members of some pairs have the same English translation equivalent (used transitively and intransitively).

| | |
|---|---|
| इस्तेमाल होना †*istemāl honā*, be used | इस्तेमाल करना †*istemāl karnā*, use |
| शुरू होना †*śurū honā*, begin | शुरू करना †*śurū karnā*, begin |
| आरंभ होना *ārambh honā*, begin | आरंभ करना *ārambh karnā*, begin |
| ख़त्म होना †*khatm honā*, finish | ख़त्म करना †*khatm karnā*, finish |
| समाप्त होना *samāpt honā*, finish | समाप्त करना *samāpt karnā*, finish |
| प्राप्त होना *prāpt honā*, be available, obtained | प्राप्त करना *prāpt karnā*, obtain |
| पैदा होना †*paidā*[1] *honā*, be born, produced | पैदा करना †*paidā*[1] *karnā*, produce, give birth to |
| बिदा होना *bidā*[1] *honā*, depart | बिदा करना *bidā*[1] *karnā*, dispatch; see off |
| रवाना होना †*ravānā*[1] *honā*, depart | रवाना करना †*ravānā*[1] *karnā*, dispatch; see off |
| वापस होना †*vāpas honā*, be returned | वापस करना †*vāpas karnā*, give back |

गरमियाँ अगले महीने में शुरू होंगी *garmiyāṁ agle mahīne meṁ śurū hoṁgī*, The hot weather will begin during next month.

छुट्टी कल ख़त्म हुई। *chuṭṭī kal khatm huī*, The vacation finished yesterday.

मेरी बेटी अप्रैल में पैदा हुई। *merī beṭī aprail meṁ paidā huī*, My daughter was born in April.

मेरी किताब जल्दी वापस कीजिए। *merī kitāb jaldī vāpas kījie*, Please return my book quickly.

(*c*) Some of the expressions (the first four pairs cited) noted in (*b*) above are based on nouns, and may be termed 'conjunct verbs' in that the nouns in these expressions have lost their syntactic identity, and are connected syntactically only with the following करना *karnā* or होना *honā*, with which they form enlarged verbal units. Note that these are different in their syntax from another, very large class of verbal expressions showing nouns in looser association with करना *karnā* and होना *honā*. The noun in these latter expressions can be directly associated with preceding expressions involving different postpositions (usually the possessive का *kā*). Some

[1] Final *-ā* in these words is invariable.

examples follow of verbal expressions showing nouns that can be preceded by this postposition, which of course shows normal concord:

इंतज़ार करना †*intazār*[1] *karnā*, wait (for)
प्रतीक्षा करना *pratīkṣā karnā*, wait (for)
प्रयोग होना, करना *prayog honā, karnā*, be used, use
प्रशंसा होना, करना *praśaṃsā honā, karnā*, be praised, praise

मैं उसका इंतज़ार करूँगा । *maiṁ uskā intazār karūṁgā*, I shall wait for him.

मैं उसकी प्रतीक्षा करूँगा । *maiṁ uskī pratīkṣā karūṁgā*, I shall wait for him.

मैं दस बजे तक इंतज़ार करूँगा । *maiṁ das baje tak intazār karūṁgā*, I shall wait till ten o'clock.

आजकल इस मशीन का प्रयोग होता है । *ājkal is maśīn kā prayog hotā hai* Nowadays this machine is used.

उसकी प्रशंसा सारे देश में हो रही है । *uskī praśaṃsā sāre deś meṁ ho rahī hai* He is being praised over the whole country.

(*d*) Some expressions based on nouns are used either with preceding का *kā* or as conjunct verbs. Examples are तलाश करना †*talāś karnā* 'look for', and इस्तेमाल करना †*istemāl karnā* 'use' (most commonly conjunct verbs).

मैं किताब (की) तलाश करूँगा । *maiṁ kitāb (kī) talāś karūṁgā*, I shall look for the book.

(*e*) Note the adjectival use of the word ख़त्म *khatm* in the expression ख़त्म है *khatm hai* 'it's finished'. (This usage and the tendency noted in (*d*) above for expressions based on nouns to be used as conjunct verbs are due to influence of the adjectival type of syntax of expressions like बंद होना *band honā* on expressions based on nouns.)

(*f*) In sentences of neutral style and emphasis negatives usually precede verb components of conjunct verbs, but sometimes precede their noun components. Negatives used with the other types of verbal expression discussed in this section regularly precede their verb components in such sentences.

[1] Pronounced with unstressed *i* in second syllable in Urdu-influenced usage; less often so otherwise. Similar pronunciations are found in other Arabic loanwords originally containing the vowel sequence *i — i — ā*.

मैं नौ बजे काम शुरू नहीं करता । *maiṁ nau baje kām śurū nahīṁ kartā*, I don't start work at nine o'clock.

मैं नौ बजे दरवाज़ा बंद नहीं करूँगा । *maiṁ nau baje darvāzā band nahīṁ karūṁga*, I shan't shut the door at nine o'clock.

वह मेरा इंतज़ार नहीं करेगा । *vah merā intazār nahīṁ karegā*, He won't wait for me.

## VOCABULARY

पता *patā*, m., track, trace; address
इतिहास *itihās*, m., history
कहानी *kahānī*, f., story, short story
नौ बजे *nau baje*, at nine o'clock
अप्रैल *aprail*, m., April
छुट्टी *chuṭṭī*, f., holiday, leave, vacation
वर्ष *varṣ*, m., year
हिंदू *hindū*, m., Hindu
ज्ञान *jñān*, m., knowledge
आना *ānā*, m., anna ($\frac{1}{16}$ rupee, old style)
ऋग्वेद *ṛgved*, m., Rigveda
इंद्र *indra*, m., Indra
अनाज *anāj*, m., grain
लंबा *lambā*, long; tall
बंद *band*, closed
हर (एक) दिन *har (ek) din*, every day
तलाश करना †*talāś karnā*, look for
पसंद आना †*pasand ānā*, be pleasing to; मुझे . . . पसंद आता है *mujhe . . . pasand ātā hai*, I like . . .
गिनना *ginnā*, count
का उल्लेख होना *kā ullekh honā*, be mentioned
का इंतज़ार करना *kā* †*intazār karnā*, wait for
की प्रतीक्षा करना *kī pratīkṣā karnā*, wait for
का प्रयोग करना *kā prayog karnā*, use
की प्रशंसा करना *kī praśaṃsā karnā*, praise
अच्छी तरह, *acchī tarah*, अच्छी तरह से *acchī tarah se*, well
आजकल *ājkal*, nowadays
आम †*ām*, ordinary
आम तौर पर/से *ām* †*taur par/se*, in general, usually
ठीक वक़्त पर *ṭhīk vaqt par*, at the correct time, punctually
क्योंकि *kyoṁki*, because

## EXERCISE 19

वह अपनी बहन से हिंदी बोलता है । आपको अपना कमरा पसंद आता है? वह और उसकी पत्नी दोनों हर एक दिन वहाँ जाते हैं । मेरी अपनी पुस्तकें सब हिंदी की हैं । वह आज अपने देश को लौट रहा है । काम आठ बजे शुरू होता है । मैं अब काम शुरू कर रहा हूँ । अब काम ख़त्म करें । आप इस पुस्तक से हिंदी का कुछ ज्ञान प्राप्त करेंगे । आजकल आने इस्तेमाल नहीं होते, लेकिन गाँव के लोग अभी तक आनों में गिनते हैं । क्या ऋग्वेद में इंद्र का उल्लेख है? आप कल तक मेरी किताब वापस कीजिए । मैं रोज़ यहाँ उसका इंतज़ार करता हूँ, लेकिन आम तौर से वह ठीक वक़्त पर नहीं आता ।

## EXERCISE 20

He always puts his books on that table. I shall give you my book. I shall give you[1] back your book. He went to London yesterday because his brother was arriving from India. My wife and I hope that you will write us[1] a letter when you arrive home. Which month were you born in? Have you any mangoes? No, they're finished. I shall finish your book tomorrow. Why is the door shut? I was looking for[2] you yesterday. He set off yesterday. I shall see them off. Does your country produce a lot of grain?

[1] The pronoun need not be expressed here.

[2] Either ढूँढ़ना *ḍhūṁṛhnā* or तलाश करना *talāś karnā*; with a personal object, as here, the former is perhaps slightly more natural.

# LESSON XI

## NUMERALS

### 1. *Cardinals*

| | | |
|---|---|---|
| 1 | एक | *ek* |
| 2 | दो | *do* |
| 3 | तीन | *tīn* |
| 4 | चार | *cār* |
| 5 | पाँच | *pāṁc* |
| 6 | छह, छः, छै | *chah, chaḥ, chai* |
| 7 | सात | *sāt* |
| 8 | ग्राठ | *āṭh* |
| 9 | नौ | *nau* |
| 10 | दस | *das* |
| 11 | ग्यारह | *gyārah*[1] |
| 12 | बारह | *bārah* |
| 13 | तेरह | *terah* |
| 14 | चौदह | *caudah* |
| 15 | पंद्रह | *pandrah* |
| 16 | सोलह | *solah* |
| 17 | सत्रह, सत्तरह | *satrah, sattrah* |
| 18 | ग्रठारह | *aṭhārah* |
| 19 | उन्नीस | *unnīs* |
| 20 | बीस | *bīs* |
| 21 | इक्कीस | *ikkīs* |
| 22 | बाईस | *bāīs* |
| 23 | तेईस | *teīs* |
| 24 | चौबीस | *caubīs* |
| 25 | पच्चीस | *paccīs* |
| 26 | छब्बीस | *chabbīs* |
| 27 | सत्ताईस | *sattāīs* |
| 28 | ग्रट्ठाईस | *aṭṭhāīs* |
| 29 | उनतीस | *untīs* |
| 30 | तीस | *tīs* |
| 31 | इकत्तीस | *ikattīs* |
| 32 | बत्तीस | *battīs* |
| 33 | तैंतीस | *taiṁtīs* |
| 34 | चौंतीस | *cauṁtīs* |
| 35 | पैंतीस | *paiṁtīs* |
| 36 | छत्तीस | *chattīs* |
| 37 | सैंतीस | *saiṁtīs* |
| 38 | ग्रड़तीस | *aṛtīs* |
| 39 | उनतालीस | *untālīs* |
| 40 | चालीस | *cālīs* |
| 41 | इकतालीस | *iktālīs* |
| 42 | बयालीस | *bayālīs* |
| 43 | तैंतालीस | *taiṁtālīs* |
| 44 | चवालीस | *cavālīs* |
| 45 | पैंतालीस | *paiṁtālīs* |
| 46 | छियालीस | *chiyālīs* |
| 47 | सैंतालीस | *saiṁtālīs* |
| 48 | ग्रड़तालीस | *aṛtālīs* |
| 49 | उनचास | *uncās* |
| 50 | पचास | *pacās* |
| 51 | इक्यावन | *ikyāvan* |
| 52 | बावन | *bāvan* |
| 53 | तिरपन | *tirpan* |
| 54 | चौवन | *cauvan* |
| 55 | पचपन | *pacpan* |
| 56 | छप्पन | *chappan* |
| 57 | सत्तावन | *sattāvan* |
| 58 | ग्रट्ठावन | *aṭṭhāvan* |
| 59 | उनसठ | *unsaṭh* |
| 60 | साठ | *sāṭh* |
| 61 | इकसठ | *iksaṭh* |
| 62 | बासठ | *bāsaṭh* |
| 63 | तिरसठ | *tirsaṭh* |
| 64 | चौंसठ | *cauṁsaṭh* |

[1] The numerals 11–18, ending in *-ah,* have common variant pronunciations with long *ā* and no aspiration in final syllable.

| | | | | | |
|---|---|---|---|---|---|
| 65 | पैंसठ | *paiṁsaṭh* | 87 | सत्तासी, सतासी | *sattāsī, satāsī* |
| 66 | छियासठ | *chiyāsaṭh* | 88 | अट्ठासी, अठासी | *aṭṭhāsī, aṭhāsī* |
| 67 | सरसठ | *sarsaṭh* | 89 | नवासी | *navāsī* |
| 68 | अड़सठ | *aṛsaṭh* | 90 | नव्वे, नब्बे | *navve, nabbe* |
| 69 | उनहत्तर | *unhattar* | 91 | इक्यानवे | *ikyānve* |
| 70 | सत्तर | *sattar* | 92 | बानवे | *bānve* |
| 71 | इकहत्तर | *ik'hattar*[1] | 93 | तिरानवे | *tirānve* |
| 72 | बहत्तर | *bahattar* | 94 | चौरानवे | *caurānve* |
| 73 | तिहत्तर | *tihattar* | 95 | पचानवे | *pacānve* |
| 74 | चौहत्तर | *cauhattar* | 96 | छियानवे | *chiyānve* |
| 75 | पचहत्तर | *pac'hattar*[1] | 97 | सत्तानवे | *sattānve* |
| 76 | छिहत्तर | *chihattar* | 98 | अट्ठानवे | *aṭṭhānve* |
| 77 | सतहत्तर | *sat'hattar*[1] | 99 | निन्यानवे | *ninyānve* |
| 78 | अठहत्तर | *aṭhhattar* | 100 | सौ | *sau* |
| 79 | उन्यासी, उन्नासी | *unyāsī, unnāsī* | 101 | एक सौ एक | *ek sau ek* |
| 80 | अस्सी | *assī* | 121 | एक सौ इक्कीस | *ek sau ikkīs* |
| 81 | इक्यासी | *ikyāsī* | 200 | दो सौ | *do sau* |
| 82 | बयासी | *bayāsī* | 1,000 | (एक) हज़ार | (*ek*) *hazār* |
| 83 | तिरासी | *tirāsī* | | (एक) सहस्र | (*ek*) **sahasra* |
| 84 | चौरासी | *caurāsī* | 2,000 | दो हज़ार | *do hazār* |
| 85 | पचासी | *pacāsī* | 100,000 | एक लाख | *ek lākh* |
| 86 | छियासी | *chiyāsī* | 10,000,000 | एक करोड़ | *ek karoṛ* |

(*a*) Divided into crores and lakhs the number 13,478,241 reads 1,34,78,241:

एक करोड़ चौंतीस लाख अठहत्तर हज़ार दो सौ इकतालीस *ek karoṛ cauṁtīs lākh aṭhhattar hazār do sau iktālīs.*

(*b*) There are variant pronunciations and spellings for a considerable number of the cardinal numerals; only a few are indicated above.

(*c*) हज़ार *hazār* and सहस्र *sahasra* are usually used as nouns, and prefixed by एक *ek*; लाख *lākh* and करोड़ *karoṛ* as single terms are always prefixed by एक *ek*: e.g.

उस ज़िले में एक लाख आदमी रहते हैं। *us zile meṁ ek lākh ādmī rahte haiṁ,* A hundred thousand people live in that district.

[1] Note the pronunciation and transliteration of these forms. The apostrophe of the transliterations indicates that *h* is separate syllabically from the preceding consonant, and is voiced.

(*d*) Cardinal numbers (and other adjectives) are often followed by collective singular nouns, where the objects concerned are not of individual importance: e.g.

दो प्याला चाय *do pyālā cāy*, two cups of tea

तीन रुपया *tīn rupayā*, three rupees

छह महीने में *chah mahīne meṁ*, in six months

Compare the use of singular nouns possible, for instance, after reduplicated क्या *kyā*: e.g.

आप उनसे क्या क्या बात करेंगे? *āp unse kyā kyā bāt kareṁge?* What will you talk to him about?

(*e*) Cardinal numerals are often combined in pairs, usually hyphenated, expressive of an approximate number, e.g. दो-चार *do-cār*, दस-पाँच *das-pāṁc*. Note unhyphenated दो एक *do ek* 'about two', i.e. 'very few', and the analogous use of suffixed एक *ek* in the sense 'approximately' with other numerals.

2. *Ordinals*

| | | | | | |
|---|---|---|---|---|---|
| 1st | पहला | *pahlā* | 6th | छठा | *chaṭhā* |
| 2nd | दूसरा | *dūsrā* | 7th | सातवाँ | *sātvāṁ* |
| 3rd | तीसरा | *tīsrā* | 8th | आठवाँ | *āṭhvāṁ* |
| 4th | चौथा | *cauthā* | 9th | नवाँ | *navāṁ* |
| 5th | पाँचवाँ | *pāṁcvāṁ* | | | |

(*a*) In formal Hindi, especially the written language, Sanskrit ordinals are sometimes found, especially for the lower numbers, viz.

| | | | | | |
|---|---|---|---|---|---|
| 1st | प्रथम | *pratham* | 3rd | तृतीय | *tṛtīy* |
| 2nd | द्वितीय | *dvitīy* | 4th | चतुर्थ | *caturth* |

Others occur occasionally, e.g. in the names of certain Hindu festivals, chapter numbers of some books, etc. But use of the ordinals in *-vāṁ* (regular from सातवाँ *sātvāṁ* on) is rarely inappropriate.

(*b*) 101st is एक सौ एकवाँ *ek sau ekvāṁ*
102nd is एक सौ दोवाँ *ek sau dovāṁ*
103rd is एक सौ तीनवाँ/तीसरा *ek sau tīnvāṁ/tīsrā*

3. *Fractions*

$\frac{1}{2}$ आधा *ādhā*
$\frac{1}{3}$ एक तिहाई *ek tihāī*
$\frac{1}{4}$ एक चौथाई *ek cauthāī*
$\frac{1}{5}$ पाँचवाँ भाग, हिस्सा *pāṁcvāṁ bhāg, †hissā*; एक बटे पाँच *ek baṭe pāṁc*
$\frac{2}{5}$ दो बटे पाँचवाँ हिस्सा *do baṭe pāṁcvāṁ †hissā*; दो बटे पाँच *do baṭe pāṁc*
$4\frac{7}{8}$ चार सात बटे आठवाँ हिस्सा *cār sāt baṭe āṭhvāṁ †hissā*; चार सात बटे आठ *cār sāt baṭe āṭh*

आधी किताबें *ādhī kitābeṁ*, half the books
उसका आधा *uskā ādhā*, half of that
एक चौथाई किताबें *ek cauthāī kitābeṁ*, a quarter of the books
दुनिया की तीन चौथाई *duniyā kī tīn cauthāī*, three-quarters of the world

(*a*) As the examples show, आधा *ādhā* is used as an adjective and a noun, while the other fractions given are used as nouns only, often as 'measure nouns' (i.e. with an immediately following noun denoting a substance of which an amount is measured).[1]

(*b*) एक आध *ek ādh* (with singular noun) means 'about one, one or two': e.g. मैं भारत में एक आध महीना बिताऊँगा। *maiṁ bhārat meṁ ek ādh mahīnā bitāūṁgā*, I shall spend a month or so in India.

(*c*) Note particularly the following invariable expressions:

पौन *paun*, three-quarters of
पौने *paune*, less a quarter
सवा *savā*, plus a quarter; $1\frac{1}{4}$ times[2]
डेढ़ *ḍeṛh*, one and a half; $1\frac{1}{2}$ times[2]
ढाई *ḍhāī*, two and a half; $2\frac{1}{2}$ times[2]
साढ़े *sāṛhe*, plus a half (from $3\frac{1}{2}$)
पौन सेर दूध *paun ser dūdh*, three-quarters of a seer of milk
पौने पच्चीस *paune paccīs*, $24\frac{3}{4}$
सवा रुपया *savā rupayā*, $1\frac{1}{4}$ rupees
सवा सौ *savā sau*, 125
डेढ़ रुपया *ḍeṛh rupayā*, $1\frac{1}{2}$ rupees

[1] Other expressions of quantity are also used in this way, e.g. तीन सेर दूध *tīn ser dūdh* 'three seers of milk', दो प्याला चाय *do pyālā cāy* 'two cups of tea', कितने सेर दूध? *kitne ser dūdh?* 'how many seers of milk?'

[2] With the words सौ *sau*, हज़ार *hazār*, लाख *lākh*, करोड़ *karoṛ*.

डेढ़ सौ *ḍeṛh sau*, 150
ढाई चम्मच *ḍhāī cammac*, 2½ spoons(full)
ढाई हज़ार *ḍhāī hazār*, 2,500
साढ़े ग्यारह *sāṛhe gyārah*, 11½

पौन *paun* is used as a measure noun; its sphere of usage is rather restricted. पौने *paune* and साढ़े *sāṛhe* are used with numerals only. The other forms given are used with both nouns and numerals.

4. *Aggregatives*

दोनों *donoṁ*, both
तीनों *tīnoṁ*, all three
चारों *cāroṁ*, all four
बीसों *bīsoṁ*, all twenty
बीसियों *bīsiyoṁ*, scores of
सैकड़ों *saikṛoṁ*, hundreds of
हज़ारों *hazāroṁ*, thousands of

हम तीनों जाएँगे । *ham tīnoṁ jāeṁge*, The three of us will go.

शहर के चारों ओर देहात है । *śahr ke cāroṁ or dehāt hai*, All around the village lies the countryside.

नदी में सैकड़ों आदमी नहीं, हज़ारों आदमी स्नान करते हैं । *nadī meṁ saikṛoṁ ādmī nahīṁ, hazāroṁ ādmī snān karte haiṁ*, Not hundreds but thousands of men bathe in the river.

(*a*) Note that aggregatives are based both on cardinal numerals and on nouns expressing numerical quantity such as बीसी *bīsī* 'a score', सैकड़ा *saikṛā* 'an amount of a hundred'; as well as occasionally on nouns which have no numerical connotation, e.g. महीना *mahīnā*:

महीनों बीत गए । *mahīnoṁ bīt gae*, Months passed.[1]

5. *Multiplicatives*

These are chiefly formed with the adjectival suffix *-gunā*. Often they are followed by adjectives. Some variant forms for lower multiplicatives are found, almost all based on unmodified cardinal numerals.

दुगुना, दूना *dugunā, dūnā*, twofold
तिगुना *tigunā*, threefold

[1] बीत गए *bīt gae* 'passed': compound verb. See lesson XVII.

चौगुना *caugunā*, fourfold
पचगुना *pacgunā*, fivefold
छैगुना, छगुना *chaigunā*, *chagunā*, sixfold
सतगुना *satgunā*, sevenfold
अठगुना *aṭhgunā*, eightfold
नौगुना *naugunā*, ninefold
दसगुना *dasgunā*, tenfold
ग्यारहगुना *gyārahgunā*, elevenfold

दिल्ली इलाहाबाद से दुगुना बड़ा शहर है । *dillī ilāhābād se dugunā baṛā śahr hai*, Delhi is twice as big a city as Allahabad.[1]

## TIME

1. The word घंटा *ghaṇṭā* means a period of one hour. Hours of the clock are expressed by means of the perfective participle of the verb बजना *bajnā* 'to sound, resound', as follows:

एक बजा *ek bajā*, one o'clock
एक बजा है । *ek bajā hai*, It is one o'clock.
एक बजे *ek baje*, at one o'clock
दो बजे *do baje*, two o'clock
दो बजे हैं । *do baje haiṁ*, It is two o'clock.
दो बजे *do baje*, at two o'clock

(*a*) The use of पौन *paun*, सवा *savā*, डेढ़ *ḍeṛh*, ढाई *ḍhāī*, and साढ़े *sāṛhe* in expressions of time is illustrated by the following examples:

पौन बजा *paun bajā*, 12.45
पौन बजा है । *paun bajā hai*, It is 12.45.
पौन बजे *paun baje*, at 12.45
सवा बजा *savā bajā*, 1.15
सवा बजा है । *savā bajā hai*, It is 1.15.
सवा बजे *savā baje*, at 1.15

Similarly

डेढ़ बजा *ḍeṛh bajā*, 1.30
पौने दो बजे *paune do baje*, 1.45
पौने दो बजे हैं । *paune do baje haiṁ*, It is 1.45.
पौने दो बजे *paune do baje*, at 1.45

[1] The use of से *se* in comparisons is explained in Lesson XVI.

Similarly

सवा दो बजे *savā do baje*, 2.15
ढाई बजे *ḍhāī baje*, 2.30
साढ़े तीन बजे *sāṛhe tīn baje*, 3.30

2. Minutes before and after the hour can be expressed as in the following examples:

पाँच बजने में दस मिनट *pāṁc bajne meṁ das minaṭ*, 4.50
पाँच बजने में दस मिनट बाक़ी हैं। *pāṁc bajne meṁ das minaṭ bāqī haiṁ*, It is 4.50.
पाँच बजने से दस मिनट पहले *pāṁc bajne se das minaṭ pahle*, at 4.50
पाँच बजकर दस मिनट *pāṁc bajkar das minaṭ*, 5.10
पाँच बजकर दस मिनट हुए हैं। *pāṁc bajkar das minaṭ hue haiṁ*, It is 5.10.
पाँच बजकर दस मिनट पर *pāṁc bajkar das minaṭ par*, at 5.10

(*a*) The hours 4.50 and 5.10 may also be expressed as चार पचास *cār pacās* and पाँच दस *pāṁc das*. This is normal timetable usage but is also fairly common elsewhere.

3. Translation equivalents of the locutions 'a.m.', 'p.m.' are illustrated in the following examples:

पाँच बजे सुबह को *pāṁc baje subah ko*, 5 a.m.
सुबह के पाँच बजे *subah ke pāṁc baje*, at 5 a.m.
दो बजे दिन को *do baje din ko*, 2 p.m.
दिन के दो बजे *din ke do baje*, at 2 p.m.
पाँच बजे शाम को *pāṁc baje śām ko*, 5 p.m.
शाम के पाँच बजे *śām ke pāṁc baje*, at 5 p.m.
दो बजे रात को *do baje rāt ko*, 2 a.m.
रात के दो बजे *rāt ke do baje*, at 2 a.m.

(*a*) सुबह *subah* runs from daybreak to about 11 a.m., दिन to about 3 or 4 p.m., शाम *śām* to about 9 p.m. Colloquially, the postpositions को *ko* and के *ke* in these usages are sometimes dropped.

(*b*) Note the form of expressions which refer to a day as well as a time of day:

आज सुबह (को) पाँच बजे *āj subah* (*ko*) *pāṁc baje*, at 5 a.m. today
कल शाम (को) पाँच बजे *kal śām* (*ko*) *pāṁc baje*, at 5 p.m. yesterday, or tomorrow
परसों रात (को) तीन बजे *parsoṁ rāt* (*ko*) *tīn baje*, at 3 a.m. two days ago, or ahead

(*c*) The word पहर *pahr*, meaning a 'watch of the day or night', i.e. three hours, is in common use in a number of expressions. Some of these are:

(ठीक) दोपहर (*ṭhīk*) *dopahr*, midday (i.e. the end of the second watch)
तीसरा पहर *tīsrā pahr*, the early afternoon
दोपहर के बाद *dopahr ke bād*, in the afternoon
पहर रात (को) *pahr rāt* (*ko*), late at night
आठों पहर *āṭhoṁ pahr*, twenty-four hours long

DATES

1. Days of the week, and months of the year (Christian and Vikramāditya):

रविवार *ravivār*, इतवार *itvār*, Sunday
सोमवार *somvār*, Monday
मंगलवार *maṅgalvār*, Tuesday
बुधवार *budhvār*, Wednesday
बृहस्पतिवार *bṛhaspativār*, गुरुवार *guruvār*, Thursday
शुक्रवार *śukravār*, Friday
शनिवार *śanivār*, Saturday

| | | | |
|---|---|---|---|
| जनवरी | *janvarī* | चैत | *cait* |
| फ़रवरी | *farvarī* | बैसाख | *baisākh* |
| मार्च | *mārc* | जेठ | *jeṭh* |
| अप्रैल | *aprail* | असाढ़ | *asāṛh* |
| मई | *maī* | सावन | *sāvan* |
| जून | *jūn* | भादों | *bhādoṁ* |
| जुलाई | *julāī* | क्वार | *kvār* |
| अगस्त | *agast* | कार्त्तिक | *kārttik* |
| सितंबर | *sitambar* | अगहन | *ag'han*[1] |
| अक्तूबर | *aktūbar* | पूस | *pūs* |
| नवंबर | *navambar* | माघ | *māgh* |
| दिसंबर | *disambar* | फागुन | *phāgun* |

(*a*) Expressions of time involving days of the week show को *ko*, those involving months में *meṁ*: e.g.

सोमवार को *somvār ko*, on Monday
अक्तूबर में *aktūbar meṁ*, in October

[1] See p. 62, n. 1.

(*b*) The dates of Hindu rites and festivals are determined according to the विक्रमादित्य *vikramāditya* calendar, which is based on lunar months, each with a 'bright phase' (शुक्ल पक्ष *śukl pakṣ*) and a 'dark phase' (कृष्ण पक्ष *kṛṣṇ pakṣ*). Months begin with the full moon, the कृष्ण पक्ष *kṛṣṇ pakṣ* following. A thirteenth intercalary month is added every thirty months to keep these months in step with the seasons. The month चैत *cait* begins in mid-March or earlier.

The Sanskrit forms and some variant Hindi forms of the names of the विक्रमादित्य *vikramāditya* lunar months are also found alongside the Hindi ones given above.

2. The word तारीख़ *tārīkh* (f.) means 'date'. It is implied in expressions of date such as

पहली जनवरी *pahlī janvarī*, January 1st
पहली जनवरी को *pahlī janvarī ko*, on January 1st
दूसरी मार्च *dūsrī mārc*, March 2nd
दूसरी मार्च को *dūsrī mārc ko*, on March 2nd

(*a*) For dates other than the first or second of a month cardinals are generally used: e.g.

आठ सितंबर *āṭh sitambar*, September 8th
आठ सितंबर को *āṭh sitambar ko*, on September 8th

(*b*) The word तारीख़ *tārīkh* can also be used in alternative forms of the above expressions: e.g.

जनवरी की पहली तारीख़ *janvarī kī pahlī tārīkh*
सितंबर की आठ तारीख़ को *sitambar kī āṭh tārīkh ko*

3. Years of the Christian era are usually denoted by the numeral preceded by the designation सन् *san*, derived from Arabic and meaning 'year': e.g. सन् उन्नीस सौ इकसठ की सत्रह मई को *san unnīs sau iksaṭh kī satrah maī ko*, on 17th May 1961

(*a*) Years of the विक्रमादित्य *vikramāditya* era (57 or 58 years ahead of the Christian) are similarly prefixed by the noun संवत् *saṃvat*. Other systems of dating include the शक *śak* era (77 or 78 years behind the Christian), used officially by the Indian government in conjunction with the Christian era.

## VOCABULARY

ज़िला *zilā*, m., administrative district
प्याला *pyālā*, m., cup
चाय *cāy*, f., tea
भाग *bhāg*, m., part
हिस्सा †*hissā*, m., part
सेर *ser*, m., seer (measure of weight, approximately 1 kg.)
मन *man*, m., maund (measure of weight, = 40 seers)
चम्मच *cammac*, m., spoon
देहात *dehāt*, m., country(side)
इलाहाबाद *ilāhābād*, m., Allahabad
समुद्र *samudr*, m., sea, ocean
घड़ी *ghaṛī*, f., watch; मेरी घड़ी में *merī ghaṛī meṁ*, by my watch
भाषण *bhāṣaṇ*, f., speech, lecture
घटना *ghaṭnā*, f., incident, happening
नया *nayā*, new
ख़राब †*kharāb*, bad; spoiled
बाक़ी †*bāqī*, remaining, left over (invariable)
स्नान करना *snān karnā*, bathe
बीतना *bītnā*, pass by (of time)
बिताना *bitānā*, spend (time)
के चारों ओर/तरफ़ *ke cāroṁ or/taraf*, on all four sides, all around

## EXERCISE 21

मेरे पास पचहत्तर नए पैसे[1] हैं। बारह आने पचहत्तर नए पैसे होते हैं। तीन चौथाई दुनिया समुद्र है। ढाई सौ। पाँच सौ इकत्तीस। दो हज़ार दो सौ बाईस। तीन लाख चार हज़ार आठ सौ सैंतालीस। तीन करोड़ इकतालीस लाख पैंसठ हज़ार तीन सौ सात। मैं उससे दुगुना काम करता हूँ। वह छठी क्लास में पढ़ती है। अगले साल सातवीं में पढ़ेगी। मनों अनाज ख़राब हुआ। पौने चार बजे हैं। जी नहीं, मेरी घड़ी में चार बजने में दस मिनट बाक़ी हैं। गाड़ी छह बजकर तीन मिनट पर पहुँचती है। आज शाम को साढ़े आठ बजे एक भाषण है। मैं तेईस जून को घर जा रहा हूँ। यह घटना सन् उन्नीस सौ उनतीस की चौबीस अक्तूबर को हुई।

## EXERCISE 22

I've been learning Hindi for a month or so. 150. 754. 9,876. 15,378,492. 9,132,444. He does twice as much work as me. Thousands of people will come here next month. I arrived at 3.30. It's now twenty-five past seven. I'm going at twenty to eight. Come at 5.30 p.m. Come at 8.30 p.m. tomorrow. My son was born on April 1st. We shall begin work on Wednesday.

[1] नया पैसा *nayā paisā*, one-hundredth of a rupee in the reformed currency; with the disappearance of the old currency, the word पैसा *paisā* is increasingly used without the adjective.

# LESSON XII

## CONSTRUCTIONS WITH THE POSTPOSITION ने *ne*

1. THE sentence

वह किताब लिख रहा था *vah kitāb likh rahā thā*

means 'he was writing the book', but 'he wrote the book' is translated

उसने किताब लिखी *usne kitāb likhī.*

In this sentence, in which the verb is transitive and perfective, we find, first, that in the initial position in the sentence, which we have seen is taken characteristically by sentence subjects in sentences of neutral style and emphasis, there occurs not the direct case form वह *vah*, but the oblique case form उस *us*, with the postposition ने *ne*. Secondly, the verb shows concord not with this form but with the word किताब *kitāb*, which, with regard to its non-initial position, may be classified as its direct object.

Constructions showing the postposition ने *ne* with positionally-determined oblique case sentence subjects, and the form of the verb determined with reference to sentence *objects*, not subjects, are regular in Hindi (with various qualifications which will be stated) where finite verbs are transitive and perfective.[1]

2. Note the importance of the form taken by the object in constructions involving ने *ne*. If an indefinite object[2] is present, or implied, the verb is in concord with it, as in the above example; but otherwise (i.e. if the object is definite,[2] or if no specific direct object is expressed or implied) the

[1] These constructions have evolved from constructions in the earlier language which showed inflected agentive forms in initial sentence position, and past participles in concord with non-initial grammatical subjects, in other words, constructions which expressed 'he wrote the book' as 'by him the book was written'. As the language evolved, however, the position of nouns and pronouns in sentences became a more important marker of their role as subject or object than their grammatical form, so that for modern Hindi it is advisable in general to consider initially occurring forms with ने *ne* as sentence subjects, and non-initial forms as direct objects determining the form of verbs in their sentences; although certain modern usages current in Delhi, western U.P., and the Panjab, which are not introduced in this book, may be interpreted as showing specifically agentive forms and verb concord with subjects, and thus still indicate the historical origins of the construction.

[2] See Lesson IX, p. 49.

verb always shows final *-ā* (and is better thought of as a 'neutral' or 'impersonal' form than as a 'third singular masculine'): e.g.

हमने अपने शत्रु को मारा। *hamne apne śatru ko mārā*, We killed our enemy.[1]

हमने अपने शत्रुओं को मारा। *hamne apne śatruoṁ ko mārā*, We killed our enemies.[1]

उसने कहा कि . . . *usne kahā ki . . .*, He, she said that . . .

उसने मेरी ओर देखा। *usne merī or dekhā*, He, she looked in my direction.

The following examples illustrate the types of construction described above:

उसने पत्र लिखा। *usne patr likhā*, He, she wrote the letter, a letter.

उसने पत्र लिखे। *usne patr likhe*, He, she, wrote the letters, some letters.

इस लड़के ने पुस्तक कल पढ़ी थी। *is laṛke ne pustak kal paṛhī thī*, This boy read the book yesterday.

उन लड़कियों ने किताबें पढ़ीं। *un laṛkiyoṁ ne kitābeṁ paṛhīṁ*, Those girls read the books.

उसने मकान बेचा होगा। *usne makān becā hogā*, He, she will have sold the house.

उसने उन स्त्रियों को पहले देखा था। *usne un striyoṁ ko pahle dekhā thā*, He, she had seen those women before.

इस लड़की ने उसे कल वहाँ देखा था। *is laṛkī ne use kal vahāṁ dekhā thā*, This girl saw him, her there yesterday.

उसने कुछ समय सोचा। *usne kuch samay socā*, He, she thought for some time.

3. ने *ne* stands slightly apart from the other postpositions in the forms it requires of some personal and other pronouns, viz.

मैंने *maiṁne*
तूने *tūne*
उन्होंने *unhoṁne* (plural of वह *vah*)
इन्होंने *inhoṁne* (plural of यह *yah*)
किन्होंने *kinhoṁne* (plural of कौन *kaun*)
जिन्होंने *jinhoṁne* (plural of जो *jo*)
कइयों ने *kaiyoṁ ne*

4. Almost all verbs which are transitive, i.e. can take direct objects, are used in construction with ने *ne* in perfective forms (except in certain cases

[1] The student can, if he wishes, visualize the impersonal nature of such constructions by bearing in mind their historical origins (see previous footnote) and mentally recasting 'we killed our enemy' as 'by us it was killed in respect of our enemy', etc.

when members of composite verbal expressions, noted in due course). The construction of a few verbs varies. Some notes on the construction of perfective forms of individual verbs and verbal expressions follow.

(*a*) कहना *kahnā* 'say' and पूछना *pūchnā* 'ask, inquire' are always used in construction with ने *ne*; बोलना *bolnā* 'speak, talk' only rarely so. (The use of बोलना *bolnā* as a transitive verb is rather restricted.)

मैंने कहा कि मैं कल वहाँ था । *maiṁne kahā ki maiṁ kal vahāṁ thā*, I said I was there yesterday.

उसने मुझसे कई प्रश्न पूछे । *usne mujhse kaī praśn pūche*, He, she asked me several questions.

वह मुझसे हिंदी में बोलीं *vah mujhse hindī meṁ bolīṁ*, She, they spoke to me in Hindi.

उसने मुझसे सब कुछ कहा । *usne mujhse sab kuch kahā*, He, she told me everything.

उसने झूठ बोला । *usne jhūṭh bolā*, He lied (spoke falsehood).

(*b*) Conjunct verbs formed with करना *karnā* and a preceding noun, and other verbal expressions involving करना *karnā*[1] are all used in construction with ने *ne*. Note that English translation equivalents of these are usually but not invariably transitive.

मैंने काम शुरू किया । *maiṁne kām śurū kiyā*, I started work.

मैंने दरवाज़ा बंद किया । *maiṁne darvāzā band kiyā*, I closed the door.

मैंने उसका इंतज़ार किया । *maiṁne uskā intazār kiyā*, I waited for him, her.

मैंने उसकी प्रतीक्षा की । *maiṁne uskī pratīkṣā kī*, I waited for him, her.

उन्होंने शत्रु पर आक्रमण किया । *unhoṁne śatru par ākramaṇ kiyā*, They attacked the enemy.

(*c*) The verb समझना *samajhnā* 'understand' is used in both constructions. Some Hindi speakers prefer to use it in construction with ने *ne* in most cases where a direct object is expressed, especially if this is of some prominence, or if it is implied that the act of understanding leads to a consequence. Where समझना *samajhnā* means 'understand something to be the case' it is regularly used in construction with ने *ne*.

(आप) समझे? (*āp*) *samjhe?* Do you understand? (masculine reference)[2]

[1] See Lesson X, pp. 56 ff.
[2] Literally 'have you understood, grasped (the question)'.

आप मेरी बात समझे? *āp merī bāt samjhe?* Do you understand what I said?

आपने मेरी बात समझी? *āpne merī bāt samjhī?* Do you understand what I said?

मैंने आपकी बातें समझी हैं, और उनपर अमल किया है । *maiṁne āpkī bāteṁ samjhī haiṁ, aur unpar amal kiyā hai*, I understand what you told me and have acted on it.

मैंने आपको अपना भाई समझा । *maiṁne āpko apnā bhāī samjhā*, I thought of you as my own brother.

(*d*) लाना *lānā* 'bring' and भूलना *bhūlnā* 'forget' are not used in construction with ने *ne*.

वह दो पुस्तकें लाया । *vah do pustkeṁ lāyā*, He brought two books.

(*e*) The expressions ले आना *le ānā* 'bring' and ले जाना *le jānā*, ले चलना *le calnā* 'take away' are collocations of absolutives with the intransitive verbs आना *ānā*, जाना *jānā* (see Lesson VII), and so of course are not used in construction with ने *ne*.

(*f*) The expressions दिखाई देना *dikhāī denā* 'be visible, appear', and सुनाई देना *sunāī denā* 'be audible' are not used in construction with ने *ne*, although based on transitive देना *denā*.

शहर दूर पर दिखाई दिया । *śahr dūr par dikhāī diyā*, The city came into view in the distance.

उसे तीन औरतें अचानक दिखाई दीं । *use tīn aurteṁ acānak dikhāī dīṁ*, He, she suddenly saw three women.[1]

(*g*) पढ़ना *paṛhnā* 'read' is usually not used in construction with ने *ne* when it has the sense 'follow a course of study in a subject'.

वह इलाहाबाद में हिंदी पढ़े । *vah ilāhābād meṁ hindī paṛhe*, He studied Hindi in Allahabad.

(*h*) नहाना *nahānā* 'wash, bathe' is used in both constructions without difference of sense, but usually without ने *ne*.

मैं (ने) ठंडे पानी से नहाया । *maiṁ(ne) ṭhaṇḍe pānī se nahāyā*, I washed in cold water.

(*i*) Some verbs, such as मुसकराना *muskarānā* 'smile' and रोना *ronā* 'weep', which usually do not take direct objects or occur in construction with

[1] Literally 'three women suddenly appeared to him, her'.

ने *ne*, may occasionally take 'cognate objects', i.e. nouns meaning 'smile', 'tears', etc., and may then sometimes occur in construction with ने *ne*, especially if an object is of some prominence.

वह मुसकराया । *vah muskarāyā*, He smiled.

वह विजय की मुसकराहट मुसकराया । *vah vijay kī muskarāhaṭ muskarāyā*, He smiled a smile of triumph.

उसने विजय की मुसकराहट मुसकराई । *usne vijay kī muskarāhaṭ muskarāī*, He smiled a smile of triumph.

(*j*) Other verbs, such as सोना *sonā* 'sleep' and हँसना *hamsnā* 'laugh, smile' are not used in construction with ने *ne* even if 'cognate objects' are expressed.

वह बेफ़िक्री की नींद सोया । *vah befikrī kī nīṁd soyā*, He slept an untroubled sleep.

## VOCABULARY

शत्रु *śatru*, m.f., enemy
प्रश्न *praśn*, m., question
आक्रमण *ākramaṇ*, m., attack
लाइब्रेरी *lāibrerī*, f., library
झगड़ा *jhagṛā*, m., quarrel
कारण *kāraṇ*, m., cause
तस्वीर †*tasvīr*, f., picture
सामान *sāmān*, m., belongings, goods, things
दिलचस्प †*dilcasp*, interesting
मारना *mārnā*, beat; kill
आक्रमण करना *ākramaṇ karnā* (*par*), attack
लाना *lānā*, bring
भूलना *bhūlnā*, forget
दिखाई देना *dikhāī denā*, be visible
सुनाई देना *sunāī denā*, be audible
ख़रीदना *kharīdnā*, buy
पाना *pānā*, get, obtain; find
सिखाना *sikhānā*, teach
सोचना *socnā*, think
कुछ समय *kuch samay*, for some time
ठंडा *ṭhaṇḍā*, cold; cool [ठंढा *ṭhaṇḍhā*]
अचानक *acānak*, suddenly
अमल *amal*, m., act, action; अमल करना *amal karnā*, act, take action
मुसकराना *muskarānā*, smile [मुस्कराना *muskarānā*]
मुसकराहट *muskarāhaṭ*, f., smile [मुस्कराहट *muskarāhaṭ*]
रोना *ronā*, cry, weep
हँसना *hamsnā*, laugh; smile
विजय *vijay*, f., victory, triumph
नींद *nīṁd*, f., sleep
बेफ़िक्री †*befikrī*, f., carefreeness
भेजना *bhejnā*, send

## EXERCISE 23

मैंने उसे कल देखा। वह एक किताब पढ़ रहा था। वह उसे लाइब्रेरी से ले आया था। उसने किताब पिछले हफ़्ते पढ़ी थी। मैंने ग्यारह बजे खाया। आप समझीं? उसने मुझे मेरे दफ़्तर में पाया। मैं उससे हिंदी बोला। उसने उसे हिंदी सिखाई। उसने उसे सिखाया। मैंने उसे झगड़े का कारण बताया। वह कल शाम को मेरे मकान के दरवाज़े पर दिखाई दी।

## EXERCISE 24

Have you written those letters? We bought several things in[1] that shop. Then we brought them home. I finished work at 5 p.m. The men put the boxes on the table. The villagers worked all day in the fields. By evening they had brought maunds of grain into the village. They used to wait for me here. In the picture several interesting things are to be seen. They took all their things away.

[1] से *se* 'from'.

# LESSON XIII

## THE FORM चाहिए *cāhie*

THIS very common verbal form is historically an old passive meaning 'is wished, is necessary'. It usually appears in constructions involving oblique case nouns or pronouns + को *ko* (or equivalent pronominal object forms) and (*a*) further nouns or pronouns only; or (*b*) infinitive or subjunctive forms of verbs. The former express want, lack or need, the latter duty or advisability. There are also other ways of expressing these ideas, which are noted below, together with the usages of चाहिए *cāhie.*

1. चाहिए cāhie *in association with nouns and pronouns only*

Note that words answering to the subjects of English translation equivalents are, if expressed,[1] in the oblique case with को *ko* (or in the equivalent object form, if pronouns). The verbal form चाहिए *cāhie* is in concord with Hindi subjects, though this concord is normally only explicit in the imperfective past tense, see (*b*) below.

आपको क्या चाहिए? *āpko kyā cāhie?* What do you want?

क्या चाहिए? *kyā cāhie?* What do you want?

मुझे कुछ दूध चाहिए। *mujhe kuch dūdh cāhie*, I want some milk.

मुझे एक किताब चाहिए। *mujhe ek kitāb cāhie*, I want a book.

उस आदमी को दस अंडे चाहिए। *us ādmī ko das aṇḍe cāhie*, That man wants ten eggs.

हमें ये पुस्तकें नहीं चाहिए। *hameṁ ye pustkeṁ nahīṁ cāhie*, We don't need these books.

(*a*) An alternative construction, perhaps somewhat less common than that with चाहिए *cāhie*, is with the feminine nouns ज़रूरत †*zarūrat* and आवश्यकता *āvaśyaktā*, both meaning 'necessity'.

मुझे दूध की ज़रूरत है। *mujhe dūdh kī zarūrat hai*, I want, need, some milk.

मुझे दस पुस्तकों की आवश्यकता है। *mujhe das pustkoṁ kī āvaśyaktā hai*, I require ten books.

(*b*) These constructions can be used in the imperfective past tense. The verbal forms are then चाहिए था *cāhie thā*, etc. (चाहिए *cāhie* functioning as

[1] See p. 12.

an equivalent of an imperfective participle), and थी *thī* in the construction with ज़रूरत *zarūrat*, आवश्यकता *āvaśyaktā*. Negatives precede चाहिए in sentences of neutral style and emphasis.

मुझे पानी चाहिए था। *mujhe pānī cāhie thā*, I needed water, some water.

हमें पानी नहीं चाहिए था। *hameṁ pānī nahīṁ cāhie thā*, We didn't need any water.

उनको एक किताब चाहिए थी। *unko ek kitāb cāhie thī*, They wanted a book.

आपको कितने अंडे चाहिए थे? *āpko kitne aṇḍe cāhie the?* How many eggs did you need?

मेरे भाई को दो कापियाँ चाहिए थीं। *mere bhāī ko do kāpiyāṁ cāhie thīṁ*, My brother needed two exercise books.

उसे दूध की ज़रूरत थी। *use dūdh kī zarūrat thī*, He needed milk, some milk.

(*c*) Elsewhere only the construction with ज़रूरत *zarūrat*, आवश्यकता *āvaśyaktā* is used, with forms of the verbs होना *honā* or पड़ना *paṛnā*; those of the latter verb tend to convey slightly more emphasis.

आपको मच्छड़दानी की ज़रूरत होगी। *āpko macchaṛdānī kī zarūrat hogī*, You'll need a mosquito net.

मुझे सहायता की आवश्यकता पड़ेगी। *mujhe sahāytā kī āvaśyaktā paṛegī*, I shall require asistance.

मुझे क़लम और काग़ज़ की ज़रूरत पड़ी। *mujhe qalam aur kāgaz kī zarūrat paṛī*, I needed, found I needed, pen and paper.

2. चाहिए cāhie *in association with infinitives or subjunctive forms*

In the standard written language and for the most part in the spoken language, transitive infinitives show adjectival concord with a preceding noun or pronoun, unless this is a definite direct object, in which case they show final *-nā*. Intransitive infinitives show final *-nā*, except as indicated in note (*a*) below. Negatives precede infinitives in sentences of neutral style and emphasis.

आपको यहाँ रहना चाहिए। *āpko yahāṁ rahnā cāhie*, You ought to stay here.

उन्हें हिंदी सीखनी चाहिए। *unheṁ hindī sīkhnī cāhie*, They should learn Hindi.

मेरे पिता जी को समाचारपत्र पढ़ने चाहिए। *mere pitā jī ko samācārpatr paṛhne cāhie*, My father ought to read the papers.

आपको ये पुस्तकें नहीं पढ़नी चाहिए। *āpko ye pustkeṁ nahīṁ paṛhnī cāhie*, You shouldn't read these books.

आपको उन्हें पढ़ना चाहिए। *āpko unheṁ paṛhnā cāhie*, You ought to read them.

(*a*) Nouns of non-personal reference, however, are not very often used with को *ko* in sentences containing intransitive infinitives. Such nouns are more usually used as subjects of चाहिए *cāhie* in sentences which do not contain any noun or pronoun + को *ko*, and infinitives are in adjectival concord with them.

क्या हिंदी राष्ट्रभाषा होनी चाहिए? *kyā hindī rāṣṭrabhāṣā honī cāhie?* Should Hindi be the national language?

यह किताब हमेशा मेज़ पर रहनी चाहिए । *yah kitāb hameśā mez par rahnī cāhie,* This book should always stay on the table.

(*b*) An alternative construction shows चाहिए *cāhie* linked by the conjunction कि *ki* to a following subject noun or pronoun and a verb in the subjunctive.

आपको चाहिए कि आप यहाँ रहें । *āpko cāhie ki āp yahāṁ raheṁ*, You ought to stay here.

चाहिए कि वह हिंदी सीख ले । *cāhie ki vah hindī sīkh le*, He ought to learn Hindi.[1]

(*c*) The verbal construction can, like the nominal, be used in the imperfective past tense. Note its special implication.

मुझे दिल्ली जाना चाहिए था । *mujhe dillī jānā cāhie thā*, I should have gone to Delhi.

उसको यह नहीं करना चाहिए था । *usko yah nahīṁ karnā cāhie thā*, He ought not to have done this.

उन्हें हिंदी सीखनी चाहिए थी । *unheṁ hindī sīkhnī cāhie thī*, They should have learned Hindi.

आपको दस अंडे ख़रीदने चाहिए थे । *āpko das aṇḍe k͟harīdne cāhie the,* You should have bought ten eggs.

आपको अपनी पुस्तकें लानी चाहिए थीं । *āpko apnī pustkeṁ lānī cāhie thīṁ*, You ought to have brought your books.

तुम्हें उनको देखना चाहिए था । *tumheṁ unko dekhnā cāhie thā*, You should have looked at them.

The imperfective reference of था *thā* stresses the fact that obligation continued over a period, and implies rather that it was not met than that

[1] सीख ले *sīkh le* 'should learn'; compound verb. See Lesson XVII.

it kept recurring. Expression of recurring obligation is dealt with in the following section.

## THE VERBS पड़ना *paṛnā* AND होना *honā* EXPRESSIVE OF OBLIGATION

The idea of compulsion or of positive obligation is expressed by association of the infinitive form of a verb with a following part of the verbs पड़ना *paṛnā*, meaning literally, 'fall' or 'be found', or होना *honā*. Use of पड़ना *paṛnā* may express a marginally stronger compulsion or obligation. Concord operates in the same way as in sentences showing चाहिए *cāhie* in association with infinitives. The form of पड़ना *paṛnā* or होना *honā* used determines the aspect, tense, and modal reference of the whole expression. Negatives precede infinitives in sentences of neutral style and emphasis.

आपको यहाँ रहना पड़ेगा/होगा । *āpko yahāṁ rahnā paṛegā/hogā*, You'll have to stay here, you must stay here.

आपको अपनी चाबी लानी पड़ेगी/होगी । *āpko apnī cābī lānī paṛegī/hogī*, You'll have to, must, bring your own key.

मुझे घर नहीं जाना पड़ा । *mujhe ghar nahīṁ jānā paṛā*, I didn't have to go home.

मुझे शाम छह बजे घर जाना पड़ता था । *mujhe śām chah baje ghar jānā paṛtā thā*, I used to have to go home at 6 p.m.

मुझे पाँच बजे तक काम करना पड़ता है । *mujhe pāṁc baje tak kām karnā paṛtā hai*, I have to work till five o'clock (daily).

मुझे पाँच बजे तक काम करना है । *mujhe pāṁc baje tak kām karnā hai*, I have to work till five o'clock (today).

(*a*) Note that constructions with the future tense of पड़ना *paṛnā* or होना *honā* are the normal means of rendering English sentences with 'must' (which anticipate future actions).

(*b*) Note the sense contrast in the last two examples, where पड़ता है *paṛtā hai* contrasts with है *hai*. The sense of the first of these two examples might have been expressed by use of होता है *hotā hai* if it had been desired to use होना *honā* instead of पड़ना *paṛnā*.

(*c*) The perfective forms of होना *honā*, viz. हुआ *huā*, हुआ था *huā thā*, etc., are not generally used in this construction.

## VOCABULARY

अंडा *aṇḍā*, m., egg

कापी *kāpī*, f., exercise book

मच्छड़दानी *macchaṛdānī*, f., mosquito net

सहायता *sahāytā*, f., help

मदद †*madad*, f., help

राष्ट्र *rāṣṭra*, m., state

राष्ट्रभाषा *rāṣṭrabhāṣā*, f., state language

समाचार *samācār*, m., (sg. and pl.) news

समाचारपत्र *samācārpatr*, m., newspaper

चाबी *cābī*, f., key

टोपी *ṭopī*, f., hat

हवाई पत्र *havāī patr*, m., air letter

क़मीज़ *qamīz*, f., shirt

बाज़ार जाना *bāzār jānā*, go to the bazaar, go shopping

फ़ोन *fon*, m., telephone; मैं उसे फ़ोन करूँगा *maiṁ use fon karūṁgā*, I shall phone him

के क़रीब *ke* †*qarīb*, about, approximately

कान्ता *kāntā*, Kāntā (girl's name)

## EXERCISE 25

मुझे एक नई टोपी चाहिए। आपको क्या चाहिए? मुझे पाँच हवाई पत्र चाहिए। उन्हें पानी चाहिए था। उसको आपकी मदद की ज़रूरत होगी। उस लड़के को क्या चाहिए? आपको ये पुस्तकें पढ़नी चाहिए थीं। मेरे भाई को भी उन्हें पढ़ना चाहिए था। मुझे उसे एक चिट्ठी लिखनी चाहिए। उनको अपना काम ख़त्म करना चाहिए। आपको इस गाँव के लोगों से हिंदी बोलनी पड़ेगी।

## EXERCISE 26

I need two shirts. Rādhā needed Kāntā's books. You ought to go to India. I ought to speak Hindi. You should have learned Hindi. I have to buy some newspapers. I'll have to go at about 11 o'clock. I must go at about 11 o'clock. I had to go at 11 o'clock. I used to have to go shopping every day. I have to phone him. I'll need ten rupees.

# LESSON XIV

## RELATIVE-CORRELATIVE CONSTRUCTIONS

RELATIVE-CORRELATIVE constructions have been mentioned above in connection with the relative pronoun and adjective जो *jo*. They are extremely common in Hindi, and are discussed more fully here. Note, first, that an English sentence made up of principal and relative clause will very often have as Hindi equivalent two clauses in the reverse order: the relative clause, containing the appropriate relative pronoun, adverb or adjective, followed by the principal clause containing a correlative to it, though this may be omitted in informal usage. The following examples of English relative sentences transposed to illustrate the structure of their Hindi equivalents should make this pattern quite clear.

I shall go when you tell me: When you tell me, then I shall go.
I didn't understand what he said: What he said, I didn't understand that.
I am reading the book you suggested: The book which you suggested, I am reading it.
Read as many books as you can: As many books as you can, read as many as that.

1. Some of the commonest relatives are listed here, together with their correlatives:

| | | |
|---|---|---|
| जब *jab*, when | — | तब *tab*, then |
| जब भी *jab bhī*, whenever | — | तब *tab*, ,, |
| जब से *jab se*, since (of time), from the time when | — | तब से *tab se*, since then |
| जब तक *jab tak*, as long as | — | तब तक *tab tak*, until then |
| जैसा *jaisā*, of such a sort as; that which | — | वैसा (ही) *vaisā (hī)*, in that way; it |
| जैसे ही *jaise hī*, as soon as | — | वैसे ही *vaise hī*, then |
| जितना *jitnā*, as many, much as; however many, much | — | उतना (ही) *utnā (hī)*, so many, much |
| जहाँ *jahāṁ*, where | — | वहाँ *vahāṁ*, there |
| जहाँ भी *jahāṁ bhī*, wherever | — | वहाँ *vahāṁ*, ,, |
| जो *jo*, the one who, which | — | वह *vah*, he, it, etc. |
| जो कोई *jo koī*, whoever, whichever | — | वह *vah*, ,, |
| जो कुछ *jo kuch*, whatever | — | वह *vah*, ,, |

2. Examples of their use follow, with further comment where necessary:

जब आप मुझसे कहेंगे, तब मैं जाऊँगा। *jab āp mujhse kaheṁge, tab maiṁ jāūṁgā*, I shall go when you tell me.

जब भी दिल्ली जाता हूँ, तब हिंदी ही बोलता हूँ। *jab bhī dillī jātā hūṁ, tab hindī hī boltā hūṁ*, Whenever I go to Delhi I speak Hindi, of course.

जब से आप चले गए थे, तब से मैं हिंदी नहीं बोला। *jab se āp cale gae the, tab se maiṁ hindī nahīṁ bolā*, I haven't spoken Hindi since you went away.[1]

जब तक मैं यहाँ रहूँगा, तब तक वे काम करेंगे। *jab tak maiṁ yahāṁ rahūṁgā, tab tak ve kām kareṁge*, They will work as long as I stay here.

जैसा आप मुझसे कहेंगे, वैसा (ही) करूँगा। *jaisā āp mujhse kaheṁge, vaisā (hī) karūṁgā*, I shall do (just) as you tell me.

जैसे ही आप मुझसे कहेंगे, वैसे ही कर दूँगा। *jaise hī āp mujhse kaheṁge, vaise hī kar dūṁgā*, I'll do it as soon as you tell me.[2]

मेरे पास जितने पैसे हैं, उनके पास उतने ही हैं। *mere pās jitne paise haiṁ, unke pās utne hī haiṁ*, He has just as much money as I.

वह मकान जितना महँगा है, उतना (ही) महँगा यह भी है। *vah makān jitnā mahaṁgā hai, utnā (hī) mahaṁgā yah bhī hai*, This house is (just) as dear as that.

आप जितना काम करेंगे, उतना ही जानेंगे। *āp jitnā kām kareṁge, utnā hī jāneṁge*, The more you work the more you'll know.

जितनी बड़ी आबादी कलकत्ते की है, उतनी बड़ी दिल्ली की नहीं है। *jitnī baṛī ābādī kalkatte kī hai, utnī baṛī dillī kī nahīṁ hai*, The population of Delhi is not as great as that of Calcutta.

जहाँ हिंदी बोली जाती है, मैं वहाँ रहना चाहता हूँ। *jahāṁ hindī bolī jātī hai, maiṁ vahāṁ rahnā cāhtā hūṁ*, I want to live where Hindi is spoken.[3]

जहाँ भी जाता हूँ, वहाँ अँग्रेज़ी बोलता हूँ। *jahāṁ bhī jātā hūṁ, vahāṁ aṁgrezī boltā hūṁ*, Wherever I go I speak English.

आप जो कह रहे हैं, मैं उसपर विश्वास नहीं करता। *āp jo kah rahe haiṁ, maiṁ uspar viśvās nahīṁ kartā*, I don't believe what you're saying.

जिस आदमी ने यह पत्र लिखा, वह भारतीय होगा। *jis ādmī ne yah patr likhā, vah bhārtīy hogā*, The man who wrote this letter is probably an Indian.

जो कोई आए, उसे यह ख़बर दीजिए। *jo koī āe, use yah khabar dījie*, Please tell this to whoever comes.

[1] For चले गए थे *cale gae the* 'went away' see Lesson XVII, p. 100.

[2] कर दूँगा *kar dūṁgā* 'shall do'; compound verb. See Lesson XVII.

[3] For बोली जाती है *bolī jātī hai* 'is spoken', see Lesson XIX, p. 116.

जिस किसी के पास यह पुस्तक नहीं है, उसे और किसी की पुस्तक पढ़नी पड़ेगी । *jis kisī ke pās yah pustak nahīṁ hai, use aur kisī kī pustak paṛhnī paṛegī,*[1] Whoever hasn't got this book will have to read someone else's.

जो कुछ करना चाहिए, उसे आप कीजिए । *jo kuch karnā cāhie, use āp kījie*, Please do whatever has to be done.

(*a*) Note that whereas जब तक *jab tak* means 'as long as', the sense 'until' is expressed by जब तक . . . न *jab tak . . . na*, followed by a subjunctive form if the reference is to a future action, and usually a perfective form if to a past action.[2]

जब तक राम न आएँ, तब तक मैं यहाँ रहूँगा । *jab tak rām na āeṁ, tab tak maiṁ yahāṁ rahūṁgā*, I shall stay here till Rām comes.

जब तक राम न आए, तब तक मैं वहाँ रहा । *jab tak rām na āe, tab tak maiṁ vahāṁ rahā*, I stayed there until Rām came.

(*b*) Concerning जैसा *jaisā* and its use, one might have expected the oblique case pair जैसे . . . वैसे *jaise . . . vaise* to cover the adverbial idea of the English 'in such a way as', etc. But in fact the direct case forms are usually used to express this idea, as well as sometimes serving as near equivalents of the जो-वह *jo . . . vah* pair, and the use of जैसे *jaise* (usually with ही *hī*) and its correlative is specialized in the sense 'as soon as . . . then'.

(*c*) जैसे *jaise* alone is, however, used in the adverbial senses 'like, just as, as if'. With preceding nouns and pronouns it functions as either a simple postposition or the main component of a compound postposition: e.g.

उन जैसे लोग *un jaise log*, } people like them.
उनके जैसे लोग *unke jaise log*, }

जैसे मैंने कहा, वह दूसरे ही दिन चला गया । *jaise maiṁne kahā, vah dūsre hī din calā gayā*, As I said, he left on the very next day.

उनकी आँखें भीगी थीं, जैसे वह रोनेवाली हो । *unkī āṁkheṁ bhīgī thīṁ, jaise vah ronevālī ho*, Her eyes were moist, as if she were about to cry.[3]

[1] और *aur* is stressed; see Lesson VIII, p. 43, n. 1.

[2] Sometimes नहीं *nahīṁ* is substituted for न *na*, in which case a future verb replaces a subjunctive.

[3] For रोनेवाली *ronevālī* 'about to cry' see Lesson XXV, pp. 152 ff.

(*d*) Note in the sentences showing the pairs जितना ... उतना (ही) *jitnā* ... *utnā* (*hī*), जैसा ... वैसा (ही) *jaisā* ... *vaisā* (*hī*), how equality is stressed by the use of ही *hī* with the correlative, or of भी *bhī* in the correlative clause; also in the last example showing जितना *jitnā*, how this form and उतना *utnā* can be used with adjectives.

(*e*) From the sentences showing the pair जो ... वह *jo* ... *vah* (additional to those given in Lesson VIII) note that the correlative as well as the relative may occur in either case.

3. Though the pattern described above is a basic one, the principal clause will not infrequently be found initially, followed by the relative clause. Some cases when this can occur are:

(*a*) In sentences where जो *jo* correlates with a noun preceded by a word of indefinite reference, such as एक *ek*, कोई *koī*; English translation equivalents contain an indefinite, rather than a definite, article. See Lesson VIII, p. 47, first example.

(*b*) In more complicated sentences, to simplify their presentation, especially those containing disyllabic relatives and correlatives. Thus with three of the examples listed in section 2 above compare the following:

यह मकान उतना ही महँगा है जितना (कि) वह मकान (है)। *yah makān utnā hī mahaṁgā hai jitnā* (*ki*) *vah makān* (*hai*).[1]

दिल्ली की आबादी उतनी बड़ी नहीं है जितनी (कि) कलकत्ते की (है)। *dillī kī ābādī utnī baṛī nahīṁ hai jitnī* (*ki*) *kalkatte kī* (*hai*).

मैं वहाँ रहना चाहता हूँ जहाँ हिंदी बोली जाती है। *maiṁ vahāṁ rahnā cāhtā hūṁ jahāṁ hindī bolī jātī hai.*

(*c*) Where prominence is given to a constituent of a principal clause, rather than of a subordinate clause; e.g. in the following sentence, in which the negatived verb is the most prominent sentence constituent:

वह आदमी नहीं आया जिसके बारे में हम बात कर रहे थे। *vah ādmī nahīṁ āyā jiske bāre meṁ ham bāt kar rahe the*, The man we were talking about didn't come.

[1] A pleonastic *ki* is sometimes found in conjunction with relatives in colloquial usage. Further examples are given in Supplement III, p. 183.

Compare with this sentence

हम जिस आदमी के बारे में बात कर रहे थे, वह नहीं आया । *ham jis ādmī ke bāre meṁ bāt kar rahe the, vah nahīṁ āyā*, The man we were talking about didn't come,

where the identity of the man concerned is stressed, and the fact that there had been a conversation about him.

4. Sometimes there is no explicit correlation of relative with principal clause, as in English. Compare with the eleventh example on p. 83

हिंदुस्तान, जहाँ हिंदी बोली जाती है, बहुत बड़ा देश है । *hindustān, jahāṁ hindī bolī jātī hai, bahut baṛā deś hai*, India, where Hindi is spoken, is a very large country.

5. Note particularly that in colloquial usage correlation is very often not expressed, though it is understood: e.g.

जिस किसी का जो जी चाहे, करे । *jis kisī kā jo jī cāhe, kare*, Everyone may do whatever he likes (whatever his soul [जी *jī*, m.] desires).

Many of the correlatives in the sentences given above could be omitted colloquially.

6. Note that frequently relative words and phrases, especially in initial clauses, may stand in first place in their clauses or may follow subjects, without the emphasis of the sentence being very greatly altered. Compare, for instance, with the fourth example listed in section 2 above the sentence

मैं जब तक यहाँ रहूँगा, तब तक वे काम करेंगे । *maiṁ jab tak yahāṁ rahūṁga, tab tak ve kām kareṁge*

of similar emphasis. Further illustrations will be found in the exercises to this Lesson.

## VOCABULARY

आबादी *ābādī*, f., population
विश्वास *viśvās*, m., faith, confidence
खबर †*k͟habar*, f., news, information
तार *tār*, m., wire; telegram, cable
भीगा *bhīgā*, wet
विश्वास करना *viśvās karnā* (*par*), believe, believe to be true
की कोशिश करना *kī* †*kośiś karnā*, try

## EXERCISE 27

आप जब भी आना चाहें, तब आइए। जब तक आप यहाँ रहना चाहें, तब तक रहिए। मैंने जब तक चाहा, तब तक वहाँ रहा। मैं जब तक भारत न गया था, तब तक मैंने हिंदी[1] पढ़ी। आप जैसे ही इलाहाबाद पहुँचें, वैसे ही मुझे तार भेजिए। कल जितने लोग यहाँ थे, आज उतने नहीं थे। आप जहाँ भी जाएँ, आपको वहाँ के लोगों की भाषा बोलने की कोशिश करनी चाहिए।

## EXERCISE 28

I wasn't at home when you came. I didn't understand what he said. I shall study Hindi until I go to India. As soon as I saw him I recognized him. I have as many English books as you have Hindi books. Do whatever he says. The men we saw here yesterday don't live in this village.

[1] The pronoun with ने *ne* is expressed, not understood, following the preceding subject concord construction. This usage is not obligatory, but is somewhat preferred by careful speakers.

# LESSON XV

## THE VERB सकना *saknā* 'to be able to . . .'

1. THIS verb is used as an auxiliary with verb stems. It is never used alone.

मैं हिंदी बोल सकता हूँ । *maiṁ hindī bol saktā hūṁ*, I can speak Hindi.

मैं हिंदी नहीं बोल सकता । *maiṁ hindī nahīṁ bol saktā*, I can't speak Hindi.

मैं अपना काम नहीं कर सका । *maiṁ apnā kām nahīṁ kar sakā*, I couldn't do my work.

(*a*) In sentences of neutral style and emphasis negatives precede stems of simple verbs with auxiliary सकना *saknā*, rather than intervening between stem and auxiliary. A sentence such as मैं सो न(हीं) सका *maiṁ so na(hīṁ) sakā* 'I couldn't sleep' is somewhat affective in character.

(*b*) Stems of transitive verbs with perfective forms of auxiliary सकना *saknā* are not used in construction with ने *ne* (सकना *saknā* itself not being transitive).

2. Sentences showing an imperfective past tense form of सकना *saknā* may be ambiguous: e.g.

मैं भारत जा सकता था । *maiṁ bhārat jā saktā thā*, I could have gone to India (but didn't),

or

I used to be able to go to India.

This ambiguity depends on the fact that the locution जा सकता था *jā saktā thā* expresses only continued ability to go, leaving open the question whether this ability was exercised or not. But in practice the majority of sentences of this kind refer to an ability not exercised.

3. सकना *saknā* may also occur in sentences expressing grant of permission, or possibility.

आप जा सकते हैं । *āp jā sakte haiṁ*, You may go.

मैं कल बनारस जा सकता हूँ । *maiṁ kal banāras jā saktā hūṁ*, I may go to Banaras tomorrow.

## THE VERB चुकना *cuknā*

This is an intransitive verb meaning 'to finish'; its characteristic use, however, is as an auxiliary with verb stems to stress that the action described by a stem is completed, has already taken place.

मैं गरमियों में कश्मीर जा रहा हूँ । नैनीताल जा चुका हूँ । *maiṁ garmiyoṁ meṁ kaśmīr jā rahā hūṁ; nainītāl jā cukā hūṁ*, In the summer I'm going to Kashmir; I've already been to Nainital.

मैं खा चुका हूँ । *maiṁ khā cukā hūṁ*, I've already eaten, I've had my meal.

मैं हिंदुस्तान में रह चुका हूँ । *maiṁ hindustān meṁ rah cukā hūṁ*, I've lived in India.

मैं अगले हफ़्ते तक यह पत्र लिख चुकूँगा । *maiṁ agle hafte tak yah patr likh cukūṁgā*, I shall write, get this letter written, by next week.

(*a*) Note that frequently an English verb with the adverb 'already' has the force of a Hindi verb stem with auxiliary चुकना *cuknā*; but also that चुकना *cuknā* with verb stems has no one English translation equivalent.

(*b*) Stems of transitive verbs with perfective forms of auxiliary चुकना *cuknā* are not used in construction with ने *ne* (चुकना *cuknā* itself not being transitive).

## THE VERB मिलना *milnā*

This intransitive verb means basically 'to accrue' or 'to be available', and is used in a variety of sentence types.

1. In conjunction with a subject and an expressed or implied noun or pronoun in the oblique case with को *ko* (or an equivalent pronominal object form), it answers frequently to the English verbs 'get', 'receive', 'meet', etc., although the syntax of these verbs is quite different, since they are transitive. The noun or pronoun with को *ko*, or equivalent object form, usually precedes the subject, except where मिलना *milnā* has the sense '(happen to) meet', where it normally follows it: e.g.

(मुझे) आपका पत्र मिला । *(mujhe) āpkā patr milā*, I got your letter (your letter accrued to me).

आपको उस दूकान में अच्छी मिठाइयाँ मिलेंगी । *āpko us dūkān meṁ acchī miṭhāiyāṁ mileṁgī*, You'll get excellent sweets in that shop.

उस काम के लिए उसे सौ रुपए मिले । *us kām ke lie use sau rupae mile*, He got 100 rupees for that work.

कल शहर में वह मुझे संयोग से मिला था। *kal śahr meṁ vah mujhe saṃyog se milā thā*, Yesterday I ran across him in the city.[1]

**2.** It also answers to English intransitive expressions such as 'to be available', 'to be found'. Here, मिलना *milnā* likewise being intransitive, the syntax of Hindi and English equivalent sentences is very similar.

भारत में बहुत सस्ती सिग्रेटें मिलती हैं। *bhārat meṁ bahut sastī sigreṭeṁ miltī haiṁ*, Very cheap cigarettes can be had in India.

कश्मीर के पहाड़ों में भालू मिलते हैं। *kaśmīr ke pahāṛoṁ meṁ bhālū milte haiṁ*, Bears are found in the mountains of Kashmir.

**3.** मिलना *milnā* is generally used in construction with से *se* to refer to meeting other than by chance; also to express resemblance.

उनसे मिलकर बातें होंगी। *unse milkar bāteṁ hoṁgī*, I'll meet him and we'll have a talk.

क्या मैं आपसे दस बजे मिल सकता हूँ? *kyā maiṁ āpse das baje mil saktā hūṁ?* May I see you at 10 o'clock?

कल शहर में वह मुझसे मिला था। *kal śahr meṁ vah mujhse milā thā*, Yesterday he met me, came to see me, in the city.

(Compare with this last example the last example given in section 1, showing मिलना *milnā* in construction with को *ko*.)

मैं शकल से अपने भाई से नहीं मिलता। *maiṁ śakl se apne bhāī se nahīṁ miltā*, I don't look like my brother.

**4.** Sometimes the verb मिलना *milnā* is linked in a conventionalized way with an 'echoing verb', जुलना *julnā*[2]: e.g.

हमें पड़ोसियों से मिल-जुलकर रहना चाहिए। *hameṁ paṛosiyoṁ se mil-julkar rahnā cāhie*, We should live on good terms with our neighbours.

आप चेहरे से अपने भाई से बिलकुल मिलते-जुलते हैं। *āp cehre se apne bhāī se bilkul milte-julte haiṁ*, You look just like your brother.

[1] संयोग से *saṃyog se* 'by chance'.

[2] The linking of verbs in this way is common in Hindi. In some cases the second member of such a verb pair has an independent meaning of its own which reinforces that of the main verb, but frequently it is merely based on a rhyming or echoing syllable. Often use of a verb pair is slightly affective in character. Participles, infinitives, and absolutives are the most usual components of verb pairs; absolutive pairs always show the first absolutive in stem form (as in the first example).

## VOCABULARY

मिठाई *miṭhāī*, f., sweet
संयोग *saṃyog*, m., chance; संयोग से *saṃyog se*, by chance
भालू *bhālū*, m., bear
पड़ोसी *parosī*, m., neighbour
चेहरा *cehrā*,[1] m., face, features
शकल *śakl*, f., face, features; form
कोश *koś*, m., dictionary
भूल *bhūl*, f., error
उत्तर *uttar*, m., answer; पत्र का उत्तर देना *patr kā uttar denā*, answer a letter
सूचना *sūcnā*, f., information
पुरस्कार *puraskār*, m., reward
के अलावा †*ke alāvā*, apart from
बिलकुल †*bilkul*, completely, quite

## EXERCISE 29

आप जब भी आ सकें, तब आइए। जब तक मैं रह सका, तब तक रहा। मुझे बहुत अफ़सोस है कि मैं कल आपसे न मिल सका। हिंदी के अलावा हम भारत में कई और[2] भारतीय भाषाएँ सीख सकते थे। आप चाय पी चुके? वह हिंदी कोश आसानी से नहीं मिलता। हम कब मिल सकते हैं? यह कपड़ा उससे मिलता-जुलता है।

## EXERCISE 30

I can't write Hindi very easily. Whenever I write, I make mistakes. When I got there he had already left.[3] I answered his letter as soon as I got it. Anyone who can give[4] information about this will receive a reward. You can get Hindi books in that shop.

[1] First vowel usually short [ɛ].

[2] और *aur* is stressed.

[3] जाना *jānā*.

[4] Use future tense.

# LESSON XVI

## COMPARISON

SOME types of comparative expression involving relatives were noted in Lesson XIV. Most of the others are considered here.

1. Adjectives, when used in non-explicit comparisons, usually show the words और *aur* or और भी *aur bhī* preceding them. और *aur* is stressed in these usages: e.g.

वह बड़ा है, लेकिन आप और (भी) बड़े हैं । *vah baṛā hai, lekin āp aur (bhī) baṛe haiṁ*, He is big, but you are bigger (even bigger).

और बड़ा संदूक़ ले आओ । *aur baṛā sandūq le āo*, Bring a bigger box.

2. When comparison is explicit (i.e. when an English translation equivalent makes use of the word 'than') the noun or pronoun with which the comparison is made is associated with the postposition से *se*, followed by the adjective in normal concord: e.g.

आप उससे बड़े हैं । *āp usse baṛe haiṁ*, You are bigger than he.

3. Collocations of adjective with preceding सबसे *sabse* (usually written as one unit) may be compared with superlatives in English. They are used both attributively and predicatively.

वह बड़ा है, मैं भी बड़ा हूँ, लेकिन आप सबसे बड़े हैं । *vah baṛā hai, maiṁ bhī baṛā hūṁ, lekin āp sabse baṛe haiṁ*, He is big and so am I, but you are the biggest (of us all).

कलकत्ता पहले भारत का सबसे बड़ा शहर था । *kalkattā pahle bhārat kā sabse baṛā śahr thā*, Calcutta used to be the biggest city in India (India's biggest city).

(*a*) Occasionally for the word सब *sab* in these locutions the adjective itself may occur. Such expressions are affective in tone, unlike those with सब *sab*, except in the case of a few standardized adverbial expressions.

उसके पास अच्छी से अच्छी किताबें हैं । *uske pās acchī se acchī kitābeṁ haiṁ*, He's got excellent, really good books.

कम से कम *kam se kam*, at least

4. Adjectives which are direct borrowings from Sanskrit may form comparatives with the suffix *-tar* and/or superlatives with the suffix *-tam*. Some such forms found are:

| | |
|---|---|
| उच्च *ucc*, high (cf. ऊँचा *ūṁcā*, the common Hindi word) | उच्चतर *uccatar*, higher |
| प्रिय *priy*, dear, beloved | प्रियतम *priytam*, dearest |
| अनन्य *ananya*, unique | अनन्यतम *ananyatam*, quite unique, peerless |
| आधुनिक *ādhunik*, modern | आधुनिकतम *ādhuniktam*, most modern |

वह उच्चतर अध्ययन के लिए आक्स्फ़र्ड चले गए । *vah uccatar adhyayan ke lie āksfarḍ cale gae*, He went to Oxford for advanced study.

These forms are comparatively rare except in verse, and are elsewhere largely confined to the written language. To use the forms described in sections 1–3 above is never really incorrect.

5. Occasionally other Sanskrit superlative forms are met with in Hindi, not always preserving strict superlative sense, and again usually in the written language. The commonest are:

| | |
|---|---|
| ज्येष्ठ *jyeṣṭh*, older, eldest | कनिष्ठ *kaniṣṭh*, younger, youngest |
| श्रेष्ठ *śreṣṭh*, very good, best | बलिष्ठ *baliṣṭh*, very strong |
| सर्वश्रेष्ठ *sarvśreṣṭh*, foremost, supreme | |

6. Much more common are a limited number of Persian comparatives and superlatives. The latter likewise have intensive force as much as superlative.

बेहतर †*behtar* better[1]
बेहतरीन †*behtarīn* best, choice[1]
बदतर †*badtar* worse
ज़्यादातर †*zyādātar* most (of); most commonly, very much

आपको इस दूकान में हिंदुस्तान के बेहतरीन कपड़े मिलेंगे । *āpko is dūkān meṁ hindustān ke behtarīn kapṛe mileṁge*, You'll find India's choicest fabrics (on sale) in this shop.

ज़्यादातर विद्यार्थी हिंदी पढ़ते हैं । *zyādātar vidyārthī hindī paṛhte haiṁ*, Most of the students study Hindi.

मैं ज़्यादातर यहाँ बैठता हूँ । *maiṁ zyādātar yahāṁ baiṭhtā hūṁ*, I very often sit here.

[1] The first vowel of these words is usually short [ɛ].

## COMPARATIVE AND OTHER EXPRESSIONS WITH ज़्यादा †*zyādā* AND अधिक *adhik*

1. The invariable and equivalent words ज़्यादा †*zyādā* and अधक *adhik* are common as adjectives, pronouns, and adverbs in locutions whose English equivalents contain expressions of quantity such as

| | | |
|---|---|---|
| more; | (very) many; | too many; |
| much; | very much; | too much |

इस साल अधिक विद्यार्थी हैं । *is sāl adhik vidyārthī haiṁ*, There are more, very many students this year.
आप ज़्यादा काम न कीजिए । *āp zyādā kām na kījie*, Please don't do any more work, too much work.
आप ज़्यादा न खाइए । *āp zyādā na khāie*, Don't eat any more, too much.
मैं अब वहाँ ज़्यादा जाता हूँ । *maiṁ ab vahāṁ zyādā jātā hūṁ*, I go there a lot now.

Their emphasis can be increased by prefixing them with बहुत (ही) *bahut* (*hī*): e.g.

इस साल बहुत (ही) ज़्यादा विद्यार्थी हैं । *is sāl bahut* (*hī*) *zyādā vidyārthī haiṁ*, There are a very great number of students, too many students, this year.
मैं अब वहाँ बहुत ज़्यादा जाता हूँ । *maiṁ ab vahāṁ bahut zyādā jātā hūṁ*, I go there a great deal now.

The translation of expressions containing ज़्यादा *zyādā* and अधिक *adhik* depends, of course, on the context. Since they can occur in a wide range of contexts, translation equivalents can vary considerably.

(*a*) Note that as adjectives and pronouns ज़्यादा *zyādā* and अधिक *adhik* signify 'a large amount of' or 'a greater amount of than', and are not normally exact equivalents of और *aur*, which means 'additional'. Compare the sentences

और लीजिए । *aur lījie*, Please take some more.
ज़्यादा लीजिए । *zyādā lījie*, Please take a larger helping, please take a lot.

(*b*) Note the frequent use of इतना *itnā* 'as many, as much, as this', with following pleonastic ज़्यादा *zyādā* or अधिक *adhik*: e.g.

आपको इतना ज़्यादा काम न करना चाहिए । *āpko itnā zyādā kām na karnā cāhie*, You shouldn't work as hard as this.

उतना *utnā*, the corresponding adjective of distant reference, is used in a similar way.

2. Preceding adjectives, ज़्यादा *zyādā* and अधिक *adhik* have the senses 'rather', 'very', or 'too' (this last especially when emphasized by बहुत *bahut*): e.g.

भारत का जलवायु ज़्यादा गरम है । *bhārat kā jalvāyu zyādā garm hai*, India's climate is very hot.

मेरे लिए भारत का जलवायु बहुत ज़्यादा गरम है । *mere lie bhārat kā jalvāyu bahut zyādā garm hai*, India's climate is too hot for me.

## REPORTS OF STATEMENTS AND QUESTIONS

Reports of statements made and questions asked are very frequently made by citing the exact words attributed to the speaker, linked by the conjunction कि *ki* to the principal clause of the sentence. Two English sentences are rephrased below to illustrate the structure of their Hindi equivalents.

I said (that) I would write the letter: I said that I shall write the letter.
I asked him when he had come: I asked him that when did you come.

1. *Statements*

उसने कहा कि मैं सच बोलूँगा । *usne kahā ki maiṁ sac bolūṁgā*, He said he would speak the truth.

मैंने उनसे कहा कि आप अच्छी हिंदी बोलते हैं । *maiṁne unse kahā ki āp acchī hindī bolte haiṁ*, I told him he spoke Hindi well.

उसने मुझसे कहा कि आप अच्छी हिंदी बोलते हैं । *usne mujhse kahā ki āp acchī hindī bolte haiṁ*, He told me that I spoke Hindi well.

(*a*) The construction can be ambiguous (as can the English construction, though the ambiguities are not the same). The sentence 'I told him you spoke Hindi well', for instance, is also a possible translation equivalent of the second example given. This is so because third person pronouns are not normally used in this construction to denote a speaker or a person actually addressed.

(*b*) As far as pronouns are concerned a thoroughly systematic use of this construction is not felt to be obligatory, especially in language that is at all removed from the colloquial, and notably in the Western-influenced, literary prose language. Where pronouns are not used in accordance with the logic of the construction, verb concord of course varies accordingly. An equivalent of the first example above could thus be

उसने कहा कि वह सच बोलेगा । *usne kahā ki vah sac bolegā.*

(*c*) Sentences expressing a person's train of thought are usually cast in the same form as reports of statements and questions: e.g.

उसने सोचा कि मैं दिल्ली जाऊँगा । *usne socā ki maiṁ dillī jāūṁgā*, He thought he would go to Delhi.

(*d*) Linking कि *ki* is very frequently omitted in colloquial usage.

2. *Questions*

उसने मुझसे पूछा कि आप कैसे हैं? *usne mujhse pūchā ki āp kaise haiṁ?* He asked me how I was.

मैं उनसे पूछूँगा कि क्या आप दिल्ली जा रहे हैं? *maiṁ unse pūchūṁgā ki kyā āp dillī jā rahe haiṁ?* I shall ask him if he is going to Delhi.

क्या आप जानते हैं कि क्लास कब शुरू होती है? *kyā āp jānte haiṁ ki klās kab śurū hotī hai?* Do you know when the class begins?

(*a*) The notes to the preceding section also apply to this section. Note the alternative English equivalents of the first two examples: 'He asked how you were' and (assuming a suitable context) 'I shall ask him if you are going to Delhi'.

## INDIRECT COMMANDS

A request or command which is to be passed on to another person may be expressed by a subordinate clause containing a third person subjunctive verb, linked to its principal clause by the conjunction कि *ki*. An English sentence is rephrased below to illustrate the structure of its Hindi equivalent.

Tell him to stop work: Tell him that he should stop work.

उनसे कहिए कि वे मुझे एक पत्र लिखें । *unse kahie ki ve mujhe ek patr likheṁ*, Please ask, tell, him to write me a letter.

मैंने उससे कहा कि वह काम ख़त्म करे । *maiṁne usse kahā ki vah kām khatm kare*, I asked, told, him to stop work.

(*a*) Alternatively an infinitive in oblique case may be used with either of the postpositions के लिए *ke lie* or को *ko*. The request or command is then rather more direct in tone: e.g.

मैंने उनसे यहाँ आने को कहा । *maiṁne unse yahāṁ āne ko kahā*, I told, asked, him to come here.

मैंने उनसे यहाँ आने के लिए कहा । *maiṁne unse yahāṁ āne ke lie kahā*, I told, asked, him to come here.

(*b*) कहना *kahnā* expressing indirect commands is normally used in construction with से *se*, as in other cases. Used in construction with को *ko* it implies a distinctly peremptory command: e.g.

उसको यहाँ आने को कहो । *usko yahāṁ āne ko kaho*, Tell him to come here.

(*c*) The verb पूछना *pūchnā* means 'ask' in the sense 'inquire', not 'request', and is thus of course not used in expressing indirect commands.

## VOCABULARY

अध्ययन *adhyayan*, m., study
जलवायु *jalvāyu*, m., climate
तमिल *tamil*, f., Tamil
जीवन *jīvan*, m., life
विषय *viṣay*, m., subject, matter, topic
पन्ना *pannā*, m., page
गली *galī*, f., narrow street, alley
गंगा *gaṅgā*, f., River Ganges
यमुना *yamunā*, f., River Jumna
पुस्तकालय *pustakālay*, m., library
मित्र *mitr*, m., friend
कम से कम *kam se kam*, at least

## EXERCISE 31

हिंदी तमिल से आसान है । हिंदी तमिल से आसान भाषा है । क्या शहर का जीवन गाँव के जीवन से दिलचस्प होता है? उस विषय पर कम से कम तीन पन्ने लिखिए । जितने लोग हिंदी बोलते हैं, उतने कोई दूसरी भारतीय भाषा नहीं बोलते । भारत दुनिया के सबसे दिलचस्प देशों में से[1] एक है । उसे भारत के बारे में बहुत कुछ मालूम है । मैंने उनसे कहा कि आपको इससे बहुत ज़्यादा काम करना पड़ेगा । उसने मुझसे पूछा कि क्या कपड़ा बाज़ार की उस गली में मिल सकता है । क्या आपने उनसे कहा कि मैं कल नहीं आ सकूँगा? मैंने उससे कहा कि वह काम कल तक ख़त्म करे ।

[1] में से *meṁ se*, literally 'from among'. This usage is discussed in Supplement III, p. 178.

## EXERCISE 32

The Ganges is longer than the Jumna. Bombay is nowadays the biggest city in India. It seems that you do more work than he. You'll meet several Indian students there. I need more books. This library is too small. He told his friends that he had already eaten. He told his friends to come to[1] his house at 6.15 p.m. As soon as I got your letter I told him that you were coming to Delhi.

[1] पर *par*.

# LESSON XVII

## COMPOUND VERBS

COMPOUND verbs are composites of verb stems with one of a small number of auxiliary verbs; their basic meaning is that of the verb stem, modified or made specific in some sense by the particular auxiliary used. The independent meaning of an auxiliary is not present, or is only figuratively present, in compound verbs. The auxiliaries may thus be called 'dependent auxiliaries'. Compound verbs are used very freely in most styles of Hindi, and the student must learn to use them reasonably accurately if his Hindi is to seem at all convincing to a native speaker. This takes time and effort. The first difficulty is that the common auxiliaries do not always lend one and the same additional shade of meaning to all the stems with which they may be used; the force of the auxiliaries is conditioned by the sense and range of usage of individual stems. Furthermore, similar modifications of the sense of stems can sometimes be brought about by more than one auxiliary, though the student will rarely have a free choice of these in conjunction with any given verb. Finally the use or non-use of compound verbs is frequently a matter of style or taste. The student must train himself to observe just which collocations are used by native speakers or writers, and in which contexts.

The following discussion of the main dependent auxiliaries, with the attached general notes, should give sufficient guidance for most ordinary collocations to be intelligible.

### 1. जाना *jānā*

जाना *jānā* in general stresses the fact that an action is completed or carried through as a process. It stresses the element of action inherent in such intransitive verbs as होना *honā*, रहना *rahnā*, बैठना *baiṭhnā*, which may express both action and non-active state. It occurs with both intransitive and transitive verbs. It is particularly common with verbs of motion.

वह दो बजे यहाँ आ जाएगा । *vah do baje yahāṁ ā jāegā*, He will arrive, get here, at two.

वह मर गया । *vah mar gayā*, He died, he's dead.

मैं ठीक समय पर दिल्ली पहुँच गया । *maiṁ ṭhīk samay par dillī pahuṁc gayā.* I arrived punctually in Delhi.

बारिश में घास हरी हो जाती है। *bāriś meṁ ghās harī ho jātī hai*, When it rains the grass turns green.

हो गया? *ho gayā?* Have you finished? (your work, meal, etc.).[1]

मैं सब रोटियाँ खा गया। *maiṁ sab roṭiyāṁ khā gayā*, I ate all the rotis (finished them, ate them up).

वह कुरसी पर बैठ गया। *vah kursī par baiṭh gayā*, He sat down on a chair.

बैठ जाइए! *baiṭh jāie!* Take a seat, please.

बरसात में पानी यहाँ रह जाता है। *barsāt meṁ pānī yahāṁ rah jātā hai*, During the rainy season water collects here.

आप मेरी बात समझ गए होंगे। *āp merī bāt samajh gae hoṁge*, You will have understood, grasped, what I've been saying.

लड़का पूरा पन्ना पढ़ गया। *laṛkā pūrā pannā paṛh gayā*, The boy read through the entire page.

(*a*) जाना *jānā* is only rarely used with the stem of the verb चलना *calnā* 'move, go'; चल जाना *cal jānā* has the sense 'begin, get going'. The senses 'move along, go away' are expressed by चला जाना *calā jānā*: e.g.

तीन आदमी रास्ते में चले जा रहे थे। *tīn ādmī rāste meṁ cale jā rahe the*, Three men were walking along the road.

See further Supplement II, pp. 172 f.

**2. लेना *lenā***

लेना *lenā* has a general reflexive sense, suggesting that the given action is of particular interest to the doer, and often carrying an implication that it is carried out with difficulty, cleverly contrived, etc. It is often used with its own stem *le*. It is rare with intransitive verbs.

मैं ग्यारह बजे खा लेता हूँ। *maiṁ gyārah baje khā letā hūṁ*, I have my meal at 11 o'clock.

मैं एक मकान ख़रीद लूंगा। *maiṁ ek makān kharīd lūṁgā*, I'm going to buy, going to buy myself, a house.

मैंने यह निश्चय कर लिया कि वह यहाँ नहीं रह सकता। *maiṁne yah niścay kar liyā ki vah yahāṁ nahīṁ rah saktā*, I decided that he couldn't stay here (after some thought).

आपने बहुत हिंदी सीख ली। *āpne bahut hindī sīkh lī*, You've learned a lot of Hindi.

[1] Literally 'has (it) become (finished)'.

राम से ले लो, और श्याम को दे दो । *rām se le lo, aur śyām ko de do*, Take it from Rām and give it to Śyām.[1]

मैं उसके साथ हो लिया । *maiṁ uske sāth ho liyā*, I went (along) with him, accompanied him.

3. देना *denā*

देना *denā* is frequently complementary to लेना *lenā*, suggesting that the given action particularly concerns some other person than the doer. Sometimes it simply stresses that an action is complete and done with. Note the common दे देना *de denā*; cf. ले लेना *le lenā* above. देना *denā* is not very common with intransitive verbs.

जज ने यह निर्णय कर दिया कि वह निरपराध है । *jaj ne yah nirṇay kar diyā ki vah niraparādh hai*, The judge decided, determined, that he was innocent.

लड़के ने पूरा पन्ना पढ़ दिया । *laṛke ne pūrā pannā paṛh diyā*, The boy read out the entire page.

उसने अपने मित्र को छोड़ दिया । *usne apne mitr ko choṛ diyā*, He abandoned his friend.

चल दिए? *cal die?* You're off?[2]

गाड़ी चल दी । *gāṛī cal dī*, The train left.

दरवाज़ा बंद कर दीजिए । *darvāzā band kar dījie*, Please close the door.

लड़की रो दी । *laṛkī ro dī*, The girl burst into tears (could not hold back her tears).

4. पड़ना *paṛnā*, उठना *uṭhnā*

These verbs, meaning literally 'fall' or 'be found', and 'rise', are often used with stems which themselves denote actions of falling and rising respectively (either literally or figuratively). They also often stress the idea of a change of circumstance, particularly a sudden one. The majority of relevant stems collocate with either one or the other, but with some stems both are used, and may express different degrees of the given action.

काग़ज़ फ़र्श पर गिर पड़ा । *kāgaz farś par gir paṛā*, The paper fell to the floor.

गाड़ी चल पड़ी । *gāṛī cal paṛī*, The train began to move.

लड़का पानी में कूद पड़ा । *laṛkā pānī meṁ kūd paṛā*, The boy jumped into the water.

[1] For दे दो *de do* 'give' see following section.

[2] For perfective forms used with reference to future time, as exemplified by दिए *die* here, see Supplement II, pp. 170 f.

अंत में वह घर से बाहर निकल पड़ा। *ant meṁ vah ghar se bāhar nikal paṛā*, Finally he emerged from the house.

कवि की आवाज़ कमरे में गूँज उठी। *kavi kī āvāz kamre meṁ gūṁj uṭhī*, The poet's voice rang out in the room.

वह बोल उठा कि ... *vah bol uṭhā ki . . .*, He (suddenly) said, blurted out, that . . .

लड़की रो पड़ी। *laṛkī ro paṛī*, The girl burst into tears.

लड़की रो उठी। *laṛkī ro uṭhī*, The girl began to sob bitterly.

मैं हँस पड़ा। *maiṁ haṁs paṛā*, I burst out laughing.

हम हँस उठे। *ham haṁs uṭhe*, We roared with laughter.

वह शोर से चौंक पड़ा। *vah śor se cauṁk paṛā*, He started at the noise.

वह शोर से चौंक उठा। *vah śor se cauṁk uṭhā*, He started violently at the noise.

5. डालना *ḍālnā*

डालना *ḍālnā*, meaning literally 'throw down', may suggest either that the given action is violent, decisive, or drastic, or that it is done in an off-hand, casual way.

उसने अपने भाई को मार डाला। *usne apne bhāī ko mār ḍālā*, He killed his brother.

उसने अपना सब माल बेच डाला। *usne apnā sab māl bec ḍālā*, He sold up, sold off, all his goods.

(*a*) मारना *mārnā* used alone often means 'beat, strike'; मार डालना *mār ḍālnā* regularly means 'kill'.

6. बैठना *baiṭhnā*

बैठना *baiṭhnā*, meaning literally 'sit', most often suggests something anti-climactic, a deterioration of some kind. Often it implies that an action is censurable, e.g. done foolishly, thoughtlessly, maliciously or with cunning.

वह रास्ते में अपना सारा माल खो बैठा। *vah rāste meṁ apnā sārā māl kho baiṭhā*, He lost all his belongings on the way.

अरे यह क्या कर बैठे हैं? *are yah kyā kar baiṭhe haiṁ?* Oh, what have you done, gone and done, now?[1]

[1] यह *yah* is used in a vague demonstrative way here, referring to the whole unpleasant situation.

देशद्रोही एक षड्यंत्र रच बैठे थे। *deśdrohī ek ṣaḍyantra rac baiṭhe the*, The traitors laid a plot.

सहसा वह उठ बैठा। *sahsā vah uṭh baiṭhā*, Suddenly he started up (involuntarily).

वह अपनी माँ से लड़ बैठा। *vah apnī mām̐ se laṛ baiṭhā*, He quarrelled with his mother.

7. आना *ānā*

आना *ānā* is complementary to जाना *jānā* (though not nearly as common), suggesting the completion or emphasizing the carrying through of actions directed towards a place, literal or figurative, from which they are considered. It is of course most common with verbs of motion.

मैं दो बजे पहुँच आया। *maiṁ do baje pahum̐c āyā*, I arrived at two o'clock.

बीस मिनट चलकर वह शहर से निकल आया। *bīs minaṭ calkar vah śahr se nikal āyā*, After walking twenty minutes he came out of the town.

दीवार पर लताएँ उग आई हैं। *dīvār par latāeṁ ug āī haiṁ*, Creepers have grown, grown up, over the wall.

(*a*) आना *ānā* is not used with the stem of the verb चलना *calnā* 'move, go'; note the collocation चला आना *calā ānā*, parallel to चला जाना *calā jānā*.

यह परंपरा हज़ारों बरस से चली आ रही है। *yah paramparā hazāroṁ baras se calī ā rahī hai*, This tradition has been carried on for thousands of years.

See further Supplement II, pp. 172 f.

8. चलना *calnā*

This verb is sometimes used to stress the progressive element in an action.

शाम का समय था। अँधेरा हो चला था। *śām kā samay thā. aṁdherā ho calā thā*, It was evening. Darkness was drawing on (it was getting dark).

9. निकलना *nikalnā*

निकलना *nikalnā*, meaning literally 'emerge', sometimes suggests suddenness or unexpectedness of the given action, much as पड़ना *paṛnā*, with verbs of motion.

वह अचानक मेरे घर के सामने आ निकला। *vah acānak mere ghar ke sāmne ā niklā*, He suddenly appeared in front of my house.

बैल रस्सी तुड़ाकर भाग निकला। *bail rassī tuṛākar bhāg niklā*, The ox broke the rope and escaped.

10. पहुँचना *pahuṁcnā*

पहुँचना *pahuṁcnā*, used with श्राना *ānā* and also जाना *jānā*, stresses the implications of arrival rather than the performance of the given action.

वह दो बजे श्रागरे श्रा पहुँचा । *vah do baje āgre ā pahuṁcā*, He reached Agra at two o'clock (after a long journey, for an impending meeting, etc.).

11. पाना *pānā*

पाना *pānā*, meaning literally 'get, find', stresses not so much ability to perform an action (cf. सकना *saknā*) as possibility of performing it, ability to complete it. Compound verbs containing पाना *pānā* are very often negatived.

मैं यह काम नहीं कर पाया । *maiṁ yah kām nahīṁ kar pāyā*, I wasn't able to do this work (couldn't manage it).

12. रखना *rakhnā*

रखना *rakhnā* underlines the fact that the action results in the achievement of a state of some duration.

मैं पाँच बजे तक सोच रखूँगा । *maiṁ pāṁc baje tak soc rakhūṁgā*, I shall make my mind up, decide, by five o'clock.

मैंने एक जगह रोक रखी है । *maiṁne ek jagah rok rakhī hai*, I've reserved a place, seat.

लड़की ने साड़ी पहन रखी है । *laṛkī ne sāṛī pahn rakhī hai*, The girl has on, is wearing, a sari.

*General notes*

(*a*) Note particularly that although the force of compound verbs can often best be brought out by the use of English translation equivalents of colloquial character, compound verb usage in Hindi has nothing exclusively colloquial about it.

(*b*) Compound verbs (other than those with auxiliary पाना *pānā*) are relatively rarely negatived in sentences of neutral style and emphasis. In so far as negatives occur in such sentences they precede stems; but in affective contexts they frequently occur between stem and auxiliary.

(*c*) Compound verbs are used in construction with ने *ne* when both the stem verb and the auxiliary are themselves used independently with ने *ne*, except that no compound verbs with auxiliary पाना *pānā* are used in construction with ने *ne*. Of these verbs which are used independently both with and without ने *ne*, at least one can be used in either construction with transitive auxiliaries, viz. रो देना *ro denā* (usually without, sometimes with ने *ne*). See the examples above for illustrations.

(*d*) In some cases questions of syllable economy and a feeling for the balance of a given sentence may be sufficient to decide whether a compound verb will or will not be used. Sometimes the position of a verb in non-final or final clause is a deciding factor. A Hindi speaker will often feel that an idea expressed by means of a simple verb is somehow incomplete and presupposes something following in the same sentence, whereas use of a compound verb rounds off a sentence more effectively.

(*e*) Compound verbs do not normally form absolutives in *-kar/-ke*. Compare the following sentences:

वह बैठ गया। *vah baiṭh gayā*, He sat down.
वह बैठकर बोला कि . . . *vah baiṭhkar bolā ki* . . ., He sat down and said that . . .

(*f*) Note that compound verbs are in form identical with collocations of unextended absolutive with following finite verb (from which they derive historically). In some cases the same form of words can be interpreted in different ways, dependent on its context, and, usually, intonation: e.g.

वह खाना खा गया है। *vah khānā khā gayā hai*

could mean 'He's finished his meal', or, possibly 'he's eaten and left'.

(*g*) Compound verbs may be formed on the stems of conjunct verbs (see pp. 57 ff.) just as on other verb stems: e.g.

मैंने काम शुरू कर दिया है *maiṁne kām śurū kar diyā hai*, I've started work (compound verb formed on शुरू करना *śurū karnā*).

## VOCABULARY

घास *ghās*, f., grass
रोटी *roṭī*, f., bread (chapatti)
निश्चय *niścay*, m., decision, resolve
निर्णय *nirṇay*, m., decision (between alternatives)
फ़र्श *farś*, m., floor
अंत *ant*, m., end
कवि *kavi*, m., poet
आवाज़ †*āvāz*, f., voice
शोर *śor*, m., noise
माल *māl*, m., goods, belongings
देशद्रोही *deśdrohī*, m., traitor

षड्यंत्र *ṣaḍyantra, m., plot
लता latā, f., creeper
परंपरा paramparā, f., tradition
बरस baras, m., year
अँधेरा aṁdherā, m., darkness; adj., dark
बैल bail, m., ox, bullock
रस्सी rassī, f., rope; string
साड़ी sāṛī, f., sari
जगह †jagah, f., place
निरपराध niraparādh, innocent
छोड़ना choṛnā, leave, abandon
गिरना girnā, fall
कूदना kūdnā, leap, jump
निकलना nikalnā, emerge
गूंजना gūṁjnā, resound
हँसना haṁsnā, laugh
चौंकना cauṁknā, start, be startled
रचना racnā, create, produce
उठना uṭhnā, rise
लड़ना laṛnā, fight; quarrel
उगना ugnā, grow (intransitive)
रोकना roknā, stop, check
तुड़ाना tuṛānā, break, cause to be broken
पहनना pahnnā, put on (clothes); पहन रखना pahn rakhnā, have on, be wearing
खोना khonā, lose
सहसा sahsā, suddenly
अरे are, oh! etc. (exclamation, often of surprise; also to attract attention)

# LESSON XVIII

## GROUPS OF VERBS OF RELATED STEM

MANY Hindi verbs may be classified in pairs or larger groups according to a similarity in the form of their stems, reflecting a loose semantic relationship. The larger groups may be built up from a consideration of related pairs, the characteristic types of which are discussed in sections 1 and 2 below. The most commonly contrasting pairs are of one intransitive and one transitive verb, or of two transitive verbs; members of a pair are distinguished from each other by one of a number of broadly regular vocalic alternations.

1. *Intransitive and transitive verbs*

A. The second member of the pair shows -*ā*- medially or finally in its stem; the corresponding stem syllable in the first member either shows -*a*-, or is normally non-realized,[1] with a preceding short vowel.

(i) *Second member shows -ā- medially in the stem*

| | |
|---|---|
| मरना *marnā*, die | मारना *mārnā*, beat; kill |
| निकलना *nikalnā*, emerge | निकालना *nikālnā*, eject; extract |
| फटना *phaṭnā*, tear | फाड़ना *phāṛnā*, tear |
| लदना *ladnā*, be laden | लादना *lādnā*, load |
| उतरना *utarnā*, descend, get down | उतारना *utārnā*, take down, off |
| छपना *chapnā*, be printed | छापना *chāpnā*, print |

(ii) *Second member shows -ā- finally in the stem*

| | |
|---|---|
| बनना *bannā*, be made, exist, become | बनाना *banānā*, make |
| जलना *jalnā*, burn | जलाना *jalānā*, burn |
| उठना *uṭhnā*, rise | उठाना *uṭhānā*, raise |
| खिलना *khilnā*, bloom | खिलाना *khilānā*, make bloom |
| मिलना *milnā*, accrue, be available | मिलाना *milānā*, bring together, cause to meet |

(*a*) Note in the pair फटना *phaṭnā* — फाड़ना *phāṛnā* the extra distinctive feature of alternation between retroflex plosive *ṭ* and flapped *ṛ*, and see other similar examples below.

[1] See p. xxiv.

B. The second member shows *-ā-* finally in the stem and a short vowel in the preceding syllable; the corresponding stem syllables in the first member show normally non-realized *-a-*[1], and a long vowel. (The usual vowel alternations are: *ā — a*; *ai* or *e — i*; *o — u*; *ū — u*).

| | |
|---|---|
| जागना *jāgnā*, be awake, waken | जगाना *jagānā*, waken |
| घूमना *ghūmnā*, wander, turn | घुमाना *ghumānā*, convey about, drive round; turn |
| बैठना *baiṭhnā*, sit | बिठाना *biṭhānā*, give a seat to[2] |
| लेटना *leṭnā*, lie down | लिटाना *liṭānā*, put lying down[3] |
| सोना *sonā*, sleep | सुलाना *sulānā*, put, rock to sleep |
| रोना *ronā*, weep | रुलाना *rulānā*, make weep |

(*a*) Where stems of first members end in long vowels second members show a glide consonant (*l* in two examples above).

(*b*) Occasional transitives in *-o-* exist alongside transitives in *-ā-*, and may be preferred: e.g.

| | |
|---|---|
| भीगना *bhīgnā*, be wet | भिगोना *bhigonā* (भिगाना *bhigānā*), make wet |

C. The second member shows *-ū-* or (more commonly) *-o-* medially in the stem[4] where the first shows *-u-* or *-ū-*; or *-e-* where the first shows *-i-* or *-ī-*; or *-ī-* where the first shows *-i-*.

| | |
|---|---|
| रुकना *ruknā*, stop | रोकना *roknā*, stop |
| खुलना *khulnā*, open | खोलना *kholnā*, open |
| लुटना *luṭnā*, be looted | लूटना *lūṭnā*, loot |
| टूटना *ṭūṭnā*, break | तोड़ना *toṛnā*, break |
| छूटना *chūṭnā*, leave | छोड़ना *choṛnā*, leave, abandon |
| फूटना *phūṭnā*, burst | फोड़ना *phoṛnā*, burst |
| धुलना *dhulnā*, be, get washed | धोना *dhonā*, wash |
| दीखना *dīkhnā*, दिखना *dikhnā*, be visible | देखना *dekhnā*, see |
| पिटना *piṭnā*, be beaten | पीटना *pīṭnā*, beat |
| खिंचना *khiṁcnā*, be drawn, pulled | खींचना *khīṁcnā*, pull |
| घिरना *ghirnā*, be surrounded | घेरना *ghernā*, surround; besiege |
| बिकना *biknā*, be sold | बेचना *becnā*, sell |

[1] See p. xxiv.

[2] Also बैठाना *baiṭhānā*.

[3] Also लेटाना *leṭānā*.

[4] Finally in धोना *dhonā* 'wash'.

(*a*) Note the consonantal alternations in the pairs टूटना *ṭūṭnā* — तोड़ना *toṛnā*; छूटना *chūṭnā* — छोड़ना *choṛnā*; फूटना *phūṭnā* — फोड़ना *phoṛnā*; बिकना *biknā* — बेचना *becnā*; also *l* in धुलना *dhulnā*, with which cf. धुलाना *dhulānā* below.

(*b*) Occasional transitives in *-e-* pair with intransitives from Group A: e.g.

| | |
|---|---|
| बिखरना *bikharnā*, be scattered | बिखेरना *bikhernā*, scatter |
| सिमटना *simaṭnā*, shrink, contract | समेटना *sameṭnā*, collect together |

2. *Pairs of transitive verbs*

These are classified according to the same criteria used for the pairs of one intransitive and one transitive verb in section 1 above.

A (ii).

| | |
|---|---|
| समझना *samajhnā*, understand | समझाना *samjhānā*, explain |
| पढ़ना *paṛhnā*, read | पढ़ाना *paṛhānā*, teach |
| सुनना *sunnā*, hear | सुनाना *sunānā*, relate, tell |
| करना *karnā*, do | कराना *karānā*, effect, bring about, cause to be done |

B.

| | |
|---|---|
| लादना *lādnā*, load | लदाना *ladānā*, cause to be laden |
| देखना *dekhnā*, see | दिखाना *dikhānā*, show |
| सीखना *sīkhnā*, learn | सिखाना *sikhānā*, teach |
| तोड़ना *toṛnā*, break | तुड़ाना *tuṛānā*, break, cause to be broken |
| छोड़ना *choṛnā*, leave, abandon | छुड़ाना *chuṛānā*, cause to leave |
| पीना *pīnā*, drink | पिलाना *pilānā*, give to drink |
| खेलना *khelnā*, play | खिलाना *khilānā*, cause to play |
| खाना *khānā*, eat | खिलाना *khilānā*, feed |
| लेना *lenā*, take | लिवाना *livānā*, cause to be taken, brought |
| देना *denā*, give | दिलाना *dilānā*, cause to be given |
| धोना *dhonā*, wash | धुलाना *dhulānā*, cause to be washed |
| बोलना *bolnā*, speak, say | बुलाना *bulānā*, call, summon; invite |

(*a*) Where stems of first members end in long vowels second members show a glide consonant (usually *l*, but also *v*; note लिवाना *livānā*).

(*b*) Note the vowel alternation *ī* — *i* in पीना *pīnā* — पिलाना *pilānā*, etc., of which no common example was adduced in section 1B above. The alternation in खाना *khānā* — खिलाना *khilānā* is exceptional.

(*c*) The verbs बताना *batānā* 'relate, inform' and कमाना *kamānā* 'earn' may be noted here. They do not pair formally with other verbs, but are relatable to the nouns बात *bāt* (and the verbal expression बात करना *bāt karnā*) and काम *kām*.

(*d*) The second member of a pair occasionally has an alternative form with *-l-* in final stem syllable, e.g. सिखलाना *sikhlānā*, दिखलाना *dikhlānā*, and बतलाना *batlānā*, equivalent in sense to the corresponding forms without *-l-*; and कहलाना *kahlānā*, common in the sense 'to be called, named'.

(*e*) Many second members of transitive pairs are used in construction with two sentence objects, a direct case object and an indirect (oblique case) object with को *ko*, which usually precedes it. Others are used with one object and agentive expressions containing the postposition से *se*. See the following examples, and the further discussion of these types of construction in the section on causative verbs, below.

वह घर से अभी नहीं निकला? तो निकाल दो! *vah ghar se abhī nahīṁ niklā? to nikāl do!*[1] He hasn't come out of the house yet? Then drive him out!

पुस्तक अगले हफ़्ते छप जाएगी। *pustak agle hafte chap jāegī*, The book will be printed next week.

मैं उसे छापूँगा। *maiṁ use chāpūṁgā*, I shall print it.

यह लकड़ी नहीं जलती। *yah lakṛī nahīṁ jaltī*, This wood doesn't burn.

उसने तरकारी जलाई। *usne tarkārī jalāī*, He burned the curry.

सूरज से फूल खिलते हैं। *sūraj se phūl khilte haiṁ*, The sun brings the flowers out.[2]

मैं आपको अपनी गाड़ी में लंदन घुमाऊँगा। *maiṁ āpko apnī gāṛī meṁ landan ghumāūṁgā*, I'll drive you round London in my car.[3]

[1] For तो *to* see Lesson XXIII, pp. 140 f.

[2] Agentive expressions containing the postposition से *se* can be used with many intransitive verbs, as in this sentence.

[3] The word लंदन *landan* is here used adverbially, not as an object of the verb; see Supplement I, p. 168.

माँ ने बच्चों को गेंद खिलाई । *mām̐ ne baccoṁ ko geṁd khilāī*, The mother got her children to play ball.

मैं उससे बात करना चाहता हूँ । उसे बुलाइए । *maiṁ usse bāt karnā cāhtā hūṁ. use bulāie*, I want to speak to him. Please call him.

यह छड़ी आसानी से नहीं टूटती । *yah chaṛī āsānī se nahīṁ ṭūṭtī*, This stick doesn't break easily.

मैं उसे तोड़ूँगा । *maiṁ use toṛūṁgā*, I shall break it.

गाड़ी एक बजे छूटती है । *gāṛī ek baje chūṭtī hai*, The train leaves at one o'clock.

उसे छोड़ दो! *use choṛ do!* Leave that, him, alone!

हर सोमवार को कपड़े धुलते हैं । *har somvār ko kapṛe dhulte haiṁ*, Monday, washday.

बहुत दिनों से आप दिखे नहीं । *bahut dinoṁ se āp dikhe nahīṁ*, I haven't seen you, you haven't been about, for a good while.

हमने चित्र देखे । *hamne citr dekhe*, We looked at the pictures.

मैं हिंदी पढ़ रहा हूँ । *maiṁ hindī paṛh rahā hūṁ*, I am studying, reading, Hindi.

मैं अपने बेटे को हिंदी पढ़ा रहा हूँ । *maiṁ apne beṭe ko hindī paṛhā rahā hūṁ*, I'm teaching my son Hindi.

मैंने उसे एक कहानी सुनाई । *maiṁne use ek kahānī sunāī*, I told him a story.

मैं आपसे यह काम कराऊँगा । *maiṁ āpse yah kām karāūṁgā*, I'll get you to do this work, get this work done by you.

मैं आपका उससे परिचय कराऊँगा । *maiṁ āpkā usse paricay karāūṁgā*, I'll introduce you to him (cause your acquaintance with him to be brought about).[1]

उसने दो आदमियों से गाड़ी चारे से लदा दी । *usne do ādmiyoṁ se gāṛī cāre se ladā dī*, He got the wagon loaded up with fodder by two men.

मुझे अपनी पुस्तक दिखाइए । *mujhe apnī pustak dikhāie*, Please show me your book.

बैल रस्सी को तुड़ाकर भाग निकला । *bail rassī ko tuṛākar bhāg niklā*, The ox broke the rope and escaped.

मैं इस दूकान पर दस रुपए का नोट तुड़ाऊँगा । *maiṁ is dūkān par das rupae kā noṭ tuṛāūṁgā*, I shall change a 10 rupee note in this shop.

[1] Cf. the simpler मैं आपको उससे मिलाऊँगा *maiṁ āpko usse milāūṁgā.*

राजा ने क़िले से शत्रु के छक्के छुड़ाए । *rājā ne qile se śatru ke chakke churāe*, The rajah drove off the enemy's detachments from the fort.

उसने मुझे एक गिलास पानी पिलाया । *usne mujhe ek gilās pānī pilāyā*, He gave me a glass of water (to drink).

उन्होंने आपको क्या खिलाया? *unhoṁne āpko kyā khilāyā?* What did they give you to eat?

मैंने दूकान से कुछ चीज़ें लिवाईं । *maiṁne dūkān se kuch cīzeṁ livāīṁ*, I had some things brought from the shop.

भारत की राजधानी दिल्ली कहलाती है । *bhārat kī rājdhānī dillī kahlātī hai*, The capital of India is called Delhi.

Before leaving this section, note that not all verbs in *-ānā* are transitive. A considerable number are intransitive, including most of those based on nouns or adjectives: e.g.

लजाना *lajānā*, be ashamed, embarrassed, modest
सुस्ताना *sustānā*, rest

Note also that some verbs are used intransitively and transitively without difference of form: e.g.

बदलना *badalnā*, change
भरना *bharnā*, be filled; fill
घबराना *ghabrānā*, be perturbed; make anxious

3. *Three-member groups*

Certain verbs figure in the above tables as both the second member of an intransitive-transitive pair and the first of a transitive-transitive pair. Thus triads of associated verbs can be set up: e.g.

| | | |
|---|---|---|
| लदना *ladnā* | लादना *lādnā* | लदाना *ladānā* |
| टूटना *ṭūṭnā* | तोड़ना *toṛnā* | तुड़ाना *tuṛānā* |
| छूटना *chūṭnā* | छोड़ना *choṛnā* | छुड़ाना *chuṛānā* |
| धुलना *dhulnā* | धोना *dhonā* | धुलाना *dhulānā* |
| दिखना *dikhnā* / दीखना *dīkhnā* | देखना *dekhnā* | दिखाना *dikhānā* |

The student may find it helpful to think of the last verb of such a triad as a causative formed on the first, and of the second verb of transitive pairs as a causative referable either to a non-existent intransitive or passive verb or directly to the first transitive verb of the pair. But since both the construction of these verbs and the clarity with which they are seen to express 'causation' varies, only the verbs described in the following section, which show a distinctive marker syllable and uniform construction, are described as causatives here.

## CAUSATIVE VERBS

Verbs showing final stem syllable *-vā-* are almost all used in construction with agentive expressions containing the postposition से *se*. These verbs are conveniently described as causatives, and are all associated with two- or three-member groups of verbs of related stem. The following examples may be compared with forms given above.

मरवाना *marvānā*, have killed, arrange the killing of (by someone)

निकलवाना *nikalvānā*, to have put out, etc. ( ,, )

फड़वाना *phaṛvānā*, to have torn ( ,, )

लदवाना *ladvānā*, to have loaded ( ,, )

छपवाना *chapvānā*, to get printed ( ,, )

बनवाना *banvānā*, to get made ( ,, )

Similarly सुनवाना *sunvānā*; पिलवाना *pilvānā*; खिलवाना *khilvānā*; रुकवाना *rukvānā*; खुलवाना *khulvānā*; तुड़वाना *tuṛvānā*; करवाना *karvānā*; बुलवाना *bulvānā*; फुड़वाना *phuṛvānā*; छुड़वाना *chuṛvānā*, etc.

मैं पुस्तक छपवाऊँगा । *maiṁ pustak chapvāūṁgā*, I shall have the book printed.

मैं अपने भाई से पुस्तक छपवाऊँगा । *maiṁ apne bhāī se pustak chapvāūṁgā*, I shall get my brother to print the book.

मैं अपने बेटे को अच्छे अध्यापक से हिंदी पढ़वा रहा हूँ । *maiṁ apne beṭe ko acche adhyāpak se hindī paṛhvā rahā hūṁ*, I'm having my son taught Hindi by a good teacher.

यह काम अच्छे मिस्तरी से करवाइए! *yah kām acche mistrī se karvāie!* Get a good workman to do this job!

मैं आपका उससे परिचय करवाऊँगा । *maiṁ āpkā usse paricay karvāūṁgā*, I'll get you introduced to him.

राम कुमार को बुलवाइए । *rām kumār ko bulvāie*, Please send for Rām Kumār (have him sent for).

उसने अपने शत्रु का मकान जलवा दिया । *usne apne śatru kā makān jalvā diyā*, He had his enemy's house burnt down.

मैं मुलज़िम को पुलिस से छुड़वा दूंगा । *maiṁ mulzim ko pulis se chuṛvā dūṁgā*, I shall get the police to set the accused free.

(*a*) Where a causative verb associates with a three-member group of verbs of related stem it will not be readily distinguishable in sense from the third member if the latter is also used in construction with से *se*. Thus the verbs लदवाना *ladvānā*, धुलवाना *dhulvānā* are semantic and syntactical equivalents of लदाना *ladānā* and धुलाना *dhulānā* respectively, whereas दिखवाना *dikhvānā* is distinct in construction and sense from दिखाना *dikhānā* and दिखलाना *dikhlānā*.

मैं आपको पत्र दिख(ल)ाऊँगा । *maiṁ āpko patr dikh(l)āūṁgā*, I shall show you the letter.

मैं आपको मंत्री से पत्र दिखवाऊँगा । *maiṁ āpko mantrī se patr dikhvāūṁgā*, I shall get the secretary to show you the letter.

(*b*) Where a causative verb associates with a pair only of verbs of related stem, it is normally distinct in construction and sense from the second member of the pair, e.g. पढ़वाना *paṛhvānā*, सुनवाना *sunvānā*. But note that कराना *karānā* and करवाना *karvānā* show the same construction and, though they may be clearly distinguishable in sense in certain contexts (see examples above), are not necessarily so. The following two sentences, for example, may be interchangeable:

मैं आपसे यह काम कराऊँगा । *maiṁ āpse yah kām karāūṁgā*, I'll get you to do this work.

मैं आपसे यह काम करवाऊँगा । *maiṁ āpse yah kām karvāūṁgā*, I'll get you to do this work.

A semantic distinction is possible, however, between these sentences according to the attitude which they imply on the part of the speaker; the second could well be less circumspect, implying greater authority on the speaker's part, or power to get the work done.

(*c*) Where third and fourth members of a group of verbs are both used in construction with से *se*, the *-vā-* form tends to be the more common.

## VOCABULARY

लकड़ी *lakṛī*, f., wood
तरकारी *tarkārī*, f., curry
सूरज *sūraj*, m., sun
फूल *phūl*, m., flower
गेंद *gemd*, f., ball
छड़ी *chaṛī*, f., stick, cane
चित्र *citr*, m., picture
चारा *cārā*, m., fodder
नोट *noṭ*, m., note (money)
छक्का *chakkā*, m., squad, detachment (literally 'group of six')
गिलास *gilās*, m., glass (for drinking)

अध्यापक *adhyāpak*, m., teacher
मिस्तरी *mistrī*, m., mechanic, (skilled) workman
मुलज़िम *mulzim*, m., accused person
पुलिस *pulis*, f., police
बिस्तर *bistar*, m., bedding
सीट *sīṭ*, f., seat; नीचे की सीट *nīce kī sīṭ*, lower seat
गधा *gadhā*, m., donkey, ass
धोबी *dhobī*, m., washerman
वाक्य *vākya*, m., sentence
लेख *lekh*, m., essay, article
तुड़ाना *tuṛānā*, break, cause to be broken; get change for (money)
बिछाना *bichānā*, spread
बहुत दिनों से *bahut dinoṁ se*, for (i.e. since) a long time
परिचय *paricay*, m., acquaintance
पीछे से *pīche se*, from behind, from the rear

## EXERCISE 33

जैसे ही गाड़ी छटी, वैसे ही मैंने नीचे की सीट पर अपना बिस्तर बिछा दिया। फिर कपड़े बदलकर मैं लेट गया। उस गधे पर किसी से सामान लदवाओ। उसने अखबार में जो लेख छपवाया था, उसे पढ़कर वे हँस पड़े। उसे समझाइए कि वह अपना काम हमेशा समय पर ख़तम करे। मैं उसे बुलाकर उसका आपसे परिचय कराऊँगा। अपने लड़के को किसी अच्छे स्कूल में पढ़वाइए। मैं आपको लंदन घुमाना चाहता हूँ। आप उस दूकान में अच्छे कपड़े बनवा सकते हैं।

## EXERCISE 34

I got off the train at Allahabad. Kindly collect your luggage from the rear (of the bus).[1] Show me what you've written. What have you gone and done? You've broken the chair! You've learned a lot of Hindi. Who taught you? We get our clothes washed by a dhobi. The train doesn't stop here. The train has just left. I get you to write a few sentences in Hindi every day.

[1] Luggage from the roof storage rack of buses is often handed down to passengers at the rear. Use the verb उतारना *utārnā*.

# LESSON XIX

## PASSIVE FORMS

COMPOSITE verbal expressions with passive force are used in the majority of aspectual, tense, and modal patterns and as infinitives. They consist of perfective participles collocating with appropriate following forms of the verb जाना *jānā*. Both parts of the composite show concord with subjects, except in impersonal constructions (see below). The action of an agent is expressed by use of the postposition से *se*. Negatives precede both parts of the composite in sentences of neutral style and emphasis.

वे शत्रु से मारे जाएँगे । *ve śatru se māre jāeṁge*, They will be killed by the enemy.

पत्र डाक से भेजा गया था । *patr ḍāk se bhejā gayā thā*, The letter was sent, had been sent by post.

हिंदी भारत में बोली जाती है । *hindī bhārat meṁ bolī jātī hai*, Hindi is spoken in India.

हिंदी इस देश में नहीं बोली जाती । *hindī is deś meṁ nahīṁ bolī jātī*, Hindi isn't spoken in this country.

### 1. *Passives of compound verbs*

These are very frequently met with. The stem of the given verb (simple or conjunct) is followed by a passive form of the dependent auxiliary verb.

पत्र डाक से भेज दिया जाएगा । *patr ḍāk se bhej diyā jāegā*, The letter will be forwarded by post (passive of भेज देना *bhej denā*).

हिंदी बहुत लोगों से राष्ट्रभाषा के रूप में स्वीकार कर ली गई थी *hindī bahut logoṁ se rāṣṭrabhāṣā ke rūp meṁ svīkār kar lī gaī thī*, Hindi was accepted as the national language by many people[1] (passive of स्वीकार कर लेना *svīkār kar lenā*).

### 2. *Impersonal passives*

These are found for both transitive and intransitive verbs. They are 'neutral' in respect of concord (this 'neutrality' being expressed by the use of 3rd singular masculine concord forms in conjunction with absence of a sentence subject).

[1] के रूप में *ke rūp meṁ* 'in the form, capacity, of'; स्वीकार करना *svīkār karnā* 'accept' (conjunct verb).

कहा जाता है कि प्रेम अंधा होता है। *kahā jātā hai ki prem andhā hotā hai*, It is said that love is blind.

चला जाए? *calā jāe?* Shall we go (should it be gone)?

मुझसे सोया नहीं गया। *mujhse soyā nahīṁ gayā*, I couldn't sleep, couldn't get to sleep (it was not slept by me).

मुझसे अभी बाज़ार नहीं जाया जाएगा। *mujhse abhī bāzār nahīṁ jāyā jāegā*, I shan't be able to go to the bazaar just now (it won't be gone by me).

मुझे हिंदुस्तान भेज दिया गया था। *mujhe hindustān bhej diyā gayā thā*, I was sent to India (it was sent to India with respect to me).

(*a*) Note from the fourth example above that passive forms of the verb जाना *jānā* show जाया *jāyā*, not गया *gayā*, as first element.

(*b*) Only a slight change in emphasis distinguishes the above impersonal sentences from corresponding sentences showing personal subjects, viz.

कहते हैं कि प्रेम अंधा होता है। *kahte haiṁ ki prem andhā hotā hai*, People say that love is blind.

चलें? *caleṁ?* Shall we go?

मैं सो नहीं सका। *maiṁ so nahīṁ sakā*, I couldn't sleep.

मैं हिंदुस्तान भेज दिया गया था। *maiṁ hindustān bhej diyā gayā thā*, I was sent to India.

The second example here is slightly less circumspect, because personal in its reference, than the corresponding impersonal expression. The last example somewhat stresses the identity of the subject referend by comparison with the corresponding impersonal expression, in which attention is focused less on the referend of the object मुझे *mujhe* than on the performance of the action itself.

3. *A limitation on the use of the passive*

An English passive form frequently has as its most natural translation equivalent not a passive, but an intransitive verb. Thus the sentence 'only one man was saved' will generally be rendered

सिर्फ़ एक ही आदमी बच गया। *sirf ek hī ādmī bac gayā.*

This states the fact of the man's escape, whereas the possible alternative

सिर्फ़ एक ही आदमी बचाया गया। *sirf ek hī ādmī bacāyā gayā*

places more emphasis than the English might warrant on the actual action of his rescue.

## CONJUNCT VERBS NOT INVOLVING करना *karnā*, होना *honā*

The use of pairs of conjunct verbs involving the verbal elements करना *karnā*, होना *honā* was noted in Lesson X. Other conjuncts, both transitive and intransitive, involve different verbal elements. Some examples follow.

1. याद रखना *yād rakhnā* 'bear in mind, remember'.

मैं यह बात हमेशा याद रखूंगा । *maiṁ yah bāt hameśā yād rakhūṁgā*, I shall always remember this (never forget it).

2. याद आना *yād ānā* 'come to mind'. Note that this intransitive expression is common in sentences whose English translation equivalent contains the transitive verb 'remember'.

उस समय मुझे राम याद आया । *us samay mujhe rām yād āyā*, At that moment I remembered Rām.

3. याद रहना *yād rahnā* 'remain in mind, be remembered'.

आज का दिन मुझे हमेशा याद रहेगा । *āj kā din mujhe hameśā yād rahegā*, I shall always remember today.

(*a*) Note that the noun याद *yād*, f., meaning 'memory, recollection' can be used in nominal-verbal constructs in which its grammatical identity is maintained, as well as in conjunct verbs proper; e.g. in conjunction with रहना *rahnā*:

उन दिनों की याद मेरे दिल में हमेशा के लिए ताज़ी रहेगी । *un dinoṁ kī yād mere dil meṁ hameśā ke lie tāzī rahegī*, The memory of those days will remain fresh in my heart for ever.

(*b*) For convenience, and because their sphere of usage is delimited by the existence of the above forms, mention of याद होना *yād honā* and याद करना *yād karnā* is also made here.

याद होना *yād honā* 'be in mind; be, become remembered'.

आपको मेरा नाम याद होगा । *āpko merā nām yād hogā*, You probably remember my name.

मुझे रामचरितमानस की सौ पंक्तियाँ याद हो गई हैं । *mujhe rāmcaritmānas kī sau paṅktiyāṁ yād ho gaī haiṁ*, I've learned a hundred lines of the *Rāmcaritmānas* by heart.

याद करना *yād karnā* 'recollect; learn by heart'.

यह घटना मेरे शहर में अभी तक याद की जाती है। *yah ghaṭnā mere śahr meṁ abhī tak yād kī jātī hai*, This incident is still remembered in my town.

उसने रामचरितमानस की सौ पंक्तियाँ याद कीं। *usne rāmcaritmānas kī sau paṅktiyāṁ yād kīṁ*, He learned a hundred lines of the *Rāmcaritmānas* by heart.

4. दान देना *dān denā* 'give (as charity), donate'.

मैंने भिखारी को तीन पैसे दान दिए। *maiṁne bhikhārī ko tīn paise dān die*, I gave the beggar three pice.

5. मोल लेना *mol lenā* 'buy'.

उसने मकान मोल लेकर उसमें रहना शुरू किया। *usne makān mol lekar usmeṁ rahnā śurū kiyā*, He bought a house and moved into it (started to live in it).

6. दिखाई देना *dikhāī denā* 'be visible, come into sight'.

सुनाई देना *sunāī denā* 'be audible'.
(See Lesson XII, p. 74.)

## SOME USES OF INFINITIVES

1. Infinitives characteristically have nominal function in Hindi. As nouns they may be equated formally with masculines in *-ā* (predominantly singular). They are negatived with preceding न *na*.

आपका घर लौटना आवश्यक है। *āpkā ghar lauṭnā āvaśyak hai*, Your return home is necessary.

ऐसा करना मना है। *aisā karnā manā hai*, To do this is forbidden.

ऐसा करने से आप सफल होंगे। *aisā karne se āp saphal hoṁge*, By doing this you'll be successful.

आपका यहाँ न रहना हमें बड़ी असुविधा का कारण होगा। *āpkā yahāṁ na rahnā hameṁ baṛī asuvidhā kā kāraṇ hogā*, Your not staying here will be a cause of great inconvenience to us.

(*a*) Compare also the formal parallelism of the following locutions, of which one contains a noun in initial position, the other an infinitive.

नाले का पानी *nāle kā pānī*, stream water
पीने का पानी *pīne kā pānī*, drinking water

2. Some further examples of the very common sequence of oblique case infinitive with following postposition are given here.

उनके जाने के बाद मुझसे मिलिए। *unke jāne ke bād mujhse milie*, (Come and) see me after he goes.

ऐसा होने पर भी आप नहीं जा सकते। *aisā hone par bhī āp nahīṁ jā sakte*, Even so (in spite of this being so) you can't go.

मैं बाहर जाने को हूँ। *maiṁ bāhar jāne ko hūṁ*, I am about to go out.

उसने हिंदी सीखने की कोशिश की। *usne hindī sīkhne kī kośiś kī*, He tried to learn Hindi.

उसने हिंदी सीखने का प्रयत्न किया। *usne hindī sīkhne kā prayatn kiyā*, He tried to learn Hindi.

उसने मुझे सहायता देने से इनकार किया। *usne mujhe sahāytā dene se inkār kiyā*, He refused to help me.

मैंने उसे आने पर मजबूर किया। *maiṁne use āne par majbūr kiyā*, I compelled him to come.

मैंने उसे आने पर बाध्य किया। *maiṁne use āne par bādhya kiyā*, I compelled him to come.

(*a*) Note particularly the force of को *ko* in the third example above; also the frequency of oblique infinitives in construction with nominal-verbal expressions based on nouns or adjectives (fourth example onwards).

(*b*) Note also from the above examples that infinitives are linked to nominal-verbal expressions in varying ways; most frequently, but not always, with का *kā* where nouns are involved (fourth, fifth, and sixth examples) and with other postpositions (never का *kā*) where adjectives are involved (last two examples).

3. In sentences expressive of purpose, oblique case infinitives may occur alone, or with following को *ko*, or with following के लिए *ke lie*.

मैं हिंदी सीखने भारत गया था। *maiṁ hindī sīkhne bhārat gayā thā*, I went to India to learn Hindi.

मैं हिंदी सीखने को भारत गया था। *maiṁ hindī sīkhne ko bhārat gayā thā*, I went to India to learn Hindi.

मैं हिंदी सीखने के लिए भारत गया था। *maiṁ hindī sīkhne ke lie bhārat gayā thā*, I went to India to learn Hindi.

वह खाना खाने बैठा। *vah khānā khāne baiṭhā*, He sat down to eat his meal.

(*a*) The oblique infinitive alone is the most common of these means of expressing purpose in the spoken language (being the most concise), but broadly speaking they are interchangeable. Feeling for sentence rhythm may lead to preference for one type of expression over the others in any given sentence.

4. Occasionally को *ko* and के लिए *ke lie* following an oblique case infinitive and preceding an adjective are interchangeable.

क्या आप जाने के लिए तैयार हैं? *kyā āp jāne ke lie taiyār haiṁ?* Are you ready to go?

क्या आप जाने को तैयार हैं? *kyā āp jāne ko taiyār haiṁ?* Are you ready to go?

मैं आपकी सेवा के लिए प्रस्तुत हूँ । *maiṁ apkī sevā ke lie prastut hūṁ*, I am at your service (ready for, to do your service).

मैं आपकी सेवा को प्रस्तुत हूँ । *maiṁ āpkī sevā ko prastut hūṁ*, I am at your service.

## VOCABULARY

डाक *ḍāk*, f., post, postal service
प्रेम *prem*, m., love, affection
नाम *nām*, m., name
पंक्ति *paṅkti*, f., line; row
भिखारी *bhikhārī*, m., beggar
असुविधा *asuvidhā*, f., inconvenience
नाला *nālā*, m., stream
सेवा *sevā*, f., service
आंदोलन *āndolan*, m., movement (social, political, etc.)
बुराई *burāī*, f., badness, wickedness; की बुराई करना *kī burāī karnā*, slander
बुरा *burā*, bad, wicked
दिल †*dil*, m., heart
पैदावार †*paidāvār*, f., produce
सावधानी *sāvdhānī*, f., care; सावधानी से *sāvdhānī se*, carefully
सावधान *sāvdhān*, adj., careful
कविता *kavitā*, f., poem
फ़र्ज़ †*farz*, m., duty
अभ्यास *abhyās*, m., practice; का अभ्यास करना *kā abhyās karnā*, practise
प्रवेश *praveś*, m., entry, entrance; प्रवेश करना *praveś karnā* (*meṁ*), enter
प्रयत्न *prayatn*, m., attempt; का प्रयत्न करना *kā prayatn karnā*, try
रामचरितमानस *rāmcaritmānas*, m., name of a work by the medieval poet Tulsīdās
इनकार *inkār*, m., refusal; इनकार करना *inkār karnā* (*se*), refuse
स्वीकार करना *svīkār karnā*, accept
मोल लेना *mol lenā*, buy
मजबूर करना †*majbūr karnā* (*par*, *ke lie*), compel
बाध्य करना *bādhya karnā* (*par*, *ke lie*), compel
लेटना *leṭnā*, lie down

रूप *rūp*, m., form; के रूप में *ke rūp meṁ*, as, in the capacity of
भेजना *bhejnā*, send
बचाना *bacānā*, save, rescue
आराम *ārām*, m., rest, comfort; आराम करना *ārām karnā*, rest
अंधा *andhā*, blind
ताज़ा *tāzā*, fresh
मना *manā* (invariable), forbidden
प्रस्तुत **prastut*, ready, prepared
स्वाभाविक *svābhāvik*, natural
दूसरा *dūsrā*, second; other
ऐसा *aisā*, adj. and pron., of this sort; this sort of thing
सफल *saphal*, successful

## EXERCISE 35

मेरी पुस्तकें एक महीने बाद भेज दी गई थीं। मुझसे न रहा गया। मुझे याद नहीं है। रास्ते में गाड़ियों का शोर सुनाई दे रहा था। हिंदी के लिए इस आंदोलन का होना स्वाभाविक है। सच बोलने पर भी दूसरे लोग आपकी बुराई करेंगे। उन्होंने उसे सच बोलने पर मजबूर किया। आप बाहर जाने को हैं? इस तस्वीर में आपको एक बैलगाड़ी दिखाई देती है। किसान आम तौर से ऐसी गाड़ियों पर अपनी पैदावार बाजार ले जाते हैं।

## EXERCISE 36

It can be said that Hindi will one day be accepted as India's national language. India, where Hindi and other languages also are spoken, is a most interesting country. I carefully remembered what you had said. When I saw him I remembered his face. You should learn some Hindi poems by heart. His books are being praised these days. I began work yesterday at nine o'clock. I shan't wait for you tomorrow. To speak the truth is a man's duty. By practising speaking you'll learn our language. The enemy tried to enter the fort. He went to the station to meet his friend. He lay down to rest.

# LESSON XX

## SUBORDINATE CONJUNCTIONS AND CLAUSES

SOME subordinate conjunctions (words identifying subordinate clauses) have been given and their use in complex sentences illustrated in Lessons XIV and XVI. The other chief subordinate conjunctions, whose use in sentences is discussed here, are found in broadly similar sentence patterns, i.e. they frequently introduce or occur in second position[1] in a subordinate clause, against which is balanced a following principal clause introduced by a linking word or phrase; but in certain cases a principal clause precedes a subordinate clause.

### A. अगर †*agar*, यदि *yadi* 'if'

These forms correlate with the conjunction तो *to* introducing the principal clause.

1. Future, subjunctive, and general present verbs are all commonly used in the subordinate clause when the verb in the principal clause is future (but see also section 3 below). Use of the subjunctive in these circumstances implies that the event in question is not envisaged as definitely as when a future or general present verb is used, but does not at all imply that it is unlikely to come about.

अगर मेहनत करोगे तो सफल होगे । *agar mehnat karoge to saphal hoge*, If you work you'll succeed.

अगर आप हिंदुस्तान आ जाएँ तो मैं आपको ताज महल ज़रूर दिखाऊँगा । *agar āp hindustān ā jāeṁ to maiṁ āpko tāj mahl zarūr dikhāūṁgā*, If you come to India I shall certainly show you the Taj Mahal.

अगर आप चाहें तो मैं आपसे हिंदी बोलूँगा । *agar āp cāheṁ to maiṁ āpse hindī bolūṁgā*, If you like I'll speak Hindi to you.

अगर आप चाहते हैं तो मैं आपसे हिंदी बोलूँगा । *agar āp cāhte haiṁ to maiṁ āpse hindī bolūṁgā*, If you want me to I'll speak Hindi to you.

2. The verb in the subordinate clause is fairly regularly subjunctive and sometimes general present when the verb in the principal clause is not future (but see also sections 3 and 4 below).

[1] As indicated above for relatives, see p. 86.

अगर विदेशी अच्छी हिंदी न बोलें तो हम उनको कभी कभी नहीं समझते । *agar videśī acchī hindī na boleṁ to ham unko kabhī kabhī nahīṁ samajhte*, If foreigners don't speak good Hindi we sometimes don't understand them.

अगर वह आए तो मेरा उससे परिचय कराइए । *agar vah āe to merā usse paricay karāie*, If he comes please introduce me to him.

अगर आपको दिल्ली जाना है तो ज़रूर जाइए । *agar āpko dillī jānā hai to zarūr jāie*, If you must go to Delhi, do so by all means.

3. Very commonly, however, perfective forms are used rather than futures or subjunctives in the subordinate clauses of sentences of the types illustrated above. This usage is especially common colloquially, and is an interesting illustration of the importance of aspect in the Hindi verbal system. By describing the action of the subordinate clause with a perfective verb and so stressing its completion, while that of the main clause is described with a non-perfective verb, one very adequately expresses the semantic relationship of the clauses in this type of sentence, in which the first clause describes a condition of action, and the second an action which ensues if the condition is met.

Perfective forms are not used in subordinate clauses referring to relatively unlikely happenings (whose completion is hardly envisaged) or to continuing events (specifically non-completed).

अगर मेहनत की तो सफल होगे । *agar mehnat kī to saphal hoge*, If you work you'll succeed.

अगर वह आया तो मेरा उससे परिचय कराइए । *agar vah āyā to merā usse paricay karāie*, If he comes please introduce me to him.

अगर उससे मुलाक़ात हुई तो मैं आपको बताऊँगा । *agar usse mulāqāt huī to maiṁ āpko batāūṁgā*, If I meet him I'll tell you.

4. To express an unrealised condition in the past, or a distinctly improbable one in the future, a special construction is used, the verb form in both clauses being an imperfective participle, or alternatively, if the reference is to past time, a perfective participle followed by the imperfective participle of होना *honā*.

अगर मैं भारत जाता तो ज़्यादा हिंदी ज़रूर सीखता । *agar maiṁ bhārat jātā to zyādā hindī zarūr sīkhtā*, Had I gone to India I should certainly have learned more Hindi.

or, If I (should happen to) go to India I would certainly learn more Hindi.

अगर मैं भारत गया होता तो मैंने ज़्यादा हिंदी ज़रूर सीखी होती । *agar maiṁ bhārat gayā hotā to maiṁne zyādā hindī zarūr sīkhī hotī*, Had I gone to India I should certainly have learned more Hindi.

5. (*a*) Introductory अगर *agar*, यदि *yadi* is very frequently omitted in informal usage. The presence of the linking तो *to* serves to establish the sentence type in such cases (though not entirely unambiguously, there being some possibility of confusion with sentences in which जब *jab* 'when' has been similarly omitted).

(*b*) In English the word 'if' may introduce an indirect question as well as a clause expressing a condition. In such cases its translation equivalent is of course always कि *ki*; see Lesson XVI.

उससे पूछो कि समझते हो या नहीं । *usse pūcho ki samajhte ho yā nahīṁ*, Ask him if he understands or not.

B. ज्योंही *jyoṁhī* 'as soon as'

This form correlates with त्योंही *tyoṁhī* introducing the principal clause.

ज्योंही *jyoṁhī*, like its equivalent जैसे ही *jaise hī*, is used with a following future or subjunctive verb in the same way as अगर *agar*, यदि *yadi*. It is also used with perfective and general present forms in reference to past and present time.

ज्योंही आप वहाँ पहुँचें, त्योंही पत्र लिखिए । *jyoṁhī āp vahāṁ pahuṁceṁ, tyoṁhī patr likhie*, Please write as soon as you get there.

ज्योंही वहाँ पहुँचूँगा, त्योंही पत्र लिखूँगा । *jyoṁhī vahāṁ pahuṁcūṁgā, tyoṁhī patr likhūṁgā*, I'll write as soon as I get there.

ज्योंही मैं वहाँ पहुँचा, त्योंही काम शुरू किया । *jyoṁhī maiṁ vahāṁ pahuṁcā, tyoṁhī kām śurū kiyā*, I started work as soon as I got there.

C. जब *jab* 'when'; जब तक *jab tak* 'as long as' (contd.)

Note that जब *jab* may correlate with तो *to* as well as with तब *tab*. जब *jab* and जब तक *jab tak* introducing references to future events are followed by subjunctive or future verbs in much the same way as अगर *agar*, यदि *yadi*; use of future verbs is somewhat more frequent.

जब वह आएगा तो मैं जाऊँगा । *jab vah āegā to maiṁ jāūṁgā*, When he comes I'll go.

जब वह आए तो मुझे ख़बर दीजिए । *jab vah āe to mujhe khabar dījie*, When he comes please let me know.

जब तक मैं यहाँ रहूँगा तब तक वे चुप रहेंगे । *jab tak maiṁ yahāṁ rahūṁgā tab tak ve cup raheṁge*, As long as I'm here they'll keep quiet.

(*a*) Introductory जब *jab* is quite often omitted in informal usage. See discussion of the similar and more frequent omission of अगर *agar*, यदि *yadi* above, par. A 5 (*a*).

D. अगरचे †*agarce*, यद्यपि **yadyapi* 'although'

The first of these conjunctions usually correlates with फिर भी *phir bhī*, पर *par* or लेकिन *lekin*, the second usually, but not exclusively, with the form तथापि **tathāpi*.

The subjunctive is not used in the subordinate clause unless doubt is implied in the concession (e.g. by the introduction of some such word as शायद *śāyad* 'perhaps', संभव *sambhav* 'possible'. For the use of the subjunctive in sentences containing these words see Lesson XXI, pp. 130 f.).

अगरचे मैं कम हिंदी जानता हूँ, फिर भी बोलने की कोशिश करता हूँ । *agarce maiṁ kam hindī jāntā hūṁ, phir bhī bolne kī kośiś kartā hūṁ*, Although I don't know much Hindi I still try to speak it.

यद्यपि पंचवर्षीय योजना सफल होगी, तथापि और प्रयत्न आवश्यक होंगे । *yadyapi pañcvarṣīy yojnā saphal hogī, tathāpi aur prayatn āvaśyak hoṁge*, Although the five-year plan will be successful, further efforts will be needed.[1]

यद्यपि पंचवर्षीय योजना कदाचित् पूर्णतः सफल हो, तथापि और अधिक प्रयत्न आवश्यक होंगे । *yadyapi pañcvarṣīy yojnā kadācit pūrṇtaḥ saphal ho, tathāpi aur adhik prayatn āvaśyak hoṁge*, Although the five-year plan will perhaps be completely successful, even further efforts will be needed.[1]

अगरचे इस क्लास के लड़के कभी चुप नहीं रहते, फिर भी अच्छे लड़के हैं । *agarce is klās ke laṛke kabhī cup nahīṁ rahte, phir bhī acche laṛke haiṁ*, Although the boys in this class are never quiet they're a good lot.[2]

(*a*) अगरचे *agarce* is very frequently omitted, its correlative supplying the idea of the concession. Omission of यद्यपि *yadyapi* before its natural correlative तथापि *tathāpi* is less common.

[1] और *aur* is stressed.

[2] कभी . . . नहीं *kabhī . . . nahīṁ* 'never'.

(*b*) The form हालाँकि †*hālāṁki* is very common in informal usage for अगरचे *agarce*.

E. चूंकि †*cūṁki*, क्योंकि *kyoṁki* 'because, since'

चूंकि *cūṁki* correlates chiefly with इसलिए *islie* 'for this reason', or an expression of equivalent sense.

चूंकि आप हिंदी जानते हैं, इसलिए आप उत्तर भारत में हर जगह जा सकेंगे। *cūṁki āp hindī jānte haiṁ, islie āp uttar bhārat meṁ har jagah jā sakeṁge*, Since you know Hindi you'll be able to go everywhere in northern India.

(*a*) The initial conjunction may be omitted; and the locutions इस वजह से *is* †*vajah se* 'for this cause', or the equivalent इस कारण (से) *is kāraṇ (se)*, may be substituted for इसलिए *islie*.

आप हिंदी जानते हैं, इस कारण से आप उत्तर भारत में हर जगह जा सकेंगे। *āp hindī jānte haiṁ, is kāraṇ se āp uttar bhārat meṁ har jagah jā sakeṁge*, You know Hindi, and therefore you'll be able to go everywhere in northern India.

(*b*) An alternative construction to that with चूंकि *cūṁki* shows the clause-order inverted, with the subordinate clause introduced in midsentence by the conjunction क्योंकि *kyoṁki*.

आप उत्तर भारत में हर जगह जा सकेंगे, क्योंकि हिंदी जानते हैं। *āp uttar bhārat meṁ har jagah jā sakeṁge, kyoṁki hindī jānte haiṁ*, You'll be able to go everywhere in northern India because you know Hindi.

Occasionally clauses introduced by क्योंकि *kyoṁki* occur initially in their sentences, with following principal clauses.

(*c*) Also very common is the use of an inflected infinitive followed by the locutions की वजह से *kī vajah se* or के कारण *ke kāraṇ*.

आप हिंदी जानने के कारण उत्तर भारत में हर जगह जा सकेंगे। *āp hindī jānne ke kāraṇ uttar bhārat meṁ har jagah jā sakeṁge*, Because you know Hindi you'll be able to go everywhere in northern India.

F. जिससे *jisse*, ताकि †*tāki*, 'so that'

These forms introduce clauses expressing purpose and containing subjunctive verbs; in sentences of neutral style and emphasis they follow principal clauses. For ताकि *tāki* कि *ki* alone is sometimes found.

वह बैठ गया, जिससे वह और आसानी से पढ़ सके । *vah baiṭh gayā, jisse vah aur āsānī se paṛh sake*, He sat down so that he could read more easily.[1]

मैं पीछे हट गया कि वह पहले हाथ धो ले । *maiṁ pīche haṭ gayā ki vah pahle hāth dho le*, I stepped back so that she could wash her hands first.[2]

## VOCABULARY

मेहनत †*mehnat*[3], f., labour, effort

विदेशी *videśī*, m.f., foreigner; adj., foreign

मुलाक़ात †*mulāqāt*, f., meeting, encounter; मुलाक़ात होना *mulāqāt honā* (*se*), meet

योजना *yojnā*, f., scheme, plan; पंचवर्षीय योजना *pañcvarṣīy yojnā*, five-year plan

उत्तर *uttar*, m., north

दक्षिण *dakṣiṇ*, m., south

फ़ोन *fon*, m., telephone; मेरा फ़ोन आया *merā fon āyā*, someone telephoned me; मैं उसको फ़ोन करूँगा *maiṁ usko fon karūṁgā*, I shall telephone him.

फ़सल *fasl*, f., crop

जेब *jeb*, f., pocket

जवाब †*javāb*, m., answer; चिट्ठी का जवाब देना, *ciṭṭhī kā javāb denā*, answer a letter

सवाल †*savāl*, m., question

स्टेशन *sṭeśan*, m., station

विचार *vicār*, m., thought; opinion

चुप *cup*, silent

आवश्यक *āvaśyak*, necessary

ज़रूरी †*zarūrī*, necessary

हटना *haṭnā*, move away, withdraw

पकना *paknā*, ripen

काटना *kāṭnā*, cut; harvest; bite (of animals)

का काम देखना *kā kām dekhnā*, see to, take care of (someone's) work

कभी कभी *kabhī kabhī*, sometimes

ज़रूर †*zarūr*, indeed, certainly, by all means

कदाचित् **kadācit*, perhaps

पूर्णत: **pūrṇtaḥ*[4], fully

देर *der*, f., delay, lapse of time; पाँच मिनट देरे से आना *pāṁc minaṭ der se ānā*, come five minutes late

कम *kam*, adj., little (of quantity), few; adv. little

गरम *garm*, hot; warm

हर जगह *har jagah*, everywhere

दूसरी बार *dūsrī bār*, a second time, again

या *yā*, or

[1] और *aur* is stressed.

[2] From the novel बड़ी बड़ी आँखें *Baṛī baṛī āṁkheṁ* by Upendranath Ashk.

[3] First vowel usually short [ɛ].

[4] See Supplement III, p. 179.

## EXERCISE 37

अगर आप आ सकें, तो आइए। अगर मेरा फ़ोन आए तो यह[1] कह दीजिए कि मैं फिर फ़ोन करूँगा। अगर वह मुझे उस दिन मिलता तो मैं उसे पहचान लेता। जब आप दिल्ली पहुँचेंगे तो मैं आपको अपने कई मित्रों से मिलाऊँगा। ज्योंही किसानों की फ़सलें पक जाती हैं, त्योंही वे उन्हें काट लेते हैं। अगरचे गाड़ी ठीक समय पर छूटी, फिर भी पाँच मिनट देर से पहुँची। चूँकि उस समय उसे कुछ काम नहीं करना था, इसलिए उसने पत्र जेब से निकालकर दूसरी बार पढ़ना शुरू किया। वह आज मेरा काम देखेगा ताकि आपको दिल्ली घुमा सकूँ।

## EXERCISE 38

If he writes to me I shall certainly answer his letter. If he had written to me before coming I'd have met him at[2] the station. Ask him if this is the right road or not. If I were to meet him I should certainly ask his opinion about this matter. Tell me when you're ready to go. Although I tried very hard I couldn't learn your language. I left Delhi in May because the weather was growing very hot then. I haven't seen you since you went to Delhi.

[1] यह *yah* here anticipates the following clause introduced with कि *ki*. This use of यह *yah* is very common, especially where following clauses are lengthy, or where their sense is emphasized.

[2] पर *par*.

# LESSON XXI

## USES OF THE SUBJUNCTIVE

THE main uses of the subjunctive, apart from those in subordinate clauses, are noted or recapitulated here. The general consideration governing the use of the subjunctive is that it presents actions as in some way contingent or uncertain, rather than as objectively realised or envisaged.

1. In asking questions or making suggestions:

मैं जाऊँ? *maiṁ jāūṁ?* May I go?
चलें? *caleṁ?* Shall we go?
चला जाए? *calā jāe?* Shall we go?[1]
अपना हाल लिखें। *apnā hāl likheṁ*, Please write (saying) how you are (please write your state).

2. In indirect commands and elsewhere where a wish is expressed about the activity of another person or thing:

नेहरू जी की जय हो! *nehrū jī kī jay ho!* Long live Nehru Ji!
उनसे कहिए कि यहाँ आएँ। *unse kahie ki yahāṁ āeṁ*, Tell him to come here.
उसे चाहिए कि यह किताब पढ़े। *use cāhie ki yah kitāb paṛhe*, He ought to read this book.
संदूक़ गिर न जाए, इसलिए उसे रस्से से बैलगाड़ी पर बाँधा गया। *sandūq gir na jāe, islie vse rasse se bailgāṛī par bāṁdhā gayā*, So that the box would not fall it was tied on to the ox-cart with a rope.
मैं चाहता हूँ कि वह हिंदी सीख ले। *maiṁ cāhtā hūṁ ki vah hindī sīkh le*, I want him to learn Hindi.

(*a*) Cf. with the last example the construction of चाहना *cāhnā* with an infinitive noted in Lesson VI, and used in simple sentences (i.e. where a person's wish to carry out an action himself is expressed).

मैं हिंदी सीखना चाहता हूँ। *maiṁ hindī sīkhnā cāhtā hūṁ*, I want to learn Hindi.

3. In many locutions expressive of uncertainty; often in sentences containing the words शायद *śāyad* 'perhaps', संभव *sambhav* 'possible':
वह शायद आए, पता नहीं। *vah śāyad āe, patā nahīṁ*, Perhaps he'll come, I don't know.

[1] See Lesson XIX, p. 117.

संभव है कि वह फ़ेल हो गया हो । *sambhav hai ki vah fel ho gayā ho*, It's possible that he may have failed.[1]

जो हो, सो हो । *jo ho, so ho*, What is to be, will be.[2]

मैं क्या कहूँ? *maiṁ kyā kahūṁ?* What am I to say?

एक सवारी और ले लूँ, फिर चलता हूँ । *ek savārī aur le lūṁ, phir caltā hūṁ*[3], I shall (just) collect one more fare, then I'm going.

(*a*) Note that शायद *śāyad*, संभव *sambhav*, and the adverb संभवतः *sambhavataḥ*[4] are also used to express probability, and in this case are not followed by a subjunctive.

संभव है कि वह फ़ेल हो गया है । *sambhav hai ki vah fel ho gayā hai*, He's probably failed.

यह किताब शायद आपके पास है । *yah kitāb śāyad āpke pās hai*, I expect you've got this book.

4. Often where an object is presented generically, as typical of a class, rather than as an individual entity:

मुझे एक ऐसी किताब चाहिए जो बच्चों के लिए उपयुक्त हो *mujhe ek aisī kitāb cāhie jo baccoṁ ke lie upayukt ho*, I want a book suitable for children.

5. Often in hypothetical comparisons involving such expressions as जैसे *jaise*, मानों *mānoṁ* 'as if':

बच्चा दरवाज़े पर खड़ा था जैसे किसी के इंतज़ार में हो । *baccā darvāze par khaṛā thā jaise kisī ke intazār meṁ ho*, The boy was standing at the door as if waiting for someone.

6. With the expressions आवश्यक है *āvaśyak hai*, ज़रूरी है *zarūrī hai* 'it is necessary', उचित है *ucit hai*, मुनासिब है †*munāsib hai* 'it is appropriate', and others which in greater or less degree partake of the nature of directives:

आवश्यक है कि हम आज पूर्व के बारे में कुछ जानें । *āvaśyak hai ki ham āj pūrv ke bāre meṁ kuch jāneṁ*, It is necessary for us to know something about the East today.

[1] For perfective subjunctive forms such as हो गया हो *ho gayā ho* see Supplement II, p. 172.

[2] सो *so* is an old demonstrative, little used in the standard language except in proverbial and gnomic expressions.

[3] और *aur* is stressed.

[4] See Supplement III, p. 179.

ग्रौर उचित है कि इस उद्देश्य से एक भारतीय भाषा सीख लें। *aur ucit hai ki is uddeśya se ek bhārtīy bhāṣā sīkh lem̐*, And it is appropriate that with this purpose we should learn an Indian language.

## THE VERB लगना *lagnā*

The basic meaning of this intransitive verb can be generalized as 'to be applied'. It occurs in a very wide range of expressions, a selection of which is given below. The common collocation of लगना *lagnā* with a preceding oblique case infinitive is noted separately.

1. The following sentences exemplify very common usages of लगना *lagnā*. Subjects of equivalent English expressions showing transitive verbs usually correspond to oblique case nouns or pronouns with को *ko* (or equivalent pronominal object forms), in initial sentence position in sentences of neutral style and emphasis. Such oblique case forms are often not expressed if the sense of a sentence is clear.

ग्रापको हिंदुस्तान कैसा लगता है? *āpko hindustān kaisā lagtā hai?* How do you like India?

ग्रच्छा लगता है। *acchā lagtā hai*, I like it.

यहाँ मन लगता है। *yahām̐ man lagtā hai*, I feel at home here (my heart is engaged, attached, here).

लगता है (कि) यह मकान खाली है। *lagtā hai (ki) yah makān k͟hālī hai*, It seems as if this house is empty.[1]

बच्चा माँ जैसा लगता है। *baccā mām̐ jaisā lagtā hai*, The child looks like his mother.[2]

डाकखाने जाने में कितनी देर लगेगी? *ḍākk͟hāne jāne mem̐ kitnī der lagegī?* How long will it take to get to the post office?

कोई पाँच मिनट लगेंगे। *koī pām̐c minaṭ lagem̐ge*, It'll take about five minutes.

उसको चोट लगी। *usko coṭ lagī*, He got hurt.

उसे ठंड लगी है। *use ṭhaṇḍ lagī hai*, He's got a cold.

मुझे ठंड लग रही है। *mujhe ṭhaṇḍ lag rahī hai*, I'm cold; I'm getting cold.

पत्थर के मकानों में भी ग्राग लग सकती है। *patthar ke makānom̐ mem̐ bhī āg lag saktī hai*, Even stone houses can catch fire.

[1] Linking कि *ki*, जैसे *jaise* introducing clauses dependent on लगना *lagnā*, मालूम होना *mālūm honā*, etc., are frequently dropped in colloquial usage; see p. 96.

[2] जैसा *jaisā* is used postpositionally with माँ *mām̐* here; see p. 84.

मुझे भूख लगी है। *mujhe bhūkh lagī hai*, I am hungry.

मुझे प्यास लगी है। *mujhe pyās lagī hai*, I am thirsty.

(*a*) Note the use of the perfective participle in the last two sentences. Cf. the following sentences:

मुझे ग्यारह बजे के क़रीब भूख लगती है। *mujhe gyārah baje ke qarīb bhūkh lagtī hai*, I get hungry about eleven o'clock.

मुझे प्यास लग रही है। *mujhe pyās lag rahī hai*, I'm getting thirsty.

2. Collocating with a preceding oblique case infinitive, लगना *lagnā* has the sense 'begin'. This type of collocation is extremely frequent.

कुछ क्षण चुप रहने के बाद वह बोलने लगा। *kuch kṣaṇ cup rahne ke bād vah bolne lagā*, After a few moments' silence he began to speak.

उसको प्यास लगने लगी। *usko pyās lagne lagī*, He began to feel thirsty.

दिन लंबे होने लगे। *din lambe hone lage*, The days started getting long, longer.

(*a*) Where personal subjects are involved collocations of oblique case infinitive with following लगना *lagnā* are equivalent in sense to, and usually interchangeable with, those of infinitive with following शुरू, आरंभ करना *śurū, ārambh karnā*, e.g. in the first example above. Where non-personal subjects are involved, e.g. in the last two examples, use of लगना *lagnā* is normal.

(*b*) Collocations of oblique case infinitive with following लगना *lagnā* are negatived only rather rarely; any negative precedes the infinitive in sentences of neutral style and emphasis.

(*c*) लगना *lagnā*, being intransitive, is of course not used in construction with ने *ne*.

## THE VERBS देना *denā* AND पाना *pānā* WITH PRECEDING OBLIQUE CASE INFINITIVES

1. देना *denā* often collocates with preceding oblique case infinitives in locutions expressing the granting of permission, and containing pronouns or nouns in oblique case with को *ko* (or equivalent pronominal object forms). It occurs in both active and passive (impersonal) constructions.

मैंने उसे जाने दिया। *maiṁne use jāne diyā*, I let him go, allowed him to go.

उसको जाने दिया गया था। *usko jāne diyā gayā thā*, He was allowed to go (it was granted to him to go).

मेरे पिता जी मुझे सिग्रेट नहीं पीने देते थे। *mere pitā jī mujhe sigreṭ nahīṁ pīne dete the*, My father used not to let me smoke cigarettes.

मैंने उसे जाने नहीं दिया। *maiṁne use jāne nahīṁ diyā*, I didn't let him go.

(*a*) In sentences of neutral style and emphasis, negatives tend on the whole to precede infinitives, but some speakers feel that they can often also be placed between infinitives and the verb देना *denā* without acquiring particular affective value.

(*b*) Collocations of perfective forms of देना *denā* with oblique case infinitives are used in construction with ने *ne*.

2. पाना *pānā* collocating with preceding oblique case infinitives expresses possibility of performing an action; these collocations are equivalent to compound verbs with पाना *pānā* as dependent auxiliary, and are giving ground to the latter in the modern language.

मैं बनारस नहीं जाने पाया, क्योंकि मुझे इलाहाबाद में ही काम था। *maiṁ banāras nahīṁ jāne pāyā, kyoṁki mujhe ilāhābād meṁ hī kām thā*, It was impossible for me to go to Banaras, because I had work in Allahabad.

(*a*) Note that collocations of पाना *pānā* with oblique case infinitives are, like compound verbs showing पाना *pānā*, not used in construction with ने *ne*, and that they are very often negatived, the negative most commonly preceding the infinitive in sentences of neutral style and emphasis.

## VOCABULARY

हाल †*hāl*, m., state, condition
जय *jay*, f., victory; . . . की जय हो . . . *kī jay ho*, long live . . .
रस्सा *rassā*, m., rope
मुझे पता नहीं (है) *mujhe patā nahīṁ* (*hai*), I don't know, have no idea
सवारी *savārī*, f., passenger; vehicle
पूर्व *pūrv*, m., east
पश्चिम *paścim*, m., west
उद्देश्य **uddeśya*, m., aim, intention
मन *man*, m., mind; heart
डाकख़ाना †*ḍākk͟hānā*, m., post office
डाकघर *ḍākghar*, m., post office
पत्थर *patthar*, m., stone
आग *āg*, f., fire
भूख *bhūkh*, f., hunger
प्यास *pyās*, f., thirst
ठंड *ṭhaṇḍ*, f., cold; a cold

क्षण *kṣaṇ*, m., moment, instant
मदद †*madad*, f., help; मदद देना *madad denā* (*ko*), help
प्रगति *pragati*, f., progress
धूप *dhūp*, f., sun's heat or light
लू *lū*, f., hot, dusty wind which blows in north India in May and June; लू लगना *lū lagnā* (*ko*), get sunstroke.
संस्कृति *saṃskṛti*, f., culture
बर्फ़ *barf*, f., ice, snow
उपयुक्त *upayukt*, suitable
उचित *ucit*, appropriate
मुनासिब †*munāsib*, appropriate
ख़ाली *khālī* (invariable), empty; free (not engaged)
बाँधना *bāṁdhnā*, tie, bind
फ़ेल होना *fel honā*, fail (examination)
पिघलना *pighalnā*, intr., melt
संभवत: *sambhavataḥ*, probably, perhaps
आसान *āsān*, easy, simple
बुनियादी *buniyādī* (invariable), basic; elementary
का अध्ययन करना *kā adhyayan karnā*, study

## EXERCISE 39

मैं चाहता हूँ कि आप उसे वह पत्र दिखाएँ। मैं उसको मदद देना चाहता था। वह शायद कल आए। वह शायद कल आएगा। उचित ही है कि आप भारत जाने से पहले एक भारतीय भाषा बोल सकें। मुझे वहाँ जाने में आधा घंटा लगा। लौटने में कितना समय लगेगा? अगर मैं सीधा जाऊँ तो इससे कम समय लगेगा। मालूम होता है, आप हिंदी लिखने में प्रगति कर रहे हैं। मुझे प्यास लगी है। चूँकि उसने सुबह से कुछ नहीं खाया था, इसलिए उसे भूख लगने लगी। सारा दिन धूप में रहने से उसे लू लग गई।

## EXERCISE 40

I want to study Indian culture. I want my son to study Indian culture. Would you like me to show him that letter? Shall I ask[1] him to write you a letter? It will probably take you at least a month to learn to read and write[2] elementary Hindi. The snow began to melt in February. We're cold. His mother didn't let him go until his father had returned.[3]

[1] कहना *kahnā*.
[2] Use सीखना *sīkhnā* with preceding direct case infinitives.
[3] Perfective verb, rather than perfective past.

# LESSON XXII

## COMPOSITE VERBAL EXPRESSIONS WITH रहना *rahnā*, जाना *jānā* (contd.), करना *karnā*, चाहना *cāhnā*

1. *With* रहना rahnā

COLLOCATIONS of participles (almost always imperfective) with following forms of the verb रहना *rahnā* stress the element of continuity in an action extending over a period of time. They are extremely common. Tense and aspectual and modal reference are determined by the form of रहना *rahnā* used.

वह दिन भर काम करता रहा । *vah din bhar kām kartā rahā*, He kept working, worked, all day long.[1]

वह दिन भर काम करती रहती थी । *vah din bhar kām kartī rahtī thī*, She used to work all day long.

वे दिन भर काम करते रहते हैं । *ve din bhar kām karte rahte haiṁ*, They work all day long.

जागते रहो! *jāgte raho!* Keep alert! (the night watchman's cry)

(*a*) Only those few perfective participles which express present state (see p. 19) are used in this way.

लड़की एक घंटा वहाँ बैठी रही । *laṛkī ek ghaṇṭā vahāṁ baiṭhī rahī*, The girl stayed sitting there for an hour.

वहाँ किसी के न मिलने के बावुजूद वे ठहरे रहे । *vahāṁ kisī ke na milne ke bāvujūd ve ṭhahre rahe*, They went on waiting in spite of not finding anyone there.

वह दिन भर बिस्तर पर पड़ा रहेगा । *vah din bhar bistar par paṛā rahegā*, He'll lie on his bed (bedding) all day.

2. *With* जाना jānā (*contd.*)

Similar collocations of imperfective participles with forms of the verb जाना *jānā* stress rather the progressive nature of an action extending over a period of time, the way in which it advances from stage to stage. They too are extremely common.

वह काम करता गया, और मैं देखता गया । *vah kām kartā gayā, aur maiṁ dekhtā gayā*, He carried on with his work, and I kept on watching.

[1] For दिन भर *din bhar* see Supplement III, p. 179.

(*a*) The same English sentence may often serve as translation equivalent of Hindi sentences containing composite verbal expressions with either रहना *rahnā* or जाना *jānā*, but there is a difference in the implication of such Hindi sentences.

3. *With* करना karnā

Collocations of perfective participles showing invariable final -*ā* with following forms of the verb करना *karnā* stress the habitual nature of a given action. These also are very common.

हम हिंदी ही बोला करते हैं, इसलिए अब अच्छी तरह बोलने लगे हैं । *ham hindī hī bolā karte haiṁ, islie ab acchī tarah bolne lage haiṁ*, We normally talk in Hindi, so now we're beginning to speak well.

पहले मेरे यहाँ आया करती थी, अब नहीं आती । *pahle mere yahāṁ āyā kartī thī, ab nahīṁ ātī*, She used to visit me frequently but doesn't any more.[1]

अपना काम अच्छी तरह किया करो । *apnā kām acchī tarah kiyā karo*, Always do your work well.

(*a*) Collocations of this type based on the verb जाना *jānā* show जाया *jāyā* (not गया *gayā*) as first element.

दिल्ली में रहता हूँ, लेकिन कलकत्ते जाया करता हूँ । *dillī meṁ rahtā hūṁ, lekin kalkatte jāyā kartā hūṁ*, I live in Delhi, but I'm always going to Calcutta.

(*b*) Perfective forms of these collocations are relatively rare, and where they occur are not used in construction with ने *ne* (their sense being fundamentally the expression of habitual action).

तुम्हारे पूर्वज घास छीला किए! *tumhāre pūrvaj ghās chīlā kie!* Your forefathers scraped grass! (did menial work)

4. *With* चाहना cāhnā

Collocations of perfective participles showing invariable final -*ā* with following forms of the verb चाहना *cāhnā* express the idea that a given action is about to occur. There are other, more common ways of expressing

[1] मेरे यहाँ *mere yahāṁ*, adverbial phrase meaning 'at, to, my place, house'. Similarly आपके यहाँ *āpke yahāṁ*, उसके यहाँ *uske yahāṁ*, etc.

this idea,[1] and these collocations are much less frequent than any of the above three types.

दो बजा चाहते हैं । *do bajā cāhte haiṁ*, It's about to strike two, two is about to strike.

(*a*) Collocations of this type based on the verb जाना *jānā* show जाया *jāyā* as first element.

मैं बाहर जाया चाहता हूँ । *maiṁ bāhar jāyā cāhtā hūṁ*, I'm about to go out.

## VOCABULARY

पूर्वज *pūrvaj*, m., ancestor
घास *ghās*, f., grass
राजपूत *rājpūt*, m., and adj., Rajput
छीलना *chīlnā*, scrape, pare
दिन भर *din bhar*, all day
ज्यों-ज्यों . . . त्यों-त्यों *jyoṁ-jyoṁ* . . . *tyoṁ-tyoṁ*, in proportion as . . . so
के बावुजूद *ke* †*bāvujūd*, in spite of
हर कोई *har koī*, everyone

## EXERCISE 41

बारिश दो दिन होती रही । जब तक हम भारत न गए तब तक हिंदी पढ़ते रहे । हिंदी पढ़ते रहिए! ज्यों-ज्यों दिन लंबे होते जाते हैं, त्यों-त्यों रातें छोटी होती जाती हैं । जब मैं उत्तर भारत में रहता हूँ तो हिंदी बोला करता हूँ ।

## EXERCISE 42

I lie in bed till eight o'clock each day. At that time war was always going on between the Rajput rajahs. We began to speak in Hindi and went on in Hindi until the end of the hour.[2] Please make a habit of learning ten new words every day. I keep asking everyone this question. What is the answer to it?[3]

[1] See Lessons XIX, p. 120; XXV, p. 154.

[2] घंटे के ख़त्म होने तक *ghaṇṭe ke khatm hone tak* 'until the hour's ending'.

[3] To it: use इसका *iskā*.

# LESSON XXIII

## REDUPLICATIVE EXPRESSIONS

REDUPLICATION is a frequent syntactic device in Hindi sentences, and generally has a distributive connotation. Words belonging to a wide range of grammatical categories may be reduplicated, and types of translation equivalent vary greatly. Reduplicative expressions will often be found hyphenated. Careful users of Hindi will in general hyphenate those which they feel refer to a collective unity more readily than those which they feel refer to an aggregate of individual items.

आपने उनसे क्या क्या बातें कीं? *āpne unse kyā kyā bātem̐ kīm̐?* What (various things) did you talk about with them?

वहाँ कौन कौन लोग थे? *vahām̐ kaun kaun log the?* Who were there?

गाड़ियाँ किस किस वक़्त चलती हैं? *gāṛiyām̐ kis kis vaqt caltī haim̐?* When do the trains leave?

उनमें कोई कोई हँसता था, कोई कोई रोता था। *unmem̐ koī koī ham̐stā thā, koī koī rotā thā,* Some of them were laughing, some were weeping.

किन्हीं किन्हीं गाँवों में तालाब नहीं है। *kinhīm̐ kinhīm̐ gām̐vom̐ mem̐ tālāb nahīm̐ hai,* In some (few, or unimportant) villages there's no tank.[1]

भारत में कहाँ कहाँ घूमे? *bhārat mem̐ kahām̐ kahām̐ ghūme?* Where have you been in India? (to what different places)

लड़कों को पचास पचास पैसे मिले। *laṛkom̐ ko pacās pacās paise mile,* The boys got fifty pice each.

एक एक लड़के को पचास पचास पैसे मिले। *ek ek laṛke ko pacās pacās paise mile,* Each boy got fifty pice.

आपको लंदन में तरह तरह के मुहल्ले मिलेंगे। *āpko landan mem̐ tarah tarah ke muhalle milem̐ge,* You'll find various types of suburb in London.

मैं रास्ते के किनारे किनारे चला। *maim̐ rāste ke kināre kināre calā,* I kept to the edge of the road (all the way).

वे अपने अपने कामों में व्यस्त हैं। *ve apne apne kāmom̐ mem̐ vyast haim̐,* They're busy with their (respective) tasks.

उसके बड़े बड़े कान हैं। *uske baṛe baṛe kān haim̐,* He has big ears.

आप धीरे धीरे बोलेंगे तो मैं समझूँगा। *āp dhīre dhīre bolem̐ge to maim̐ samjhūm̐gā,* If you speak slowly I'll understand.

[1] For किन्हीं *kinhīm̐* see p. 44.

लड़की ने सिसक सिसकर अपनी कहानी सुनाई । *laṛkī ne sisak sisakkar apnī kahānī sunāī*, Sobbing continuously, the girl told her story.[1]

हम धूप में चलते चलते थक गए । *ham dhūp meṁ calte calte thak gae*, We got tired walking in the sun (walking so long, continuously, etc.).

(*a*) In some cases reduplication does have intensive force: e.g.

गरम गरम चाय ले आओ! *garm garm cāy le āo!* Bring some tea, really hot!

But in most such cases a distributive idea is already present in the sentence: e.g.

उस खेत में बहुत-से बड़े बड़े पेड़ हैं । *us khet meṁ bahut-se baṛe baṛe peṛ haiṁ*, There are a lot of very big trees in that field.[2]

(*b*) A few expressions of reduplicative structure are based on oblique case forms: e.g.

दिनों-दिन *dinoṁ-din*, day by day

के बीचों-बीच *ke bīcoṁ-bīc*, in the very middle of

(*c*) One or two common expressions contain the Persian preposition ब *ba* or a corrupted form of it: e.g.

दिनबदिन †*dinbadin*, day by day
रंगबिरंगा †*raṅgbiraṅgā*, many-coloured
हफ़्ते बहफ़्ते †*hafte bahafte*, week by week

## THE CONJUNCTION तो *to*

Correlative usages of this conjunction have been noted above.[3] It is also often used in non-correlative constructions, as a link between loosely connected sentences or parts of one sentence. Two general types of usage of तो *to* can be distinguished.

1. In initial sentence or clause position, तो *to* furnishes a semantically colourless link with what precedes. (Its correlative usages fall under this heading.) English translation equivalents depend on the sentence context.

अगर वह आए, तो मुझे खबर दीजिए । *agar vah āe, to mujhe k͟habar dījie*, If he comes, please let me know.

[1] Reduplicated absolutives show the first absolutive in stem form; cf. p. 90, n. 2.
[2] The form बहुत-से *bahut-se* 'many' is explained in Lesson XXIV, pp. 147 f.
[3] Lesson XX, pp. 123 ff.

वे चलने लगे, तो मुझे उनसे बात करने का अवसर मिला। *ve calne lage, to mujhe unse bāt karne kā avasar milā*, He was going off when I got the chance to have a few words with him.

सभ्यता मनुष्यों को सब प्रकार से आराम देती है, तो भी वे असंतुष्ट रहते हैं। *sabhyatā manuṣyoṁ ko sab prakār se ārām detī hai, to bhī ve asantuṣṭ rahte haiṁ*, Civilisation gives men all kinds of comforts, but still they are unsatisfied.[1]

(*a*) Note the very common expression नहीं तो *nahīṁ to* 'otherwise', representing (अगर) नहीं, तो . . . (*agar*) *nahīṁ, to* . . . 'if not, then . . .'. Colloquially this expression is often contracted to the single word नहीं *nahīṁ* in initial position in its clause.

अपना काम देखो, नहीं (तो) अच्छा न होगा! *apnā kām dekho, nahīṁ* (*to*) *acchā na hogā!* Pay attention to your work, or there'll be trouble!

2. In non-initial sentence or clause position, तो *to* usually suggests that the given sentence or clause expresses an idea at variance in some way with what precedes (whether the content of a locution, an unexpressed thought or an action), or modifying it in some way.

बात तो यह है कि . . . *bāt to yah hai ki* . . . The fact is that . . . (contrary to what has been supposed)

नहीं, नहीं, मैं तो वैसे ही मज़ाक़ कर रहा था! *nahīṁ, nahīṁ, maiṁ to vaise hī mazāq kar rahā thā!* No, no, I was just joking![2]

(*a*) तो *to* may occur both initially and non-initially in a phrase or sentence.

हामिद के लिए कुछ नहीं है, तो दो पैसे का दूध तो चाहिए ही। *hāmid ke lie kuch nahīṁ hai, to do paise kā dūdh to cāhie hī*, There is nothing (available) for Hamid, but he does certainly need two pice worth of milk.[3]

(*b*) तो *to* may occur in non-initial position in a sentence not connected with any preceding utterance or action.

आप अच्छे तो हैं? *āp acche to haiṁ?* Are you getting on all right? (I expect you are, but please confirm it)

Here the force of तो *to* is to reduce the content of the inquiry, which is quite conventionalised and hardly a request for information.

[1] For तो भी *to bhī* 'but even so' see further Supplement III, p. 180.

[2] For वैसे ही *vaise hī* see Supplement III, p. 167.

[3] From the short story ईदगाह *Īdgāh*, by Premcand (1880–1936).

## THE EMPHATIC ENCLITIC ही *hī* (contd.)

The general function of ही *hī* as an enclitic of restrictive force, stressing the importance of the word or syntactic group immediately preceding it in a sentence, has been indicated above.[1]

1. Some examples illustrating its use with different grammatical forms, and its wide range of possible translation equivalents, are given in this section.

बनारस के लोग हिंदी ही बोलते हैं । *banāras ke log hindī hī bolte haiṁ*, The people of Banaras of course speak Hindi.

शहर पास ही है । *śahr pās hī hai*, The city is quite near, very near.

आपने जो इंतज़ाम किया है, वह बहुत ही अच्छा है । *āpne jo intazām kiyā hai, vah bahut hī acchā hai*, The arrangements you've made are excellent.

वह अपनी ही किताब लाया । *vah apnī hī kitāb lāyā*, He brought his own book.

वह अच्छे आदमी नहीं थे, लेकिन वकील तो अच्छे थे ही । *vah acche ādmī nahīṁ the, lekin vakīl tō acche the hī*,[2] He wasn't a good man, but certainly was a good lawyer.

वह मन ही मन सोचने लगा कि . . . *vah man hī man socne lagā ki . . .*, The thought occurred to him that . . . (he started to think in his heart that . . .)

उस काम के लिए तीन ही आदमी कम होंगे । *us kām ke lie tīn hī ādmī kam hoṁge*, Three men, only three men, will be too few for that job.

उसे उस काम के लिए एक ही रुपया मिला । *use us kām ke lie ek hī rupayā milā*, He only got one rupee for that work.

मैं आपसे जो कह रहा हूँ, उसे समझ ही गए होंगे । *maiṁ āpse jo kah rahā hūṁ, use samajh hī gae hoṁge*, You'll certainly have understood what I'm saying to you.

2. ही *hī* coalesces with some personal and demonstrative pronominal forms. The emphatic forms of the personal and demonstrative pronouns are as follows:

| | | | | | | |
|---|---|---|---|---|---|---|
| Sg. Dir. | मैं ही | *maiṁ hī* | तू ही | *tū hī* | वही | *vahī* |
| Obl. | मुझी | *mujhī* | तुझी | *tujhī* | उसी | *usī* |
| Obj. | मुझे ही | *mujhe hī* | तुझे ही | *tujhe hī* | उसे ही | *use hī* |
| Poss. | मेरा ही | *merā hī* | तेरा ही | *terā hī* | उसी का | *usī kā* |

[1] Lesson V, pp. 27 f.

[2] Affective word-order.

| | | | | | | | |
|---|---|---|---|---|---|---|---|
| Pl. | Dir. | हम ही | *ham hī* | तुम ही | *tum hī* | वे ही | *ve hī* |
| | Obl. | हमीं | *hamīṁ* | तुम्हीं | *tumhīṁ* | उन्हीं | *unhīṁ* |
| | Obj. | हमें ही | *hameṁ hī* | तुम्हें ही | *tumheṁ hī* | उन्हें ही | *unheṁ hī* |
| | Poss. | हमारा ही | *hamārā hī* | तुम्हारा ही | *tumhārā hī* | उन्हीं का | *unhīṁ kā* |

| | | | | | |
|---|---|---|---|---|---|
| Sg. | Dir. | यही | *yahī* | आप ही | *āp hī* |
| | Obl. | इसी | *isī* | आप ही | *āp hī* |
| | Object | इसे ही | *ise hī* | आपको ही | *āpko hī* |
| | Possessive | इसी का | *isī kā* | आपका ही | *āpkā hī* |
| Pl. | Dir. | ये ही | *ye hī* | आप ही | *āp hī* |
| | Obl. | इन्हीं | *inhīṁ* | आप ही | *āp hī* |
| | Object | इन्हें ही | *inheṁ hī* | आपको ही | *āpko hī* |
| | Possessive | इन्हीं का | *inhīṁ kā* | आपका ही | *āpkā hī* |

आप उन्हीं पुस्तकों को पढ़िए । *āp unhīṁ pustkoṁ ko paṛhie*, Please read those same books, those very books.

यही कारण है कि हम आपका प्रस्ताव नहीं स्वीकार कर सकते । *yahī kāraṇ hai ki ham āpkā prastāv nahīṁ svīkār kar sakte*, This is the reason we can't accept your suggestion.

हम आपका प्रस्ताव इसीलिए नहीं स्वीकार कर सकते । *ham āpkā prastāv isīlie nahīṁ svīkār kar sakte*, We can't accept your suggestion for this reason.

उसी समय मेरे पिता जी आगरे में थे । *usī samay mere pitā jī āgre meṁ the*, At that very time, that particular time, my father was in Agra.

उन्हीं दिनों में उनके शत्रु लड़ाई की तैयारियाँ कर रहे थे । *unhīṁ dinoṁ meṁ unke śatru laṛāī kī taiyāriyāṁ kar rahe the*, During that very period their enemies were making preparations for war.

मैं लाल मिर्च खा ही नहीं सकता । *maiṁ lāl mirc khā hī nahīṁ saktā*, I can't eat red pepper at all.

3. Note that while emphatic ही *hī* may separate parts of composite and other verbal expressions (see last example above) it does not normally separate a word that it stresses from any post-position associated with it.

कवि के ही शब्दों में *kavi ke hī śabdoṁ meṁ*, in the poet's own words, the words of the poet himself

हम लड़ाई के पहले से ही यहाँ आया करते हैं । *ham laṛāī ke pahle se hī yahāṁ āyā karte haiṁ*, We've been coming here since even before the war.

But while this is the most general usage, it is not invariably followed.

4. Notice particularly the frequent collocation of oblique case imperfective participles in *-e* with following ही *hī*, in sentences whose most direct English translation equivalent usually contains the phrase 'as soon as'. Its use is straightforward in sentences which refer throughout to activity on the part of the same persons or things. Whatever the gender and number of the sentence subject, the participle is always in the *-e* form (these being adverbial, not adjectival expressions).

मैं आते ही काम करने लगा। *maiṁ āte hī kām karne lagā*, I started work as soon as I arrived.

आते ही मैं काम करने लगा। *āte hī maiṁ kām karne lagā*, As soon as I arrived I started work.

मैं आते ही काम करने लगी। *maiṁ āte hī kām karne lagī*, I started work as soon as I arrived (f. sg. subject).

हम आते ही काम करने लगीं। *ham āte hī kām karne lagīṁ*, We started work as soon as we arrived (f. pl. subject).

(*a*) Where a sentence of this sort describes the activity of different persons or things we usually find not a direct case noun or pronoun associated with the participle, but the corresponding possessive form. Again the participle is always in the *-e* form.

वह मेरे आते ही काम करने लगा। *vah mere āte hī kām karne lagā*, He started work as soon as I arrived.

मेरी बहन के आते ही मैंने आपका हाल पूछा। *merī bahn ke āte hī maiṁne āpkā hāl pūchā*, As soon as my sister came I asked how you were.

There are exceptions to this, however, especially where non-personal subjects and participles of intransitive verbs are involved: e.g.

नज़र मिलते ही उसने आँखें झुका लीं। *nazar milte hī usne āṁkheṁ jhukā līṁ*, As soon as (my) glance met (hers) she lowered her eyes.

5. Some common adverbs formed with ही *hī* are:

अभी *abhī*, now, at this particular time (see Lesson V)

तभी *tabhī*, then, at that particular time

कभी *kabhī*, sometimes; at some time

यहीं *yahīṁ*, here, at this particular place (यहाँ *yahāṁ* + ही *hī*)

वहीं *vahīṁ*, there, at that particular place (वहाँ *vahāṁ* + ही *hī*)

मैं कभी वहाँ गया था । *maiṁ kabhī vahāṁ gayā thā*, I went there once (on one occasion).

मैं कभी कभी वहाँ जाता था । *maiṁ kabhī kabhī vahāṁ jātā thā*, I used to go there sometimes.

वह इन दिनों कभी वहाँ नहीं जाता । *vah in dinoṁ kabhī vahāṁ nahīṁ jātā*, He never goes there these days.

मैं इलाहाबाद में विद्यार्थी था । वहीं हिंदी सीखी । *maiṁ ilāhābād meṁ vidyārthī thā. vahīṁ hindī sīkhī.* I was a student at Allahabad. It was there that I learned Hindi.

(*a*) Note from the third example the use of कभी *kabhī* in negatived sentences whose translation equivalent usually contains the word 'never'.

## VOCABULARY

मुहल्ला *muhallā*, m., suburb

किनारा *kinārā*, m., bank, edge

नज़र †*nazar*, f., sight; glance

कान *kān*, m., ear

नाक *nāk*, f., nose

अवसर *avasar*, m., opportunity, occasion

सभ्यता *sabhyatā*, f., civilisation

प्रकार *prakār*, m., type, kind; सब प्रकार से *sab prakār se*, in every way

मज़ाक़ *mazāq*, m., joke; मज़ाक़ करना *mazāq karnā*, joke

इंतज़ाम †*intazām*, m., arrangement, arrangements

वकील *vakīl*, m., lawyer

प्रस्ताव *prastāv*, m., suggestion

तैयारियाँ *taiyāriyāṁ*, f. pl., preparations; की तैयारियाँ करना *kī taiyāriyāṁ karnā*, prepare for

शब्द *śabd*, m., word

सिपाही *sipāhī*, m., soldier

तरक़्क़ी †*taraqqī*, f., progress

विश्वविद्यालय *viśvavidyālay*, m., university

माँग *māṁg*, f., request

व्यस्त *vyast*, busy

संतुष्ट *santuṣṭ*, satisfied

असंतुष्ट *asantuṣṭ*, dissatisfied

मिर्च *mirc*, f., pepper; chilli

सिसकना *sisaknā*, sob

झुकाना *jhukānā*, lower

धीरे, धीरे धीरे *dhīre, dhīre dhīre*, slowly

(के) लायक़ (*ke*) †*lāyaq*, suitable for; देखने लायक़ *dekhne lāyaq*, worth seeing (के *ke* is very often omitted in construction with infinitives)

मनुष्य *manuṣya*, m., man, human being

## EXERCISE 43

आप लोग[1] रोज़ दस दस नए शब्द सीखा कीजिए । हर एक राजपूत ने शत्रु के कई कई सिपाहियों को मार डाला । लोग दूर दूर से गंगा में स्नान करने के लिए इलाहाबाद आते हैं । आप तो हिंदी समझते हैं? गाड़ी छूटी तो ठीक वक़्त पर, लेकिन वह पाँच मिनट देर से पहुँची । आप रोज़ दस ही शब्द सीखने पर भी तरक़्क़ी करेंगे । मैंने उस रेस्टरेंट में कभी खाना नहीं खाया । मैं देखते ही आपको पहचान गया । उसके बैठते ही हम उससे तरह तरह के प्रश्न पूछने लगे ।

## EXERCISE 44

What did you do in the vacation? What people did you meet at the University yesterday? You'll find small villages in the countryside around the city which are worth seeing. He usually spoke slowly, but even then[2] I didn't always[3] understand. Speak slowly, otherwise I shan't understand. If you want to learn Hindi you should speak Hindi. On that very day my father arrived from Delhi. On hearing his request they burst out laughing. As soon as the train left I started reading my paper.

[1] For आप लोग *āp log*, pl., see Supplement I, p. 165.

[2] तब भी *tab bhī*.

[3] कभी कभी *kabhī kabhī*.

# LESSON XXIV

## THE ADJECTIVAL PARTICLE सा *sā*

THIS particle, which shows normal adjectival flexion, is found suffixed to various parts of speech, most commonly adjectives. It is used in a variety of ways, to express the notion of 'general resemblance'. It is usually written hyphenated to the word to which it is suffixed.

1. Suffixed to most adjectives it denotes, broadly speaking, a reduced degree of a quality.

यमुना नदी का नीला-सा पानी । *yamunā nadī kā nīlā-sā pānī*, the bluish water of the river Jumna

मैं एक अच्छी-सी किताब पढ़ रहा हूँ । *maiṁ ek acchī-sī kitāb paṛh rahā hūṁ*, I'm reading a rather good book, quite a good book.

मुझे दोनों मकान एक-से दिखाई देते हैं । *mujhe donoṁ makān ek-se dikhāī dete haiṁ*, Both houses look similar, much the same, to me.

2. Suffixed to quantitative adjectives (e.g. बहुत *bahut*, थोड़ा *thoṛā* 'a little') and sometimes other adjectives expressing bulk or size (especially बड़ा *baṛā*, छोटा *choṭā*), it introduces an element of vagueness to the interpretation of the quantity or size.

उसने मुझे बहुत रुपया दिया था । *usne mujhe bahut rupayā diyā thā*, He gave me a lot of money.

उसने मुझे बहुत-सा रुपया दिया था । *usne mujhe bahut-sā rupayā diyā thā*, He gave me a lot of money (it doesn't matter how much, more than sufficient, etc.).

माघ मेले में बहुत-से लोग आते हैं । *māgh mele meṁ bahut-se log āte haiṁ*, Many people come to the Māgh Melā.

उसने दो हिरण और एक बड़ा-सा शेर मारा । *usne do hiraṇ aur ek baṛā-sā śer mārā*, He killed two deer and a big tiger.

पहले उसकी एक छोटी-सी दूकान थी । *pahle uskī ek choṭī-sī dūkān thī*, Formerly he used to have a little shop.

(*a*) Note particularly that the form बहुत-से/सी *bahut-se/sī*, pl., 'many' is an adjective only, whereas unsuffixed बहुत *bahut* may be either an adjective or an adverb, and before an adjective is always interpreted as an adverb.

Compare the following sentences:

उस खेत में बहुत बड़े पेड़ हैं । *us khet meṁ bahut baṛe peṛ haiṁ*, There are some very big trees in that field.

उस खेत में बहुत-से बड़े पेड़ हैं । *us khet meṁ bahut-se baṛe peṛ haiṁ*, There are many big trees in that field.

(*b*) A sentence such as

मैं एक बहुत अच्छी-सी किताब पढ़ रहा हूँ । *maiṁ ek bahut acchī-sī kitāb paṛh rahā hūṁ*

means 'I am reading a very good book', not 'I am reading quite a good book'. Here सी *sī* is associated with the entire locution बहुत अच्छी *bahut acchī*, rather than with अच्छी *acchī* alone.

(*c*) Note the use of कोई-सा *koī-sā* 'any out of a number of possibilities or choices':

विद्यार्थी कोई-से तीन विषय पढ़ सकते हैं । *vidyārthī koī-se tīn viṣay paṛh sakte haiṁ*, Students can read any three subjects (of a syllabus, etc.).

(*d*) Similarly कौन-सा *kaun-sā* means 'which out of a number of possibilities or choices'.[1]

मैं श्रीवास्तव बोल रहा हूँ । – कौन-सा? *maiṁ śrīvāstav bol rahā hūṁ.—kaun-sā?* This is Śrīvāstav speaking.—Which Śrīvāstav?

3. Suffixed to other forms it expresses likeness.

उसका शेर-सा दिल है । *uskā śer-sā dil hai*, He has a heart like a lion.

उसका शेर का-सा दिल है । *uskā śer kā-sā dil hai*, He has a heart like a lion('s).

मुझ-सा ग़रीब आदमी यह कैसे कर सकता है? *mujh-sā garīb ādmī yah kaise kar saktā hai?* How can a poor man like me do this?

कुत्ते-से जीवन जीने से मर जाना बेहतर है । *kutte-se jīvan jīne se mar jānā behtar hai*. It is better to die than live one's life like a dog.[2]

बंदर दीवार पर नाच-सा उठा । *bandar dīvār par nāc-sā uṭhā*, The monkey started a kind of dance on the wall.[3]

[1] See p. 45.

[2] कुत्ते-से *kutte-se* 'like a dog'; से *se* in concord with कुत्ते *kutte*. Where सा *sā* suffixed to a noun has no other referend in its sentence than that noun, it regularly shows concord with it.

[3] नाच उठना *nāc uṭhnā* compound verb. सा *sā* shows the same concord as the verb.

(*a*) Note from the third and fourth examples above that सा *sā* is suffixed to oblique case forms of pronouns and nouns.

(*b*) In this type of expression the form जैसा *jaisā* is usually interchangeable with सा *sā*; also the rather less common सरीखा *sarīkhā* (with nouns and pronouns).

## INVERTED COMPOUND POSTPOSITIONS

The distinctive elements of certain compound postpositions whose first element is के *ke* will often be found dissociated from के *ke*, and preceding the word with which the compound postposition as a whole is syntactically related. This inversion is common colloquially, but is also not unknown in the more formal language. It is most frequent with the postpositions के बिना *ke binā* 'without', के मारे *ke māre* 'because of', के सिवा(य) *ke †sivā(y)* 'except for', के अलावा *ke †alāvā* 'apart from', के बग़ैर *ke †bagair* 'without', and के बजाय *ke †bajāy* 'instead of'.

1. Some examples of both constructions with nouns follow.

बिना आपकी सहायता के हम सफल न हो सके । *binā āpkī sahāytā ke ham saphal na ho sake*, We couldn't have been successful without your help.

आपकी सहायता के बिना हम सफल न हो सके । *āpkī sahāytā ke binā ham saphal na ho sake*, We couldn't have been successful without your help.

वह मारे ख़ुशी के नाचने लगा । *vah māre khuśī ke nācne lagā*, He began to dance for joy.

सिवा आपके मेरा कोई मित्र नहीं है । *sivā āpke merā koī mitr nahīṁ hai*, I have no friend but you.

आपके सिवा मेरा कोई मित्र नहीं है । *āpke sivā merā koī mitr nahīṁ hai*, I have no friend but you.

2. In the case of such postpositions associated with verbs there are further variations in the construction. The distinctive element of the postposition usually precedes an oblique case perfective participle (-*e* form) without following के *ke* (i.e. functions as a preposition). Most of the postpositions concerned may also be used according to the normal postpositional pattern, with preceding के *ke* and an oblique case infinitive (-*e* form).

सिवा यह कष्ट उठाए और क्या चारा है? *sivā yah kaṣṭ uṭhāe aur kyā cārā hai?* What can be done, what recourse is there, except to go to this trouble?[1] (there is no way of avoiding it)

[1] और *aur* is stressed in this and the following example.

यह कष्ट उठाने के सिवा ग्रौर क्या चारा है? *yah kaṣṭ uṭhāne ke sivā aur kyā cārā hai?* What can be done except to go to this trouble?

(*a*) Note that with preceding verbs the compound forms के बिना *ke binā*, के बग़ैर *ke bagair* are normally replaced by बिना *binā*, बग़ैर *bagair* alone, and that the verb forms in question are oblique case perfective participles (-*e* form), not infinitives.

बिना तकलीफ़ उठाए हम तरक़्क़ी नहीं करेंगे । *binā taklīf uṭhāe ham taraqqī nahīṁ kareṁge,* Without making an effort we won't progress.

तकलीफ़ उठाए बिना हम तरक़्क़ी नहीं करेंगे । *taklīf uṭhāe binā ham taraqqī nahīṁ kareṁge,* Without making an effort we won't progress.

## VOCABULARY

मेला *melā*, m., festival; fair; माघ मेला *māgh melā*, bathing festival held at the confluence of the Ganges and Jumna at Allahabad in the month of Māgh

हिरण *hiraṇ*, m., deer

शेर †*śer*, m., tiger; lion

दिल †*dil*, m., heart

कुत्ता *kuttā*, m., dog

बंदर *bandar*, m., monkey

कष्ट *kaṣṭ*, m., difficulty, inconvenience

तकलीफ़ †*taklīf*, f., difficulty, inconvenience

चारा *cārā*, m., recourse, course of action

डर *ḍar*, m., fear

पाँव *pāṁv*, m., foot, leg

संकोच *saṅkoc*, m., shyness, embarrassment

दाढ़ी *dāṛhī*, f., beard

कोट *koṭ*, m., coat

नीला *nīlā*, blue; dark blue or green

थोड़ा *thoṛā*, a little; थोड़ी-सी हिंदी *thoṛī-sī hindī*, a little Hindi

नाचना *nācnā*, dance

बँधना *baṁdhnā*, be tied, bound

नहाना *nahānā*, bathe

## EXERCISE 45

उन्होंने कई लंबी-सी कहानियाँ लिखी हैं । बहुत-से लोग हर एक दिन नदी में नहाते हैं । मैं थोड़ी-सी हिंदी जानता हूँ । उसके पाँव डर के कारण बँध-से गए । उसके ग्रलावा वहाँ कोई ग्रौर नहीं था । बिना काम किए किसी को तरक़्क़ी करने की ग्राशा नहीं हो सकती । संकोच के मारे वह ग्रक्सर हिंदी नहीं बोलता ।

## EXERCISE 46

He has quite a long beard. Many important people[1] work in that building. Apart from myself there was no one else there. Don't go out without putting on a coat.

[1] बड़े लोग *baṛe log.*

# LESSON XXV

## REFLEXIVE PRONOUNS

THE common reflexive pronouns are आप *āp* and its equivalents: the Persian loanword ख़ुद †*khud*, and the Sanskrit loanword स्वयं **svayaṃ*. These refer to nouns and pronouns in their sentences, in the same way as the possessive अपना *apnā*, and all have various translation equivalents: 'myself', 'yourself', 'himself', etc. Note that स्वयं *svayaṃ* is pronounced with final [m].[1]

1. All the above forms are used in direct case, often with following ही *hī*.

मैं यह काम आप (ही) करूँगा। *maiṁ yah kām āp (hī) karūṁgā*, I shall do this work myself.

हमने यह खाना ख़ुद ही बनाया। *hamne yah khānā khud (hī) banāyā*, We made this food ourselves, all on our own.

मैं कल आप दिल्ली जाऊँगी। *maiṁ kal āp dillī jāūṁgī*, I shall go to Delhi myself tomorrow. (f. subject)

तब वह स्वयं परलोक सिधारे। *tab vah svayaṃ parlok sidhāre*, Then he himself passed away (departed to the other world).

2. As oblique case forms of आप *āp* both अपने *apne* and अपने आप *apne āp* are found, the latter most commonly in conjunction with को *ko*. ख़ुद *khud* and स्वयं *svayaṁ*, which are invariable, are less freely used than these forms in oblique case.

मैं अपने को सहनशील आदमी समझता हूँ। *maiṁ apne ko sahnśīl ādmī samajhtā hūṁ*, I consider myself a tolerant man.

चोर ने अपने आप को छत पर छिपा लिया। *cor ne apne āp ko chat par chipā liyā*, The thief hid himself on the roof.

अपने लिए ऐसा करेंगे, दूसरों के लिए नहीं। *apne lie aisā kareṁge, dūsroṁ ke lie nahīṁ*, He'll do it for himself, but not for others.

(*a*) Since अपना *apnā* is itself a possessive, it and अपने आप *apne āp* combine differently with compound postpositions whose first element is के *ke*; see the last example above, and cf. Lesson VI, p. 34.

[1] Use of *anusvāra* to indicate final [m] is a Sanskrit spelling device.

(*b*) अपने आप *apne āp* is also used adverbially without following post-position, in the sense 'of one's own accord'.

मैं हिंदी अपने आप सीखने लगा । *maiṁ hindī apne āp sīkhne lagā*, I started learning Hindi of my own accord.

(*c*) Note that अपने आप *apne āp* is also used to some extent as a direct case form of the same force as आप *āp*, खुद *khud*, स्वयं *svayaṃ*. The sentence

मैंने यह काम अपने आप किया था । *maiṁne yah kām apne āp kiyā thā*

can mean either 'I did this work of my own accord' or (less commonly) 'I did this work myself'.

3. The collective noun आपस *āpas* 'kindred, fraternity' is used in locutions expressing mutuality or reciprocity of action, often with the postpositions में *meṁ*, का *kā*. An invariable adjectival derivative आपसी *āpsī* 'mutual, one another's' is also found.

भाइयों के लिए आपस में लड़ना-झगड़ना अच्छा नहीं है । *bhāiyoṁ ke lie āpas meṁ larṇā-jhagarṇā acchā nahīṁ hai*, It's not good for brothers to be fighting and quarrelling among themselves.

उनके आपसी संबंध अच्छे थे । *unke āpsī sambandh acche the*, They were on good terms with one another.

(*a*) Note the adverb and adjective परस्पर **paraspar*, a Sanskrit loanword synonymous with आपस में *āpas meṁ*, आपसी *āpsī* which is common in the written language.

4. An oblique case form आपे *āpe* is used as a noun meaning 'oneself' in some expressions with postpositions.

वह छोटी छोटी बात पर आपे से बाहर हो जाता है । *vah choṭī choṭī bāt par āpe se bāhar ho jātā hai*, He gets beside himself over trifles.

## THE FORMATIVE ELEMENT -वाला *-vālā*

This formative element makes derivatives used as both adjectives and nouns; it is particularly common colloquially, in association chiefly with nouns, the oblique form of infinitives, and adverbs. Some examples of its use follow:

1. With nouns and adverbs it indicates that these are in a general adjectival relationship to a following noun, expressed or understood.

टोपीवाला लड़का सबसे पीछे बैठा है। *ṭopīvālā laṛkā sabse pīche baiṭhā hai*, The boy with the hat is sitting right at the back.

मुझे एक पंद्रह पैसेवाला टिकट चाहिए। *mujhe ek pandrah paisevālā ṭikaṭ cāhie*, I want a 15 pice stamp, please.

लाल साड़ीवाली औरत कुएँ के पास बैठी थी। *lāl sāṛīvālī aurat kueṁ ke pās baiṭhī thī*, A woman wearing a red sari was sitting by the well.

वह ऊपरवाले कमरे में काम कर रहा है। *vah ūparvāle kamre meṁ kām kar rahā hai*, He is working in the room upstairs.

गाँववाले कभी शहर आ जाते हैं। *gāṁvvāle kabhī śahr ā jāte haiṁ*, The villagers sometimes come to the city.

स्टेशन के बाहर एक ही रिक्शेवाला इंतज़ार कर रहा था। *sṭeśan ke bāhar ek hī rikśevālā intazār kar rahā thā*, There was just one rickshaw-wallah waiting outside the station.

(*a*) Note that use of -वाला *-vālā* is often the simplest and concisest way of expressing what would be adjective phrases, or relative clauses involving expressions such as 'the one who', etc. in English.

(*b*) Nouns on which -वाला *-vālā* derivatives are formed show oblique case frequently. This usage is regular in the plural: e.g.

यह मकान चारा काटने की मशीनोंवाले सरदार लहना सिंह का है। *yah makān cārā kāṭne kī maśīnoṁvāle sardār lahnā siṃh kā hai* (*Ashk*), This house belongs to Sardār Lahnā Singh, the fodder-cutting-machine man.

In the singular the only nouns whose case is apparent are the masculines in final *-ā*; these sometimes, but not always, show oblique *-e* in conjunction with -वाला *-vālā*. Thus alongside रिक्शेवाला *rikśevālā* the form रिक्शावाला *rikśāvālā* exists, and is quite acceptable.

(*c*) Note that -वाला *-vālā*, being of adjectival force, is usually superfluous with adjectives themselves, but that it is sometimes used in informal language with adjectives.

उसकी दाढ़ी पहलेवाले साधु की तरह लंबी है। *uskī dāṛhī pahlevāle sādhu kī tarah lambī hai*, His beard is long, like (that of) the first *sādhu*.[1]

[1] पहलेवाले साधु की तरह *pahlevāle sādhu kī tarah*: the syntax of this phrase is explained in Supplement III, p. 178, paragraph (*b*).

(*d*) Quite frequently the two parts of -वाला *-vālā* derivatives are written or printed as separate words.

2. With verbs it has agentive force.

मैं इलाहाबाद का रहनेवाला हूँ। *maiṁ ilāhābād kā rahnevālā hūṁ*, I'm a resident of Allahabad.

हम भारत के रहनेवाले हैं। *ham bhārat ke rahnevāle haiṁ*, We are citizens of India.

हिंदी सीखनेवाले विद्यार्थियों को मेरी ओर से बधाई दीजिएगा। *hindī sīkhnevāle vidyārthiyoṁ ko merī ōr se badhāī dījiegā*, Please give my congratulations (congratulations from my side) to the students who are learning Hindi.

स्त्रियों और बच्चों पर तोड़े जानेवाले अत्याचारों की खबरों ने इस आग पर तेल का काम किया। *striyoṁ aur baccoṁ par toṛe jānevāle atyācāroṁ kī khabaroṁ ne is āg par tel kā kām kiyā* (Ashk), The news of the excesses being committed against the women and children added fuel to this fire.[1]

मैं यूनिवर्सिटी जानेवाला हूँ। *maiṁ yūnivarsiṭī jānevālā hūṁ*, I am about to go to the University; I am on my way to the University.

राधा भारत जानेवाली थी कि बीमार पड़ गई। *rādhā bhārat jānevālī thī ki bīmār paṛ gaī*, Rādhā was about to go to India when she fell ill.[2]

(*a*) Note the syntactic convenience of the use of -वाला *-vālā* with verbs, as with nouns and adverbs, in forming equivalent expressions to adjective phrases and relative clauses.

(*b*) Note from the second last example above that -वाला *-vālā* verbal derivatives followed by a form of the verb होना *honā* have the sense either 'to be about to . . .' or 'to be engaged in . . .', depending on context.

(*c*) The two parts of -वाला *-vālā* verbal derivatives can be separated by the enclitic ही *hī* (though some users of Hindi may prefer always to place ही *hī* after -वाला *-vālā*): e.g.

राधा भारत जाने ही वाली थी कि बीमार पड़ गई। *Rādhā bhārat jāne hī vālī thī ki bīmār paṛ gaī*, Rādhā was on the very point of leaving for India when she fell ill.

[1] तोड़े जानेवाले *toṛe jānevāle*, literally 'being broken'; तोड़ा जाना *toṛā jānā*, passive infinitive of तोड़ना *toṛnā*.

[2] For the use of कि *ki* here see Supplement III, p. 183.

But even where no ही *hī* intervenes they are, like -वाला *-vālā* derivatives based on nouns and adverbs, quite often written or printed as separate words.

## VOCABULARY

परलोक *parlok*, m., the other world, next world; परलोक सिधारना *parlok sidhārnā*, depart for the next world
चोर *cor*, m., thief
छत *chat*, f., roof
संबंध *sambandh*, m., connection, relationship
टिकट *ṭikaṭ*, m.f., stamp
साड़ी *sāṛī*, f., sari
रिक्शा *rikśā*, m., rickshaw
ताँगा *tāṁgā*, m., tonga (two-wheeled horse-drawn vehicle) [टाँगा *ṭāṁgā*]
मशीन *maśīn*, f., machine
बधाई *badhāī*, f., congratulations
तेल *tel*, m., oil
यूनिवर्सिटी *yūnivarsiṭī*, f., university
अत्याचार *atyācār*, m., excess, harsh action
सहनशील *sahnśīl*, tolerant
बीमार *bīmār*, ill
बनाना *banānā*, make, construct
छिपाना *chipānā*, trans., hide
झगड़ना *jhagaṛnā*, quarrel
मिलाना *milānā* (*se*), introduce (to), cause to meet with
पार करना *pār karnā*, trans., cross
पैदल *paidal*, adv., on foot
पैदल चलनेवाला *paidal calnevālā*, pedestrian

## EXERCISE 47

हम आपको अपने मित्रों से मिलाने के लिए स्वयं ले चलेंगे। ताँगावाले, मुझे कितने पैसे में स्टेशन ले चलोगे? उस लाल फूलवाले पेड़ का क्या नाम है? राजाओं में परस्पर लड़ाइयाँ होती रहती थीं।

## EXERCISE 48

He did this work himself, without anyone's help. Pedestrians must cross the street here.[1] Although the lower rooms are small, they are more comfortable than the upper ones. I'm going out. Give me five fifteen paise stamps, please.

[1] यहीं *yahīṁ* if 'here' is stressed; otherwise यहाँ *yahāṁ* (with different sense).

# LESSON XXVI

## NON-FINITE PARTICIPIAL CONSTRUCTIONS

IMPERFECTIVE and perfective participles frequently occur otherwise than as bases for members of the conjugational patterns of finite verbs noted in Lessons IV and V. They function then as independent (non-finite) units in sentences, and their syntax shows adjectival, substantival, and adverbial characteristics. The form हुआ *huā* may occur following and in the same concord as non-finite participles, in most cases where there is a clear implication that the participles denote a certain condition or a continued state of activity. If such an implication is strong, हुआ *huā* is more likely than not to occur.

The chief types of non-finite participial construction are illustrated below under separate headings according as they show (either wholly or predominantly) adjectival, substantival, or adverbial characteristics.

### 1. *Adjectival constructions*

The great majority of these are quite straightforward. Imperfective and perfective participles may be used attributively (preceding and forming syntactic units with nouns) or predicatively (otherwise).

चलती (हुई) गाड़ी से कूद पड़ना बेवक़ूफ़ी है । *caltī (huī) gāṛī se kūd paṛnā bevaqūfī hai*, To jump from a moving train is stupid, stupidity.

अच्छी तरह पढ़ी (हुई) किताब कभी भूली नहीं जाती । *acchī tarah paṛhī (huī) kitāb kabhī bhūlī nahīṁ jātī*, A book well read is never forgotten.

औरत गाती (हुई) आई । *aurat gātī (huī) āī*, The woman came singing, was singing as she came.

लड़का दौड़ा (हुआ) आया । *laṛkā dauṛā (huā) āyā*, The boy came running, at a run.

एक साधु ज़मीन पर बैठा (हुआ) दिखाई दे रहा था । दूसरा खड़ा (हुआ) था । *ek sādhu zamīn par baiṭhā (huā) dikhāī de rahā thā. dūsrā khaṛā (huā) thā.* One holy man could be seen sitting on the ground. The other was standing.[1]

यह किताब मेरी पढ़ी (हुई) है । *yah kitāb merī paṛhī (huī) hai*, I've read this book, this book is one I've read.

[1] The word खड़ा *khaṛā* 'standing' is an adjective, not a participle, but can be followed by हुआ *huā*.

(*a*) In the last example note the possessive form preceding the participle and denoting the activity of an agent other than the referend of the sentence subject.

(*b*) Note that some expressions showing adjectival concord of participles are adverbial in force, and that in these हुआ *huā* does not appear.

लौटते समय हम बात करने लगे । *lauṭte samay ham bāt karne lage*, On the way back we began to talk (at returning-time).

मैं जाती दफ़ा आपको अपनी पुस्तक दे दूंगा । *maiṁ jātī dafā āpko apnī pustak de dūṁgā*, I shall give you my book when I go (at going-time).

वह नाश्ता करते समय समाचारपत्र पढ़ता था । *vah nāśta karte samay samācarpatr paṛhtā thā*, He used to read the paper while he was having his breakfast.

चोर दबे पाँव मकान में घुस गया । *cor dabe pāṁv makān meṁ ghus gayā*, The thief crept stealthily into the house (with 'suppressed footsteps').

(*c*) Note particularly that participles qualifying oblique case nouns or pronouns are for the most part used only attributively. Predicative usages of participles with oblique case nouns or pronouns are adverbial, and are discussed below.

(*d*) Reduplicated participles are sometimes used adjectivally: e.g.

मैं दिल्ली में पड़ा पड़ा बेज़ार हो गया । *maiṁ dillī meṁ paṛā paṛā bezār ho gayā*, I got fed up with staying all the time in Delhi.

Adverbial construction of reduplicated participles, especially imperfective participles, is more common, however, as these tend to express states of activity engaged in, rather than to describe attributes of a person or object adjectivally. Examples are given below. Reduplicated participles are never extended with हुआ *huā*.[1]

2. *Substantival constructions*

The following sentences show participles functioning syntactically as nouns in that they are preceded by possessive forms or by the possessive postposition, or are followed by other postpositions, or function as sentence subject or object. The implication of the participles is frequently such that they are extendable with हुआ *huā*, while like other nouns they may serve

[1] No doubt because the reduplication itself already emphasizes the continuing nature of a condition or action.

also as the basis for oblique case adverbial constructions. Both direct and oblique case participles are found; of the latter, note particularly those preceded by a possessive form or expression, which characteristically denotes the activity of an agent other than the referend of the sentence subject.

*Direct case*

मरता क्या न करता? *martā kyā na kartā?* What wouldn't a dying man do?[1]

आप मेरा कहा (हुआ) मानिए। *āp merā kahā* (*huā*) *mānie*, Please accept what I say (what I have said).[2]

*Oblique case*

हम तकलीफ़ उठाए बिना आगे नहीं बढ़ेंगे। *ham taklīf uṭhāe binā āge nahīṁ baṛheṁge.* Without making an effort, taking trouble, we won't advance.[3]

गिरों को (गिरे हुओं को) उठाओ, सोतों को (सोते हुओं को) जगाओ! *giroṁ ko* (*gire huoṁ ko*) *uṭhāo, sotoṁ ko* (*sote huoṁ ko*) *jagāo!* Raise up the fallen, awaken the sleeping!

उसके आते ही मैं काम करने लगा। *uske āte hī maiṁ kām karne lagā*, As soon as he came I started work.[4]

वह मेरे रोके (हुए) न रुका। *vah mere roke* (*hue*) *na rukā*, I didn't succeed in stopping him (he didn't stop despite my trying to stop him).

सीता के जीते (हुए) घर में कोई कमी नहीं होती थी। *sītā ke jīte* (*hue*) *ghar meṁ koī kamī nahīṁ hotī thī*, While Sītā lived no want was felt in the home.

3. *Adverbial constructions*

It has been convenient to mention certain adverbial constructions above, but the majority can be most clearly presented in a separate section. In these constructions participles show final *-e* irrespective of the gender of the word to which they refer. Their function is to indicate that in conjunction with the action denoted by the finite verb a certain further condition or state of activity obtains. This function is usually not clearly

[1] For the use of करता *kartā* in this expression see Supplement II, p. 170.

[2] But आप मेरा कहना मानिए *āp merā kahnā mānie* would be a more common expression. मानना *mānnā* 'consider, accept as; believe; obey'.

[3] See Lesson XXIV, pp. 149 f.

[4] See Lesson XXIII, p. 144.

distinguishable from that of हुआ *huā*, and as a result most adverbial usages of participles may show following हुए *hue*.

In the case of adverbial constructions of participles it is useful to distinguish those based on imperfective from those based on perfective participles.

*Based on imperfective participles*

(i) In conjunction with direct case forms.

मैं आते ही काम करने लगा । *maiṁ āte hī kām karne lagā*, As soon as I arrived I started work.[1]

मैं यह कहते (हुए) डरता हूँ । *maiṁ yah kahte (hue) ḍartā hūṁ*, I'm afraid to say this.

औरत गाते (हुए) आ रही थी । *aurat gāte (hue) ā rahī thī*, The woman was coming along singing.

दोनों लड़कियाँ काम करते करते थक गईं । *donoṁ laṛkiyāṁ kām karte karte thak gaīṁ*, The two girls grew tired as they worked on.

लड़की दौड़ते दौड़ते आई । *laṛkī dauṛte dauṛte āī*, The girl came running up.

(*a*) Reduplicated participles are never extended with हुआ *huā*; see above.

(ii) In conjunction with oblique case forms.

राम ने किताबें मेज़ पर रखते (हुए) कहा कि . . . *rām ne kitābeṁ mez par rakhte (hue) kahā ki . . .*, (As he was) putting the books down on the table Rām said . . .

आप उसे आते (हुए) देखेंगे । *āp use āte (hue) dekheṁge*, You will see him, her, coming.

(*a*) Adverbial construction of predicatively used participles is normal in these cases, except that where definite direct objects are involved some Hindi speakers may optionally use participles in 'neutral' or 'impersonal' *-ā*, and might accordingly replace the second example above with the sentence

आप उसे आता (हुआ) देखेंगे । *āp use ātā (huā) dekheṁge.*

(*b*) Note especially the construction of participles with noun and pronoun forms followed by को *ko* (or equivalent pronominal object forms) which

[1] See Lesson XXIII, p. 144.

are not definite direct objects (cf. second example in subsection (ii) above); this construction typically expresses passage of time.

उसको विश्वविद्यालय में पढ़ते (हुए) दो वर्ष हो चुके हैं। *usko viśvavidyālay meṁ paṛhte (hue) do varṣ ho cuke haiṁ*, He has been studying at the university for two years now (two years have already passed while he has been studying at the university).

There are parallel usages of perfective participles; see below.

*Based on perfective participles*

Adverbial construction of perfective participles of transitive verbs is extremely common to denote states arising from the carrying out of actions.

(i) In conjunction with direct case forms.

लड़की साड़ी पहने (हुए) है। *laṛkī sāṛī pahne (hue) hai*, The girl is wearing a sari (in the state of having put on a sari).

लड़का टोपी पहने (हुए), चादर ओढ़े (हुए) था। *laṛkā ṭopī pahne (hue), cādar oṛhe (hue) thā*, The boy was wearing a hat and had a shawl wrapped round himself.

एक आदमी पाँव पर पाँव रखे (हुए) फ़र्श पर बैठा (हुआ) था। *ek ādmī pāṁv par pāṁv rakhe (hue) farś par baiṭhā (huā) thā*, A man was sitting on the floor with his legs crossed.

साधु हाथ उठाए (हुए) मंत्र जप रहा था। *sādhu hāth uṭhāe (hue) mantra jap rahā thā*, The holy man, hand held in the air, was reciting incantations.

मैं समझे (हुए) था कि ... *maiṁ samjhe (hue) thā ki . . .*, I thought, had thought that . . .

(*a*) Note that in very many cases where participles in this construction are followed by other verbs than होना *honā* they are replaceable with absolutives: e.g.

एक आदमी पाँव पर पाँव रखकर फ़र्श पर बैठा (हुआ) था। *ek ādmī pāṁv par pāṁv rakhkar farś par baiṭhā (huā) thā.*

(*b*) Compare with the first example in subsection (i) above the following sentences, showing ने *ne* and participles used as parts of finite verbs in concord with sentence objects:

लड़की ने साड़ी पहनी है। *laṛkī ne sāṛī pahnī hai*, The girl has put on a sari.

लड़की ने साड़ी पहन रखी है । *laṛkī ne sāṛī pahn rakhī hai*, The girl is wearing, has on a sari.[1]

(ii) In conjunction with oblique case forms.

उसने किताब हाथ में लिए (हुए) कहा कि . . . *usne kitāb hāth meṁ lie* (*hue*) *kahā ki* . . . , While holding the book in his hand he said . . .

उसने उसे सोए (हुए) देखा । *usne use soe* (*hue*) *dekhā*, He saw him, her, asleep.

(*a*) Adverbial construction is normal here, as with imperfective participles.

(*b*) Note the common adverbial construction of perfective participles (transitive or intransitive) with noun or pronoun forms followed by को *ko* (or equivalent pronominal object forms) which are not definite direct objects; this typically expresses passage of time. Cf. the parallel usage of imperfective participles illustrated above.

उसको विश्वविद्यालय में पढ़े (हुए) दो वर्ष हो चुके हैं । *usko viśvavidyālay meṁ paṛhe* (*hue*) *do varṣ ho cuke haiṁ*, Two years have (already) passed since he finished studying at the university.

मुझे यहाँ आए (हुए) एक महीना हो गया है । *mujhe yahāṁ āe* (*hue*) *ek mahīnā ho gayā hai*, It's a month since I came, I've been here a month.

आपको बनारस गए (हुए) कितने दिन हुए हैं? *āpko banāras gae* (*hue*) *kitne din hue haiṁ?* How long is it since you went to, have been in Banaras?

## VOCABULARY

बेवकूफ़ †*bevaqūf*, stupid

बेवकूफ़ी †*bevaqūfī*, f., stupidity

ज़मीन †*zamīn*, f., land

दफ़ा †*dafā*, f., time, occasion

नाश्ता *nāśtā*, m., breakfast, first light meal of the day

कमी *kamī*, f., want, shortage, deficiency

चादर *cādar*, f., shawl; sheet

मंत्र *mantra*, m., incantation, verse or utterance of religious significance

पुल *pul*, m., bridge

कुरता *kurtā*, m., collarless shirt

पाजामा *pājāmā*, m., light cotton trousers

गाय *gāy*, f., cow

लाठी *lāṭhī*, f., staff

बेज़ार *bezār*, displeased, bored

[1] For रखना *rakhnā* as dependent auxiliary see Lesson XVII, p. 104. (Note that this sentence is an equivalent of the first sentence given in subsection (i) above, but not of the sentence immediately preceding it in note (*b*.)

यूरोपीय *yūropīy*, noun (m.f.) and adj., European

तीखा *tīkhā*, sharp, piercing

नीचा *nīcā*, low; नीचा करना *nīcā karnā*, lower

दबना *dabnā*, be suppressed, restrained; दबे पाँव *dabe pāṁv*, stealthily

घुसना *ghusnā*, creep, slink

दौड़ना *dauṛnā*, run

बढ़ना *baṛhnā*, advance; rise

ओढ़ना *oṛhnā*, wrap round, wrap about one

जपना *japnā*, repeat mechanically (a god's name, an incantation)

कटना *kaṭnā*, be cut, cut off

चरना *carnā*, graze

देर से आना *der se ānā*, arrive late

## EXERCISE 49

बनारस से गाड़ियाँ गंगा का पुल पार करती हुई[1] देखी जा सकती हैं। एक कटा हुआ पेड़ मकान के सामने ज़मीन पर पड़ा था। लड़की रोती हुई मेरे पास आई। मैं यह कहते डरता हूँ। जब मैं उससे कल मिला, तब वह कुरता और पाजामा पहने था। आज तो वह संभवतः यूरोपीय कपड़े पहने होगा। मैंने उसे कभी दफ़्तर में देर से आते नहीं देखा। आपको भारत आए कितने दिन हो गए हैं? हमें मिले बहुत दिन हो गए हैं। मेरी ओर तीखी नज़र से देखते हुए उन्होंने कहा "मैं इसीलिए आपको वहाँ भेज रहा हूँ"। वह किताब हाथ में लिए कमरे के बाहर चला गया।

## EXERCISE 50

I saw a cow grazing. The women were singing as they worked. A holy man was sitting in front of the temple door with head bowed. The old man stood up, and walked off in the direction of the village with his staff in his hand. I've been studying Hindi for a month. It's two days since she finished the work.

[1] Or करते हुए *karte hue.*

# SUPPLEMENT

# I

## FURTHER ASPECTS OF THE GRAMMAR OF NOMINAL FORMS

1. *Feminine forms of nouns*

Words referring to animate beings often show variation in form to denote male and female sex. The most common feminine endings are:

(*a*) -*ī*

| | | | | | |
|---|---|---|---|---|---|
| लड़का | *laṛkā*, | boy | लड़की | *laṛkī*, | girl |
| बेटा | *beṭā*, | son | बेटी | *beṭī*, | daughter |
| पुत्र | *putr*, | son | पुत्री | *putrī*, | daughter |
| बंदर | *bandar*, | monkey | बंदरी | *bandarī*, | female monkey |

Sanskrit loanwords may show -*ī* as well as native Hindi words, e.g. पुत्री *putrī* above.

(*b*) -*iyā*

| | | | | | |
|---|---|---|---|---|---|
| बेटा | *beṭā*, | son | बिटिया | *biṭiyā*, | daughter |
| बूढ़ा | *būṛhā*, | old man | बुढ़िया | *buṛhiyā*, | old woman |
| कुत्ता | *kuttā*, | dog | कुतिया | *kutiyā*, | bitch |

Note that long vowels are frequently modified and double consonants shortened before -*iyā*; also that -*iyā* feminines may exist alongside -*ī* feminines. In this case they may have diminutive (affectionate or pejorative) force, but the use made of the forms varies.

(*c*) -*in*

| | | | | | |
|---|---|---|---|---|---|
| लोहार | *lohār*, | blacksmith | लोहारिन | *lohārin*, | blacksmith's wife |
| नाई | *nāī*, | barber | नाइन | *nāin*, | barber's wife |
| दूल्हा | *dūlhā*, | bridegroom | दुल्हिन | *dulhin*, | bride[1] |
| बाघ | *bāgh*, | tiger | बाघिन | *bāghin*, | tigress |
| मालिक | *mālik*, | master | मालकिन | *mālkin*, | mistress |

(*d*) -*nī*

| | | | | | |
|---|---|---|---|---|---|
| बाघ | *bāgh* | tiger | बाघनी | *bāghnī*, | tigress |
| हाथी | *hāthī*, | elephant | हथनी | *hathnī*, | she-elephant[2] |
| मास्टर | *māsṭar*, | schoolmaster | मास्टरनी | *māsṭarnī*, | schoolmistress |

[1] Note short -*u*-.
[2] Note short -*a*-.

For *-nī* the Sanskritic spelling *-inī* sometimes appears, e.g. in हथिनी *hathinī*. Note that *-nī* feminines may exist alongside *-in* feminines.

(*e*) *-āin*

| | | | |
|---|---|---|---|
| पंडित *paṇḍit*, | pandit | पंडिताइन *paṇḍitāin*, | pandit's wife |
| साह, साहु *sāh*, *sāhu*, | merchant | सहुआइन *sahuāin*, | merchant's wife[1] |

(*f*) *-ānī*

| | | | |
|---|---|---|---|
| नौकर *naukar*, | servant | नौकरानी *naukrānī*, | female servant |

(*g*) *-ā*

| | | | |
|---|---|---|---|
| छात्र *chātr*, | student | छात्रा *chātrā*, | student (f.) |

This suffix represents the common *-ā* ending of Sanskrit feminine nouns, see Lesson I. (A very few Persian or Arabic loanwords also happen to show feminines in *-ā*).

(*h*) *-trī*

| | | | |
|---|---|---|---|
| अभिनेता *abhinetā*, | actor | अभिनेत्री *abhinetrī*, | actress |

This suffix pairs almost exclusively with *-tā* of some masculine loanwords from Sanskrit (exemplified by दाता *dātā*, Lesson I).

(*i*) *-ikā*

| | | | |
|---|---|---|---|
| अध्यापक *adhyāpak*, | teacher | अध्यापिका *adhyāpikā*, | schoolmistress |
| लेखक *lekhak*, | writer | लेखिका *lekhikā*, | writer (f.) |

This suffix pairs with agentive *-ak* of Sanskrit loanwords.

(*j*) *-inī*

| | | | |
|---|---|---|---|
| विद्यार्थी *vidyārthī*, | student | विद्यार्थिनी *vidyārthinī* | student (f.) |

This suffix is quite rare in the spoken language (but see (*d*) above and section 8 following).

[1] Note short *-a-*.

Words referring to inanimate objects also sometimes occur in pairs; feminine members of such pairs usually denote smaller or more delicate varieties of objects. Some examples are:

| | | | | | |
|---|---|---|---|---|---|
| घंटा | *ghaṇṭā*, | bell; hour | घंटी | *ghaṇṭī*, | small bell |
| थाल | *thāl*, | large platter | थाली | *thālī*, | platter |
| रस्सा | *rassā*, | rope | रस्सी | *rassī*, | rope; string |

2. *Periphrastic plurals*

Periphrastic plurals, formed with the plural noun लोग *log* 'people', are quite common for nouns denoting members of classes or types of persons.

साधु लोग हर साल यहाँ आ जाते हैं । *sādhu log har sāl yahāṁ ā jāte haiṁ*, Holy men come here every year.

The locutions तुम लोग *tum log*, आप लोग *āp log* are very common where the reference of the pronouns is to a plural number of persons and not merely honorific, similarly हम लोग *ham log* where the reference is to more than two persons.

आप लोगों का कहना ठीक है । *āp logoṁ kā kahnā ṭhīk hai*, What you people say is correct.

3. *Two common usages of the pronoun* हम ham

(*a*) Quite frequently, especially in the eastern part of the Hindi language area, the first personal plural form हम *ham* is used with singular reference, i.e. as an equivalent of मैं *maiṁ*. This usage cannot be called 'incorrect', but should perhaps be avoided by foreigners.

(*b*) हम *ham* is quite often used by women in masculine plural verb concord, especially where an activity is felt to have a somewhat collective character.

4. *Use of adjectives as nouns*

This is common.

बेचारी क्या करेगी? *becārī kyā karegī?* What will the poor woman do?

हमारे जवान देश की रक्षा करेंगे । *hamāre javān deś kī rakṣā kareṁge*, Our soldiers will defend the country.[1]

[1] जवान *javān* 'young; young man; soldier'.

थानेवालों ने आकर कितनों को पकड़ा! *thānevālom̐ ne ākar kitnom̐ ko pakṛā!* What a lot of people the police came and arrested![1]

5. *Masculine nouns in final* -iyā: *orthography*

Nouns like डाकिया *ḍākiyā* 'postman', पहिया *pahiyā* 'wheel', etc. show alternative oblique singular and direct plural spellings without *-y-*, viz. डाकिए *ḍākie*, पहिए *pahie* etc., which are often preferred by careful users of the language. (The *-y-* represents a glide between vowels, whose presence between *i* and *e* is less obtrusive than between *i* and *ā*.)

6. *Concords implying unexpressed feminine nouns*

Such concords imply a noun of generalised sense, such as बात *bāt*, बार *bār*, as being understood, and are common colloquially: e.g.

उसकी एक भी नहीं चलती । *uskī ek bhī nahīm̐ caltī*, Nothing he wants to do is successful.

उसकी आजकल ख़ूब चल रही है । *uskī ājkal khūb cal rahī hai*, He's getting on splendidly these days.[2]

पिछले साल नैनीताल गया था । अबकी कश्मीर जाऊँगा । *pichle sāl nainītāl gayā thā. abkī kaśmīr jāūm̐gā*, Last year I went to Nainital. This time I'm going to Kashmir (on vacation, etc.)

7. *Some usages of pronominal adjectives*

(*a*) इतना *itnā* 'as many, much, as this'. This form, like most pronominal adjectives, functions as pronoun and adverb as well as adjective. Some further examples of its use are:[3]

इतना तो कहा जा सकता है कि . . . *itnā to kahā jā saktā hai ki* . . . , This much, at least, can be said, that . . .

इतने में मेरी बहन कमरे में आ गई । *itne mem̐ merī bahn kamre mem̐ ā gaī*, With this, with that, my sister came into the room.

वह अँधेरे से इतना डरती है कि . . . *vah am̐dhere se itnā ḍartī hai ki* . . . , She is so afraid of the dark that . . .

Note (last example) that इतना *itnā* may be used adverbially in direct case.

[1] थाना *thānā*, m., '(small) police station'.

[2] ख़ूब *khūb* 'splendid(ly), excellent(ly)'.

[3] See also p. 94.

(*b*) ऐसा *aisā* 'of this sort'; वैसा *vaisā* 'of that sort'.

मैंने कहा था कि वह फ़ेल हो जाएगा। और ऐसा ही हुआ। *maiṁne kahā thā ki vah fel ho jāegā. aur aisā hī huā*, I said he would fail. And that is just what happened.

वह ऐसे बोला कि मुझे ग़ुस्सा आ गया। *vah aise bolā ki mujhe gussā ā gayā*, He spoke in such a way that I grew angry.

ऐसा आदमी किसी काम के क़ाबिल नहीं है। *aisā ādmī kisī kām ke qābil nahīṁ hai*, Such a man is not capable of anything.

वैसे तो वह सच्चा बनता है, लेकिन वह झूठा आदमी है। *vaise to vah saccā bantā hai, lekin vah jhūṭhā ādmī hai*, It's like this: he seems to be a trustworthy person but is not.[1]

वैसे मैं बोलने आनेवाला नहीं था, लेकिन बोलना पड़ रहा है। *vaise maiṁ bolne ānevālā nahīṁ thā, lekin bolnā paṛ rahā hai*, Well, I didn't come to speak, but (I see) I have to.

मेरी बात बुरी न मानें, मैंने वैसे ही कह दी थी। *merī bāt burī na māneṁ, maiṁne vaise hī kah dī thī*, Don't take what I said amiss, I said it without thinking, casually.[2]

Note particularly the use of introductory वैसे *vaise*, वैसे तो *vaise to*, and वैसे ही *vaise hī* 'merely, simply; casually'. All these expressions are extremely common in the spoken language.

(*c*) कम *kam* 'little (of quantity), few'.

मैं कम हिंदी जानता हूँ। *maiṁ kam hindī jāntā hūṁ*, I know little Hindi.

वह कम किताबें पढ़ता है। *vah kam kitābeṁ paṛhtā hai*, He reads few books.

मैं अब वहाँ कम जाता हूँ। *maiṁ ab vahāṁ kam jātā hūṁ*, I go there little now.

(*d*) थोड़ा *thoṛā* 'a little; little'.

मुझे थोड़ी हिंदी आती है। *mujhe thoṛī hindī ātī hai*, I know a little Hindi.

मैं यह थोड़े ही जानता था कि आप यहाँ होंगे। *maiṁ yah thoṛe hī jāntā thā ki āp yahāṁ hoṁge*, I little knew that you would be here.

[1] बनना *bannā*, which is often a close equivalent of हो जाना *ho jānā*, here has the sense 'appear as, make a pretence of being . . .'; झूठा *jhūṭhā* 'false, lying; a liar'.

[2] मानना *mānnā* 'consider, accept as; believe; obey'.

थोड़ा *thoṛā* is mainly used adjectivally; as an adverb कम *kam* is more common.

The compound adjective थोड़ा-बहुत *thoṛā-bahut* is used in the sense 'a certain amount of'.

मैं थोड़ी-बहुत हिंदी जानता हूँ । *maiṁ thoṛī-bahut hindī jāntā hūṁ*, I know a certain amount of Hindi.

8. *Some Sanskrit endings used adjectivally in Hindi*

The Sanskrit feminine inflexional endings *-ā*, *-inī* (see 1(*g*), (*j*) above) and *-matī*, *-vatī* (with corresponding masculines in *-mān*, *-vān*, see pp. 196 f.) are sometimes used adjectivally, chiefly in formal language: e.g.

नागरी प्रचारिणी सभा *nāgarī pracāriṇī sabhā*, Society for the Propagation of Nāgarī (a title)[1]

सुशीला स्त्री *suśīlā strī*, a virtuous woman

श्रीमती वर्मा *śrīmatī varmā*, Mrs. Varmā

दीप्तिमती प्रतिभा *dīptimatī pratibhā*, brilliant genius

कलावती नर्तिका *kalāvatī nartikā*, a gifted, artistic, dancer

युवती स्त्री *yuvatī śtrī*, young woman[2]

9. *Some expressions of place*

Names of towns are sometimes used colloquially without postpositions as expressions of place, equivalent to expressions showing the postposition में *meṁ*: e.g.

जब मैं इलाहाबाद था, तो रोज़ काफ़ी हाउस जाता था । *jab maiṁ ilāhābād thā, to roz kāfī hāus jātā thā*, When I was in Allahabad I used to go everyday to the Coffee House.

उस समय मैं आगरा रहता था । *us samay maiṁ āgrā rahtā thā*, At that time I was living in Agra.

10. *Multiplicatives (contd.)*

Some other multiplicatives than those given in Lesson XI are

इकहरा *ikahrā*, 'onefold'; thin

[1] For *ṇ* in the word प्रचारिणी *pracāriṇī* see p. 189.

[2] The corresponding masculine form is युवा *yuvā* 'young; a youth or young man'.

दोहरा, दुहरा *dohrā*, *duhrā*, twofold; ample; fat

तेहरा, तिहरा *tehrā*, *tihrā*, threefold[1]

चौहरा *cauhrā*, fourfold

मैं आपसे दोहरा (दुगुना) काम करता हूँ। *maiṁ āpse dohrā* (*dugunā*) *kām kartā hūṁ*, I do twice as much work as you.

उस कंबल में चौहरी तह लगाना! *us kambal meṁ cauhrī tah lagānā!* Fold that blanket into four![2]

(*a*) A few fractional forms in *-ā* are also found:

पौना *paunā*, $\frac{3}{4}$ the amount of

सवाया *savāyā*, $1\frac{1}{4}$ times the amount of

ड्योढ़ा *ḍyoṛhā* $1\frac{1}{2}$ times the amount of

उसे पिछले हफ़्ते सवाई तनख़ाह मिली। *use pichle hafte savāī tankhāh milī*, Last week he got one and a quarter times his (usual) wage.

[1] The first vowel of this word is usually short [ɛ], sometimes [i].
[2] तह *tah*, f. 'fold'.

## II

### FURTHER ASPECTS OF THE GRAMMAR OF VERBS

1. *Routine imperfective*

In past narration imperfective participles are commonly used without auxiliaries to describe routines of action, i.e. not actions presented as actually occurring, but actions presented as those which would typically occur, in given circumstances.

बूढ़ा शाम को रोज़ बाग़ में घूमने जाता। *būṛhā śām ko roz bāg meṁ ghūmne jātā*, The old man would go for a walk in the park every evening.

डाइनिंग हाल में खाना मैं पहले भी खाता था, और कई बार उस पाँत में भी खाता था, जिसमें देवा जी और उनका परिवार रहता। *ḍāiniṅg hāl meṁ khānā maiṁ pahle bhī khātā thā, aur kaī bār us pāṁt meṁ bhī khātā thā, jismeṁ devā jī aur unkā parivār rahtā* (Ashk), I had used to eat in the dining hall before that, too, several times in the very row in which Devā Jī and his family would sit (to eat).

2. *Use of imperfective participles to denote hypothetical events (contd.)*

It was noted in Lesson XX that imperfective participles are used in conditional sentences to denote hypothetical events or events very unlikely to occur. Some illustrations of similar usages in non-conditional sentences are:

काश (कि) मैं वहाँ जा सकता! *kāś (ki) maiṁ vahāṁ jā saktā!* How I wish I could go there![1]

मैं तुमसे क्यों न ईर्ष्या करता? *maiṁ tumse kyoṁ na īrṣyā kartā?* Why should I not have envied you?[2]

इतना चाहता हूँ कि वह मुझसे मिलने आता। *itnā cāhtā hūṁ ki vah mujhse milne ātā*, I long for him to come to see me (but I fear he will not).

3. *Usages of perfective participles*

(*a*) The use of perfective participles with future time reference in conditional sentences has been noted in Lesson XX. It is common elsewhere, usually with an affective value.

[1] काश (कि) †*kāś* (*ki*) 'would that . . .'. This expression also occurs with subjunctive verbs.

[2] ईर्ष्या *īrṣyā*, f. 'envy; jealousy'.

पानी लाओ! –लाया, साहब! *pānī lāo! — lāyā, sāhab!* Bring some water! Very good, sir![1]

मैं अभी आया। *maiṁ abhī āyā*, I'll be back in a moment.

तो चल दिए? *to cal die?* You're off, then?

(*b*) Note the common use of रहा *rahā*, rather than a form of होना *honā*, in affective expressions serving to point out an object in a certain place.

देखिए, वह रहा मंदिर! *dekhie, vah rahā mandir!* Look, there's a temple! (over there).[2]

(*c*) Note the use of हुआ *huā* in concord with preceding nouns in the adverbial sense 'ago' (i.e. expressing the completion of a period of time).

| | | |
|---|---|---|
| एक साल हुआ | *ek sāl huā,* | a year ago |
| एक हफ़्ता हुआ | *ek haftā huā,* | a week ago |
| दो हफ़्ते हुए | *do hafte hue,* | two weeks ago |

4. *Subjunctive usages*

(*a*) Note the very common use of न जाने *na jāne*, and colloquially, unnegatived जाने *jāne*, in the sense 'one cannot tell', 'Heaven knows', etc.

न जाने क्यों मैं उसे देख नहीं सकता। *na jāne kyoṁ maiṁ use dekh nahīṁ saktā*, For some reason I can't stand the sight of him.

और जाने क्या क्या कहा। *aur jāne kyā kyā kahā*, Heaven knows what else he said.

गीत विरह का था, पर जाने क्यों मुझे करुण नहीं लगा। *gīt virah kā thā, par jāne kyoṁ mujhe karuṇ nahīṁ lagā* (Ashk), The song was one of separation, but for some reason it did not strike me as sad.

(*b*) The form चाहे *cāhe* 'one may wish' is used reduplicated, with subjunctive verbs, in the conjunctival sense 'whether . . . or'; also singly with a correlative such as लेकिन *lekin*, etc.

[1] An alternative expression would be लाता हूँ *lātā hūṁ*; this would convey less of the idea that the servant is about to carry out, and complete, the action at the given time.

[2] वह *vah* is here not the subject of रहा *rahā*, but is used in a vague demonstrative way similar to that exemplified for यह *yah* on p. 102; the subject of रहा *rahā* is मंदिर *mandir*.

चाहे वह बुरा हो, चाहे अच्छा हो, फिर भी हमारा बेटा ही है। *cāhe vah burā ho, cāhe acchā ho, phir bhī hamārā beṭā hī hai*, Whether he be good or bad, he is still our son.

चाहे आप यहाँ रहें, लेकिन मैं नहीं रहूँगा। *cāhe āp yahāṁ raheṁ, lekin maiṁ nahīṁ rahūṁgā*, You can stay if you like, but I shan't.

(*c*) Perfective subjunctive forms are available to define verbal actions as of possible occurrence, completed. They show perfective participles with subjunctive forms of होना *honā* as auxiliaries.

तुमने जो कुछ लिखा हो, उसे दिखाना। *tumne jo kuch likhā ho, use dikhānā*, Show me whatever you've written.

(*d*) Imperfective and continuous subjunctive forms are also available: e.g.

अगर मैं लिखता होऊँ तो मुझे न बुलाना। *agar maiṁ likhtā hoūṁ to mujhe na bulānā*, If I'm writing don't call me.

अगर वह आ रहा हो तो आप भी आ जाइएगा! *agar vah ā rahā ho to āp bhī ā jāiegā!* If he's coming (going to come), you come too by all means!

5. *Negatived sentences with verb unexpressed*

Present tense forms of the verb होना *honā* are often felt to be superfluous in sentences negatived with नहीं *nahīṁ*, and are omitted, especially in informal usage.

कुएँ में पानी नहीं। *kueṁ meṁ pānī nahīṁ*, There's no water in the well.

6. *Intensives*

Forms which may be described as 'intensives' exist associated with compound verbs and some other composite verbal expressions. They usually stress in some way that an action is in progress or is immediately impending at a particular time. Intensives of intransitive verbs are usually based on perfective participles in adjectival concord with subjects, those of transitive verbs regularly on adverbially used *-e* forms of perfective participles.

(i) *Intensives showing perfective participles in concord*

बर्फ़ पिघली जाती है! *barf pighlī jātī hai!* The ice is melting! (Something should be done about it.)

उसकी माँ उसके पीछे मरी जाती है। *uskī māṁ uske pīche marī jātī hai*, His mother works herself to death for him.

(*a*) Intensives of verbs of motion are quite common, stressing that the action is in progress, e.g. चला जाना *calā jānā* move (along), go (away)'; भागा जाना *bhāgā jānā* flee (away)'. They usually have less affective force than other intensives (this applies especially to चला जाना *calā jānā*.)

(ii) *Intensives showing* -e *forms*

मैं आपसे यह कहे देता हूँ कि . . . *maiṁ āpse yah kahe detā hūṁ ki* . . . , I tell you this . . .

मुझे बचाओ, यह मुझे मारे डालता है! *mujhe bacāo, yah mujhe māre ḍāltā hai!* Save me, this fellow is killing me!

बच्चे का तुतलाना मन को मोहे लेता था। *bacce kā tutlānā man ko mohe letā thā*, The baby's prattling used to be absolutely delightful.[1]

बच्चे का तुतलाना आपके मन को मोहे लेगा। *bacce kā tutlānā āpke man ko mohe legā*, The baby's prattling will absolutely delight you.

(*a*) Intensives containing the auxiliaries देना *denā*, लेना *lena*, and डालना *ḍālnā* show imperfective participles of these verbs in the great majority of cases.

(*b*) Intensives in which the *-e* form is followed by जाना *jānā* express very much the same sense as composites of imperfective participle + जाना *jānā* (see p. 136), but often with a slightly different emphasis which may be characterised in general as 'intensive'. They differ in their range of occurrence from the intensives already noted in this subsection, in that जाना *jānā* often occurs in non-imperfective forms.

बर्फ़ पिघले जाती है! *barf pighle jātī hai!* The ice is melting![2]

वह सारे दिन रामचरितमानस पढ़े जाता है, करता कुछ नहीं *vah sāre din rāmcaritmānas paṛhe jātā hai, kartā kuch nahīṁ*, He does nothing but read the Rāmcaritmānas all day.

जब तक मुझमें शक्ति है, मैं काम किए जाऊँगा। *jab tak mujhmeṁ śakti hai, maiṁ kām kie jāūṁgā*, As long as I have the strength I shall press on with the work (actively).

मैं उसे हज़ार रुपया महीना दिए जाऊँगा। *maiṁ use hazār rupayā mahīnā die jāūṁgā*, I shall give him a thousand rupees a month (unconditionally, positively).

[1] तुतलाना *tutlānā* 'babble, lisp'; मोहना *mohnā* 'enchant, charm'.

[2] An equivalent of the sentence given on p. 172.

(*c*) Note that verbal expressions showing जाना *jānā* following an *-e* form are not necessarily intensives as defined above; their contexts may require that the verb जाना *jānā* be interpreted in its literal sense 'go': e.g.

उसे क्यों छोड़े जाती है? *use kyoṁ choṛe jātī hai?* Why is she going off and leaving him?

7. *Syntax of absolutive expressions*

(*a*) Note the frequency of unrelated absolutives in passive constructions (most usually impersonal passive constructions).

मशीन गिर न जाए, इसलिए उसे रस्सियों से कसकर बाँधा गया। *maśīn gir na jāe, islie use rassiyoṁ se kaskar bāṁdhā gayā* (Ashk), So that the machine would not fall off it was tied on tightly with ropes (pulled tight and tied on with ropes)[1]

(*b*) Note that verbs and other parts of sentences often intervene between absolutives and clauses dependent on them.

मुझे यह सुनकर बड़ी ख़ुशी है कि . . . *mujhe yah sunkar baṛī khuśī hai ki . . .*, I'm very glad to hear that . . .

वह अपने बच्चों से कहकर जाती कि तुम किसान की बातें सुनकर मुझे बताना। *vah apne baccoṁ se kahkar jātī ki tum kisān kī bāteṁ sunkar mujhe batānā*, On leaving she would tell her children to listen to what the farmer said and report it to her.

(*c*) Note the common collocations जान पड़ना *jān paṛnā* 'seem', देख पड़ना *dekh paṛnā* 'be visible', सुन पड़ना *sun paṛnā* 'be audible' showing stem absolutives.[2]

(मुझे) जान पड़ता है कि . . . (*mujhe*) *jān paṛtā hai ki . . .*, It seems (to me) that . . .

मुझे कोने में एक साँप देख पड़ा। *mujhe kone meṁ ek sāṁp dekh paṛā*, I caught sight of a snake in the corner.

(*d*) Where there is an implication that the action denoted by an absolutive is closely associated with that denoted by a finite verb, stem absolutives (rather than extended absolutives showing *-kar*, *-ke*) are common. This is clear in collocations of stem absolutive + finite verb such as ले जाना *le*

[1] कसना *kasnā* 'bind, pull tight'.

[2] Equivalents of मालूम होना *mālūm honā*, दिखाई देना *dikhāī denā*, and सुनाई देना *sunāī denā* respectively.

*jānā*, etc., but note that stem absolutives do not necessarily immediately precede finite verbs of their sentences: e.g.

वह अमर का हाथ पकड़ कमरे में ले गया । *vah amar kā hāth pakaṛ kamre meṁ le gayā*, Taking Amar by the hand he led him into the room.

8. *Variants of inflexional forms*

More than one spelling is current for many verb forms. These variant spellings usually involve analogical extensions of the graph *y*, representing a semi-vocalic glide between vowels, from spellings of forms in whose pronunciation the glide is prominent. Spellings without *y* are often preferred by careful users of the language. Some representative pairs of spellings of forms of the verb आना *ānā* are:

| | | | | |
|---|---|---|---|---|
| आई | *āī* | आयी | *āyī* | (influence of आया *āyā*) |
| आए | *āe* (perfective and subjunctive) | आये | *āye* | (influence of आया *āyā*) |
| आईं | *āīṁ* | आयीं | *āyīṁ* | (influence of आया *āyā*) |
| आएगा | *āegā* | आयेगा | *āyegā* | (influence of आये *āye*) |

Similar pairs are:

| | | | |
|---|---|---|---|
| पिए | *pie* | पिये | *piye* |
| सिओ | *sio* | सियो | *siyo* |
| बोलिए | *bolie* | बोलिये | *boliye* |
| चाहिए | *cāhie* | चाहिये | *cāhiye*, etc. |

A few variant spellings depend on the de-stressing of final or medial syllables of inflexional forms. For example alongside

| | | | | | | |
|---|---|---|---|---|---|---|
| जाए | *jāe* | जाये | *jāye* | also occurs | जाय | *jāy* |
| जाएँ | *jāeṁ* | जायें | *jāyeṁ* | ,, | जायँ | *jāyaṁ* |
| जाएगा | *jāegā* | जायेगा | *jāyegā* | ,, | जायगा | *jāygā*, etc. |

Third person subjunctive forms of verbs whose stem ends in *-ā* sometimes show a glide *v* in both pronunciation and spelling, for example alongside

| | | | | |
|---|---|---|---|---|
| आए | *āe* | occurs | आवे | *āve* |
| पाए | *pāe* | ,, | पावे | *pāve* |
| दिखाएँ | *dikhāeṁ* | ,, | दिखावें | *dikhāveṁ*, etc. |

Forms of this last type are relatively frequent in speech, less so in the written language.

9. -ie *and* -iegā *forms (contd.)*

These forms, which were discussed for convenience under the heading 'Imperative forms', are, as was stated in that section, very far from being true imperatives in force, their force being equatable much rather with that of the subjunctive forms of modern Hindi. They in fact represent third person singular passive subjunctive, and earlier passive indicative forms of the older language. Their affiliation with subjunctives is clearly seen in the fact that they often occur in questions which cannot be construed as requests, and even in subordinate clauses. Their use emphasises (sometimes with irony) that questions and statements are circumspect or considerate in some way. Sometimes, as in the last example below, their original passive force is quite clear.

(आप) अंडा कैसे खाइएगा? *(āp) aṇḍā kaise khāiegā?* How would you like your egg?

फिर आप कहाँ जाइएगा? *phir āp kahāṁ jāiegā?* Where are you going next?

फिर आप चलिएगा कहाँ? *phir āp caliegā kahāṁ?* Where *are* you going then? (please be so good as to tell me).

अगर आप दिल्ली चलिए(गा), तो मैं भी हो लूँ। *agar āp dillī calie(gā), to maiṁ bhī ho lūṁ*, If you should go to Delhi, I'd like to go with you.

किताबें न ख़रीद सकिए(गा), तो लाइब्रेरी में जाकर पढ़िए। *kitābeṁ na kharīd sakie(gā), to lāibrerī meṁ jākar paṛhie*, If you can't buy the books, go and study in the library.

जी चाहता था, वहीं सो रहिए। *jī cāhtā thā, vahīṁ so rahie*, I longed to lie down and sleep right there.

10. *Concord of infinitives*

Infinitives of transitive verbs immediately preceding such verbs as सीखना *sīkhnā*, चाहना *cāhnā*, and शुरू करना *śurū karnā* usually show the same concord as these when they are in construction with ने *ne*.

उन्होंने हिंदी लिखनी सीखी। *unhoṁne hindī likhnī sīkhī*, He learned to write Hindi.

उन्होंने किताब बेचनी चाही। *unhoṁne kitāb becnī cāhī*, They wanted, tried to sell the book.[1]

[1] वे किताब बेचना चाहे *ve kitāb becnā cāhe* is also possible, चाहना *cāhnā* not being always used in construction with ने *ne*.

मैंने किताब पढ़नी शुरू की । *maiṁne kitāb paṛhnī śurū kī*, I began to read the book.

But in some persons' usage, especially spoken usage, þoth infinitive and finite verb show *-ā*. Thus for the last sentence

मैंने किताब पढ़ना शुरू किया । *maiṁne kitāb paṛhnā śurū kiyā*

is also possible.

## III

## FURTHER ASPECTS OF THE GRAMMAR OF POSTPOSITIONS, ADVERBS, AND CONJUNCTIONS

### 1. *Postpositional usages*

(*a*) Postpositions do not always occur singly. A particularly common postpositional pair is में से *meṁ se* 'from inside, from among'; note also pairs showing final का *kā*, e.g. पर का *par kā* 'the . . . on'.

इन किताबों में से आप दो-तीन चुन लें। *in kitāboṁ meṁ se āp do-tīn cun leṁ*, Please pick out two or three of these books.

कुएँ में से पानी निकालने के लिए बालटी इस्तेमाल हो सकती है। *kueṁ meṁ se pānī nikālne ke lie bālṭī istemāl ho saktī hai*, A bucket can be used for drawing water from a well.

गाड़ी पर का सामान उतरवा दो। *gāṛī par kā sāmān utarvā do*, Get the luggage on the car unloaded.

(*b*) The postposition का *kā* does not occur in first position in postpositional pairs. Note the syntax of such a sentence as

मेरी निगाहें फिर उससे जा मिलीं। *merī nigāheṁ phir usse jā milīṁ* (Ashk), My eyes once more met hers (literally, 'met her'),[1]

and the difference between the syntax of the following sentence, in which the word कुरसी *kursī* is repeated, and that of its English translation equivalent:

मेरी कुरसी पर न बैठकर उसकी कुरसी पर बैठिए। *merī kursī par na baiṭhkar uskī kursī par baiṭhie*, Don't sit in my chair, sit in his.

(*c*) Constructions involving the postposition का *kā* can sometimes be confusing, in that between का *kā* and a noun with which it is in concord other parts of a sentence may intervene.

मकान का ऊपर का कमरा। *makān kā ūpar kā kamrā*, the room at the top of the house

पित्तो के ज़िंदा रहते, मुझे नगर के उस शोर-शराबे और भीड़-भब्भर का कभी अहसास न हुआ था। *pitto ke zindā rahte, mujhe nagar ke us śor-śarābe aur bhīṛ-bhabbhaṛ kā kabhī ahsās na huā thā* (Ashk), While Pitto was alive, I had never noticed that din and turmoil of the city.[2]

[1] निगाह †*nigāh*, f. 'look, glance'.

[2] ज़िंदा *zindā*, see p. 7; शोर-शराबा *śor-śarābā*, भीड़-भब्भर *bhīṛ-bhabbhaṛ*, see p. 201; अहसास †*ahsās*, m. 'perception, feeling'.

(*d*) Where more than one oblique case noun is associated with a single postposition this is usually expressed with the last noun only: e.g.

वे अपने दोस्तों और रिश्तेदारों से मिलने आए थे। *ve apne dostoṁ aur riśtedāroṁ se milne āe the*, They had come to meet their friends and relatives.

2. *Formation of adverbs*

Note the common use of the collocation . . . रूप से . . . *rūp se*, and the use of the suffix -तः *-taḥ*, in forming adverbs from adjectives in the more formal language; also the Sanskrit inflexional ending *-yā* which occasionally forms adverbs from borrowed feminine nouns in *-ā*. Certain other Sanskrit inflexional endings are also very occasionally used in the same way.

सामान्य रूप से *sāmānya rūp se*, in general
विशेष रूप से *viśeṣ rūp se*, in particular
संभवतः *sambhavataḥ*, probably, possibly
पूर्णतः *pūrṇtaḥ*, fully, in full
पूर्णतया *pūrṇtayā*, „ „ „
कृपया *kṛpayā*, kindly, of your kindness[1]

3. शायद ही śāyad hī; तक tak; भर bhar

(*a*) Note the use of शायद ही *śāyad hī* in the senses 'scarcely; scarcely ever'.

मेरे जीवन में ऐसा शायद ही कभी हुआ हो कि . . . *mere jīvan meṁ aisā śāyad hī kabhī huā ho ki* . . . (Premcand), It can scarcely ever have happened in my life that . . .

(*b*) तक *tak* is used adverbially in the sense 'even' with preceding direct, not oblique, case nouns.

मेरे पास पैसा तक न रहा। *mere pās paisā tak na rahā*, I didn't have a pice left.

(*c*) भर *bhar*, i.e. the stem of the verb भरना *bharnā* 'fill', is used in various adverbial expressions with preceding nouns in oblique case.

दिन भर *din bhar*, all day
हफ़्ते भर *hafte bhar*, all week
पेट भर खाना *peṭ bhar khānā*, eat one's fill[2]
पल भर *pal bhar*, (for) just a moment

[1] In making somewhat formal requests.

[2] Very occasionally भर *bhar* is used as a prefix, e.g. भरपेट खाना *bharpeṭ khānā*, synonymous with the above expression.

4. भी bhī (*contd.*)

Most of the usages of this enclitic will be found to give little difficulty of interpretation if its inclusive force, complementary to that of restrictive ही *hī*, and its general translation equivalents 'also', 'even' are borne in mind. Some further examples of the use of भी *bhī*, in construction with verbs and in some standardised locutions, are given here.

चलिए भी! *calie bhī!* Come on then, do come on!

उसे रहने भी दो। *use rahne bhī do*, Do leave that alone, for goodness sake leave that alone.[1]

दफ़्तर में काम करते, मित्र-शत्रुओं, अफ़सरों या चपरासियों से बातें करते हुए भी, आँखें उसको देखती रहती थीं। *daftar meṁ kām karte, mitr-śatruoṁ, afsaroṁ yā caprāsiyoṁ se bāteṁ karte hue bhī, āṁkheṁ usko dekhtī rahtī thīṁ* (*Ashk*), Even when (I was) working in the office, talking to friends and enemies, officers or messengers, I kept seeing her in my mind's eye.[2]

कुछ भी *kuch bhī*, anything at all

कोई भी *koī bhī*, anyone at all

अब भी *ab bhī*, even now

और भी *aur bhī*, even more

तो भी *to bhī*, but even so

भी . . . भी *bhī . . . bhī*, both . . . and

वह बच्चों के लिए किताबें भी लाया और खिलौने भी। *vah baccoṁ ke lie kitābeṁ bhī lāyā aur khilaune bhī*, He brought both books and toys for the children.

5. कहीं kahīṁ '*somewhere*'

Note that कहीं *kahīṁ* is not an interrogative, despite its apparent connection with कहाँ *kahāṁ*. Some common locutions showing कहीं *kahīṁ* are given here, and others in section 7 below.

कहीं नहीं *kahīṁ nahīṁ*, nowhere
सब कहीं *sab kahīṁ*, everywhere
कहीं भी *kahīṁ bhī*, anywhere at all
जहाँ कहीं *jahāṁ kahīṁ*, wheresoever
कहीं और *kahīṁ aur*, somewhere else
कहीं कहीं *kahīṁ kahīṁ*, in different places

[1] Or 'leave him alone'.

[2] Literally '. . . (my) eyes kept seeing her'. भी *bhī*, though expressed only with the second participle, is to be taken with the first also.

6. *Affective usages of* न na

Affective usages of न *na* are very common, especially with imperatives, in the locution जो है न *jo hai na* in informal speech, and in certain reduplicative expressions: e.g.

'बताइए न संगीत जी', उसने फिर आग्रह के साथ कहा। '*batāie na saṅgīt jī*', *usne phir āgrah ke sāth kahā*, 'Please do tell (me), Saṅgīt jī', she repeated eagerly.[1]

वहाँ जो गाड़ी खड़ी है न, वह मेरी है। *vahāṁ jo gāṛī khaṛī hai na, vah merī hai*, You see that car over there? It's mine.[1]

कोई न कोई *koī na koī*, someone or other

कुछ न कुछ *kuch na kuch*, something or other

कभी न कभी *kabhī na kabhī*, at one time or another

कहीं न कहीं *kahīṁ na kahīṁ*, somewhere or other

7. *Other affective usages*

Many affective usages of interrogative words are similar to English affective usages and give no difficulty, especially those involving कैसा *kaisā* and कितना *kitnā*, and many with क्या *kyā*: e.g.

वे कैसे अच्छे आदमी हैं! *ve kaise acche ādmī haiṁ!* What a good man he is!

राजपूतों की वीरता का क्या कहना! *rājpūtoṁ kī vīrtā kā kyā kahnā!* What stories there are of the Rajputs' heroism![2]

Others, especially those involving कहाँ *kahāṁ*, कहीं *kahīṁ*, and कब *kab*, are more difficult. Note कहीं *kahīṁ* used with न *na* in the sense 'lest', and कितना ही . . . क्यों न *kitnā hī . . . kyoṁ na* 'however much'.

वह कहाँ जगाए जगाए उठता था? *vah kahāṁ jagāe jagāe uṭhtā thā?* Would he ever get up, even after being repeatedly wakened (where, in what case, used he to get up)?[3]

यह पुस्तक उससे कहीं अच्छी है। *yah pustak usse kahīṁ acchī hai*, This book is far better than that (better to how great an extent).

[1] न *na* following verb forms has a rising intonation.

[2] कहना *kahnā* is used as a noun; plural कहने *kahne* (with के *ke*) is also possible here.

[3] जगाए जगाए *jagāe jagāe* here represents (किसी के) जगाए जगाए (*kisī ke*) *jagāe jagāe* 'on being wakened (by someone)'.

चलो यहाँ से, बदमाश कहीं का! *calo yahāṁ se, badmāsh kahīṁ kā!* Clear out of here, you villain (villain of how great a degree)!

मुझे डर था कि कहीं सब पुस्तकें गिर न जाएँ। *mujhe ḍar thā ki kahīṁ sab pustkeṁ gir na jāeṁ*, I was afraid that (it might happen that) all the books would fall.

नहीं तो मैं दिल्ली कब का चला गया होता। *nahīṁ to maiṁ dillī kab kā calā gayā hotā*, Otherwise I would have gone to Delhi long since (at what time would I have gone? — Long since).

उनके पास कितना ही पैसा क्यों न हो, फिर भी कोई उनका आदर नहीं करता। *unke pās kitnā hī paisā kyoṁ na ho, phir bhī koī unkā ādar nahīṁ kartā*, However much money he may have, no one respects him.[1]

उसे हिंदी तो क्या, बँगला भी आती है। *use hindī to kyā, baṁglā bhī ātī hai*, He knows Hindi of course, and Bengali too (what of Hindi, he also knows Bengali).

काम शुरू कर रहे हैं?—हाँ, और क्या? *kām śurū kar rahe haiṁ? — hāṁ, aur kyā?* Are you starting work? — Yes, of course![2]

8. *Conjunctions: forms and usages*

(*a*) Alongside और *aur* 'and' there are the equivalent Sanskrit loanwords तथा *tathā* and एवं *evaṃ*[3] in the formal language. Alongside पर *par*, लेकिन *lekin* 'but' the Sanskrit loanwords परंतु *parantu*, किंतु *kintu* and the Persian loanword मगर †*magar* occur, and alongside या *yā* 'or' the Sanskrit loanword (अथ)वा (*ath*)*vā* occurs. Note also the Persian forms -ओ- *-o-*, व *va*, used in expressions of a more or less stereotyped nature, the first very largely in expressions of specifically Urdu character, the second more widely.

दिलोजान से *dilojān se*, with heart and soul

आबोहवा *ābohavā*, climate (water and air)

नाम व पता *nām va patā*, name and address

ये जानवर दिन में व रात में शिकार करते हैं। *ye jānvar din meṁ va rāt meṁ śikār karte haiṁ*, These animals hunt (both) by day and by night.

[1] कितना ही . . . क्यों न *kitnā hī . . . kyoṁ na* is often followed by फिर भी *phir bhī*, लेकिन *lekin*, etc.; and the word कितना *kitnā* may be preceded by concessive चाहे *cāhe*.

[2] और *aur* is stressed.

[3] Pronounced with final [m].

(*b*) The following pairs of conjunctions are common. Note that तो *to* usually occurs following the first member of these pairs in sentences of neutral style and emphasis.

या . . . या *yā . . . yā*, either . . . or

न . . . न *na . . . na*, neither . . . nor

मैं या तो बनारस जाऊँगा, या इलाहाबाद । *maiṁ yā to banāras jāūṁgā, yā ilāhābād*, I shall go either to Banaras or Allahabad.

मैं न तो बनारस जाऊँगा, न इलाहाबाद । *maiṁ na to banāras jāūṁgā, na ilāhābād*, I shall go neither to Banaras nor to Allahabad.

मैं न बनारस जाऊँगा, न तो इलाहाबाद । *maiṁ nā banāras jāūṁgā, na to ilāhābād*, I shall not go to Banaras, nor to Allahabad either.

(*c*) The form बल्कि *balki* means 'but, but rather, in addition' and is common after negative clauses. The forms वरन् **varan*, अपितु **apitu* are also found.

वह किताब लाया ही नहीं, बल्कि उसने मुझे उसे पढ़ने में मदद दी । *vah kitāb lāyā hī nahīṁ, balki usne mujhe use paṛhne meṁ madad dī*, He not only brought the book but helped me to read it.

(*d*) The form कि *ki*, which is really a link of non-specific force between parts of sentences, is often used instead of जब *jab* 'when' to join clauses when the action described in the second clause is a sudden, fresh development in the context of that described in the first. It is also common for या *yā* in the locution या नहीं *yā nahīṁ* 'or not'.

राधा भारत जानेवाली थी कि बीमार पड़ गई । *rādhā bhārat jānevālī thī ki bīmār paṛ gaī*, Radha was about to go to India when she fell ill.

यह ठीक रास्ता है कि नहीं? *yah ṭhīk rāstā hai ki nahīṁ?* Is this the right road or not?

Its use pleonastically with relative words (usually, but not always, following these) is common colloquially.

वह एक ऐसा आदमी है जो कि बहुत दूर जाएगा । *vah ek aisā ādmī hai jo ki bahut dūr jāegā*, He is a man who will go far.

जैसे कि मैं आपसे कह रहा था . . . *jaise ki maiṁ āpse kah rahā thā . . .*, As I was telling you . . .

The locution न कि *na ki* has the sense 'and not' in such a sentence as

उसने बँगला सीखी थी, न कि हिंदी। *usne bamglā sīkhī thī, na ki hindī*, He learned Bengali, not Hindi.

(*e*) As an equivalent of the expression नहीं तो *nahīṁ to* 'otherwise' the Arabic loanword वरना †*varnā* is common.

अपना काम देखो, वरना अच्छा न होगा! *apnā kām dekho, varnā acchā na hogā!* Do your work properly, or there'll be trouble!

# IV

## SANDHI

The word *sandhi* means 'union, junction'. The 'rules of *sandhi*' describe ways in which vowels and consonants combine or are modified in the formation of various types of Sanskrit words, chiefly compounds and derivatives. Sanskrit loanwords, and new formations in Hindi on Sanskrit words, normally show correct Sanskritic *sandhi*, and some acquaintance with the main *sandhis* will help the student in recognizing and using these words.

### 1. *Vowel* sandhi

(*a*)

Skt. *a, ā + a, ā > ā*
Skt. *i, ī + i, ī > ī*
Skt. *u, ū + u, ū > ū*

| | | |
|---|---|---|
| Skt. नियम *niyama*, rule | + अनुसार *anusāra*, usage | : H. नियमानुसार *niyamānusār*, according to rule |
| Skt. हिम *hima*, snow | + आलय *ālaya*, abode | : H. हिमालय *himālay*, Himalaya |
| Skt. आत्मा *ātmā*, self | + अभिमान *abhimāna*, pride | : H. आत्माभिमान *ātmābhimān*, self-respect; conceit |
| Skt. सुधि *sudhī*, understanding | + इन्द्र *indra*, Indra | : Skt. H. सुधीन्द्र, सुधींद्र[1] *sudhīndra* (personal name) |

(*b*)

Skt. *a, ā + i, ī > e*
Skt. *a, ā + u, ū > o*
Skt. *a, ā + ṛ > ar*

| | | |
|---|---|---|
| Skt. गण *gaṇa*, multitude | + ईश *īśa*, lord | : H. गणेश *gaṇeś* (name of a god; personal name) |
| Skt. महा *mahā*, great | + ईश *īśa*, lord | : H. महेश *maheś* (title of a god; personal name) |

[1] For the alternative spellings see p. xxviii. Use of conjuncts in cases such as this in Hindi is common where the nasal precedes dentals or labials, less common where it precedes other plosives.

| | | |
|---|---|---|
| Skt. ग्राम *grāma*, village | + उद्योग *udyoga*, endeavour | : H. ग्रामोद्योग *grāmodyog*, village industry |
| Skt. सीमा *sīmā*, border | + उल्लङ्घन *ullaṅghana*, crossing | : H. सीमोल्लंघन *sīmollaṅghan*, violation of frontier |
| Skt. महा *mahā*, great | + ऋषि *ṛṣi*, sage | : Skt. H. महर्षि *maharṣi*, great sage |

(*c*) Skt. *a*, *ā* + *e* > *ai*

Skt. *a*, *ā* + *o* > *au*

| | | |
|---|---|---|
| Skt. सदा *sadā*, always | + एव *eva*, just so | : H. सदैव *sadaiv*, always |

*ai* and *au* are called *vṛddhi* forms of *i* and *ī*, *u* and *ū* respectively.[1] The corresponding *vṛddhi* form of *a* is *ā*, and of *ṛ*, *ār*. The occurrence of *vṛddhi* forms in derivative words is noted in Supplement V.

(*d*) Skt. *i*, *ī* > *y* before vowels of different quality.

Skt. *u*, *ū* > *v* before vowels of different quality.

| | | |
|---|---|---|
| Skt. प्रति *prati* (distributive prefix) | + एक *eka*, one | : H. प्रत्येक *pratyek*, each |
| Skt. इति *iti*, thus | + आदि *ādi*, and so on | : Skt. H. इत्यादि *ityādi*, et cetera |
| Skt. अनु *anu*, according to | + अय *aya*, going | : H. अन्वय *anvay*, union |

2. *Consonant* sandhi

(*a*) Before vowels and voiced consonants other than nasals the voiceless plosives are voiced:

*k* > *g*

*c* > *j*

*ṭ* > *ḍ*

*t* > *d*

*p* > *b*

[1] That is, forms produced by the process of *vṛddhi* 'increase'.

| | | |
|---|---|---|
| Skt. जगत् *jagat*, world | + ईश *īśa*, lord | : H. जगदीश *jagdīś* (name) |
| Skt. भगवत् *bhagavat*, divine; divine being | + गीता *gītā*, song | : Skt. H. भगवदगीता *bhagavadgītā*, Song of the Lord |
| Skt. षट *ṣaṭ*, six | + ऋतु *ṛtu*, season | : Skt. H. षड्तु *ṣaḍṛtu*, the six seasons |

(*b*) Before nasal consonants all plosives become corresponding nasals:

*k*, *g* > *ṅ*
*c*, *j* > *ñ*
*ṭ*, *ḍ* > *ṇ*
*t*, *d* > *n*
*p*, *b* > *m*

| | | |
|---|---|---|
| Skt. वाक् *vāk*, speech | + मय *maya*, composed of | : H. वाङ्मय *vāṅmay*, literature[1] |
| Skt. उद् *ud*, up | + नति *nati*, bowing | : H. उन्नति *unnati*, progress |

(*c*) *t* before voiced *j* or *l* becomes *j*, *l* respectively.

| | | |
|---|---|---|
| Skt. सत् *sat*, existent, good | + जन *jana*, person | : H. सज्जन *sajjan*, good person |
| Skt. तत् *tat*, that | + लीन *līna*, attached to | : H. तल्लीन *tallīn*, absorbed in that, engrossed |

(*d*) *t* and *d* before voiceless *c* become *c*, and combine with following voiceless *ś* as *cch*.

| | | |
|---|---|---|
| Skt. सत् *sat*, being | + चित् *cit*, thought + आनन्द *ānanda*, bliss | : H. सच्चिदानंद *saccidānand*, pure being, thought and bliss |
| Skt. उद् *ud*, up | + श्वास *śvāsa*, breath | : H. उच्छ्वास *ucchvās*, sigh |

(*e*) *d* + *h* > *ddh*

| | | |
|---|---|---|
| Skt. उद् *ud*, up | + हरण *haraṇa*, carrying | : H. उद्धरण *uddharaṇ*, extract, citation |

[1] The word साहित्य *sāhitya* is much more common.

(*f*) Final *s* not preceded by *a* or *ā* becomes *r* before a vowel or voiced consonant.

| | | |
|---|---|---|
| Skt. दुस् *dus*, bad | + दैव *daiva*, fate | : H. दुर्दैव *durdaiv*, evil fate |
| Skt. निस् *nis*, not, without | + भय *bhaya*, fear | : H. निर्भय *nirbhay*, fearless |
| Skt. निस् *nis*, not, without | + आमिष *āmiṣa*, meat | : H. निरामिष *nirāmiṣ*, vegetarian |

(*g*) Before voiceless *k*, *kh*, *p* or *ph* it becomes *ṣ*; and before voiceless *c*, *ś*. Before voiceless *t* it remains in a few formations (but in Sanskrit the group often becomes *ṣṭ*).

| | | |
|---|---|---|
| Skt. निस् *nis*, not, without | + फल *phala*, fruit | : H. निष्फल *niṣphal*, fruitless |
| Skt. दुस् *dus*, bad, difficult | + कृ *kṛ* (> *kara*), do | : H. दुष्कर *duṣkar*, hard to accomplish |
| Skt. दुस् *dus*, bad, difficult | + चिन्ता *cintā*, thought | : H. दुश्चिंता *duścintā*, wicked thought |
| Skt. निस् *nis*, not, without | + तन्द्रा *tandrā*, idleness | : H. निस्तंद्र *nistandra*, unwearying |

(*h*) Final *-as* becomes *-o* before a voiced consonant.

| | | |
|---|---|---|
| Skt. मनस् *manas*, mind | + नीत *nīta*, led | : H. मनोनीत *manonīt*, preferred |
| Skt. अधस् *adhas*, down | + मुख *mukh*, face | : H. अधोमुख *adhomukh*, facing down |

(*i*) Final *-ar* or *-as* before voiceless *k*, *kh*, *p* or *ph* becomes *aḥ*; before voiceless *c*, *aś*; and before voiceless *t*, *as*.

| | | |
|---|---|---|
| Skt. अन्तर् *antar*, within | + पुर *pura*, stronghold | : H. अंतःपुर *antaḥpur*, women's quarters |
| Skt. प्रातर् *prātar*, early | + काल *kāla*, time | : H. प्रातःकाल *prātaḥkāl*, morning |
| Skt. पुनर् *punar*, again | + च *ca*, and | : H. पुनश्च *punaśca*, PS. (postscript) |
| Skt. अन्तर् *antar*, within | + तल *tala*, surface, level | : H. अंतस्तल *antastal*, heart |

Skt. अधस् *adhas*, down + पतन *patana*, falling : H. अध:पतन *adhaḥpatan*, decline

Skt. अधस् *adhas*, down + तल *tala*, surface, level : H. अधस्तल *adhastal*, lower room, level.

(*j*) Final *m* (e.g. in the prefix *sam* 'together with') before a plosive becomes the corresponding nasal.

संकोच H. *saṅkoc*, embarrassment

संजय H. *sañjay* (name)

संदेश H. *sandeś*, message

संप्रदाय H. *sampradāy*, community

Before other consonants it is pronounced variously, as indicated on p. xxviii, and always written as *anusvāra*.

संयोग H. *saṃyog*, chance

संस्था H. *saṃsthā*, organization

(*k*) Dental *n* becomes retroflex *ṇ* under the influence of a preceding retroflex *ṛ*, *ṣ*, or *r* in most cases where a palatal, retroflex or dental consonant (excluding *y*) does not intervene. This principle accounts for various spellings with *ṇ* which tend to be overlooked by learners.

(नागरी) प्रचारिणी (सभा) (*nāgarī*) *pracāriṇī* (*sabhā*), Society for the Propagation of Nāgarī

रामायण H. *rāmāyaṇ*, name of a Sanskrit poem

रमणी Skt. H. *ramaṇī*, delightful lady

# V

## FORMATION OF WORDS

Many words, chiefly nouns and adjectives, are formed by prefixation and suffixation. Some are made by modification of the form of roots or stems, or by the use of verb stems as different parts of speech.

### 1. *Prefixation*

Words formed by prefixation are mainly Sanskrit loanwords or later formations on Sanskrit models. The sense of the loanwords sometimes differs from their Sanskrit sense. Their pronunciation is very frequently somewhat Sanskritised, with 'inherent' vowels, which would be silent in words of Hindi origin of the same form, tending to be pronounced to a variable degree and with *ṣ* and *ṇ* realised as retroflexes. There are a few Persian, Arabic, and Hindi prefixes. The commonest prefixes are:

*a-*, *an-*, not, without (Skt. and H.)
अपरिचित *aparicit*, unacquainted
अनादर *anādar*, disrespect
अनेक *anek*, different (not one)
अनदेखा *andekhā*, unseen
अलग *alag*, separate, different

The form *an-* is used with Sanskrit words beginning with vowels only, but is quite common with Hindi words beginning with consonants also.

*ati-*, exceedingly (Skt.)
अतिक्षीण *atikṣīṇ*, very slight, weak

*adhas-*, down (Skt.)
अधःपतन *adhaḥpatan*, decline

*antar-*, within; internal (Skt.)
अंतःकरण *antaḥkaraṇ*, spirit
अंतर्राष्ट्रीय *antarrāṣṭrīy*, international[1]
अंतर्देशीय *antardeśīy*, inland (adj.)

[1] The spelling अंतरराष्ट्रीय *antarrāṣṭrīy* is also found. (Neither of these spellings shows correct Sanskritic *sandhi*, which would produce a form *antārāṣṭrīy*, unused in Hindi.)

*adhi*-, additional; above (Skt.)
अधिकार *adhikār*, authority

*anu*-, according to (Skt.)
के अनुसार *ke anusār*, according to
अनुवाद *anuvād*, translation

*apa*-, away, back; down (Skt.)
अपशब्द *apaśabd*, term of abuse

*abhi*-, towards; particular (Skt.)
अभियोग *abhiyog*, accusation

*ava*-, away; down (Skt.)
अवनति *avanati*, decline

*ā*-, to, towards; up to (Skt.)
आरक्षा *ārakṣā*, security
आगमन *āgaman*, arrival

*ud*-, upwards (Skt.)
उत्पादन *utpādan*, produce
उद्भव *udbhav*, origin
उन्नति *unnati*, progress

*upa*-, subsidiary (Skt.)
उपकुलपति *upakulpati*, vice-chancellor
उपभाषा *upabhāṣā*, dialect

*ku*- bad; deficient (Skt. and H.)
कुपुत्र *kuputr*, bad son
कुचाली *kucālī*, of bad conduct

*dus*-, bad; difficult (Skt.)
दुश्चिंता *duścintā*, wicked thought
दुर्दैव *durdaiv*, ill fate
दुष्कर *duṣkar*, hard to accomplish

*nis-*, without; away (Skt.)
निस्संकोच *nissaṅkoc*, without constraint
निष्पाप *niṣpāp*, sinless
निश्चल *niścal*, motionless
निष्कासन *niṣkāsan*, exile

*para-*, other (Skt.)
परतंत्र *partantra*, subjugated

*pari-*, around; abundantly (Skt.)
परिधि *paridhi*, circle
परिचित *paricit*, acquainted
परिपूर्ण *paripurṇ*, replete

*punar-*, again (Skt.)
पुनर्जागरण *punarjāgaraṇ*, renaissance

*pra-*, forward; exceedingly (Skt.)
प्रगति *pragati*, progress
प्रबंध *prabandh*, arrangement
प्रोत्साहन *protsāhan*, encouragement
प्रखर *prakhar*, very hard

*prati-*, against; every; per (Skt.)
के प्रतिकूल *ke pratikūl*, contrary to
प्रतिदिन *pratidin*, every day
प्रतिशत *pratiśat*, per cent
प्रतीक्षा *pratīkṣā*, expectation; waiting

*vi-*, apart; different, opposite; particular (Skt.)
विलग *vilag*, disconnected
विदेश *videś*, abroad, foreign lands
विमल *vimal*, without stain, pure
विशुद्ध *viśuddh*, pure, very pure
विनीत *vinīt*, humble, submissive

*sa-*, with, possessing (Skt.)
सपरिवार *saparivār*, with one's family
सहृदयता *sahṛdaytā*, good-heartedness, friendliness

*sam-*, together with; complete(ly) (Skt.)
संस्था *saṃsthā*, organisation
संयोग *saṃyog*, chance
समाप्त *samāpt*, finished
संपूर्ण *sampūrṇ*, complete

*sama-*, same, equal (Skt.)
समतल *samtal*, level
समसामयिक *samsāmayik*, contemporary[1]

*saha-*, together with (Skt.)
सहकार्यकर्ता *sahkāryakartā*, colleague
सहानुभूति *sahānubhūti*, sympathy, fellow-feeling
सहचर्य *sahcarya*, life together, married life

*su-*, good; easy (Skt. and H.)
सुपुत्र *suputr*, good son
सुगम *sugam*, accessible; easy
सुडौल *suḍaul*, well-built (physically)

*sva-* one's own (Skt.)
स्वदेश *svadeś*, one's own country
स्वभाव *svabhāv*, nature, temperament

*ġair-*, without; against (Ar.)
ग़ैरहाज़िर *ġairhāzir*, absent

*nā-*, without, non- (P.)
नाक़ाबिल *nāqābil*, incapable
नादान *nādān*, ignorant

*fī*, per (Ar.)
फ़ी सदी *fī sadī*, per cent

*be-*, without (P.)
बेकार *bekār*, unemployed; pointless

[1] *-ā-* in this form is explained on p. 195.

*lā-*, without (Ar.)

लाजवाब *lājavāb*, speechless, without an answer
लापरवाही *lāparvāhī*, carelessness
लापता *lāpatā*, of unknown whereabouts[1]

2. *Suffixation*

Words formed by suffixation include both words of Hindi origin and loanwords from Sanskrit, Persian, and Arabic.

(*a*) Common Hindi suffixes which form nouns and adjectives from verb or nominal stems (sometimes with vowel or consonant modification) are:

Forming nouns:

| | |
|---|---|
| *-āī* (f.) | पढ़ाई *paṛhāī*, reading, study |
| | लंबाई *lambāī*, length |
| *-āv* (m.) | घेराव *gherāv*, encirclement, siege |
| *-āvā* (m.) | दिखावा *dikhāvā*, evidence, display |
| *-ān* (m. f.) | उड़ान *uṛān*, flight |
| *-āvaṭ* (f.) | रुकावट *rukāvaṭ*, obstacle (cf. रोकना *roknā*) |
| *-āhaṭ* (f.) | घबराहट *ghabrāhaṭ*, confusion |
| | कड़वाहट *karvāhaṭ*, bitterness |
| *-ī* (m. f.) | फेरी *pherī*, circuit, ambit |
| | बोली *bolī*, speech, language |
| | तेली *telī*, oil seller |
| *-an* (m. f.) | सूजन *sūjan*, swelling |
| | लगन *lagan*, affection; desire |
| | चलन *calan*, motion, movement; behaviour |
| *-iyā* (m. f.) | डाकिया *ḍākiyā*, postman[2] |
| | डिबिया *ḍibiyā*, small box[2] (cf. डिब्बा *ḍibbā*) |
| | लुटिया *luṭiyā*, small brass pot (cf. लोटा *loṭā*) |
| *-erā* (m.) | सँपेरा *sam̐perā*, snake-charmer (cf. साँप *sām̐p*) |
| *-pan* (m.) | बचपन *bacpan*, childhood (cf. बच्चा *baccā*) |
| | लड़कपन *laṛakpan*, boyhood (cf. लड़का *laṛkā*) |
| | सीधापन *sīdhāpan*, simplicity[3] |
| *-pā* (m.) | बुढ़ापा *buṛhāpā*, old age (cf. बूढ़ा *būṛhā*) |

[1] Invariable (since based on the noun पता *patā*).

[2] See p. 2.

[3] Oblique case सीधेपन *sīdhepan*; similarly all derivatives of adjectives formed with this suffix.

Forming adjectives:

| | | |
|---|---|---|
| *-akkaṛ* | भुलक्कड़ *bhulakkaṛ*, forgetful (c.f. भूलना *bhūlnā*) |
| *-āū* | उपजाऊ *upjāū*, fertile<br>फिसलाऊ *phislāū*, slippery |
| *-ī* | कुचाली *kucālī*, of bad conduct |
| *-iyā* | कलकतिया *kalkatiyā*, belonging to Calcutta[1] (cf. कलकत्ता *kalkattā*)<br>बढ़िया *baṛhiyā*, good, nice |
| *-īlā* | नशीला *naśīlā*, intoxicating (cf. नशा *naśā*)<br>रसीला *rasīlā*, juicy |
| *-erā* | बहुतेरा *bahuterā*, many, much, frequent |

(*b*) Common Sanskrit suffixes in loanwords or later formations (other than some already noted) are:

***-ak*** (often agentive)

लेखक *lekhak*, writer

अध्यापक *adhyāpak*, teacher

बहुसंख्यक *bahusaṅkhyak*, numerous

***-ik*** (forms adjectives and agentive nouns from nouns, with *vṛddhi* of root or initial vowel)

धार्मिक *dhārmik*, religious (cf. धर्म *dharm*)

दैनिक *dainik*, daily (cf. दिन *din*)

औद्योगिक *audyogik*, industrial (cf. उद्योग *udyog*)

सांप्रदायिक *sāmpradāyik*, communal (cf. संप्रदाय *sampradāy*)

प्रादेशिक *prādeśik*, concerning a state (cf. प्रदेश *pradeś*)

सांस्कृतिक *sāṃskṛtik*, cultural (cf. संस्कृति *saṃskṛti*)[2]

आंशिक *āṃśik*, partial (cf. अंश *aṃś*)[2]

सैनिक *sainik*, military; soldier (cf. सेना *senā*)

(सम)सामयिक (*sam*)*sāmayik*, (con)temporary (cf. समय *samay*)

[1] Unchanged in feminine concord.

[2] Where the vowel *a* preceding a nasal consonant + a non-plosive consonant is lengthened in derivative words (or in *sandhi*) it is nasalized, usually with loss of the nasal consonant; but the spelling is with *anusvāra* not *candrabindu*. Cf. p. xxviii.
An example of such an *a* lengthened and nasalized in *sandhi* is seen in the word अधिकांश *adhikāṃś* 'majority, greater part'.

***-it*** (forms past participial adjectives)
सुरक्षित *surakṣit*, protected, preserved
परिचित *paricit*, acquainted
क्रोधित *krodhit*, angry, made angry

***-ī*** (forms nouns and adjectives)
अधिकारी *adhikārī*, official, person in authority
अभिमानी *abhimānī*, proud person
सुखी *sukhī*, happy

***-kār*** (forms agentive nouns)
साहित्यकार *sāhityakār*, writer, literary man

***-tavya*** (forms verbal nouns)
कर्तव्य *kartavya*, duty (that which is to be done)

***-tva*** (forms abstract nouns from nouns and adjectives)
पुरुषत्व *puruṣatva*, manliness
उत्तरदायित्व *uttardāyitva*, responsibility

***-pūrvak*** (forms adverbs of manner from nouns)
आदरपूर्वक *ādarpūrvak*, respectfully

***-may*** (forms adjectives of the sense 'consisting of . . .')
मधुमय *madhumay*, sweet, mellifluous

***-mān*** (forms adjectives from nouns, chiefly, of the sense 'possessed of . . ')[1]
दीप्तिमान् *dīptimān*, illuminated, brilliant
श्रीमान् *śrīmān*, sir (in address)[2]

***-ya*** (forms adjectives expressing potentiality from verbal roots; also abstract nouns from nouns or adjectives, with *vṛddhi* of root or initial vowel)
सह्य *sahya*, tolerable
प्राप्य *prāpya*, obtainable, accessible
पांडित्य *pāṇḍitya*, learning
सौभाग्य *saubhāgya*, good fortune
धैर्य *dhairya*, steadfastness

[1] For feminines of these forms see Supplement I, p. 168.
[2] The Sanskrit vocative form श्रीमन् *śrīman* is also heard in very formal style.

*-vān* (forms adjectives and nouns from nouns, chiefly, of the sense 'possessed of . . .')[1]

कलावान् *kalāvān*, artistic
विद्वान् *vidvān*, learned, a scholar

(*c*) The commonest Arabic and Persian suffixes are:

*-at* (in feminine abstract nouns)
तबीयत *tabīyat*, state of health

*-ānā* (forms adjectives, normally invariable, and nouns from nouns)
मरदाना *mardānā*, male
ज़नाना *zanānā*, female
रोज़ाना *rozānā*, daily
राजपुतानी *rājputānī*, Rajput woman

*-iś* (forms feminine abstract nouns)
सिफ़ारिश *sifāriś*, recommendation
गुंजाइश *guñjāiś*, room, space, scope

*-ī* (forms abstract nouns and adjectives from nouns and adjectives)
दोस्ती *dostī*, friendship, friendliness
ख़ुशी *khuśī*, happiness
ज़िंदगी *zindagī*, life
हिंदी *hindī*, Hindi (language of Hind)
क़ानूनी *qānūnī*, legal

*-dār* (forms nouns and adjectives from nouns)
दुकानदार *dukāndār*, shopkeeper
समझदार *samajhdār*, intelligent
दाँतदार *dāṁtdār*, toothed, cogged

*-īn* (forms adjectives from nouns)
शौक़ीन *śauqīn*, desirous, eager; cultivated

3. *Other types of word formation*

(*a*) From Hindi verb stems, by using these as nouns; monosyllabic stems

[1] For feminines of these forms see Supplement I, p. 168. The second example is based on a verbal root and does not show a feminine in -वती *-vatī*.

with short vowels usually show vowel lengthening or modification. Most verbal nouns of this type are feminine.

मार *mār*, beating; killing
लूट *lūṭ*, looting
समझ *samajh*, understanding, comprehension
चाल *cāl*, action, activity; deportment
बाढ़ *bāṛh*, flood
मेल *mel*, union; harmony
मेल-जोल *mel-jol*, association; familiarity

(*b*) In Sanskrit loanwords; *vṛddhi* derivatives without suffixation.

शैव *śaiv*, devotee of Śiva
वैष्णव *vaiṣṇav*, devotee of Viṣṇu[1]
बौद्ध *bauddh*, devotee of the Buddha
स्मार्त *smārta*, follower of *smṛti* doctrine[1]

(*c*) In Arabic loanwords through Persian; related forms may show a variety of vowel and consonant alternations, e.g. as in

| | | | | |
|---|---|---|---|---|
| ख़बर | *khabar*, news | : | अख़बार | *akhbār*, newspaper |
| तकलीफ़ | *taklīf*, trouble | : | तकल्लुफ़ | *takalluf*, formality |
| असर | *asar*, effect | : | आसार | *āsār*, signs, portents |

These alternations are of little importance in themselves for the student of Hindi. Words derived in this way are best learned individually as they occur.

[1] Words ending in *-u* or *-i* show modification of these vowels as well as *vṛddhi* of their root vowel.

# VI

## COMPOUNDING OF WORDS

Compounding is a very common device in Hindi; instances have already been noted (pp. 63, 90, 185 ff.). Most compounds give little difficulty in interpretation, but the student may find a brief outline of the chief types of compound which occur useful.

### 1. *Co-ordinative compounds*

Co-ordinative compounds are those implying a link, ग्रौर *aur* 'and', or occasionally या *yā* 'or', between the members of the compound. These may be various parts of speech, and either of Hindi origin words or loan-words. Co-ordinative compounds are usually hyphenated.

बाप-बेटा *bāp-beṭā*, father and son
बाप-दादा *bāp-dādā*, forefathers[1]
मित्र-शत्रु *mitr-śatru*, friends and enemies
छोटे-बड़े *choṭe-baṛe*, small and great

(*a*) Second members of some compounds are of identical or similar sense to first members. Such compounds usually have some degree of affective force, however slight.

बाल-बच्चे *bāl-bacce*, children
भरा-पूरा *bharā-pūrā*, well-filled, solid, bulky
मुग्ध-चकित *mugdh-cakit*, fascinated, fond (artless and astonished)
ग्रच्छा-खासा *acchā-k͟hāsā*, good, fine (cf. P. loanword खासा *k͟hāsā* 'special')

(*b*) Verb compounds are for the most part of participial, absolutive or infinitive forms. Some are of stem forms and have the force of nouns.

लोग सड़क में ग्राते-जाते हैं । *log saṛak meṁ āte-jāte haiṁ*, People come and go in the street.

मैंने यह जान-बूझकर किया । *maiṁne yah jān-būjhkar kiyā*, I did this on purpose (with knowledge and understanding).[2]

[1] In this compound दादा *dādā* is often inflected as a masculine in final *-ā*, and not as दिन *din*; cf. p. 1.

[2] For the form of the absolutive see p. 90, n. 2 (where verb compounds are referred to as 'verb pairs', to avoid any later confusion with compound verbs).

तुम लोगों का लड़ना-झगड़ना मुझे अच्छा नहीं लगता । *tum logoṁ kā laṛnā-jhagaṛnā mujhe acchā nahīṁ lagtā*, I don't like the way you people fight and quarrel.

रोक-टोक *rok-ṭok*, checking, interference

मार-काट *mār-kāṭ*, slaughter

(*c*) Two special categories of verb compounds are (i) those of perfective participles of verbs of related stem, which emphasise thoroughness of action, and (ii) those of masculine and feminine perfective participles, usually of the same verb, which emphasise reciprocity or intensity of action. These have the force of nouns and are of feminine gender.

दूल्हा देखना क्या है? मेरा देखा-दिखाया है *dūlhā dekhnā kyā hai? merā dekhā-dikhāyā hai*, What's the point of (going) to see the bridegroom? I've already seen him (and am satisfied).

बने-बनाए जूते *bane-banāe jūte*, ready-made shoes

मारा-मारी *mārā-mārī*, fight, brawl

(मेरे) देखा-देखी *(mere) dekhā-dekhī*, (in) imitation (of me)[1]

खींचा-तानी *khīṁcā-tānī*, competition; tension

2. *Determinative compounds*

In these the sense of the first member of the compound defines that of the second in some way.[2] Both words of Hindi origin and loanwords occur; the former sometimes show vowel or consonant modification. Most of these compounds may be unhyphenated, though practice varies. Compounds whose second member is a Hindi verbal form are usually hyphenated.

देवनगरवासी *devnagarvāsī*, an inhabitant of Devnagar

नदीतट *nadītaṭ*, river-bank

मनमोहक *manmohak*, heart-captivating

जी-तोड़ *jī-toṛ*, soul-destroying

शरारत-भरा *śarārat-bharā*, filled with wickedness, naughtiness

नीलकंठ *nīlkaṇṭh*, blue jay (blue-throat)

परमप्रिय *parampriy*, supremely dear

यथासंभव *yathāsambhav*, as far, much, as possible

[1] With the use here of मेरे *mere* not in concord cf. the use of के *ke* in certain postpositional expressions based on feminine nouns, noted on p. 35.

[2] A sub-classification of determinative compounds is made for Sanskrit grammar, but concerns the student of Hindi only marginally, and is therefore not given here.

कठपुतली *kaṭhputlī*, puppet (wooden doll; cf. काठ *kāṭh*, m. 'wood')
आँखों-देखा *āṁkhoṁ-dekhā*, seen with one's own eyes
लकड़बग्घा *lakaṛbagghā*, hyena (cf. बाघ *bāgh*, m. 'tiger; lion')
घुड़सवार *ghuṛsavār*, horse-rider (cf. घोड़ा *ghoṛā*)
भिखमँगा *bhikhmaṁgā*, beggar (cf. भीख *bhīkh*, f. 'alms'; माँगना *māṁgnā*, 'request')

3. *Possessive compounds*

The second member of these is characteristically a noun, and the compounds are adjectives qualifying nouns or pronouns. Though common in Sanskrit they are relatively rare in Hindi, even in the more Sanskritised language; possessives with prefixes as first member are the only type which is at all frequent. Some possessives show a final adjectival suffix. These compounds are normally unhyphenated.

हँसमुख *haṁsmukh*, cheerful, jolly
प्रगतिशील *pragatiśīl*, progressive, of progressive character
पूर्णकाम *pūrṇkām*, of fulfilled desire
निस्तंद्र *nistandra*, unwearying[1]
दुमंज़िला *dumanzilā*, two-storeyed (cf. मंज़िल *manzil*, f. 'storey')

4. *Quasi-compounds*

Many compounds exist in informal usage whose second member is rare, or used very figuratively, or meaningless independently. These usually have some degree of affective force. Second members are usually based on rhyming or echoing syllables. Some examples are:

बातचीत *bātcīt*, conversation
भीड़-भाड़ *bhīṛ-bhāṛ*, crowd, throng
भीड़-भब्भर *bhīṛ-bhabbhaṛ*, crowd, throng
ठीक-ठाक *ṭhīk-ṭhāk*, fine (answering the question 'how are you?')
शोर-शराबा *śor-śarābā*, noise and confusion
चाय-वाय *cāy-vāy*, tea, etc. (tea and something to eat)
गड़बड़-शड़बड़ *gaṛbaṛ-śaṛbaṛ*, confusion

In some cases the first element of the compound is the meaningless one.

(के) आस-पास (*ke*) *ās-pās*, near, round about; nearby

[1] See p. 188.

# READING PASSAGES

वाणी, जिसे मैं केवल[1] बारह-तेरह बरस[2] की समझता था, वास्तव में[3] पन्द्रह-सोलह साल की लड़की थी । छोटे क़द[4] की पतली,[5] दुबली,[6] बीमार-बीमार-सी! कवि अख़तर शेरानी ने जब लिखा था–'मुझे तो कुछ इन्हीं बीमार कलियों से[7] मुहब्बत[8] है'–तो शायद उसी जैसी[9] किसी लड़की को 'बीमार कली' की संज्ञा[10] दी होगी । जब पहले दिन मैं देवनगर आया था, और अपने पिता का आदेश[11] पालने[12] की उत्सुकता[13] में वाणी फुदकती[14] हुई-सी अपनी छोटी बहन के साथ दरवाज़े में आ खड़ी हुई थी,[15] तो मैंने उसकी ओर ध्यान[16] भी न दिया था । वही चाय लायी थी, लेकिन उसमें कोई भी ऐसा आकर्षण[17] न था कि देवा जी की बातें सुनते या उन्हें अपनी बातें सुनाते समय मेरा ध्यान उसकी ओर चला जाता । इसलिए यह ठीक ही था कि जब मैं तीरथराम की प्रेयसी[18] की तलाश में देवनगर के घर-घर घूमा तो वाणी की ओर मेरा ध्यान भी नहीं गया । लेकिन उस शाम के बाद वह नन्हीं[19] बीमार-सी कली अचानक मेरा ध्यान खींचने लगी ।

डाइनिंग हाल में खाना मैं पहले भी खाता था और कई बार उस पाँत[20] में भी खाता था, जिसमें देवा जी और उनका परिवार रहता[21] । लेकिन उस घटना के बाद दूसरे दिन जब मैं दोपहर का खाना खाने गया तो अचानक मेरी आँखें अगली मेज़ों की ओर उठ गयीं, जहाँ प्राय:[22] देवा जी आकर बैठते थे । देवा जी नहीं थे, न[23] उनकी पत्नी थीं–शायद वे पहली पाँत में खाना खा गये थे–लेकिन दूसरे बच्चों में घिरी वाणी बैठी थी । मैंने निगाह[24] उठायी तो मौन[25] रूप से उसे अपनी ओर तकते[26] पाया । नज़र मिलते ही[27] उसने आँखें झुका लीं, लेकिन जब मैंने फिर उसकी ओर देखा तो मेरी निगाहें फिर उससे जा मिलीं[28] ।

[1] only
[2] year (m.)
[3] in reality, in fact
[4] stature (m.)
[5] thin
[6] thin, weak
[7] कली *kalī*, f., bud; बीमार कली *bīmār kalī*, ailing, frail young thing
[8] †love (f.)
[9] See p. 84.
[10] title, appellation; noun (f.)
[11] direction, command (m.)
[12] maintain, bring up; carry out
[13] eagerness (f.)
[14] hop, skip, frolic
[15] came and stood; आ *ā*, stem absolutive
[16] attention (m.)
[17] attraction; attractiveness, charm
[18] beloved (f.)
[19] नन्हाँ *nanhāṁ*, tiny
[20] row (f.); Hindi form corresponding to Skt. loanword पंक्ति *paṅkti*.
[21] See p. 170.
[22] usually
[23] nor
[24] †glance (f.)
[25] *silent; silence (m.)
[26] look, gaze
[27] See p. 144.
[28] See p. 178.

खाना खाने के बाद थाली[1] लेकर जब मैं बाहर निकला तो कुछ इस तरह हुआ[2] कि वाणी और मैं लगभग एक साथ[3] नल[4] पर पहुँचे। मैं थाली रखकर हमाम की टोंटी[5] के नीचे हाथ धोने जा ही रहा था कि वाणी थाली रखकर आ गयी। मैं पीछे हट गया कि वह पहले हाथ धो ले। तभी मेरी नज़र सामने डचोढ़ी[6] की ओर चली गयी। तीरथराम उसी तरह[7] हाथ बग़ल[8] में दबाये[9] घूम रहा था। उसकी निगाह हमारी ओर थी, पर मुझे देखते ही वह सिर झुकाकर मुड़[10] गया।

बड़े मीठे[11] स्वर[12] में 'थैंक यू' कहते हुए वाणी हाथ धोने लगी। साबुन[13] मलते[14] और हाथ धोते हुए उसने अपनी चंचल[15] पर गहरी[16] दृष्टि मुझपर डाली और ज़रा-सा[17] मुस्कराते[18] हुए बोली—"आप उस दिन गाते ही बाहर क्यों चले गये थे?"

हाथ धोकर वह पीछे हट गयी और रूमाल[19] से उन्हें पोंछने[20] लगी। मैं हाथ धोने लगा। इस बीच[21] लगातार[22] मैं उसके प्रश्न का उत्तर सोचता रहा।

"बताइए न संगीत जी?" उसने फिर आग्रह[23] के साथ कहा।

शाम का वक़्त था। नहर[1] पर पहुँचा तो पश्चिम में सूरज डूब[2] रहा था। सर्दी सरे-शाम ही[3] उतर आयी थी और मैं ओवरकोट पहने था। तभी पश्चिम की ओर आँखें उठाते ही

[1] flat metal tray for carrying food (f.)
[2] it so happened that
[3] लगभग एक साथ *lagbhag ek sāth*, just about together
[4] pipe, conduit (m.)
[5] water-pot with spout (for washing hands); हम्माम, हमाम *ham(m)ām*, m., place for bathing, washing
[6] threshold, doorway (f.)
[7] in the same way (as before)
[8] armpit, side (f.)
[9] press (trans.)
[10] turn, turn away (intr.)
[11] sweet; pleasant
[12] voice (m.)
[13] soap (m.)
[14] rub, rub on (trans.)
[15] mobile, restless
[16] deep; grave
[17] slightly; ज़रा †*zarā* (invariable adj.) just, (just) a little
[18] smile
[19] handkerchief (m.)
[20] wipe
[21] in the meantime
[22] continuously
[23] zeal, eagerness (m.); see p. 181

[1] canal (m.)
[2] sink, set
[3] with the fall of evening; an expression of specifically Urdu character.

दिल की धड़कन[4] जैसे थम[5] गयी । कितना अकथ[6], कितना सुन्दर दृश्य[7] था! दूर, बहुत दूर खजूर[8] के एकाकी[9] पेड़ के पीछे, जो उस निर्जन[10] के सूनेपन[11] को चुनौती[12] देता हुआ-सा खड़ा था, सूरज डूब रहा था । बड़ा-बड़ा और पीला-पीला[13]– पेड़ का ऊपर का सिरा[14] ऐसे लग रहा था[15] जैसे उस पीली कुंदनी[16] थाली पर अंकित[17] हो । नहर के पानी पर सूरज का बिम्ब,[18] ऊपर आकाश के हलके[19] श्वेत[20] बादलों पर उसका रंग,[21] उस रंग से रंजित[22] दूर तक फैली नहर की पटरी[23] और अकेला[24] मैं . . . कुछ दूर चलकर बैठ गया और अचानक गाने लगा । वही अपना चिर-परिचित गीत नहीं,[25] सहगल के मधुमय[26] स्वर में सुना[27] वह कृष्ण के प्रेम में पागल[28] गोपी[29] का गीत, जो ज़रूर ही अल्हड़[30] रही होगी, छोटी उम्र[31] की होगी । गीत विरह[32] का था । पर जाने क्यों मुझे करुण[33] नहीं लगा । मन की उमंग[34] में जैसे[35] उस प्राकृतिक[36] सौन्दर्य और सुनसान[37] को भरता हुआ[38] मैं गा उठा–

[4] beating, thumping (f.)
[5] be checked, stopped
[6] indescribable ; cf. Sanskrit अकथ्य *akathya.*
[7] sight (m.)
[8] date (palm) (m.f.)
[9] solitary (invariable adj.)
[10] *deserted, unpopulated spot (m.) ; desolate
[11] emptiness (m.)
[12] challenge (f.)
[13] yellow
[14] edge; see Supplement III, p. 178.
[15] seemed
[16] made of fine gold (कुंदन *kundan*, m.)
[17] drawn, traced
[18] *reflection; halo (m.)
[19] light
[20] *white ; बादल *bādal*, m., cloud
[21] colour (m.)
[22] *coloured
[23] surface (f.) (often of road or path)
[24] alone, single
[25] not that old song of mine; अपना *apnā* depends on मैं *maiṁ* understood from the previous sentence; चिर-परिचित गीत **cir-paricit gīt*, m., song with which one is long acquainted, long-known song.
[26] *sweet (मधु *madhu*, m., honey); सहगल *sahgal*, a personal name
[27] non-finite participle, qualifying गीत *gīt*
[28] mad, crazy
[29] herdgirl; the herdgirls of Braj were enamoured of Krishna (*Kṛṣṇ*).
[30] gay
[31] †age (f.)
[32] separation (of lovers) (m.)
[33] sad, piteous
[34] enthusiasm; zeal; delight (f.)
[35] See p. 84.
[36] natural, belonging to nature (प्रकृति *prakṛti*); सौन्दर्य *saundarya*, beauty
[37] emptiness, loneliness, solitude (m.); lonely, deserted
[38] fill, pour in

सुनो सुनो रे कृषण काला[39]
सुनो सुनो रे कृषण काला

तभी कहीं निकट[40] ठहाके[41] की आवाज़ आयी–सूने[42] में सहसा बज उठने वाली घंटियों सरीखी युवा-लड़कियों के ठहाके की आवाज़। मैं चौंक उठा। पटरी पर वाणी, श्यामा और मधु न जाने किस बात पर हँसती-हँसती दोहरी होती[43] जा रही थीं। साथ उनके अठारह-बीस वर्ष का एक यवक[44] था।

उन्हें गुज़रने[45] के लिए राह[46] देने को मैं एक ओर हट गया। पर चारों की टोली[47] मेरे पास आकर रुक गयी।

"दिलजीत, यह हैं संगीत जी, बड़ा ही अच्छा गाते हैं[48]।" अपनी बड़ी-बड़ी आँखों को फैलाते[49] और शब्दों के साथ झूमते हुए वाणी ने अपने साथी[50] युवक को मेरा परिचय दिया और फिर मुझसे बोली–"यह है दिलजीत, मेरा भाई, गवर्नमेण्ट कालेज में पढ़ता है, छुट्टियों में[51] आया है।"

यह मान[1] लेने में मुझे कुछ भी संकोच नहीं कि उन चार महीनों में देवनगर से मुझे बेहद[2] प्यार[3] हो गया था। वहाँ वाणी थी और उसकी मुग्ध-चकित[4] आँखों में मेरे लिए अपार[5] स्नेह[6] और सहानुभूति[7] थी, या वहाँ देवा जी थे, जो मेरे संतप्त[8] मन को शान्ति[9] प्रदान करते थे,[10] या फिर देवनगर-वासियों[11] में वैसी सहृदयता,[12] स्नेह और प्यार था, जैसा

[39] Oh listen, dark Krishna. रे *re*, variant of अरे *are*. The form कृषण *kṛṣaṇ* shows a simplification of consonant groups typical of many Sanskrit loanwords, usually older ones.
[40] near, nearby
[41] loud laughter, guffaw (m.)
[42] emptiness, solitude (m.); empty, lonely
[43] दोहरी होती *dohrī hotī*, as a group. See p. 169.
[44] *youth, young man (m.)
[45] pass (intr.), pass by
[46] †road; way, passage (f.)
[47] group (f.)
[48] he sings very well indeed. For बड़ा *baṛā* here see p. 50.
[49] spread; (of eyes) open wide
[50] companion; accompanying (adj.)
[51] for

[1] मानना *mānnā*, accept, agree; accept as. Cf. p. 158, n. 2.
[2] †unlimited; see p. 193.
[3] love, affection (m.)
[4] See p. 199.
[5] limitless
[6] love, affection (m.)
[7] sympathy
[8] *heated, tormented
[9] peace (f.)
[10] give, donate (conjunct verb)
[11] inhabitants of Devnagar
[12] friendliness, kindliness (m.)

कहीं ग्रौर देखने में नहीं ग्राता–नहीं, इनमें से कोई बात न थी[13] । वाणी के उस स्नेह ग्रौर सहानुभूति ने मेरी उस ग्रस्थायी[14] शान्ति को, जो देवनगर के उन पहले दिनों में मुझे प्राप्त हुई थी, एक ग्रजीब-सी[15] बेचैनी[16] में बदल दिया था । देवा जी के लेखों[17] की बड़ी-बड़ी बातें भी मेरे मन के सागर[18] पर तैरती[19] हुई वृन्तहीन[20] कमलिनियों[21]-सी बहने लगी थीं । ग्रौर देवनगर के वासी! –जैसे-जैसे[22] मैं उन्हें जानता गया, मुझे लगता गया कि ऊपर से नज़र ग्रानेवाली[23] मुस्कानों[24] ग्रौर प्रकट[25] सुनायी देनेवाले प्रेम ग्रौर परस्पर[26] प्रोत्साहन[27] के दावों[28] के नीचे वही ईर्ष्या-द्वेष[29] का विष[30] छिपा हुग्रा है । लेकिन देवनगर के ग्रास-पास[31] की सुन्दरता,[32] उन देहाती[33] सुबहों ग्रौर शामों का वह सोने,[34] गुलाब[35] ग्रौर केसर[36] से धुला हुग्रा लावण्य,[37] नदी-तट[38] का वह एकांत[39], करीर[40] की उन ठिगनी[41] भरी-पूरी[42] झाड़ियों[43] के फूलों की वह जलते ग्रंगारों[44]-की-सी लाली[45]– सब मेरे मन

[13] The sense of the sentence in outline is: It was not that Vāṇī was there . . . or that Devā Jī was there . . . or that the inhabitants of Devnagar showed such warm feeling as was not found elsewhere.

[14] impermanent, short-lived (invariable adj.)

[15] †strange, curious

[16] disquiet (f.)

[17] article, writing (m.)

[18] ocean (m.)

[19] swim, float

[20] *stalkless; हीन *hīn*, deprived of, without (in compounds); wretched

[21] lotus (f.); see Supplement I, pp. 164 f.; बहना *bahnā;* flow, float

[22] in proportion as

[23] नज़र ग्राना †*nazar ānā*, be visible

[24] smile (f.)

[25] clearly, manifestly

[26] See p. 152.

[27] encouragement (m.)

[28] दावा *dāvā*, m., claim

[29] jealousy (f.) and hatred (m.)

[30] poison (m.)

[31] See p. 201.

[32] beauty (f.)

[33] country (invariable adj.)

[34] gold (m.)

[35] pink; rose (m.)

[36] saffron (m.)

[37] *savour, charm (m.)

[38] bank (m.)

[39] *quiet, privacy (m.)

[40] caper-bush (a thorny shrub) (m.)

[41] dwarfish, stumpy

[42] See p. 199.

[43] bush (f.)

[44] ग्रंगारा *aṅgārā*, m., spark

[45] redness

को कुछ इस तरह बाँधे था कि जब दिमाग़[46] कहता,[47] 'मैंने देवनगर आकर ग़लती[48] की' तो मन वहाँ से जाने के विचार-मात्र[49] से उदास[50] हो जाता।

पित्तो की मौत[1] के बाद शहर की भीड़-भाड़[2] में मेरा दम[3] घुटने[4] लगा था। असल में[5] पित्तो के ज़िन्दा रहते[6] मुझे नगर[7] के उस शोर-शराबे[8] और भीड़-भब्भड़ का कभी अहसास[9] न हुआ था। उस सारे शोर के ऊपर जैसे पित्तो की प्यारी-प्यारी बातें मेरे कानों[10] में गूंजती रहती थीं और वह सारी भीड़ पित्तो की सूरत[11] के आगे[12] एकदम[13] लुप्त[14] हो जाती थी। दफ़्तर में काम करते, मित्र-शत्रुओं, अफ़सरों[15] या चपरासियों[16] से बातें करते हुए भी आँखें उसको देखती रहती थीं। दो-चार बच्चे हो जाते[17] तो सम्भव है कि नोन,[18] तेल, लकड़ी और कपड़े की यथार्थता[19] विवाह[20] के उन शुरू के वर्षों की व्यामोहावस्था[21] को भंग कर देती,[22] लेकिन तीन वर्षों के उन तीन पल[23] बनकर बीत जानेवाले दिनों के सहचर्य[24] के बाद, जब वह मीठी आवाज़ और वह मन-मोहक[25] सूरत मौत के हाथों[26]

[46] brain (m.)
[47] See p. 170.
[48] †mistake, error (f.)
[49] at the very thought of going; मात्र *mātr (suffixed adv.), only
[50] dejected

[1] †death (f.)
[2] See p. 201.
[3] breath (m.)
[4] be choked
[5] †in reality
[6] See p. 178.
[7] city (m.)
[8] See p. 201.
[9] †perception, feeling (m.)
[10] कान *kān*, m., ear
[11] †form, face (f.)
[12] in front of, out in front of; beyond
[13] completely, simply; at once
[14] *vanished
[15] officer, official (m.)
[16] office messenger (m.)
[17] Unrealized condition; see p. 124.
[18] salt (m.); नमक *namak*, m., is a commoner word.
[19] reality (m.); 'the realities of daily life' here
[20] marriage (m.)
[21] *carefree, delighted state; = *vi* + *ā* + *moh* (m.), fascination, infatuation + *avasthā* (f.), position, state
[22] भंग करना *bhaṅg karnā*, break; conjunct verb, with dependent auxiliary देना *denā*
[23] पल *pal*, m., moment; बनना *bannā*, be made; become
[24] married life (m.); after the companionship of those three years (those three years' days) which had passed by like three seconds. उन *un* qualifies दिनों *dinoṁ*.
[25] See p. 200.
[26] at the hands of, at the onslaught of death; adverbial oblique

क्षीण[27] और विकृत[28] होकर चली गयी, तो लगा कि जैसे[29] शहर का शोर मेरे कानों के पर्दे[30] फाड़ रहा है और भीड़ मेरा गला[31] घोंटे[32] दे रही है। देवनगर के उन वीरानों[33] का वह मौन मुझे इतना अच्छा लगता कि कभी-कभी जी[34] चाहता उसी में विलीन[35] हो जाऊँ, घुल[36] जाऊँ, शरीर[37] को छोड़कर उसके कण-कण[38] में समा[39] जाऊँ।

[27] *frail, slight
[28] *spoiled, damaged
[29] लगा कि जैसे *lagā ki jaise*, it seemed that
[30] पर्दा *pardā*, m., curtain; कान का पर्दा *kān kā pardā*, eardrum
[31] throat (m.)
[32] घोंटना *ghomṭnā*, choke, throttle; see pp. 172 f.
[33] वीराना *vīrānā*, m., deserted place
[34] life, spirit (m.)
[35] immersed, absorbed
[36] be dissolved
[37] body (m.)
[38] *fragment, particle, drop (m.); see p. 139; उसके *uske* refers back to मौन *maun.*
[39] समाना *samānā*, be contained, absorbed; कण-कण में समा जाना *kaṇ-kaṇ meṁ samā jānā*, pervade thoroughly, pervade every atom of

# COMPOSITION PASSAGES

## I

A certain man had two sons. One day one son said to his father, 'Father, please give me my share[1] of[2] your wealth[3].' His father gave him his share. After this he went off to a distant land. In that country, he wasted[4] all his father's money,[5] and quickly became poor. At that time he was living in the house of an inhabitant[6] of that country. He began to work in that man's fields, because he had no money. After some time he thought,[7] 'I shall return[8] to my country, and go to my father, and tell him how greatly I have sinned.[9]' And he came back[10] to his country. His father saw him from far off, and was very happy.[11] He had waited for him a long time.[12] The servants gave him new clothes to wear, and a fat calf[13] was killed.[14] But his brother was very angry.[15] 'What's going on here?'[16] he said. His father answered that his brother had just[17] returned, and that[18] he ought to be happy.

[1] हिस्सा †*hissā*, m., भाग *bhāg*, m., part

[2] में से *meṁ se*

[3] धन *dhan*, m., दौलत †*daulat*, f., wealth, riches

[4] उड़ाना *uṛānā*, literally 'cause to fly'

[5] पैसे *paise*, m.pl.

[6] निवासी *nivāsī*, m.

[7] सोचना *socnā* (used with ने *ne*)

[8] Subjunctive possible; the idea is a proposition in the first instance.

[9] मैंने कैसा पाप किया है *maiṁne kaisā pāp kiyā hai*

[10] लौट ग्राना *lauṭ ānā*

[11] हुए *hue*, not थे *the*, describing the sudden, new development.

[12] Continuous past (emphasizing duration of the period).

[13] मोटा बछड़ा *moṭā bachṛā*, m.

[14] ज़बह करना *zabah karnā*, slaughter (conjunct verb). The word ज़बह *zabah* is often pronounced and written with *i* in first syllable.

[15] बिगड़ना *bigaṛnā*, be spoiled; be upset; perfective required here.

[16] यह क्या हो रहा है? *yah kyā ho rahā hai?* For यह *yah* here see p. 102.

[17] Distributive ग्रभी-ग्रभी *abhī-abhī* possible (the emphasis being less on the exact time of the return than on the fact that it has taken place during the immediately preceding period).

[18] Since direct speech reportage will be used here, the words 'and that' need not be represented.

## II

Allahabad is about[1] 500 miles from Delhi,[2] and[3] the train journey[4] usually takes about twelve hours. My train was an express bound for Calcutta, and it left at 7.20 a.m. At that time it was quite cool.[5] Later on, however, especially[6] in the afternoon, it grew very hot[7] and dusty in the carriage.[8] I became very tired[9] and began to feel very thirsty, and dozed off[10] several times. Apart from myself there was only one other passenger[11] in the compartment,[12] a Muslim[13] of about forty-five.[14] But I didn't have much conversation[15] with him because he was reading a book most of the time.[16] I could see[17] that the book was written in Urdu. There seemed to be quite a difference[18] between[19] the countryside near Allahabad[20] and that in the west. The monsoon had begun, but round Delhi the fields were

[1] क़रीब †*qarīb*, लगभग *lagbhag*

[2] Say '500 miles distant from Delhi'.

[3] Note that long English sentences are frequently best broken up into shorter sentences in Hindi, especially in simple style. The word और *aur* can be omitted here and a new sentence begun.

[4] Say 'going by train (रेल *rel*, f., ट्रेन *ṭren*, f.) usually takes . . .'

[5] Use the noun ठंड *ṭhanḍ*, f., 'coolness', not the adj. ठंडा *ṭhanḍā*.

[6] ख़ासकर †*k͟hāskar*, विशेषकर *viśeṣkar*

[7] Use गरमी लगना *garmī lagnā*, be hot

[8] धूल *dhūl*, f., dust; use धूल भरना *dhūl bharnā*, be dusty (of an enclosed place which can be *filled* with dust). For 'carriage' use गाड़ी *gāṛī*, f.

[9] Use थकना *thaknā*.

[10] ऊँघना *ūṁghnā*, doze; for 'doze off' use with लगना *lagnā*.

[11] यात्री *yātrī*, m.

[12] डिब्बा *ḍibbā*, m.

[13] मुसलमान *musalmān*, m.

[14] Say 'of about 45 years'.

[15] बातचीत *bātcīt*, f., conversation; मेरी उससे ज्यादा बातचीत न हो सकी *merī usse zyādā bātcīt na ho sakī*. Construction with होना *honā* is better than with करना *karnā*; use of सकना *saknā* underlines the fact that the person wished to have some conversation.

[16] ज्यादातर *zyādātar*

[17] मैंने देखा *maiṁne dekhā*. English 'I could see' does not really stress ability to see in this context, and use of सकना *saknā* is unnecessary.

[18] फ़र्क़ *farq*, m.; काफ़ी फ़र्क़ मालूम हुआ *kāfī farq mālūm huā*

[19] में *meṁ*

[20] इलाहाबाद के पास का देहात *ilāhābād ke pās kā dehāt*

still[21] rather brown[22] and dry.[23] Here[24] in the east, however, everything was green,[25] and I could see that water was lying[26] in the rice-fields.[27]

## III

At last[1] we reached Allahabad, and the train stopped[2] in the station just about right on time. A porter[3] came into the compartment and asked me how much luggage I had, and a moment later[4] I stepped out on to the platform.[5] On the platform there was a great crowd of people who[6] had come to meet[7] their friends and relatives.[8] I tried to pick out[9] my friend's brother somewhere in the crowd, but I had never met him and besides, it was getting dark,[10] so I hardly expected[11] to find him easily. I thought that he would perhaps recognise me from my photograph. And so it turned out;[12] in just a few seconds[13] a man who very much resembled my

[21] अभी भी *abhī bhī*

[22] भूरा *bhūrā*

[23] सूखा *sūkhā*

[24] इधर *idhar*, literally 'hither, out here'. (Note also उधर *udhar* 'thither' and किधर *kidhar* 'whither'.)

[25] Say 'greenness (हरियाली *hariyālī*, f.) was everywhere'.

[26] भरा हुआ *bharā huā*

[27] धान *dhān*, m., paddy

[1] आखिर (में) *ā<u>kh</u>ir (meṁ)*

[2] आ रुकी *ā rukī*, i.e. 'came in and stopped'.

[3] क़ुली *qulī*, m.

[4] एक पल बाद *ek pal bād*. See p. 35.

[5] प्लेटफ़ार्म *pleṭfārm*, m.

[6] Say 'on the platform there was a large crowd (भीड़ *bhīṛ*, f.). These people had come . . .'.

[7] Use of लेना *lenā*, i.e. '(meet and) take away with them', is possible here.

[8] रिश्तेदार *riśtedār*, m.

[9] ढूँढ़ लेना *ḍhūṁṛh lenā*. ढूँढ़ना *ḍhūṁṛhnā* often means 'search out', i.e. 'look for and find', rather than simply 'look for'.

[10] The particle भी *bhī* can be included in the translation, viz. 'darkness too was drawing on'. Hindi favours the marking of ideas which are parallel or 'additional' in a sentence by the use of भी *bhī*.

[11] मुझे कम आशा थी कि . . . *mujhe kam āśā thī ki . . .*

[12] ऐसा ही हुआ *aisā hī huā*

[13] क्षण *kṣaṇ*, m.

friend came up to me and greeted me[14] with folded hands.[15] He had had no trouble[16] at all in recognising me since I was the only European who had got off the train.[17]

## IV

When Premnāth and I came out of the station I saw that in front of the station at one side there were ten or fifteen cycle rickshaws[1] standing, and a few cars also at the other side. I had not seen cycle rickshaws before. As soon as the rickshaw-wallahs saw us several of them began to run[2] towards us, shouting out 'Rickshaw, sir!'[3] But Premnāth had a car, so[4] we did not need them on this occasion. I followed[5] him over to the car, and he got my porter to put my luggage on the back seat.[6] I did not know how much to tip[7] the porter, but Premnāth solved[8] my difficulty;[9] he gave him four annas for each big case.[10] Four annas are 25 naye paise. I expect[11] that if I had been alone the porter would have asked[12] me for very much more[13] money.

[14] नमस्ते किया *namaste kiyā*

[15] हाथ जोड़कर *hāth joṛkar*, literally 'having joined his hands'

[16] दिक़्क़त †*diqqat*, f.

[17] Say 'among those getting down from the train I was a single (अकेला *akelā*) European'.

[1] साइकिल रिक्शा *sāikil rikśā*, m.

[2] दौड़ पड़ना *dauṛ paṛnā*

[3] The commonest equivalent to the vocative 'sir' is probably the expression बाबू जी *bābū jī*, though the word साहब *sāhab* is also very common. The word बाबू *bābū*, which is often used in the sense 'clerk, government servant', means properly 'educated or distinguished person', and of course has this connotation in the expression बाबू जी *bābū jī*.

[4] इसलिए *islie*

[5] . . . के पीछे-पीछे चलना . . . *ke pīche-pīche calnā*

[6] सीट *sīṭ*, f.

[7] पैसे देना *paise denā*

[8] दूर करना *dūr karnā*

[9] Say 'this difficulty of mine': मेरी यह मुश्किल *merī yah muśkil*

[10] बक्सा *baksā*, m.

[11] मुझे लगता है *mujhe lagtā hai*

[12] माँगना *māṁgnā* (with से *se*)

[13] कहीं अधिक *kahīṁ adhik*

## V

Premnāth was a lawyer, and lived in a bungalow[1] in the Allahabad Civil Lines[2] about a mile and a half away from the station. The Civil Lines is a suburb of straight, wide (*cauṛā*) streets and large houses. We reached Premnāth's bungalow in just a few minutes, and he stopped[3] the car beside the front door. An old family[4] servant took[5] my luggage out of the car. Premnāth and I went into his office. His table was piled high[6] with law[7] books. We talked for a little while about his younger brother, who was studying medicine[8] in England. Then his son came into the room, and Premnāth introduced him to me. I did not meet[9] Premnāth's wife that evening. I was not at all hungry,[10] but very thirsty, and so I was very glad when a servant brought us some tea and biscuits.[11] After a little while I said good-night[12] to Premnāth, and went[13] out on to the verandah,[14] where the servant had put a charpoy[15] for me. I lay down and very shortly fell asleep.[16]

[1] कोठी *koṭhī*, f.

[2] इलाहाबाद की सिविल लाइन्स *ilāhābād kī sivil lāins*

[3] खड़ा करना *khaṛā karnā*

[4] परिवार *parivār*, m.

[5] उतारना *utārnā*, set down, take down

[6] Use लदना *ladnā*.

[7] क़ानून *qānūn*, m.

[8] डाक्टरी पढ़ना *ḍākṭarī* (f.) *paṛhnā*

[9] Use of सकना *saknā* with मिलना *milnā* here would underline the fact that the narrator had been expecting or hoping to meet Premnāth's wife also.

[10] मुझे ज़रा भी भूख नहीं थी *mujhe zarā bhī bhūkh nahīṁ thī*; use of लगना *lagnā* in this negatived expression is not necessary, though possible. For ज़रा *zarā* see p. 203, n. 17.

[11] बिस्कुट *biskuṭ*, m.

[12] आज्ञा लेना *ājñā* (f.) *lenā*. आज्ञा *ājñā* 'command, order' has the sense 'leave to go' in this expression and the complementary आज्ञा देना *ājñā denā* 'allow to go'.

[13] Use आना *ānā* (the centre of interest now being the verandah).

[14] बरामदा *barāmdā*, m. For 'on to' use में *meṁ*.

[15] Use चारपाई बिछा रखना *cārpāī* (f.) *bichā rakhnā*, literally 'spread a charpoy (with bedding) and place it'.

[16] नींद आना *nīṁd* (f.) *ānā* (*ko*), fall asleep

## VI

Here in Allahabad the humidity[1] was much greater than in Delhi.[2] For this reason I wasn't able to sleep terribly well, although the charpoy was very comfortable. The next morning[3] I was up very early,[4] but not as early as Premnāth and his family.[5] It was cooler, but the humidity was just the same,[6] and the sky was completely covered[7] with heavy[8] black clouds.[9] I went into the bathroom[10] and washed[11] in[12] cold water. Then I felt much better.[13] I found Premnāth in his office reading the paper. He took two papers, one English and one Hindi. We talked about the news[14] for a while, and I asked him many questions about life in Allahabad. Then the servant brought in breakfast—tea, toast, and a fried[15] egg for me. I drank[16] several cups of tea.

## VII

Premnāth's son went out into the road and called a rickshaw-wallah who brought his rickshaw up to the front of the house.[1] The two of us loaded my luggage on to the rickshaw and got in,[2] and I said good-bye to Premnāth

[1] नमी *namī*, f.

[2] Say 'was much greater than Delhi'. See p. 178, paragraph (*b*).

[3] दूसरे दिन *dūsre din*

[4] जल्दी *jaldī*

[5] प्रेमनाथ . . . से (की तरह) जल्दी नहीं *premnāth . . . se* (*kī tarah*) *jaldī nahīṁ*

[6] वैसा ही *vaisā hī*

[7] ढकना *ḍhaknā*, be covered; cover

[8] घना *ghanā*, thick, dense

[9] बादल *bādal*, m.

[10] गुस्लखाना *guslkhānā*, m.

[11] नहाना *nahānā*

[12] से *se*

[13] Use तबीयत ख़ुश होना *tabīyat* (f.) *khuś honā*.

[14] नए समाचार *nae samācār*, m.pl.

[15] फ़ाइड *frāiḍ*

[16] Concord with चाय *cāy*.

[1] रिक्शा मकान के सामने लाकर खड़ा कर दिया *rikśā makān ke sāmne lākar khaṛā kar diyā*, literally 'brought it and stopped it in front of the house'

[2] बैठना *baiṭhnā*

and thanked[3] him very much for the kindness which he had shown me.[4] We set off for the University. It took about fifteen minutes to get there. On the way[5] we passed[6] the Nehru family's house, called Ānand Bhavan; it was[7] a very imposing (*śāndār*) house with a pleasant garden.[8] Then a few minutes later we entered the University area,[9] on one side of which was Amarnāth Jhā Hostel. I had come to live in[10] Allahabad for[11] six months, so that I could improve[12] my Hindi. At the same time[13] I planned[14] to attend Hindi classes[15] in the University. We entered the hostel, and went up[16] to the Warden's house.

[3] धन्यवाद देना *dhanyavād denā (ko)*

[4] अपने सत्कार के लिए *apne satkār ke lie.* सत्कार *satkār* is here used in the sense 'kindness received by a guest'.

[5] रास्ते में *rāste meṁ*

[6] के पास से गुज़रना *ke pās se guzarnā*

[7] As well as था *thā*, है *hai* is possible here; the state of affairs still obtains.

[8] सुहावना बग़ीचा *suhāvnā bagīcā*, m.

[9] क्षेत्र *kṣetr*, m.

[10] The postposition may be omitted.

[11] के लिए *ke lie*

[12] सुधारना *sudhārnā*

[13] साथ ही *sāth hī*, 'together with this'

[14] मेरा विचार . . . ने का था *merā vicār . . . ne kā thā*

[15] Use कक्षाओं में बैठना *kakṣāoṁ meṁ baiṭhnā.* कक्षा *kakṣā*, f., class

[16] पहुँचना *pahuṁcnā*

# KEY TO EXERCISES

## 1

This is a table. The book is on the table. There is a pen on the table. There are two chairs in the room. What is this? This is a jar. Is there water in the jar? No, but there is water in the well. The books are on the table. Are the books on the tables? There is one chair here. There are two chairs there. Is this a chair? No, this isn't a chair, it's a table. The boys are in Agra, but the girls are in Calcutta. There are three men here. Where are the women? There are books on the tables.

## 2

यह क्या है? यह पुस्तक है। पुस्तक यहाँ है। पुस्तकें वहाँ हैं। पत्र कहाँ है? यहाँ दो लड़के हैं। मेज़ कमरे में है। घड़ा मेज़ पर है, और घड़े में पानी है। वह क्या है? । वह मेज़ है। चिड़िया पिंजरे में है। पिंजरे में तीन चिड़ियाँ हैं। मकान में तीन कमरे हैं। एक कमरे में मेज़ें और कुरसियाँ हैं। अख़बार मेज़ों पर हैं।

## 3

He[1] isn't here, but his[1] younger sisters are here. He isn't at home. Two small children are standing at the door. This water is very dirty. There are five books in the black box. Are the books in this black box? In that country there are many cities and villages. Sītā is in the fifth class. The Red Fort is in Delhi. These are the books belonging to those little girls. The walls of those buildings are high. The rajah's palace is in this city. It is very beautiful.

## 4

किताब[2] उस मेज़ पर है। कपड़े इस संदूक़ में हैं। किताबें उन मेज़ों पर हैं। कपड़े इन संदूक़ों में हैं। वे यहाँ हैं। वह कहाँ है? वह कहाँ है? सीता उसकी छोटी बहन है। उसकी किताब मेज़ पर है। उसकी किताबें उस कमरे में हैं। उनके कपड़े साफ़ और सफ़ेद हैं। वह क्या है? वह संदूक़ है। उसमें चार बड़ी किताबें हैं। ये किताबें उसकी हैं। उस छोटे गाँव में दो मंदिर हैं। कलकत्ता बड़ा शहर है।

[1] Also 'she', 'her'. Alternative translations depending on points of grammar already explained are not given in the Key (nor, usually, in the Lessons).

[2] Also पुस्तक *pustak*. Alternative translations depending on the existence of common lexical equivalents (see p. xi) are not given in the Key.

5

My son is now in Delhi. My son's house is very large. Your books are on that large table. He is my elder brother. Hullo, how are you? How are you, Sītā? Is everything all right? Yes, everything's all right. Mr. Prasad is here, he's sitting in that room. Our city is small. Their brothers aren't here. Is this book yours? No, its not mine, it's my father's.

6

सीता इस लड़के की बहन है। इन लड़कों की बहनें स्कूल में हैं। तुम्हारी माँ कहाँ हैं? आपकी पत्नी कैसी हैं? यह काम ठीक नहीं है। वह किताब मेरी है। सब किताबें मेरी हैं। ये सब किताबें मेरे माता-पिता की हैं। हम उनके कमरे में बैठे हैं। आप कैसे हैं, प्रसाद जी? मैं ठीक हूँ। भारत में बहुत गाँव हैं। दिल्ली भारत की राजधानी है।

7

How are you? I'm well. We are English. Our language is English. His sisters were in Agra yesterday. I was there yesterday. Will it rain today? No, it won't rain today. I am writing a letter. He speaks English to me. The leaves of that tree are green. Trees' leaves are green. I don't know Hindi. They used to speak English to us in India. He's sitting in my chair. We are going to India the day after tomorrow. Well, I'm going (now). The boy is singing a song. Why are you learning Hindi?

8

मेरे दोस्त का भाई कल यहाँ था। उनकी बहनें कमरे में नहीं थीं। क्या वे दफ़्तर में हैं? जी नहीं, घर पर होंगे। वे भारतीय विद्यार्थियों से हमेशा हिंदी बोलते हैं, लेकिन मुझसे नहीं बोलते। हम भारत की राजधानी में रहते हैं। मैं हिंदी सीख रहा हूँ। मैं उसकी पुस्तकें नहीं पढ़ता। गरमियों में दिन लंबे होते हैं। सिग्रेटें भारत में महँगी नहीं होतीं। डाकिया कब आता है? लड़कियाँ उस कमरे में सोती थीं। हम एक बहुत अच्छी पुस्तक पढ़ रहे हैं।

9

I've just arrived from Delhi. What will you say to his brother? She'll be on her way (here). Perhaps I'll write the letter tomorrow. The boy is standing in the courtyard. What am I to say to him tomorrow? The students went to Delhi, and also to Bombay. Come on, let's have some coffee in the restaurant. I shall give the boy just two rupees. I shall not give him even one rupee. How long did you stay in India? The money is lying on the table. In the cold season the weather is good. Everyone went into the house.

10

मैं दूध नहीं पिऊँगा । मैं उसका पत्र पढ़ूँ? मैं क्या कहूँ? मैं उससे पूछूँगा । उसके काग़ज़[1] मेज़ पर पड़े हैं । वह कल पहुँचा होगा । वह आपको पत्र देंगे । मैं कल सारा दिन घर पर ही रहा । मैं बरसात में यहाँ आया । वह मुझसे हिंदी बोला ।

11

The paper is underneath the books. The window is behind you. She is sitting outside. I arrived here before him. Formerly I used to live in a village. I shall ask him about this. How far is Delhi from Agra? Shall we go in ten minutes' time? A girl was standing at the window. At that time I was reading a book. I want to learn Hindi by next year. At the right-hand side of the road there's a big building. These days food isn't cheap. I slept *inside* the house last night.

12

मैं उसके साथ आया । वह मेरे साथ आया । वह हमारे लिए यह काम कर रहे हैं । मैं कल तक दिल्ली में उसके लिए ठहरा । मेरे भाई मकान के सामने खड़े हैं । पहले मैं दिल्ली में रहता था । दिल्ली हमारे शहर के काफ़ी पास है । आपका गाँव भी पास है । मैं कल से यहाँ हूँ । आप हिंदी बहुत जल्दी सीख रहे हैं । मैं रेल से जाऊँगा और कार से लौटूँगा । मैं हवाई जहाज़ से लंदन जाना चाहता हूँ ।

13

I shall write him a letter after I have eaten. What will you do in India (after you get to India)? He put all the things in the cupboard and went out of the room. Rāmādhīn, go to the bazaar and get (bring) four mangoes. He went out, with the book (taking the book). Excuse me, is this the Delhi train? Please speak slowly!

14

आप हिंदुस्तान जाकर हिंदी जल्दी सीख लेंगे । वह यह किताब हिंदुस्तान से ले आया । मैं हवाई जहाज़ से बंबई होकर गया । यह काम अभी कीजिए । इस कुरसी पर बैठिए । मुझे और दीजिए!

[1] Note also the compound noun काग़ज़-पत्र *kāgaz-patr*, common for 'papers' in this sense, and the equivalent form कागज़ात †*kāgazāt*. The latter shows an Arabic plural inflexional ending which is common in Persian and Arabic loanwords in Urdu, though rarely used in Hindi.

15

Is anyone there? I shan't say anything about that. Eight or nine men arrived with him. Several books were lying under the table. A few other books were on the table. There's no chair in my room. Whom do these books belong to (which different persons)? Whom will you speak to about this? The book I am reading is on the table. The man I was watching has just gone out. The room I shall work in is very comfortable. How long have you been in this country, and how long will you stay here? Why don't you speak Hindi?

16

मैं किसी गाँव में रहूँगा। यहाँ कोई हिंदी नहीं जानता। मैं उससे उसके बारे में कुछ पूछूँगा। कई आदमी कल यहाँ आए। कुछ लोग हर साल वहाँ जाते हैं। ये आदमी कौन हैं? आप ये किताबें किसे देंगे? जो आदमी कल यहाँ आए थे, वे मेरे दोस्त हैं। मैं जिस कुरसी पर बैठा हूँ, वह काफ़ी मज़बूत है। जिस लड़के की पुस्तक मेज़ पर है, वह मेरा बेटा है। वे किस शहर में रहते हैं? क्या आपकी तबीयत कल ठीक नहीं थी? सुनिए, आप राधा जी की बहन हैं?

17

He doesn't recognise me. I shall write those letters. I shall give you the books tomorrow. I'm going home on Friday. Do you know them? On that day I was reading a book. What do you mean by that? Do you have any paper? Please give me some. I have a friend in Calcutta. How many walls does that room have? I haven't any books.

18

हमें एक पत्र लिखिए। मैं कल आपसे इसके बारे में कुछ कहूँगा। मेरा दोस्त अगले हफ़्ते इंग्लैंड लौटेगा। मुझे उसके बारे में बहुत ख़ुशी है। मुझे आशा है कि आप भारतवर्ष जाएँगे। किसान घोड़े को ढूँढ़ रहा है। कमरे में कब जाएँगे? वह पेड़ के पास खड़ा था। आपके बच्चे हैं? मेरे दो बेटे और एक बेटी है। मेरा गाँव आगरे के काफ़ी पास है। क्या आपके पास हिंदी की किताबें हैं?

19

He speaks Hindi to his sister. Do you like your room? He and his wife go there every day. My own books are all Hindi ones. He is going back to his own country today. Work starts at eight o'clock. I'm starting work now. Let's stop work now. You will obtain some knowledge of Hindi from this book. Nowadays annas are not used, but village people still count in annas. Is Indra mentioned in the Ṛgveda? Please return my book by tomorrow. I wait for him here every day but usually he doesn't arrive on time.

20

वह अपनी किताबें उस मेज़ पर हमेशा रखते हैं। मैं आपको अपनी किताब दूंगा। मैं आपकी किताब वापस करूँगा। वह कल लंदन गया था, क्योंकि उसका भाई भारत से आ रहा था। मुझे और मेरी पत्नी को आशा है कि आप अपने घर पहुँचकर चिट्ठी लिखेंगे। आप किस महीने में पैदा हुए? आपके पास आम हैं? जी नहीं, ख़त्म हैं। मैं आपकी किताब कल ख़त्म करूँगा। दरवाज़ा क्यों बंद है? मैं कल आपको ढूंढ़ रहा था। वह कल रवाना हुआ। मैं उनको रवाना करूँगा। क्या आपका देश बहुत अनाज पैदा करता है?

21

I've got 75 nae paise. Twelve annas make 75 nae paise. Three quarters of the world consists of ocean. 250. 531. 2,222. 304,837. 34,165,307. I do twice as much work as he. She is in the sixth class. Next year she'll be in the seventh class. (Entire) maunds of grain were ruined. It's a quarter to four. No, its ten to four by my watch. The train arrives at three minutes past six. There's a lecture at 8.30 this evening. I'm going home on June 23rd. This incident occurred on October 24th 1929.

22

मैं एक आध महीने से हिंदी सीख रहा हूँ। डेढ़ सौ। सात सौ चौवन। नौ हज़ार आठ सौ छिहत्तर। एक करोड़ तिरपन लाख अठहत्तर हज़ार चार सौ बानवे। इक्यानवे लाख बत्तीस हज़ार चार सौ चवालीस। वह मुझसे दुगुना काम करता है। हज़ारों लोग अगले महीने यहाँ आएँगे। मैं साढ़े तीन बजे पहुँचा। अब सात बजकर पच्चीस मिनट हुए हैं। मैं आठ बजने से बीस मिनट पहले जा रहा हूँ। साढ़े पाँच बजे आइए। कल शाम को साढ़े आठ बजे आइए। मेरा बेटा पहली अप्रैल को पैदा हुआ। हम बुधवार को काम शुरू करेंगे।

23

I saw him yesterday. He was reading a book. He had brought it from the library. He read the book last week. I ate at eleven o'clock. Do you understand? (f. pl.) He found me in my office. I spoke Hindi to him. He taught him Hindi.[1] He taught him. I told him the cause of the quarrel. He appeared at the door of my house yesterday evening.

[1] Note the concord of the verb in this sentence with two objects. Concord in constructions involving ने *ne* is with an indefinite object if one is expressed or understood (any further object form being an indirect object).

24

क्या आपने वे पत्र लिखे? हमने उस दूकान से कई चीज़ें ख़रीदीं। फिर हम उन्हें घर ले आए। मैंने शाम के पाँच बजे काम ख़त्म किया। आदमियों ने संदूक़ मेज़ पर रखे। गाँव के लोगों ने सारा दिन खेतों में काम किया। शाम तक वे मनों अनाज गाँव में ले आए थे। वे मेरा यहाँ इंतज़ार करते थे[1]। तस्वीर में कई दिलचस्प चीज़ें दिखाई दे रही हैं। वे अपना सब सामान ले गए।

25

I need a new hat. What do you want? I want five air letters. They needed some water. He will need your help. What does that boy want? You should have read these books. My brother should have read them too. I ought to write him a letter. They ought to finish their work. You'll have to speak Hindi to the people of this village.

26

मुझे दो कमीज़ें चाहिए। राधा को कान्ता की पुस्तकों की ज़रूरत थी। आपको भारत जाना चाहिए। मुझे हिंदी बोलनी चाहिए। आपको हिंदी सीखनी चाहिए थी। मुझे कुछ अख़बार खरीदने हैं। मुझे ग्यारह बजे के क़रीब जाना पड़ेगा। मुझे ग्यारह बजे के क़रीब जाना पड़ेगा। मुझे ग्यारह बजे जाना पड़ा। मुझे रोज़ बाज़ार जाना पड़ता था। मुझे उसे फ़ोन करना है। मुझे दस रुपए की ज़रूरत होगी।

27

Please come whenever you wish. Please stay here as long as you wish. I stayed there as long as I wanted to. I studied Hindi until I went to India. Please send me a telegram as soon as you reach Allahabad. There weren't as many people here today as there were yesterday. Wherever you go you ought to try to speak the language of the people.

28

जब आप आए, तब मैं घर पर नहीं था। उसने जो कहा, मैं उसे नहीं समझा। मैं जब तक भारत न जाऊँ, तब तक हिंदी पढ़ूँगा। जैसे ही मैंने उसे देखा, वैसे ही मैंने उसे पहचाना। आपके पास जितनी हिंदी की पुस्तकें हैं, उतनी ही मेरे पास अँग्रेज़ी की पुस्तकें हैं। वह जो कुछ कहता है, उसे कीजिए। हमने जिन आदमियों को कल यहाँ देखा था, वे इस गाँव में नहीं रहते।

[1] This is the most natural word order (although यहाँ *yahāṁ* might well follow इंतज़ार *intazār*); components of possessive phrases, such as मेरा इंतज़ार *merā intazār* in this sentence, are very frequently separated by adverbs, adverbial phrases or conjunctions. Other examples will be found in later Lessons.

29

Please come whenever you can. I stayed as long as I could. I am very sorry that I couldn't see (meet) you yesterday. Apart from Hindi we could have learned several other Indian languages in India. Have you had tea? That Hindi dictionary is hard to get hold of. When can we meet? This cloth is very similar to that.

30

मैं हिंदी बहुत आसानी से नहीं लिख सकता। मैं जब भी लिखता हूँ, भूलें करता हूँ। जब मैं वहाँ पहुँचा, तब वह जा चुका था। जैसे ही उसका पत्र मुझे मिला, वैसे ही मैंने उसका उत्तर दिया। जो कोई इसके बारे में सूचना दे सकेगा, उसे पुरस्कार मिलेगा। आपको उस दूकान में हिंदी की पुस्तकें मिल सकती हैं।

31

Hindi is easier than Tamil. Hindi is an easier language than Tamil. Is city life more interesting than village life? Please write at least three pages on this subject. More people speak Hindi than any other Indian language. India is one of the world's most interesting countries. He knows a great deal about India. I told him that he would have to do considerably more work than that. He asked me if cloth was obtainable in that street of the bazaar. Did you tell him that I won't be able to come tomorrow? I told him to finish the work by tomorrow.

32

गंगा यमुना से लंबी है। बंबई आजकल भारत का सबसे बड़ा शहर है। मालूम होता है कि आप उससे ज़्यादा काम करते हैं। आपको वहाँ कई भारतीय विद्यार्थी मिलेंगे। मुझे अधिक पुस्तकें चाहिए। यह पुस्तकालय बहुत अधिक छोटा है। उसने अपने मित्रों से कहा कि मैं खा चुका हूँ। उसने अपने मित्रों से कहा कि वे शाम के सवा छै बजे उसके मकान पर आएँ। जैसे ही आपका पत्र मिला, वैसे ही मैंने उनको बताया कि आप दिल्ली आ रहे हैं।

33

As soon as the train left I spread out my bedding on the lower seat. Then I changed my clothes and lay down. Get someone to load the things on that donkey. They burst out laughing on reading the essay he had had printed in the paper. Please explain to him that he should always finish his work on time. I'll ask him here and introduce him to you. Put your boy in a good school. I want to show you round London. You can have good clothes made in that shop.

34

मैं इलाहाबाद में गाड़ी से उतर गया। सामान पीछे से उतारें। आपने जो लिखा है, मुझे दिखाइए[1]। तुम क्या कर बैठे हो! कुरसी तोड़ डाली! आपने बहुत हिंदी सीख ली। आपको किसने सिखाई?[2] हम अपने कपड़े धोबी से धुलाते हैं। गाड़ी यहाँ नहीं रुकती। गाड़ी अभी छूटी है। मैं आपसे रोज़ हिंदी में कुछ वाक्य लिखवाता हूँ।

35

My books were sent on a month later.[3] I couldn't contain myself. I don't remember. In the street the noise of vehicles could be heard. The existence of this movement in favour of Hindi is natural. Even if you speak the truth other people will slander you. They forced him to speak the truth. Are you going out now? In this picture you see an ox-cart. Farmers usually take their produce to market on carts like this.

36

कहा जा सकता है कि हिंदी एक दिन भारत की राष्ट्रभाषा के रूप में स्वीकार कर ली जाएगी। भारत, जहाँ हिंदी और दूसरी भाषाएँ भी बोली जाती हैं, एक बहुत दिलचस्प देश है। आपने जो कहा था, वह मैंने सावधानी से याद रखा। जब मैंने उसे देखा, तब उसका चेहरा मुझे याद आया। आपको हिंदी की कई[4] कविताएँ याद करनी चाहिए। उनकी पुस्तकों की इन दिनों[5] प्रशंसा हो रही है। मैंने कल नौ बजे काम शुरू किया। मैं कल आपका इंतज़ार नहीं करूँगा। सच बोलना आदमी का फ़र्ज़ है। बोलने का अभ्यास करने से आप हमारी भाषा सीख लेंगे। शत्रु ने क़िले में प्रवेश करने का प्रयत्न किया। वह अपने दोस्त से मिलने के लिए स्टेशन गया था। वह आराम करने को लेट गया।

37

Please come if you can. If there is a phone call for me please say that I'll ring back. If I had met him that day I would have recognised him. When you reach Delhi I'll introduce you to several of my friends. As soon as the farmers' crops ripen they cut them. Although the train left on time it arrived five minutes late. Since he had no work to do at the time he took the letter out of his pocket and started to read it again. He will look after my work today so that I can show you round Delhi.

[1] Correlative वह *vah* not expressed; see p. 86.

[2] Concord with the noun हिंदी *hindī* understood, see p. 220, n.

[3] See p. 35.

[4] Note the position of कई *kaī*, following the possessive.

[5] For the word order here see p. 221, n.

38

अगर वह मुझे लिखे तो मैं उसकी चिट्ठी का जवाब ज़रूर दूंगा । अगर वह आने से पहले मुझे लिखता, तो मैं उससे स्टेशन पर मिलता । उससे पूछिए कि यह ठीक रास्ता है या नहीं । अगर मैं उससे मिलता तो मैं उस विषय के बारे में उसका विचार ज़रूर पूछता । जब आप जाने के लिए तैयार हों, तो मुझसे कहिए । अगरचे मैंने बहुत ज़्यादा कोशिश की, फिर भी मैं आपकी भाषा न सीख सका । मैं मई में दिल्ली से चला गया, क्योंकि मौसम उस समय बहुत गरम हो रहा था । जब से आप दिल्ली चले गए, तब से मैं आपसे नहीं मिला ।

39

I want you to show him that letter. I wanted to help him. He may possibly come tomorrow. He'll probably come tomorrow. It's very fitting that you should be able to speak an Indian language before going to India. It took me half an hour to get there. How long will it take you to get back? Less, if I go directly. It seems as if you are making progress in writing Hindi. I'm thirsty. He began to feel hungry, not having eaten anything since morning. He got sunstroke through staying out in the sun all day.

40

मैं भारत की संस्कृति का अध्ययन करना चाहता हूँ । मैं चाहता हूँ कि मेरा बेटा भारतीय संस्कृति का अध्ययन करे । क्या आप चाहते हैं कि मैं उसे वह पत्र दिखाऊँ? मैं उससे कहूँ कि वह आपको एक पत्र लिखे? आपको बुनियादी हिंदी पढ़ना और लिखना सीखने में संभवतः कम से कम एक महीना लगेगा । बर्फ़ फ़रवरी में पिघलने लगी । हमें ठंड लग रही है । जब तक उसका पिता न लौट आया, तब तक उसकी माता ने उसे न जाने दिया ।

41

It went on raining for two days. We went on studying Hindi until we went to India. Keep studying Hindi! As the days get longer the nights get shorter. When I'm in northern India I make it a habit to speak Hindi.

42

मैं रोज़ आठ बजे तक बिस्तर पर पड़ा रहता हूँ । उस समय राजपूत राजाओं में लड़ाई होती रहती थी । हम हिंदी में बोलने लगे, और घंटे के ख़त्म होने तक हिंदी में बोलते रहे । आप हर एक दिन दस नए शब्द सीखा कीजिए । मैं हर किसी से यह सवाल पूछता जाता हूँ । इसका क्या जवाब है?

43

Each of you please make a habit of learning ten new words daily. Each Rajput killed several enemy soldiers. People come to Allahabad from far off to bathe in the Ganges. You understand Hindi, do you? The train did leave on time, but it arrived five minutes late. Even if you learn only ten words a day you'll make progress. I have never eaten a meal in that restaurant. As soon as I saw (you) I recognised you. As soon as he sat down we started asking him various questions.

44

आपने छुट्टी में क्या क्या किया? आप कल विश्वविद्यालय में किन किन लोगों से मिले? आपको शहर के चारों ओर के देहात में छोटे छोटे गाँव मिलेंगे, जो देखने लायक़ हैं। वह अक्सर धीरे धीरे बोलता था, लेकिन तब भी मैं कभी कभी नहीं समझता था। धीरे धीरे बोलिए, नहीं तो मैं नहीं समझूँगा। अगर आप हिंदी सीखना चाहें, तो आपको हिंदी ही बोलनी चाहिए। उसी दिन मेरे पिता जी दिल्ली से आ गए। उसकी माँग सुनते ही वे हँस पड़े। गाड़ी के छूटते ही मैं अपना अख़बार पढ़ने लगा।

45

He has written several rather long stories. Many people bathe in the river every day. I know a little Hindi. His legs were as if rooted to the spot by fear. Apart from him there was no one else there. Without working no one can hope to progress. Out of shyness he usually doesn't speak Hindi.

46

उसकी लंबी-सी दाढ़ी है। बहुत-से बड़े लोग उस इमारत में काम करते हैं। मेरे अलावा वहाँ कोई और नहीं था। बिना कोट पहने बाहर न जाइए।

47

We shall take you ourselves to meet (to introduce you to) our friends. Tongawallah, how much will you take me to the station for? What is the name of that tree with the red flowers? There were always wars going on between the rajahs.

48

उसने यह काम आप किया, बिना किसी की सहायता के। पैदल चलनेवालों को सड़क यहाँ पार करनी पड़ती है। नीचे के कमरे छोटे होने पर भी ऊपरवाले कमरों से आरामदेह हैं। मैं बाहर जानेवाला हूँ। मुझे पाँच पंद्रह पैसेवाले टिकट दीजिए।

49

From Banaras trains can be seen crossing the Ganges bridge. A tree which had been cut down was lying on the ground in front of the house.

The girl came to me in tears. I am afraid to say this. When I met him yesterday he was wearing a kurtā and pājāmā. But today he'll probably be wearing European clothes. I never saw him arrive at the office late. How long is it since you came to India? It's a long time since we met. Looking at me sharply he said, 'I'm sending you there for that very reason.'[1] He went out of the room with the book in his hand.

50

मैंने एक गाय को चरते हुए देखा था। औरतें काम करते हुए गा रही थीं। एक साधु सिर नीचा किए मंदिर के दरवाज़े के सामने बैठा था। बूढ़ा आदमी खड़ा हो गया और हाथ में लाठी लिए गाँव की ओर चला गया। मुझे हिंदी पढ़ते एक महीना हो गया है। उसे काम खत्म किए दो दिन हो गए हैं।

[1] For इसीलिए *isīlie* (rather than उसीलिए *usīlie*, उसी कारण से *usī kāraṇ se*, etc.) see p. 12.

# FAIR VERSIONS OF COMPOSITION PASSAGES

## I

किसी आदमी के दो बेटे थे। एक दिन एक बेटे ने अपने पिता से कहा "पिता जी, अपने धन में से मेरा हिस्सा मुझे दीजिए"। उसके पिता ने उसे उसका हिस्सा दे दिया। इसके बाद वह किसी दूर देश को चला गया। उस देश में उसने अपने पिता के सब पैसे उड़ा दिए और जल्दी ही ग़रीब हो गया। उस समय वह उस देश के एक निवासी के मकान में रहता था। वह उस आदमी के खेतों में काम करने लगा, क्योंकि उसके पास पैसे नहीं थे। कुछ समय के बाद उसने सोचा, मैं अपने देश लौट जाऊँ, और अपने पिता जी के पास जाकर यह बता दूँ कि मैंने कैसा पाप किया है। और वह अपने देश लौट आया। दूर ही से उसके पिता जी ने उसे देखा और बहुत ख़ुश हुआ। वह बहुत दिनों से उसका इन्तज़ार कर रहा था। नौकरों ने उसे नए कपड़े पहनने के लिए दिए, और एक मोटा बछड़ा ज़बह किया गया। लेकिन उसका भाई बहुत बिगड़ा। उसने कहा 'यह क्या हो रहा है?'। उसके पिता ने उत्तर दिया कि तुम्हारा भाई अभी-अभी लौटा है, तुम्हें ख़ुश होना चाहिए।

## II

इलाहाबाद दिल्ली से लगभग पाँच सौ मील दूर है। रेल से जाने में अक्सर बारह घंटे लगते हैं। मेरी ट्रेन कलकत्ते जानेवाली एक एक्सप्रेस ट्रेन थी। ट्रेन सात बजकर बीस मिनट पर छूटी। उस वक़्त काफ़ी ठंड थी। लेकिन बाद में, ख़ासकर दोपहर के बाद, गाड़ी में बहुत गरमी लगने लगी, और धूल भी भरने लगी। मैं बहुत थक गया, और मुझे बहुत प्यास लगने लगी। कई बार मैं ऊँघने भी लगा। मेरे अलावा डिब्बे में सिर्फ़ एक और यात्री था। वह क़रीब पैंतालीस साल का एक मुसलमान था। मेरी तो उससे ज़्यादा बातचीत न हो सकी, क्योंकि वह ज़्यादातर किताब पढ़ रहा था। मैंने देखा कि किताब उर्दू की थी। इलाहाबाद के पास के देहात और पश्चिम के देहात में काफ़ी फ़र्क़ मालूम होता था। बरसात शुरू हो गई थी, लेकिन दिल्ली के आस-पास खेत अभी भी भूरे-से और सूखे थे। लेकिन इधर पूर्व में हर ओर हरियाली थी, और मैंने देखा कि धान के खेतों में पानी भरा हुआ है।

## III

आख़िर हम इलाहाबाद पहुँचे, और गाड़ी क़रीब-क़रीब ठीक समय पर स्टेशन पर आ रुकी। एक क़ुली ने डिब्बे में आकर मुझसे पूछा कि आपके पास कितना सामान है। एक पल बाद मैं प्लेटफ़ार्म पर उतर आया। प्लेटफ़ार्म पर बड़ी भीड़ थी। ये लोग अपने मित्रों और रिश्तेदारों को लेने आए थे। मैंने भीड़ में कहीं अपने मित्र के भाई को ढूँढ़ लेने की कोशिश की। लेकिन मैं उनसे कभी मिला नहीं था। इसके अलावा अँधेरा भी हो चला था। इसलिए मुझे कम आशा थी कि मैं उन्हें आसानी से ढूँढ़ सकूँगा। मैंने सोचा कि वह शायद मेरी तस्वीर से मुझे पहचान लें। और ऐसा ही हुआ। कुछ ही क्षणों में एक आदमी जो मेरे मित्र से बहुत मिलता-जुलता था मेरे पास आया और हाथ जोड़कर नमस्ते किया। मुझे पहचानने में उसे कोई भी दिक़्क़त नहीं हुई क्योंकि गाड़ी से उतरनेवालों में मैं ही एक अकेला यूरोपीय था।

## IV

जब प्रेमनाथ और मैं दोनों स्टेशन के बाहर निकले, तो मैंने देखा कि स्टेशन के सामने एक तरफ़ दस-पंद्रह साइकिल रिक्शे खड़े हैं । दूसरी तरफ़ कुछ कारें भी थीं । मैंने पहले साइकिल रिक्शे नहीं देखे थे । जैसे ही रिक्शेवालों ने हमें देखा, कई 'रिक्शा, बाबू जी' चिल्लाते हुए हमारी ओर दौड़ पड़े । लेकिन प्रेमनाथ के पास गाड़ी थी, इसलिए इस बार हमें उनकी ज़रूरत नहीं थी । मैं उनके पीछे-पीछे कार की ओर चला, और उन्होंने क़ुली से मेरा सामान पीछे की सीट पर रखवाया । मुझे पता नहीं था कि क़ुली को कितने पैसे देने चाहिए । लेकिन प्रेमनाथ ने मेरी यह मुश्किल दूर कर दी । उन्होंने उसे हर बड़े बक्से के लिए चार आने दिए । चार आने पच्चीस नए पैसे होते हैं । मुझे लगता है कि यदि मैं अकेला होता, तो क़ुली ने मुझसे कहीं अधिक पैसे माँगे होते ।

## V

प्रेमनाथ वकील थे । वह स्टेशन से क़रीब डेढ़ मील दूर इलाहाबाद की सिविल लाइन्स में एक कोठी में रहते थे । सिविल लाइन्स सीधी, चौड़ी सड़कों और बड़े बड़े मकानों वाला एक मुहल्ला है । हम कुछ ही मिनटों में प्रेमनाथ की कोठी पर पहुँच गए । उन्होंने सामने के दरवाज़े के पास कार खड़ी कर दी । परिवार के एक बूढ़े नौकर ने मेरा सामान कार से उतारा । प्रेमनाथ और मैं दोनों उनके दफ़्तर में गए । उनकी मेज़ क़ानून की किताबों से लदी हुई थी । हमने थोड़ी देर तक उनके छोटे भाई के बारे में, जो इंग्लैंड में डाक्टरी पढ़ रहा था, बातें कीं । तब उनका बेटा कमरे में आया । प्रेमनाथ ने उसका मुझसे परिचय कराया । मैं उस शाम को प्रेमनाथ की पत्नी से नहीं मिला । मुझे ज़रा भी भूख नहीं थी, लेकिन प्यास बहुत लगी थी, इसलिए जब नौकर चाय और बिस्कुट ले आया, तो मुझे बहुत ख़ुशी हुई । थोड़ी देर बाद मैंने प्रेमनाथ से आज्ञा ली और बाहर बरामदे में आया जहाँ नौकर ने मेरे लिए एक चारपाई बिछा रखी थी । मैं लेट गया और थोड़ी ही देर में मुझे नींद आ गई ।

## VI

इधर इलाहाबाद में नमी दिल्ली से बहुत ज़्यादा थी । मैं इसलिए बहुत अच्छी तरह सो नहीं सका, हालाँकि चारपाई बहुत आरामदेह थी । दूसरे दिन मैं बहुत जल्दी उठा, लेकिन प्रेमनाथ और उनके परिवार से जल्दी नहीं । ठंड ज़्यादा हो गई थी । लेकिन नमी वैसी ही थी, और आकाश घने काले बादलों से बिलकुल ढका हुआ था । ग़ुस्लख़ाने में जाकर मैं ठंडे पानी से नहाया । तबीयत फिर ख़ुश हो गई । मैंने प्रेमनाथ को दफ़्तर में अख़बार पढ़ते हुए पाया । वह दो अख़बार लेते थे, एक अँग्रेज़ी का और एक हिंदी का । हमने कुछ देर तक नए समाचारों के बारे में बातें कीं, और मैंने उनसे इलाहाबाद के जीवन के बारे में बहुत-से प्रश्न पूछे । इसके बाद नौकर नाश्ता ले आया—चाय, टोस्ट, और मेरे लिए एक फ़्राइड अंडा । मैंने कई प्याले चाय पी ।

## VII

प्रेमनाथ के बेटे ने सड़क पर जाकर रिक्शेवाले को बुलाया। रिक्शेवाले ने अपना रिक्शा कोठी के सामने लाकर खड़ा कर दिया। हम दोनों मेरा सामान रिक्शे में लादकर बैठ गए। मैंने प्रेमनाथ से बिदा ली, और अपने सत्कार के लिए उन्हें बहुत धन्यवाद दिया। हम यूनिवर्सिटी की ओर चल पड़े। वहाँ पहुँचने में क़रीब पंद्रह मिनट लगे। रास्ते में हम नेहरू परिवार के मकान के पास से गुज़रे, जिसका नाम 'आनन्द भवन' है। यह एक बहुत शानदार और सुहावना बग़ीचावाला मकान है। कुछ मिनट बाद हमने यूनिवर्सिटी के क्षेत्र में प्रवेश किया, जिसके एक ओर अमरनाथ झा हास्टल है। मैं छै महीने के लिए इलाहाबाद रहने आया था ताकि मैं अपनी हिंदी सुधार सकूँ। साथ ही मेरा विचार यूनिवर्सिटी में हिंदी की कक्षाओं में बैठने का था। हम हास्टल में प्रवेश करके वार्डन के मकान पर पहुँचे।

# APPENDIX

## SOME RECENT WORKS ON ASPECTS OF HINDI GRAMMAR


Gaeffke, P., *Untersuchungen zur Syntax des Hindi* (The Hague, 1967).

Hacker, P., 'Zur Funktion einiger Hilfsverben im modernen Hindi', *Akademie der Wiss. u. der Lit.: Abh. der geistes- u. sozialwissenschaftl. Kl.*, 1958 (4) (Mainz/Wiesbaden, 1958). (Available as a separate monograph.)

Hook, P. E., *The Compound Verb in Hindi,* University of Michigan Center for South and Southeast Asian Studies, 1974.

Kachru, Y., *An Introduction to Hindi Syntax* (Urbana, 1967). (With extensive bibliography of books and articles.)

Kelkar, A. R., *Studies in Hindi-Urdu, I. Introduction and word phonology*, Deccan College Postgraduate and Research Institute (Poona, 1968).

Lienhard, S., *Tempusgebrauch und Aktionsartenbildung in der modernen Hindi*, Stockholm Oriental Studies, 1 (Stockholm, 1961).

Miltner, V., *Theory of Hindi syntax: descriptive, generative, transformational* (The Hague, 1970).

# VOCABULARIES

## HINDI–ENGLISH

Order of characters is as given on pp. xxii f.; note that vowels to which *anusvāra*, *candrabindu* or following *visarga* are attached precede the same vowels written without any of these signs.

References are to discussions of particular grammatical points in Lessons I–XXVI and in Supplements I–III.

अँग्रेज़ *aṁgrez*, m.f., Englishman, Englishwoman

अँग्रेज़ी *aṁgrezī*, adj. and f., English; the English language

अंडा *aṇḍā*, m., egg

अंत *ant*, m., end

के अंदर *ke andar*, inside

अंधा *andhā*, blind

अँधेरा *aṁdherā*, m. and adj., darkness; dark.

अक्सर *aksar*, usually [अकसर]

अख़बार *akhbār*, m., newspaper

अगर *agar*, if XX

अगरचे *agarce*, although XX

अगला *aglā*, next VI

अचानक *acānak*, suddenly

अच्छा *acchā*, good; adv., well; interj., all right, I see, etc. अच्छी तरह (से) *acchī tarah* (*se*), well VI

अत्याचार *atyācār*, m., excess, harsh action

अथवा *athvā*, or 182

अधिक *adhik*, more, many, much, etc. XVI

अध्ययन *adhyayan*, m., study; अध्ययन करना (का) *adhyayan karnā* (*kā*), to study

अध्यापक *adhyāpak*, m., teacher 164

अनन्य *ananya*, unique XVI

अनाज *anāj*, m., grain

अपना *apnā*, one's own X

अपितु *apitu*, but rather 183

अप्रैल *aprail*, m. April

अफ़सोस *afsos*, m., regret

अब *ab*, now

अभी *abhī*, now V

अभ्यास *abhyās*, m., practice; अभ्यास करना (का) *abhyās karnā* (*kā*), to practise

अमल *amal*, m., act, action; अमल करना *amal karnā*, to act, to take action

अमीर *amīr*, rich

अरे *are*, oh! etc.

अलमारी *almārī*, f., cupboard

के अलावा *ke alāvā*, apart from XXIV

अवसर *avasar*, m., opportunity; occasion

असंतुष्ट *asantuṣṭ*, dissatisfied

असुविधा *asuvidhā*, f., inconvenience

आँख *āṁkh*, f., eye

आँगन *āṁgan*, m., courtyard

आंदोलन *āndolan*, m., movement (social, political)

आक्रमण *ākramaṇ*, m., attack; आक्रमण करना (पर) *ākramaṇ karnā*

(*par*), to attack
आग *āg*, f., fire
आगरा *āgrā*, m., Agra I
आज *āj*, today
आजकल *ājkal*, nowadays
आठ *āṭh* eight
आदमी *ādmī*, m., man
आधा *ādhā*, half; a half XI
आधुनिक *ādhunik*, modern XVI
आना *ānā*, m., an anna
आना *ānā*, to come XVII
आप *āp*, you; he, she, they; oneself III XXV 165
आपस *āpas*, 'group' XXV
आपसी *āpsī*, mutual, reciprocal XXV
आबादी *ābādī*, f., population
आबोहवा *ābohavā*, f., climate 182
आम *ām*, ordinary; आम तौर पर/से *ām taur par/se*, in general, usually
आम *ām*, m., mango
आरंभ *ārambh*, m., beginning; आरंभ करना *ārambh karnā*, to begin (trans.) X
आराम *ārām*, m., rest, comfort; आराम करना *ārām karnā*, to rest
आरामदेह *ārāmdeh*, comfortable
आवश्यक *āvaśyak*, necessary XXI
आवश्यकता *āvaśyaktā*, f., necessity XIII
आवाज़ *āvāz*, f., voice
आशा *āśā*, f., hope IX
आसान *āsān*, easy, simple
आसानी *āsānī*, f., ease VI
आहिस्ता *āhistā*, आहिस्ते *āhiste*, adv., slowly

इंतज़ाम *intazām*, m., arrangement, arrangements
इंतज़ार करना (का) *intazār karnā* (*kā*), to wait (for) X
इंद्र *indra*, m., Indra
इकहरा *ikahrā*, thin 168
इतना *itnā*, as many, as much as this XVI 166
इतवार *itvār*, m., Sunday XI
इतिहास *itihās*, m., history
इनकार *inkār*, m., refusal; इनकार करना (से) *inkār karnā* (*se*), to refuse (to) XIX
इमारत *imārat*, f., building
इलाहाबाद *ilāhābād*, m., Allahabad
इसलिए *islie*, for this reason XX
इस्तेमाल *istemāl*, m., use; इस्तेमाल करना *istemāl karnā*, to use X

उगना *ugnā*, to grow (intr.)
उचित *ucit*, appropriate XXI
उच्च *ucc*, high XVI
उठना *uṭhnā*, to rise, to get up XVII
उठाना *uṭhānā*, to raise
उतरना *utarnā*, to descend, to get down
उतारना *utārnā*, to take down; to take off
उत्तर *uttar*, m., north
उत्तर *uttar*, m., answer; पत्र का उत्तर देना *patr kā uttar denā*, to answer a letter
उद्देश्य *uddeśya*, m., aim, intention
उपयुक्त *upayukt*, suitable
उल्लेख *ullekh*, m., mention; उल्लेख होना (का) *ullekh honā* (*kā*), to be mentioned

ऊँचा *ūṁcā*, high
ऊँट *ūṁṭ*, camel
के ऊपर *ke ūpar*, above, on top of

ऋग्वेद *ṛgved*, m., Rigveda

एक *ek*, one; a, an I XI
एवं *evaṃ*, and 182

ऐसा *aisā*, of this sort 167

ओढ़ना *oṛhnā*, to wrap round, to wrap about one
ओर *or*, f., direction, side; की ओर *kī or*, towards, to; की ओर देखना *kī or dekhnā*, to look at, to watch

और *aur*, and
और *aur* (stressed), extra, additional; adv., additionally VIII XVI
औरत *aurat*, f., woman

कटना *kaṭnā*, to be cut; to be cut off
कदाचित् *kadācit*, perhaps
कनिष्ठ *kaniṣṭh*, younger, youngest XVI
कपड़ा *kapṛā*, m., cloth; pl. clothes
कब *kab*, when? IV 181–2
कभी *kabhī*, sometimes; at some time XXIII
कम *kam*, little (of quantity), few; adv., little; कम से कम *kam se kam*, at least 167
कमरा *kamrā*, m., room
कमाना *kamānā*, to earn XVIII
कमी *kamī*, f., want, shortage, deficiency
क़मीज़ *qamīz*, f., shirt
करना *karnā*, to do V VII X XII XXII
कराना *karānā*, to cause to be done XVIII
के क़रीब *ke qarīb*, about, approximately
करोड़ *karoṛ*, ten million XI
कल *kal*, yesterday, tomorrow
कलकत्ता *kalkattā*, m., Calcutta I
क़लम *qalam*, f.m., pen
कवि *kavi*, m., poet
कविता *kavitā*, f., poem
कष्ट *kaṣṭ*, m., difficulty, inconvenience
कहना *kahnā*, to say, to tell IV XII XVI
कहलाना *kahlānā*, to be called XVIII
कहाँ *kahāṁ*, where? I 181
कहानी *kahānī*, f., story, short story
कहीं *kahīṁ*, somewhere 180, 181–2
का *kā*, of II IX 178
काग़ज़ *kāgaz*, m., paper
काटना *kāṭnā*, to cut; to harvest; to bite (of animals)
कान *kān*, m., ear
कान्ता *kāntā*, f., Kāntā (girl's name)
कापी *kāpī*, f., exercise book
काफ़ी *kāfī*, f., coffee [कौफ़ी *kaufī*]
काफ़ी *kāfī*, adv., quite, fairly; adj., a fair amount of
काम *kām*, m., work; काम देखना (का) *kām dekhnā* (*kā*), see to, attend to (one's work)
कार *kār*, f., car
कारण *kāraṇ*, m., cause; के कारण *ke kāraṇ*, because of XX
काला *kālā*, black
किंतु *kintu*, but 182
कि *ki*, conj., that XVI XXII 183 184
कितना *kitnā*, how much? how many? कितने दिन *kitne din*, how long? कितना ही . . . क्यों न *kitnā hī . . . kyoṁ na*, however much 181–2
किताब *kitāb*, f., book
किनारा *kinārā*, m., bank, edge
क़िला *qilā*, m., fort

किश्ती *kiśtī*, f., (small) boat
किसान *kisān*, m., farmer
कुआँ *kuāṁ*, m., well I
कुछ *kuch*, something, some; कुछ समय *kuch samay*, for some time VIII
कुत्ता *kuttā*, m., dog 163
कुमारी *kumārī*, f., 'Miss' III
कुरता *kurtā*, m., collarless shirt
कुरसी *kursī*, f., chair
कूदना *kūdnā*, to leap, to jump
कृपया *kṛpayā*, kindly 179
कैसा *kaisā*, what sort of? आप कैसे हैं? *āp kaise haiṁ?* how are you? III VI
कैसे *kaise*, how?
को *ko*, obl. case marker II V VI IX XI XIII XV XVIII XIX
कोई *koī*, someone, some VIII
कोट *koṭ*, m., coat
कोश *kos*, m., dictionary
कोशिश *kośiś*, f., attempt; कोशिश करना (की) *kośiś karnā* (*kī*), to try (to)
कौन *kaun*, who? which? कौन-सा *kaun-sā*, which one? VIII XXIV
क्या *kyā*, what? I VIII 181–2
क्यों *kyoṁ*, why? IV 181–2
क्योंकि *kyoṁki*, because, since XX
क्लास *klās*, f.m., class (school)
क्षण *kṣaṇ*, m., moment, instant

खड़ा *khaṛā*, standing XXVI
ख़त्म *k͟hatm*, m., end; ख़त्म करना *k͟hatm karnā*, to finish (trans.) X
ख़बर *k͟habar*, f., news, information
ख़राब *k͟harāb*, bad; spoiled
ख़रीदना *k͟harīdnā*, to buy
खाना *khānā*, to eat; m., food; खाना खाना *khānā khānā*, to have a meal
खिंचना *khiṁcnā*, to be drawn, pulled
खिड़की *khiṛkī*, f., window
खिलना *khilnā*, to bloom
खिलाना *khilānā*, to cause to play
खिलाना *khilānā*, to feed XVIII
खिलाना *khilānā*, to cause to bloom
खींचना *khīṁcnā*, to pull
ख़ुद *k͟hud*, oneself XXV
खुलना *khulnā*, to open (intr.)
ख़ुशी *k͟huśī*, f., happiness, pleasure IX
खेत *khet*, m., field
खोना *khonā*, to lose
खोलना *kholnā*, to open (tr.)

गंगा *gaṅgā*, f., River Ganges
गधा *gadhā*, m., donkey, ass
गरम *garm*, hot; warm
गरमियाँ *garmiyāṁ*, f. pl., hot season
ग़रीब *ġarīb*, poor
गली *galī*, f., narrow street, alley
गाँव *gāṁv*, m., village
गाड़ी *gāṛī*, f., vehicle
गाना *gānā*, to sing; m., a song
गाय *gāy*, f., cow
गिनना *ginnā*, to count
गिरना *girnā*, to fall
गिलास *gilās*, m., glass (for drinking)
गुरुवार *guruvār*, Thursday XI
गूँजना *gūṁjnā*, to resound
गेंद *geṁd*, f., ball

घंटा *ghaṇṭā*, m., an hour; a bell 165
घंटी *ghaṇṭī*, f., a small bell 165
घटना *ghaṭnā*, f., incident, happening
घड़ा *ghaṛā*, m., pot, jar
घड़ी *ghaṛī*, f., watch; मेरी घड़ी में *merī ghaṛī meṁ*, by my watch
घबराना *ghabrānā*, to be perturbed; to make anxious XVIII

घर *ghar*, m., house, home; घर पर *ghar par*, at home
घास *ghās*, f., grass
घिरना *ghirnā*, to be surrounded
घुमाना *ghumānā*, to convey about; to turn (tr.)
घुसना *ghusnā*, to creep, to slink
घूमना *ghūmnā*, to wander, to turn
घेरना *ghernā*, to surround
घोड़ा *ghoṛā*, m., horse

चतुर्थ *caturth*, fourth XI
चम्मच *cammac*, m., spoon
चरना *carnā*, to graze
चलना *calnā*, to go, to move; चला जाना *calā jānā*, to move along, to go away XVII 173
चाचा *cācā*, m., paternal uncle I
चादर *cādar*, f., shawl; sheet
चाबी *cābī*, f., key
चाय *cāy*, f., tea
चार *cār*, four; के चारों ओर/तरफ़ *ke cāroṁ or/taraf*, on all four sides of, all around
चारा *cārā*, m., recourse, course of action
चारा *cārā*, m., fodder
चाहना *cāhnā*, to wish VI XXI XXII 171 176
चाहिए *cāhie*, is wished, is necessary XIII
चिट्ठी *ciṭṭhī* f., letter
चिड़िया *ciṛiyā*, f., bird
चित्र *citr*, m., picture
चिल्लाना *cillānā*, to cry out, to shout
चीज़ *cīz*, f., thing
चुकना *cuknā*, to finish (intr.) XV
चुप *cup*, silent
चूँकि *cūṁki*, because, since XX
चेहरा *cehrā*, m., face, features
चोट *coṭ*, f., blow, knock
चोर *cor*, m., thief
चौंकना *cauṁknā*, to start, to be startled
चौथा *cauthā*, fourth
चौहरा *cauhrā*, fourfold 169

छक्का *chakkā*, m., squad, detachment
छठा *chaṭhā*, sixth
छड़ी *chaṛī*, f., stick, cane
छत *chat*, f., roof
छपना *chapnā*, to be printed
छह, छः, छै *chah*, *chaḥ*, *chai*, six
छात्र *chātr*, m., student; छात्रा *chātrā*, f. 164
छापना *chāpnā*, to print
छिपाना *chipānā*, to hide (trans.)
छीलना *chīlnā*, to scrape, to pare
छुट्टी *chuṭṭī*, f., holiday, leave, vacation
छुड़ाना *chuṛānā*, to cause to leave
छूटना *chūṭnā*, to leave (intr.)
छूना *chūnā*, to touch VI
छोटा *choṭā*, small; छोटा भाई *choṭā bhāī*, m., younger brother; छोटी बहन *choṭī bahn*, f., younger sister
छोड़ना *choṛnā*, to leave, to abandon

ज़ख्मी *zakhmī*, wounded
जगह *jagah*, f., place
जगाना *jagānā*, to waken (tr.)
जपना *japnā*, to repeat mechanically (a god's name, an incantation)
जब *jab*, (at the time) when; जब भी *jab bhī*, whenever; जब से *jab se*, since (the time when); जब तक *jab tak*, as long as XIV 183
ज़मीन *zamīn*, f., land
ज़मीनदार *zamīndār*, m., zamindar,

landlord
जय *jay*, f., victory; . . . की जय हो *kī jay ho*, long live . . .
ज़रूर *zarūr*, certainly, by all means
ज़रूरत *zarūrat*, f., necessity XIII
ज़रूरी *zarūrī*, necessary XXI
जलना *jalnā*, to burn (intr.)
जलवायु *jalvāyu*, m., climate
जलाना *jalānā*, to burn (tr.)
जल्द *jald*, f., haste, speed; जल्द (से) *jald* (*se*), quickly; soon
जल्दी *jaldī*, f., haste, speed; जल्दी (से) *jaldī* (*se*), quickly; soon
जवाब *javāb*, m., answer; चिट्ठी का जवाब देना *ciṭṭhī kā javāb denā*, to answer a letter
जहाँ *jahāṁ*, (the place) where; जहाँ भी *jahāṁ bhī*, wherever XIV
जहाज़ *jahāz*, m., ship
जागना *jāgnā*, to be awake
जानना *jānnā*, to know; जान पड़ना *jān paṛnā*, to seem 174
जाना *jānā*, to go IV V XVII XIX XXII
जायदाद *jāydād*, f., estate (land)
ज़िंदा *zindā*, alive II
जितना *jitnā*, as many as, as much as; however many, much XIV
ज़िला *zilā*, m., administrative district
जिससे *jisse*, so that XX
जी *jī*, m., soul, spirit; honorific particle III
जीना *jīnā*, to live, to be alive V
जीवन *jīvan*, m., life
जेब *jeb*, f., pocket
जो *jo*, the one who, which; जो कोई *jo koī*, whoever, whichever; जो कुछ *jo kuch*, whatever VIII XIV
जैसा *jaisā*, of such a sort as; that which XIV XXV
जैसे *jaise*, as if; जैसे ही *jaise hī*, as soon as XIV XXI
ज्ञान *jñān*, m., knowledge
ज़्यादा *zyādā*, more; many; much, etc. XVI
ज़्यादातर *zyādātar*, most (of); most commonly, very much XVI
ज्येष्ठ *jyeṣṭh*, older, eldest XVI
ज्यों-ज्यों . . . त्यों-त्यों *jyoṁ-jyoṁ . . . tyoṁ-tyoṁ*, in proportion as . . . so
ज्योंही *jyoṁhī*, as soon as XX

झगड़ना *jhagaṛnā*, to quarrel
झगड़ा *jhagṛā*, m., quarrel
झुकाना *jhukānā*, to lower
झूमना *jhūmnā*, to sway

टिकट *ṭikaṭ*, m.f., stamp
टूटना *ṭūṭnā*, to break (intr.)
टोपी *ṭopī*, f., hat

ठंड *ṭhaṇḍ*, f., cold; a cold
ठंडा *ṭhaṇḍā*, cold
ठहरना *ṭhaharnā*, to remain, to stay, to wait
ठीक *ṭhīk*, correct, all right, fine; ठीक वक़्त पर *ṭhīk vaqt par*, at the correct time, punctually

डर *ḍar*, m., fear
डरना *ḍarnā*, to fear
डाक *ḍāk*, f., post, postal service
डाकख़ाना *ḍākkhānā*, m., post office
डाकघर *ḍākghar*, m., post office
डाकिया *ḍākiyā*, m., postman 166
डाक्टर *ḍākṭar*, m., doctor
डालना *ḍālnā*, to throw down, to pour XVII
डिबिया *ḍibiyā*, f., small box I
डेढ़ *ḍeṛh*, one and a half; one and a

half times XI
ड्योढ़ा *ḍyoṛhā*, one and a half times the amount of 169

ढाई *ḍhāī*, two and a half; two and a half times XI
ढूँढ़ना *dhūṁṛhnā*, to look for, to search out

तक *tak*, up to; as far as; until, by VI XIV 179
तकलीफ़ *taklīf*, f., difficulty, inconvenience
तथा *tathā*, and 182
तथापि *tathāpi*, nevertheless XX
तब *tab*, then XIV
तबीयत *tabīyat*, f., state of health; disposition; तबीयत ठीक होना *tabīyat ṭhīk honā*, to be well
तभी *tabhī*, at that (particular) time XXIII
तमिल *tamil*, m., Tamil
तरकारी *tarkārī*, f., curry
तरक़्क़ी *taraqqī*, f., progress
तरफ़ *taraf*, f., direction, side; की तरफ़ *kī taraf*, towards; to (see page 50) VI
तरह *tarah*, f., way, manner; इस तरह (से) *is tarah (se)*, in this way VI
तलाश *talāś*, f., search; तलाश करना *talāś karnā*, to look for X
तस्वीर *tasvīr*, f., picture
ताँगा *tāṁgā*, m., tonga
ताकि *tāki*, so that XX
ताज़ा *tāzā*, fresh
तार *tār*, m., wire; telegram
तारीख़ *tārīkh*, f., date XI
ताला *tālā*, m., lock
तालाब *tālāb*, m., tank
तीखा *tīkhā*, sharp, piercing
तीन *tīn*, three
तीसरा *tīsrā*, third
तुड़ाना *tuṛānā*, to break, to cause to be broken; to get change for (money)
तुम *tum*, you III 165
तू *tū*, you III
तृतीय *tṛtīy*, third XI
तेल *tel*, m., oil
तेहरा *tehrā*, threefold 169
तैयार *taiyār*, ready XIX
तैयारियाँ *taiyāriyāṁ*, f.pl., preparations; तैयारियाँ करना (की) *taiyāriyāṁ karnā (kī)*, to prepare (for)
तो *to*, conj., then; but, etc. XX XXIII
तोड़ना *toṛnā*, to break (tr.)

थोड़ा *thoṛā*, a little; थोड़ा-सा *thoṛā-sā*, a little XXIV 167–8

दक्षिण *dakṣiṇ*, south
दफ़ा *dafā*, f., time, occasion I
दफ़्तर *daftar*, m., office
दबना *dabnā*, to be pressed down, restrained; दबे पाँव *dabe pāṁv*, stealthily
दरवाज़ा *darvāzā*, m., door; दरवाजे पर *darvāze par*, at the door
दर्ज़ी *darzī*, m., tailor
दर्द *dard*, m., pain
दस *das*, ten
दाढ़ी *dāṛhī*, f., beard
दाता *dātā*, m., a giver I
दादा *dādā*, m., paternal grandfather I
दान *dān*, m., donation; दान देना *dān denā*, to donate XIX
दाहिना *dāhinā*, right (hand); के दाहिनी (दाईं) तरफ़ *ke dāhinī (dāīṁ)*

*taraf*, on the right-hand side of VI
दिखना *dikhnā*, to be visible
दिखलाना *dikhlānā*, to show XVIII
दिखवाना *dikhvānā*, to cause to be shown (by) XVIII
दिखाई देना *dikhāī denā*, to be visible XII
दिखाना *dikhānā*, to show XVIII
दिन *din*, day; दिन भर *din bhar*, all day; दिनबदिन *dinbadin*, day by day; दिनों-दिन *dinoṁ-ḍin*, day by day VI XXII XXIII 179
दिल *dil*, m., heart
दिलचस्प *dilcasp*, interesting
दिलाना *dilānā*, to cause to be given
दिल्ली *dillī*, f., Delhi
दीखना *dīkhnā*, to be visible
दीवार *dīvār*, f., wall
दुख *dukh*, m., grief
दुनिया *duniyā*, f., world I
दुपट्टा *dupaṭṭā*, m., shawl
दूकान *dūkān*, f., shop [दुकान *dukān*]
दूध *dūdh*, m., milk
दूर *dūr*, f. and adj., distance; distant; कितनी दूर *kitnī dūr*, how far?
दूसरा *dūsrā*, second; other; दूसरी बार *dūsrī bār*, f., a second time, again
दूल्हा *dūlhā*, m., bridegroom 163
देखना *dekhnā*, to see; देख पड़ना *dekh paṛnā*, to be visible 174
देना *denā*, to give V VII XII XVII XXI
देर *der*, f., delay, lapse of time; पाँच मिनट देर से आना *pāṁc minaṭ der se ānā*, to come five minutes late
देवता *devtā*, m., deity I
देश *deś*, m., country
देशद्रोही *deśdrohī*, m., traitor
देहात *dehāt*, m., country(side)
दो *do*, two
दोनों *donoṁ*, both II
दोस्त *dost*, m., friend
दोहरा *dohrā*, twofold; fat 169
दौड़ना *dauṛnā*, to run
द्वितीय *dvitīy* second XI

धन्यवाद *dhanyavād*, thank you VII
धीरे *dhīre*, slowly (often reduplicated)
धुलना *dhulnā*, to be washed
धुलवाना *dhulvānā*, to cause to be washed (by) XVIII
धुलाना *dhulānā*, to cause to be washed XVIII
धूप *dhūp*, f., sun's heat or light
धोना *dhonā*, to wash
धोबी *dhobī*, m., washerman

न *na*, not V VII XIV 171 181 183
नज़र *nazar*, f., sight; glance
नदी *nadī*, f., river
नमस्कार *namaskār*, m., 'greetings'
नमस्ते *namaste*, m., 'greetings'
नया *nayā*, new
नहाना *nahānā*, to bathe XII
नहीं *nahīṁ*, no, not; नहीं तो *nahīṁ to*, otherwise III IV V XXIII 184
नाक *nāk*, f., nose
नाचना *nācnā*, to dance
नाम *nām*, m., name
नाला *nālā*, m., stream
नाश्ता *nāśtā*, m., breakfast, first light meal of the day
निकलना *nikalnā*, to emerge XVII
निकालना *nikālnā*, to eject; to take out, to extract; to drive out
निरपराध *niraparādh*, innocent, not guilty
निर्णय *nirṇay*, m., decision (between

alternatives)
निश्चय *niścay*, m., decision (resolve)
नींद *nīṁd*, f., sleep
नीचा *nīcā*, low; नीचा करना *nīcā karnā*, to lower; के नीचे *ke nīce*, below, underneath
नीला *nīlā*, blue; dark blue or green
ने *ne*, ppn. XII
नोट *noṭ*, m., note (money)
नौ *nau*, nine

पंक्ति *paṅkti*, f., line, row
पकड़ना *pakaṛnā*, to seize
पकना *paknā*, to ripen
पड़ना *paṛnā*, to fall; to be found; पड़ा *paṛā*, lying, placed flat IV XIII XVII
पड़ोसी *paṛosī*, m., neighbour
पढ़ना *paṛhnā*, to read; to study XII
पढ़ाना *paṛhānā*, to teach
पता *patā*, m., track, trace; address; मुझे पता नहीं (है) *mujhe patā nahīṁ (hai)*, I don't know, I have no idea
पति *pati*, m., husband
पत्ता *pattā*, m., leaf
पत्थर *patthar*, m., stone
पत्नी *patnī*, f., wife
पत्र *patr*, m., letter
पन्ना *pannā*, m., page
परंतु *parantu*, but 182
परंपरा *paramparā*, f., tradition
पर *par*, on; पर का *par kā*, (the one) on VI 178
परलोक *parlok*, m., the other world; परलोक सिधारना *parlok sidhārnā*, to depart for the next world
परसों *parsoṁ*, the day before yesterday, the day after tomorrow
परस्पर *paraspar*, mutual(ly), reciprocal(ly) XXV
परिचय *paricay*, m., acquaintance
परेशान (से) *pareśān (se)*, troubled (by)
पश्चिम *paścim*, m., west
पसंद आना (को) *pasand ānā (ko)*, to be pleasing (to)
पहचानना *pahcānnā*, to recognize
पहनना *pahnnā*, to put on (clothes); पहन रखना *pahn rakhnā*, to have on, to be wearing XVII XXVI
पहर *pahr*, m., 'a watch of the day or night' XI
पहला *pahlā*, first
के/से पहले *ke/se pahle*, before (time) VI
पहाड़ *pahāṛ*, m., mountain, hill
पहुँचना *pahuṁcnā*, to arrive XVII
पाँच *pāṁc*, five; पाँचवाँ *pāṁcvāṁ*, fifth
पाँव *pāṁv*, m., foot, leg
पाजामा *pājāmā*, m., light cotton trousers
पाना *pānā*, to get, to obtain; to find XVII XXI
पानी *pānī*, m., water
पार करना *pār karnā*, to cross (trans.)
के पास *ke pās*, beside; near; in the possession of VI IX
पिंजरा *piñjrā*, m., cage
पिघलना *pighalnā*, to melt (intr.)
पिछला *pichlā*, last
पिटना *piṭnā*, to be beaten
पिता *pitā*, m., father I
पिलाना *pilānā*, to give to drink XVIII
के पीछे *ke pīche*, behind; पीछे से *pīche se*, from behind
पीटना *pīṭna*, to beat
पीना *pīnā*, to drink VII
पुत्र *putr*, m., son

पुरस्कार *puraskār*, m., reward
पुल *pul*, m., bridge
पुलिस *pulis*, f., police
पुस्तक *pustak*, f., book
पुस्तकालय *pustakālay*, m., library
पूछना *pūchnā*, to ask, to inquire IV XII XVI
पूर्णतः *pūrṇtaḥ*, fully 179
पूर्णतया *pūrṇtayā*, fully 179
पूर्व *pūrv*, m., east
पूर्वज *pūrvaj*, m., ancestor
पेंसिल *peṃsil*, f., pencil
पेड़ *peṛ*, m., tree
पैदल *paidal*, on foot; पैदल चलनेवाला *paidal calnevālā*, a pedestrian
पैदा *paidā*, born, produced; पैदा करना *paidā karnā*, to produce; to give birth to X
पैदावार *paidāvār*, f., produce
पैसा *paisā*, m., pice; money (often pl.)
पौन *paun*, three-quarters of XI
पौना *paunā*, three-quarters the amount of 169
पौने *paune*, less a quarter XI
प्यार *pyār*, m., love VI
प्याला *pyālā*, m., cup
प्यास *pyās*, f., thirst
प्रकार *prakār*, m., type, kind; सब प्रकार से *sab prakār se*, in every way
प्रगति *pragati*, f., progress
प्रतीक्षा करना (की) *pratīkṣā karnā (kī)*, to wait (for) X
प्रथम *pratham*, first XI
प्रयत्न *prayatn*, m., attempt; प्रयत्न करना (का) *prayatn karnā (kā)*, to try (to)
प्रयोग *prayog*, m., use; प्रयोग करना (का) *prayog karnā (kā)*, to use
प्रवेश *praveś*, m., entry, entrance; प्रवेश करना (में) *praveś karnā (meṁ)*, to enter
प्रशंसा *praśaṃsā*, f., praise; प्रशंसा करना (की) *praśaṃsā karnā (kī)*, to praise X
प्रश्न *praśn*, m., question
प्रसन्नता *prasannatā*, f., pleasure IX
प्रस्ताव *prastāv*, m., suggestion
प्रस्तुत *prastut*, ready, prepared XIX
प्राप्त *prāpt*, obtained; प्राप्त करना *prāpt karnā*, to obtain X
प्रिय *priy*, dear, beloved XVI
प्रेम *prem*, m., love, affection

फटना *phaṭnā*, to tear (intr.)
फ़र्ज़ *farz*, m., duty
फ़र्श *farś*, m., floor
फ़सल *fasl*, f., crop
फाड़ना *phāṛnā*, to tear (tr.)
फिर *phir*, again, then, next; फिर भी *phir bhī*, nevertheless XX
फूटना *phūṭnā*, to burst (intr.)
फूल *phūl*, m., flower
फ़ेल होना *fel honā*, to fail (an examination)
फोड़ना *phoṛnā*, to burst (tr.)
फ़ोन *fon*, m., telephone; मैं उसे फ़ोन करूँगा *maiṁ use fon karūṁgā*, I shall phone him; मेरा फ़ोन आया *merā fon āyā*, someone telephoned me

बंद *band*, closed
बंदर *bandar*, m., monkey 163
बँधना *baṁdhnā*, to be tied, to be bound
बंबई *bambaī*, f., Bombay
के बग़ैर *ke bagair*, without XXIV
बचना *bacnā*, to be safe, saved
बचाना *bacānā*, to save, to rescue

बच्चा *baccā*, m., child; baby
के बजाय *ke bajāy*, instead of XXIV
बजे *baje*, o'clock X
बड़ा *baṛā*, large
बढ़ना *baṛhnā*, to advance; to rise
बढ़िया *baṛhiyā*, good, nice II
बतलाना *batlānā*, to relate, to inform XVIII
बताना (को) *batānā* (*ko*), to tell, to inform (one) XVII
बदतर *badtar*, worse XVI
बदलना *badalnā*, to change XVIII
बधाई *badhāī*, f., congratulations
बनना *bannā*, to be made; to become 167
बनाना *banānā*, to make, to construct
बनारस *banāras*, m., Banaras
बरस *baras*, m., year
बरसात *barsāt*, f., rainy season
बर्फ़ *barf*, f., ice, snow
बलिष्ठ *baliṣṭh*, strong, sturdy XVI
बल्कि *balki*, but rather 183
बल्ला *ballā*, m., pole
बहन *bahn*, f., sister
बहुत *bahut*, adj. and adv., much, many; very; बहुत दिनों से *bahut dinoṁ se*, for (i.e. since) a long time; बहुत-सा *bahut-sā*, much XVI XXIV
बाँधना *bāṁdhnā*, to tie, to bind
बाक़ी *bāqī*, remaining, left over
बाज़ार *bāzār*, m., bazaar; बाज़ार जाना *bāzār jānā*, to go to the bazaar, to go shopping
बात *bāt*, f., thing said; matter, concern; बात करना (से), बातें करना (से) *bāt*(*eṁ*) *karnā* (*se*), to talk (to) 166
के बाद *ke bād*, after; बाद में *bād meṁ*, afterwards VI
बाध्य *bādhya*, compelled; बाध्य करना (पर, के लिए) *bādhya karnā* (*par*, *ke lie*), to compel (to)
बायाँ *bāyāṁ*, left (hand); के बाईं तरफ़ *ke bāīṁ taraf*, on the left hand side of II VI
बार *bār*, f., time, occasion; एक बार *ek bār*, once 166
बारिश *bāriś*, f., rain; बारिश होना *bāriś honā*, to rain
के बारे में *ke bāre meṁ*, concerning
के बावुजूद *ke bāvujūd*, in spite of
के/से बाहर *ke/se bāhar*, outside VI
बिकना *biknā*, to be sold
बिखरना *bikharnā*, to be scattered
बिखेरना *bikhernā*, to scatter
बिछाना *bichānā*, to spread (trans.)
बिठाना *biṭhānā*, to give a seat XVII
बिताना *bitānā*, to spend (time)
बिदा करना *bidā karnā*, to dispatch; to see off X
बिदा होना *bidā honā*, to depart
के बिना *ke binā*, without XXIV
बिल *bil*, m., bill (account)
बिलकुल *bilkul*, completely, quite
बिस्तर *bistar*, m., bedding
बीतना *bītnā*, to pass by (of time)
बीसी *bīsī*, f., a score XI
बुधवार *budhvār*, m., Wednesday XI
बुनियादी *buniyādī*, basic; elementary
बुरा *burā*, bad, wicked
बुराई *burāī*, f., badness, wickedness; बुराई करना (की) *burāī karnā* (*kī*), to slander
बुलाना *bulānā*, to call, to summon; to invite
बूढ़ा *būṛhā*, old (of persons); m., old man
बृहस्पतिवार *bṛhaspativār*, m., Thursday XI

बेचना *becnā*, to sell
बेचारा *becārā*, adj, helpless, 'poor'
बेज़ार *bezār*, displeased, bored
बेटा *beṭā*, m., son
बेटी *beṭī*, f., daughter
बेफ़िक्री *befikrī*, f., carefreeness
बेवक़ूफ़ *bevaqūf*, stupid
बेवक़ूफ़ी *bevaqūfī*, f., stupidity
बेहतर *behtar*, better XVI
बेहतरीन *behtarīn*, best, choice XVI
बैठना *baiṭhnā*, to sit; बैठा *baiṭhā*, seated, sitting IV XVII
बैल *bail*, m., ox, bullock
बोलना *bolnā*, to speak, to talk IV XII

भरना *bharnā*, to be filled; to fill XVIII 179
भाई *bhāī*, m., brother
भाग *bhāg*, m., part
भागना *bhāgnā*, to run away, to flee
भारत *bhārat*, m., India
भारतवर्ष *bhāratvarṣ*, m., India
भारतीय *bhārtīy*, adj. and m.f., Indian
भालू *bhālū*, m., bear
भाषण *bhāṣaṇ*, m., speech, lecture
भाषा *bhāṣā*, f., language
भिखारी *bhikhārī*, m., beggar
भिगोना *bhigonā*, to make wet XVIII
भी *bhī*, emphatic enclitic V 180
भीगना *bhīgnā*, to be wet
भीगा *bhīgā*, wet
भूख *bhūkh*, f., hunger
भूल *bhūl*, f., error
भूलना *bhūlnā*, to forget XII
भेजना *bhejnā*, to send

मंगलवार *maṅgalvār*, m., Tuesday XI
मंत्र *mantra*, m., incantation
मंत्री *mantrī*, m., secretary, minister
मंदिर *mandir*, m., temple
मकान *makān*, m., house
मगर *magar*, but 182
मच्छड़दानी *macchaṛdānī*, f., mosquito net
मज़बूत *mazbūt*, strong (of objects)
मजबूर *majbūr*, compelled; मजबूर करना (पर) *majbūr karnā* (*par*), to compel (to)
मज़ाक़ *mazāq*, m., joke; मज़ाक़ करना *mazāq karnā*, to joke
मत *mat*, negative particle VII
मतलब *matlab*, m., intention, purpose
मदद *madad*, f., help; मदद देना (को) *madad denā* (*ko*), to help
मन *man*, m., a maund (= 40 seers)
मन *man*, m., mind; heart
मना *manā* (invariable), forbidden
मनुष्य *manuṣya*, m., man, human being
मरना *marnā*, to die
मशीन *maśīn*, f., machine
महँगा *mahaṁgā*, expensive
महल *mahl*, m., palace
महीना *mahīnā*, m., month VI
माँ *māṁ*, f., mother
माँग *māṁg*, f., request
माता *mātā*, f., mother; माता-पिता *mātā-pitā*, m.pl., parents
मादा *mādā*, female (adj.) II
मानों *mānoṁ*, as if
मारना *mārnā*, to beat; to kill
के मारे *ke māre*, because of XXV
माल *māl*, m., goods, belongings
मालूम *mālūm*, known; मुझे मालूम है *mujhe mālūm hai*, I know; मुझे मालूम होता है *mujhe mālūm hotā hai*, it seems to me IX
मिठाई *miṭhāī*, f., sweet

मित्र *mitr*, m., friend
मिनट *minaṭ*, m., minute
मिर्च *mirc*, f., pepper; chilli
मिलना *milnā*, to accrue; to be available; to meet; to resemble; मिलाना (से) *milānā (se)*, to bring together; to introduce (to), to cause to meet (with) XV
मिस्तरी *mistrī*, m., mechanic, (skilled) workman
मुनासिब *munāsib*, appropriate XXI
मुलज़िम *mulzim*, m., accused person
मुलाक़ात *mulāqāt*, f., meeting, encounter; मुलाक़ात होना (से) *mulāqāt honā (se)*, to meet
मुश्किल *muśkil*, f. and adj., difficulty; difficult; मुश्किल से *muśkil se*, with difficulty VI
मुसकराना *muskarānā*, to smile XII
मुसकराहट *muskarāhaṭ*, f., a smile
मुहल्ला *muhallā*, m., suburb
में *meṁ*, in; में से *meṁ se*, from among VI XI 178
मेज़ *mez*, f., table
मेला *melā*, m., festival, fair; माघ मेला *māgh melā*, m., bathing festival held at Allahabad in the month of Māgh
मेहनत *mehnat*, f., labour, effort
मेहरबानी *mehrbānī*, f., kindness VII
मैं *maiṁ*, I
मैला *mailā*, dirty
मोटर *moṭar*, f., car
मोल लेना *mol lenā*, to buy
मौसम *mausam*, m., season, weather

यदि *yadi*, if XX
यद्यपि *yadyapi*, although XX
यमुना *yamunā*, f., River Jumna
यह *yah*, this II III 171
यहाँ *yahāṁ*, here
यहीं *yahīṁ*, at this (particular) place XXIII
या *yā*, or 182 183
याद *yād*, f., memory XIX
यूनिवर्सिटी *yūnivarsiṭī*, f., university
यूरोपीय *yūropīy*, adj. and m. f., European
योजना *yojnā*, f., scheme, plan; पंचवर्षीय योजना *pañcvarṣīy yojnā*, five-year plan

रखना *rakhnā*, to put, to place; to keep XVII XXI
रचना *racnā*, to create, to produce
रवाना करना *ravānā karnā*, to dispatch; to see off X
रवाना होना *ravānā honā*, to depart X
रविवार *ravivār*, m., Sunday XI
रस्सा *rassā*, m., rope
रस्सी *rassī*, f., rope; string 165
रहना *rahnā*, to stay, to remain, to live XXII 171
राजधानी *rājdhānī*, f., capital
राजपूत *rājpūt*, m. and adj., Rajput
राजा *rājā*, m., rajah I
रात *rāt*, f., night VI
राधा *rādhā*, f., Rādhā (girl's name)
रामचरितमानस *rāmcaritmānas*, m., name of a work by Tulsīdās
राष्ट्र *rāṣṭra*, m., state, nation
राष्ट्रभाषा *rāṣṭrabhāṣā*, f., national language
रास्ता *rāstā*, m., road, street
रिक्शा *rikśā*, m., rickshaw
रुकना *ruknā*, to stop (intr.)
रुपया *rupayā*, m., rupee; money (usually pl.)
रुलाना *rulānā*, to make weep
रूप *rūp*, m., form; के रूप में *ke rūp meṁ*,

as, in the capacity of; . . . रूप से . . . *rūp se*, adv. marker 179
रोकना *roknā*, to stop, to check
रोज़ *roz*, m., day; adv., daily
रोटी *roṭī*, f., bread (chapatti)
रोना *ronā*, to cry, to weep XII
रेल *rel*, f., railway train; रेल से *rel se*, by train
रेस्टरेंट *resṭareṇṭ*, m., restaurant

लंदन *landan*, m., London
लंबा *lambā*, long; tall
लकड़ी *lakṛī*, f., wood
लगना *lagnā*, to be applied, attached, etc.; to begin XXI
लजाना *lajānā*, to be ashamed XVIII
लड़का *laṛkā*, m., boy
लड़की *laṛkī*, f., girl
लड़ना *laṛnā*, to fight; to quarrel
लड़ाई *laṛāī*, f., war
लता *latā*, f., creeper
लदना *ladnā*, to be laden
लदवाना *ladvānā*, to cause to be loaded (by) XVIII
लदाना *ladānā*, to cause to be laden XVIII
लाइब्रेरी *lāibrerī*, f., library
लाख *lākh*, one hundred thousand XI
लाठी *lāṭhī*, f., staff
लादना *lādnā*, to load
लाना *lānā*, to bring XII
लायक़ *lāyaq*, suitable (for, के *ke*); देखने लायक़ *dekhne lāyaq*, worth seeing
लाल *lāl*, red
के लिए *ke lie*, for XIX
लिखना *likhnā*, to write
लिटाना *liṭānā*, to put lying down XVIII
लिवाना *livānā*, to cause to be taken, brought
लुटना *luṭnā*, to be looted
लू *lū*, f., a hot dusty wind which blows in north India in May and June; लू लगना (को) *lū lagnā (ko)*, to get sunstroke
लूटना *lūṭnā*, to loot
ले आना *le ānā*, to bring VII XII
ले चलना *le calnā*, to take away VII
ले जाना *le jānā*, to take away VII XII
लेकिन *lekin*, but XX 171 182
लेख *lekh*, m., essay, article
लेटना *leṭnā*, to lie down
लेना *lenā*, to take V VII XVII
लोग *log*, m. pl., people; सब लोग *sab log*, everyone
लौटना *lauṭnā*, to return

वकील *vakīl*, m., lawyer
वक़्त *vaqt*, m., time
वजह *vajah*, f., reason; इस वजह से for this reason XX
वरन् *varan*, but rather 183
वरना *varnā*, otherwise 184
वर्ष *varṣ*, m., year
वह *vah*, that II III 171
वहाँ *vahāṁ*, there
वहीं *vahīṁ*, at that (particular) place XXIII
वा *vā*, or 182
वाक्य *vākya*, m., sentence
वापस करना *vāpas karnā*, to give back X
-वाला *-vālā* XXV
विचार *vicār*, m., thought; opinion
विजय *vijay*, f., victory, triumph
विदेशी *videśī*, m.f. and adj., foreigner; foreign

विद्यार्थी *vidyārthī*, m., student 164
विशेष *viśeṣ*, particular; विशेष रूप से *viśeṣ rūp se*, in particular 179
विश्वविद्यालय *viśvavidyālay*, m., university
विश्वास *viśvās*, m., faith, confidence; विश्वास करना (पर) *viśvās karnā* (*par*), to believe, to believe to be true
विषय *viṣay*, m., subject, matter, topic
वैसा *vaisā*, of that sort
वैसे *vaise*, adv., well (introductory); वैसे ही *vaise hī*, merely, casually 167
व्यस्त *vyast*, busy

शकल *śakl*, f., face, features; form
शत्रु *śatru*, m., enemy
शनिवार *śanivār*, m., Saturday XI
शब्द *śabd*, m., word
शहर *śahr*, m., city, town
शाम *śām*, f., evening, late afternoon VI XI
शायद *śāyad*, perhaps; शायद ही *śāyad hī*, scarcely ever V XXI 171
शुक्रवार *śukravār*, m., Friday XI
शुक्रिया *śukriyā*, thank you VII
शुरू करना *śurū kaṛnā*, to begin (trans.) X 176
शेर *śer*, m., tiger; lion
शोर *śor*, m., noise
श्री *śrī*, m., 'Mr.' III
श्रीमती *śrīmatī*, f., 'Mrs.' III
श्रेष्ठ *śreṣṭh*, very good, best XVI

षडयंत्र *ṣaḍyantra*, m., plot

संकोच *saṅkoc*, m., shyness, embarrassment
संतुष्ट *santuṣṭ*, satisfied
संदूक़ *sandūq*, m., box
संबंध *sambandh*, m., connection, relationship
संभव *sambhav*, possible, probable XXI
संभवत: *sambhavataḥ*, probably, possibly XXI 179
संयोग *saṃyog*, m., chance; संयोग से *saṃyog se*, by chance
संस्कृति *saṃskṛti*, f., culture
सकना *saknā*, to be able to . . . XV
सच *sac*, m., truth
सड़क *saṛak*, f., street, road
सफल *saphal*, successful
सफ़ेद *safed*, white
सब *sab*, all; सब किताबें *sab kitābeṁ*, all the books
सभ्यता *sabhyatā*, f., civilization
समझना *samajhnā*, to understand XII
समझाना *samjhānā*, to explain
समय *samay*, m., time; उस समय *us samay*, at that time
समाचार *samācār*, m. (sg. and pl.), news; समाचारपत्र *samācārpatr*, m., newspaper
समाप्त *samāpt*, finished; समाप्त करना *samāpt karnā*, to finish (trans.)
समुद्र *samudr*, m., sea, ocean
समेटना *sameṭnā*, to collect together (tr.)
सरीखा *sarīkhā*, like XXIV
सर्दियाँ *sardiyāṁ*, f. pl., cold season
सर्वश्रेष्ठ *sarvśreṣṭh*, foremost, supreme XVI
सवा *savā*, plus a quarter; one and a quarter times XI
सवाया *savāyā*, one and a quarter times the amount of 169

सवारी *savārī*, f., passenger; vehicle; fare
सवाल *savāl*, m., question
सवेरा *saverā*, m., morning VI
सस्ता *sastā*, cheap
सहनशील *sahnśīl*, tolerant
सहसा *sahsā*, suddenly
सहस्र *sahasra*, a thousand XI
सहायता *sahāytā*, f., help
सा *sā*, 'similar to' XXIV
साड़ी *sāṛī*, f., sari
साढ़े *sāṛhe*, plus a half XI
सात *sāt*, seven
के साथ *ke sāth*, together with
साधु *sādhu*, m., holy man
साफ़ *sāf*, clean; clear
के सामने *ke sāmne*, in front of
सामान *sāmān*, m., belongings, goods, things
सारा *sārā*, entire, all; सारा दिन *sārā din*, all day
साल *sāl*, m., year VI
सावधान *sāvdhān*, careful
सावधानी *sāvdhānī*, f., care; सावधानी से *sāvdhānī se*, carefully
सिखलाना *sikhlānā*, to teach XVIII
सिखाना *sikhānā*, to teach
सिग्रेट *sigreṭ*, f.m., cigarette
सिपाही *sipāhī*, m., soldier
सिमटना *simaṭnā*, to contract
सिर *sir*, m., head
सिर्फ़ *sirf*, only
के सिवा(य) *ke sivā(y)*, except for XXIV
सिसकना *sisaknā*, to sob
सीखना *sīkhnā*, to learn 176
सीट *sīṭ*, f., seat; नीचे की सीट *nīce kī sīṭ*, lower seat
सीता *sītā*, f., Sītā (girl's name)
सीधा *sīdhā*, direct, straight VI
सीना *sīnā*, to sew IV
सुंदर *sundar*, beautiful
सुनना *sunnā*, to hear; सुन पड़ना *sun paṛnā*, to be audible 174
सुनाई देना *sunāī denā*, to be audible XII
सुनाना *sunānā*, to tell, to relate
सुनिए *sunie*, excuse me! (in attracting attention)
सुबह *subah*, f., morning VI XI
सुलाना *sulānā*, to put to sleep, to rock to sleep
सुश्री *suśrī*, f., 'Miss' III
सुस्ताना *sustānā*, to rest XVIII
सूचना *sūcnā*, f., information
सूरज *sūraj*, m., sun
सूरत *sūrat*, f., face, form
से *se*, from; by, with; to; than IV VI XVI XVIII
सेर *ser*, m., a seer (approx. 1 kg.)
सेवा *sevā*, f., service
सैकड़ा *saikṛā*, an amount of a hundred, a century XI
सोचना *socnā*, to think
सोना *sonā*, to sleep XII
सोमवार *somvār*, m., Monday XI
स्कूल *skūl*, m., school; स्कूल में *skūl meṁ*, at school
स्टेशन *sṭeśan*, m., station
स्त्री *strī*, f., woman
स्थिति *sthiti*, f., position I
स्नान *snān*, m., bathing; स्नान करना *snān karnā*, to bathe
स्याही *syāhī*, f., ink
स्वयं *svayaṃ*, oneself XXV
स्वाभाविक *svābhāvik*, natural
स्वीकार *svīkār*, m., acceptance; स्वीकार करना *svīkār karnā*, to accept

हँसना *haṁsnā*, to laugh; to smile XII
हज़ार *hazār*, a thousand XI
हटना *haṭnā*, to move away, to withdraw
हफ़्ता *haftā*, m., week VI
हम *ham*, we 165
हमेशा *hameśā*, always
हर *har*, each, every; हर (एक) दिन *har (ek) din*, every day; हर कोई *har koī*, everyone; हर जगह *har jagah*, everywhere
हरा *harā*, green
हवा *havā*, f., air, wind I
हवाई जहाज़ *havāī jahāz*, m., aeroplane
हवाई पत्र *havāī patr*, m., air letter
हाँ *hām̐*, yes III
हाथ *hāth*, m., hand
हाथी *hāthī*, m., elephant 163
हाल *hāl*, m., state, condition
हालाँकि *hālām̐ki*, although XX
हिंदी *hindī*, f., Hindi
हिंदुस्तान *hindustān*, m., India
हिंदू *hindū*, m. and adj., Hindu
हिरण *hiraṇ*, m., deer
हिस्सा *hissā*, m., part
ही *hī*, emphatic enclitic V XXIII
हैं *haiṁ*, are
है *hai*, is
हुआ *huā*, became; adv., ago IV XXVI 171
होकर *hokar*, 'having been'; via VII
होना *honā*, to be, to become IV V XIII

## ENGLISH–HINDI

a, an, एक *ek*
abandon, to, छोड़ना *choṛnā*
able to, to be, सकना *saknā*
about, (approximately) के क़रीब *ke qarīb*; (concerning) के बारे में *ke bāre meṁ*
above, के ऊपर *ke ūpar*
accept, to, स्वीकार करना *svīkār karnā*; to accept (a statement, etc.) मानना *mānnā*
accompany, to, हो लेना *ho lenā*
accrue, to, मिलना *milnā*
accused person, मुलज़िम *mulzim*, m.
acquaintance, परिचय *paricay*, m.
act, to, अमल करना *amal karnā*
additional, और *aur*
address, पता *patā*, m.
advance, to, बढ़ना *baṛhnā*
aeroplane, हवाई जहाज़ *havāī jahāz*, m.
affection, प्रेम *prem*, m.
after, के बाद *ke bād*
afternoon, दो पहर के बाद *do pahr ke bād* (adv.); late afternoon, शाम *śām*, f.
again, फिर *phir*
ago, हुआ *huā*
Agra, आगरा *āgrā*, m.
aim (intention), उद्देश्य *uddeśya*, m.
air, हवा *havā*, f.; air-letter, हवाई पत्र *havāī patr*, m.
all, सब *sab*; (entire) सारा *sārā*; all the books, सब किताबें *sab kitābeṁ*; all around (sthg.), चारों ओर (के)

*cāroṁ or* (*ke*); all right (= I see), अच्छा *acchā*

Allahabad, इलाहाबाद *ilāhābād*, m.

alley, गली *galī*, f.

allow, to, -ने देना *-ne denā*

although, अगरचे *agarce*; यद्यपि *yadyapi*

always, हमेशा *hameśā*

am, हूँ *hūṁ*

ancestor, पूर्वज *pūrvaj*, m.

and, और *aur*; etc. (p. 182)

anna, आना *ānā*, m.

answer, जवाब *javāb*, m.; to answer (a person), जवाब देना (को) *javāb denā* (*ko*); (a letter), जवाब देना (का) *javāb denā* (*kā*)

apart from, के अलावा *ke alāvā*

appropriate, उचित *ucit*; मुनासिब *munāsib*

approximately, (के) क़रीब (*ke*) *qarīb*; (के) लगभग (*ke*) *lagbhag*

April, अप्रैल *aprail*, m.

are, हैं *haiṁ*

arrangement(s), इंतज़ाम *intazām*, m.

arrive, to, पहुँचना *pahuṁcnā*

article (essay), लेख *lekh*, m.

as, (in the capacity of) के रूप में *ke rūp meṁ*; as if, जैसे *jaise*

ask, to (= inquire), पूछना *pūchnā*

ass, गधा *gadhā*, m.

attack, आक्रमण *ākramaṇ*, m.; to attack, आक्रमण करना (पर) *ākramaṇ karnā* (*par*)

attempt, प्रयत्न *prayatn*, m.; to attempt, प्रयत्न करना (का) *prayatn karnā* (*kā*)

audible, to be, सुनाई देना *sunāī denā*

available, to be, मिलना *milnā*; प्राप्त होना *prāpt honā*

awake, to be, जागना *jāgnā*

baby, बच्चा *baccā*, m.

bad, ख़राब *kharāb*; (wicked) बुरा *burā*

badness (wickedness), बुराई *burāī*, f.

ball, गेंद *geṁd*, f.

Banaras, बनारस *banāras*, m.

bank, किनारा *kinārā*, m.

basic, बुनियादी *buniyādī*

bathe, to, नहाना *nahānā*; स्नान करना *snān karnā*

bazaar, बाज़ार *bāzār*, m.

bear, भालू *bhālū*, m.

beard, दाढ़ी *dāṛhī*, f.

beat, to मारना *mārnā*; पीटना *pīṭnā*

beautiful, सुंदर *sundar*

because, चूँकि *cūṁki*; क्योंकि *kyoṁki*; because of (impelled by) के मारे *ke māre*

become, to, होना *honā*; बनना *bannā*

bedding, बिस्तर *bistar*, m.

before, (time) के/से पहले *ke/se pahle*; (time and place) के/से आगे *ke/se āge*

beggar, भिखारी *bhikhārī*, m.

begin, to, शुरू करना *śurū karnā*; आरंभ करना *ārambh karnā*

beginning, शुरुआत *śuruāt*, f.; आरंभ *ārambh*, m.

behind, के पीछे *ke pīche*; from behind, पीछे से *pīche se*

believe (= put faith in), to, विश्वास करना (पर) *viśvās karnā* (*par*)

belongings, सामान *sāmān*, m.

below, के नीचे *ke nīce*

beside, के पास *ke pās*

best, बेहतरीन *behtarīn*; श्रेष्ठ *śreṣṭh*

better, बेहतर *behtar*

bicycle, साइकिल *sāikil*, f.

bill (account), बिल *bil*, m.

bind, to, बाँधना *bāṁdhnā*

bird, चिड़िया *ciṛiyā*, f.
bite (of animals), to, काटना *kāṭnā*
black, काला *kālā*
blind, अंधा *andhā*
bloom, to, खिलना *khilnā*
blow, चोट *coṭ*, f.
blue; dark blue or green, नीला *nīlā*
boat (small), किश्ती *kiśtī*, f.
Bombay, बंबई *bambaī*, f.
book, किताब *kitāb*, f., पुस्तक *pustak*, f.
bored, बेज़ार *bezār*
born, to be, पैदा होना *paidā honā*
box, संदूक़ *sandūq*, m.
boy, लड़का *laṛkā*, m.
bread (chapatti), रोटी *roṭī*, f.
break, to, टूटना *ṭūṭna* (intr.); तोड़ना *toṛnā* (tr.)
'breakfast', नाश्ता *nāśtā*, m.
bridge, पुल *pul*, m.
bring, to, ले आना *le ānā*; लाना *lānā*
broken, to cause to be, तुड़ाना *tuṛānā*
brother, भाई *bhāī*, m.
building, इमारत *imārat*, f.
bullock, बैल *bail*, m.
burn, to, जलना *jalnā* (intr.); जलाना *jalānā* (tr.)
burst, to, फूटना *phūṭnā* (intr.), फोड़ना *phoṛnā* (tr.)
busy, व्यस्त *vyast*
but, पर *par*; लेकिन *lekin*; etc. (p. 182); but rather, बल्कि *balki*
buy, to, ख़रीदना *kharīdnā*; मोल लेना *mol lenā*
by, (means or agency) से *se*; (by a future time) तक *tak*

cage, पिंजरा *piñjrā*, m.
Calcutta, कलकत्ता *kalkattā*, m.
call (summon), to, बुलाना *bulānā*
camel, ऊँट *ūṁṭ*, m.
cane, छड़ी *chaṛī*, f.
capital, राजधानी *rājdhānī*, f.
car, मोटर *moṭar*, f.; कार *kār*, f.; गाड़ी *gāṛī*, f.
care, सावधानी *sāvdhānī*, f.; carefully, सावधानी से *sāvdhānī se*
carefreeness, बेफ़िक्री *befikrī*, f.
careful, सावधान *sāvdhān*
casually, वैसे ही *vaise hī*
cause, कारण *kāraṇ*, m.
certain, a, कोई *koī*
certainly, ज़रूर *zarūr*; अवश्य *avaśya*
chair, कुरसी *kursī*, f.
chance, संयोग *saṃyog*, m.; by chance संयोग से *saṃyog se*
change, to, बदलना *badalnā*
cheap, सस्ता *sastā*
child, बच्चा *baccā*, m.
chilli, मिर्च *mirc*, f.
cigarette, सिग्रेट *sigreṭ*, f.m.
city, शहर *śahr*, m.
civilization, सभ्यता *sabhyatā*, f.
class (school), क्लास *klās*, f.m.
clean, साफ़ *sāf*
clear, साफ़ *sāf*
climate, आबोहवा *ābohavā*, f. (p. 182); जलवायु *jalvāyu*, m.
closed, बंद *band*
cloth, कपड़ा *kapṛā*, m.
clothes, कपड़े *kapṛe*, m.pl.
coat, कोट *koṭ*, m.
coffee, काफ़ी *kāfī*, f.
cold, ठंडा *ṭhaṇḍā*; (cold temperature) ठंड *ṭhaṇḍ*, f.; a cold, ठंड *ṭhaṇḍ*, f.; cold season, सर्दियाँ *sardiyāṁ*, f.pl.
come, to, आना *ānā*
comfort, आराम *ārām*, m.
comfortable,, आरामदेह *ārāmdeh*

compel, to, मजबूर करना (पर, के लिए) *majbūr karnā* (*par, ke lie*); बाध्य करना (पर, के लिए) *bādhya karnā* (*par, ke lie*)
completely, बिलकुल *bilkul*
concerning, के बारे में *ke bāre meṁ*
condition (state), हाल *hāl*, m.
confidence, विश्वास *viśvās*, m.
congratulations, बधाई *badhāī*, f.
connection, संबंध *sambandh*, m.
consider (as), to, मानना *mānnā*
construct, to, बनाना *banānā*
cool, ठंडा *ṭhaṇḍā* (q.v.)
correct, ठीक *ṭhīk*
count, to, गिनना *ginnā*
country, देश *deś*, m.
course of action, चारा *cārā*, m.
courtyard, आँगन *āṁgan*, m.
cow, गाय *gāy*, f.
create, to, रचना *racnā*
creep, to, घुसना *ghusnā*
creeper, लता *latā*, f.
crop, फ़सल *fasl*, f.
cross, to (tr.), पार करना *pār karnā*
crowd, भीड़ *bhīṛ*, f.
cry, to, रोना *ronā*
culture, संस्कृति *saṃskṛti*, f.
cup, प्याला *pyālā*, m.
cupboard, अलमारी *almārī*, f.
curry, तरकारी *tarkārī*, f.
cut, to be, कटना *kaṭnā*
cut, to, काटना *kāṭnā*

daily, रोज़ *roz*
dance, to, नाचना *nācnā*
dark, अँधेरा *aṁdherā*
darkness, अँधेरा *aṃdherā*, m.
date, तारीख़ *tārīkh*, f.
daughter, बेटी *beṭī*, f.
day, दिन *din*, m.; रोज़ *roz*, m.; all day, दिन भर *din bhar*; day after tomorrow, परसों *parsoṁ*; day before yesterday, परसों *parsoṁ*
dear (beloved), प्रिय *priy*; dearest, प्रियतम *priytam*
decision, (resolve) निश्चय *niścay*, m.; (between alternatives) निर्णय *nirṇay*, m.
deer, हिरण *hiraṇ*, m.
delay, देर *der*, f.
Delhi, दिल्ली *dillī*, f.
depart, to, बिदा होना *bidā honā*; रवाना होना *ravānā honā*
descend, to, उतरना *utarnā*
detachment (group), छक्का *chakkā*, m.
dictionary, कोश *koś*, m.
die, to, मरना *marnā*
difficult, मुश्किल *muśkil*; कठिन *kaṭhin*
difficulty, मुश्किल *muśkil*, f.; (trouble) तकलीफ़ *taklīf*, f., कष्ट *kaṣṭ*, m.
direct, सीधा *sīdhā*
direction, तरफ़ *taraf;* f.; ओर *or*, f.
dirty, मैला *mailā*
dispatch, to, बिदा करना *bidā karnā*; रवाना करना *ravānā karnā*
dissatisfied, असंतुष्ट *asantuṣṭ*
distance, दूर *dūr*, f.; दूरी *dūrī*, f.
distant, दूर *dūr*
district (administrative), ज़िला *zilā*, m.
do, to, करना *karnā*
doctor, डाक्टर *ḍākṭar*, m.
dog, कुत्ता *kuttā*, m.
donkey, गधा *gadhā*, m.
door, दरवाज़ा *darvāzā*, m.; at the door, दरवाज़े पर *darvāze par*
drink, to, पीना *pīnā*

drive around (tr.), to, घुमाना *ghumānā*

duty, फ़र्ज़ *farz*, m.

each, हर *har*

ear, कान *kān*, m.

earn, to, कमाना *kamānā*

ease, आसानी *āsānī*, f.; easily, आसानी से *āsānī se*

east, पूर्व *pūrv*, m.

easy, आसान *āsān*

eat, to, खाना *khānā*

edge, किनारा *kinārā*, m.

egg, अंडा *aṇḍā*, m.

eight, आठ *āṭh*

either . . . or, या . . . या *yā . . . yā*

eject, to, निकालना *nikālnā*

elementary, बुनियादी *buniyādī*; प्रारंभिक *prārambhik*

elephant, हाथी *hāthī*, m.

embarrassment, संकोच *saṅkoc*, m.

emerge, to, निकलना *nikalnā*

empty, ख़ाली *khālī*

end, अंत *ant*, m.

enemy, शत्रु *śatru*, m.f.

English, अँग्रेज़ी *aṁgrezī*; English language, अँग्रेज़ी *aṁgrezī*, f.; Englishman, Englishwoman, अंग्रेज़ *aṁgrez*, m.f.

entire, सारा *sārā*

entrance, प्रवेश *praveś*, m.

entry, प्रवेश *praveś*, m.; to enter, प्रवेश करना (में) *praveś karnā (meṁ)*

error, भूल *bhūl*, f.

estate (land), जायदाद *jāydād*, f.

European, यूरोपीय *yūropīy*, adj. and m.f.

evening, शाम *śām*, f.

every, हर *har*; every day, हर (एक) दिन *har (ek) din*; everyone, सब लोग *sab log*, m.pl., हर कोई *har koī*, sg.; everywhere, हर जगह *har jagah*

except for के सिवा(य) *ke sivā(y)*

excess (harsh action), अत्याचार *atyācār*, m.

excuse me, (in attracting attention) सुनिए *sunie*

exercise book, कापी *kāpī*, f.

expensive, महँगा *mahaṁgā*

explain, to, समझाना *samjhānā*

extra, और *aur*

extract, to, निकालना *nikālnā*

eye, आँख *āṁkh*, f.

face (features), चेहरा *cehrā*, m.; शकल *śakl*, f.

fail (an examination), to, फ़ेल होना *fel honā*

fair, मेला *melā*, m.

faith, विश्वास *viśvās*, m.

fall, to, पड़ना *paṛnā*; गिरना *girnā*

far as, as, तक *tak*

farmer, किसान *kisān*, m.

father, पिता *pitā*, m.

fear, डर *ḍar*, m.

fear, to, डरना *ḍarnā*

features, चेहरा *cehrā*, m.; शकल *śakl*, f.

feed, to, खिलाना *khilānā*

festival, मेला *melā*, m.

few, कम *kam*; थोड़ा *thoṛā*; a few, कुछ *kuch*, एक आध *ek ādh*

field, खेत *khet*, m.

fight, to, लड़ना *laṛnā*

fill, to, भरना *bharnā*

filled, to be, भरना *bharnā*

find, to (= succeed in meeting), पाना *pānā*

fine, O.K., ठीक *ṭhīk*

finish, to, ख़त्म करना <u>kh</u>atm karnā; समाप्त करना samāpt karnā; चुकना cuknā (intr., p. 89)
fire, आग āg, f.
five, पाँच pāṁc
floor, फ़र्श farś, m.
flower, फूल phūl, m.
fodder, चारा cārā, m.
food, खाना khānā, m.
foot, पाँव pāṁv, m.; on foot, पैदल paidal
for, के लिए ke lie
forbidden, मना manā (invariable)
foreign, विदेशी videśī
foreigner, विदेशी videśī, m.f.
foremost (supreme), सर्वश्रेष्ठ sarv-śreṣṭh
forget, to, भूलना bhūlnā
form, रूप rūp, m.; शकल śakl, f.
fort, क़िला qilā, m.
found, to be, पड़ना paṛnā; मिलना milnā
four, चार cār
free (available), ख़ाली <u>kh</u>ālī; फ़्री frī
fresh, ताज़ा tāzā
Friday, शुक्रवार śukravār, m.
friend, दोस्त dost, m.; मित्र mitr, m.
from, से se
front of, in, के सामने ke sāmne; (out in front of) के आगे ke āge
fully, पूर्णतः pūrṇtaḥ

Ganges, गंगा gaṅgā, f.
get up, to, उठना uṭhnā
girl, लड़की laṛkī, f.
give back, to, वापस करना vāpas karnā; लौटाना lauṭānā
glance, नज़र nazar, f.; दृष्टि dṛṣṭi, f.
glass (drinking), गिलास gilās, m.
go, to, जाना jānā; (move) चलना calnā; to go away, चला जाना calā jānā
good, अच्छा acchā
goods माल māl, m.; (belongings, luggage) सामान sāmān, m.
grain, अनाज anāj, m.
grass, घास ghas, f.
graze, to, चरना carnā
green, हरा harā
'greetings', नमस्ते namaste; नमस्कार namaskār
grief, दुख dukh, m.
grow, to (intr.), उगना ugnā

half, आधा ādhā, adj. and m.
hand, हाथ hāth, m.
happening, घटना ghaṭnā, f.
happiness, ख़ुशी <u>kh</u>uśī, f.; प्रसन्नता prasannatā, f.
harvest, to, काटना kāṭnā
hat, टोपी ṭopī, f.
he, वह vah
head, सिर sir, m.
health (state of), तबीयत tabīyat, f.
hear, to, सुनना sunnā
heart, दिल dil, m.; मन man, m.
help, मदद madad, f.; सहायता sahāytā, f.
help, to, मदद देना (को) madad denā (ko), etc.
here, यहाँ yahāṁ
hide, to (tr.), छिपाना chipānā
high, ऊँचा ūṁcā
hill, पहाड़ pahāṛ, m.
Hindi, हिंदी hindī, f.
Hindu, हिंदू hindū, m.
history, इतिहास itihās, m.
holiday, छुट्टी chuṭṭī, f.
holy man, साधु sādhu, m.
home, घर ghar, m.; at home, घर पर ghar par

hope, आशा *āśā*, f.
horse, घोड़ा *ghoṛā*, m.
hot, गरम *garm*; hot season, गरमियाँ *garmiyāṁ*, f.pl.
hour, घंटा *ghaṇṭā*, m.
house, मकान *makān*, m.; घर *ghar*, m.
how? (adv.) कैसे *kaise*; (adj.) कैसा *kaisā*; how far? कितनी दूर *kitnī dūr*; how long? कितने दिन *kitne din*, कब तक *kab tak*; how many? कितना *kitnā*
however much, जितना *jitnā*; जितना भी *jitnā bhī*; कितना ही . . . क्यों न *kitnā hī . . . kyoṁ na*
hunger, भूख *bhūkh*, f.
hungry, to be, भूख लगना (को) *bhūkh lagnā (ko)*
husband, पति *pati*, m.

I, मैं *maiṁ*
ice, बर्फ़ *barf*, f.
if, अगर *agar*; यदि *yadi*
ill, बीमार *bīmār*
in, में *meṁ*
incantation, मंत्र *mantra*, m.
incident, घटना *ghaṭnā*, f.
inconvenience, असुविधा *asuvidhā*, f.
India, भारत *bhārat*, m.; भारतवर्ष *bhāratvarṣ*, m.; हिंदुस्तान *hindustān*, m.
Indian, adj. and m.f., भारतीय *bhārtīy*
Indra, इंद्र *indra*, m.
inform, to, बताना *batānā*
information, ख़बर *khabar*, f.; सूचना *sūcnā*, f.
inhabitant, रहनेवाला *rahnevālā*, m.; निवासी *nivāsī*, m.
ink, स्याही *syāhī*, f.
innocent, निरपराध *niraparādh*
inquire, to, पूछना *pūchnā*
inside, के अंदर *ke andar*
instead of, के बजाय *ke bajāy*
intention, मतलब *matlab*, m.; उद्देश्य *uddeśya*, m.
interesting, दिलचस्प *dilcasp*
into, में *meṁ*
introduce, to, मिलाना (से) *milānā (se)*
invite, to, बुलाना *bulānā*
is, है *hai*
it, वह *vah*

jar, घड़ा *ghaṛā*, m.
joke, मज़ाक़ *mazāq*, m.; to joke, मज़ाक़ करना *mazāq karnā*
Jumna (Yamuna) यमुना *yamunā*, f.
jump, to, कूदना *kūdnā*
just as, जैसे *jaise*

keep, to, रखना *rakhnā*
key, चाबी *cābī*, f.
kill, to, मारना *mārnā*
kind (type), तरह *tarah*; प्रकार *prakār*, m.
know, to, जानना *jānnā*; पता होना (को) *patā honā (ko)*; see *known*
knowledge, ज्ञान *jñān*, m.
known, मालूम *mālūm*; I know, मुझे मालूम है *mujhe mālūm hai*; it seems to me, मुझे मालूम होता है *mujhe mālūm hotā hai*

labour, मेहनत *mehnat*, f.
lack, कमी *kamī*, f.
laden, to be, लदना *ladnā*
land, ज़मीन *zamīn*, f.
language, भाषा *bhāṣā*, f.
large, बड़ा *baṛā*
last, पिछला *pichlā*

late, देर से *der se* (adv.)
laugh, to, हँसना *haṁsnā*
lawyer, वकील *vakīl*, m.
leaf, पत्ता *pattā*, m.
leap, to, कूदना *kūdnā*
learn, to, सीखना *sīkhnā*
least, at, कम से कम *kam se kam*
leave, छुट्टी *chuṭṭī*, f.
leave, to, छूटना *chūṭnā* (intr.); छोड़ना *choṛnā* (tr.)
lecture, भाषण *bhāṣaṇ*, m.
left (hand) बायाँ *bāyāṁ*; on the left-hand side of, के बाईं तरफ़ *ke bāīṁ taraf*
leg, पाँव *pāṁv*, m.
lest, कहीं . . . न *kahīṁ . . . na*
letter, चिट्ठी *ciṭṭhī*, f.; पत्र *patr*, m.
library, लाइब्रेरी *lāibrerī*, f.; पुस्तकालय *pustakālay*, m.
lie down, to, लेटना *leṭnā*
life, जीवन *jīvan*, m.
line (row), पंक्ति *paṅkti*, f.
lion, शेर *śer*, m.
little (of quantity), थोड़ा *thoṛā*; कम *kam*
little, a, थोड़ा *thoṛā*
live, to, जीना *jīnā*; (reside, stay) रहना *rahnā*
load, to, लादना *lādnā*
lock, ताला *tālā*, m.
London, लंदन *landan*, m.
long, लंबा *lambā*
long as, as, जब तक *jab tak*
long live, जय हो (की) *jay ho* (*kī*)
look, to, देखना *dekhnā*; to look at, की ओर देखना *kī or dekhnā*; to look for, ढूँढ़ना *ḍhūṁṛhnā*; तलाश करना *talāś karnā* (p. 58)
loot, to, लूटना *lūṭnā*
lose, to, खोना *khonā*
love, प्रेम *prem*, m.
low, नीचा *nīcā*
lower, to, नीचा करना *nīcā karnā*; झुकाना *jhukānā*
luggage, सामान *sāmān*, m.
lying (flat), पड़ा *paṛā*

machine, मशीन *maśīn*, f.
make, to, बनाना *banānā*
man, आदमी *ādmī*, m.; (human being; mankind) मनुष्य *manuṣya*, m.
manage, to, पाना *pānā* (pp. 104,134)
mango, आम *ām*, m.
many, बहुत *bahut*; ज्यादा *zyādā*; अधिक *adhik*
maund (weight), मन *man*, m.
meal, खाना *khānā*, m.
meaning, मतलब *matlab*, m.; अर्थ *arth*, m.
mechanic, मिस्तरी *mistrī*, m.
meet, to, मिलना *milnā* (*se* or *ko*); see next
meeting, मुलाक़ात *mulāqāt*; to meet, मुलाक़ात होना (से) *mulāqāt honā* (*se*)
melt, to (intr.), पिघलना *pighalnā*
memory, याद *yād*, f.
mentioned, to be, उल्लेख होना (का) *ullekh honā* (*kā*)
merely (casually), वैसे ही *vaise hī*
milk, दूध *dūdh*, m.
mind (and heart), मन *man*, m.
minute, मिनट *minaṭ*, m.
modern, आधुनिक *ādhunik*
moment, क्षण *kṣaṇ*, m.
Monday, सोमवार *somvār*, m.
money, पैसा *paisā* (sg. or pl.)
monkey, बंदर *bandar*, m.
monsoon, बरसात *barsāt*, f.
month, महीना *mahīnā*, m.

more, ज़्यादा zyādā; अधिक adhik

morning, सेरा saverā, m.; सुबह subah, f.

mosquito net, मच्छड़दानी macchaṛdānī, f.

mostly ज़्यादातर zyādātar

mother, माता, माँ mātā, mām̐, f.

mountain, पहाड़ pahāṛ, m.

move, to, चलना calnā; to move along, चला जाना calā jānā; to move back, हटना haṭnā (intr.)

movement (social, political), आंदोलन āndolan, m.

much, बहुत bahut; ज़्यादा zyādā; अधिक adhik

mutual, आपसी āpsī; परस्पर paraspar

name, नाम nām, m.

national language, राष्ट्रभाषा rāṣṭrabhāṣā, f.

natural, स्वाभाविक svābhāvik

near, के पास ke pās

necessary, ज़रूरी zarūrī; आवश्यक āvaśyak; is necessary, चाहिए cāhie

need, ज़रूरत zarūrat, f.

neighbour, पड़ोसी paṛosī, f.

neither . . . nor, न . . . न na . . . na

never, कभी नहीं kabhī nahīm̐

new, नया nayā

news, समाचार samācār, m. (sg. and pl.); ख़बर khabar, f.

newspaper, अख़बार akhbār, m.

next, अगला aglā

nice (good), बढ़िया baṛhiyā

night, रात rāt, f.

nine, नौ nau

no, नहीं nahīm̐

noise, शोर śor, m.

north, उत्तर uttar, m.

nose, नाक nāk, f.

not, नहीं nahīm̐; न na; मत mat

note (money), नोट noṭ, m.

now, अब ab

nowadays, आजकल ājkal

obey (a command, etc.), to, मानना mānnā

obtain, to, पाना pānā; प्राप्त करना prāpt karnā

occasion, बार bār, f.; (opportunity) अवसर avasar, m.

ocean, समुद्र samudr, m.

o'clock, बजे baje; at nine o'clock, नौ बजे nau baje

of, का kā

office, दफ़्तर daftar, m.

oh! अरे are

oil, तेल tel, m.

old (of persons), बूढ़ा būṛhā

on, पर par

once, एक बार ek bār

one, एक ek; one and a half, डेढ़ ḍeṛh; one and a quarter, सवा savā (invariable)

oneself, आप āp; ख़ुद khud; स्वयं svayam

only, सिर्फ़ sirf; केवल keval

open, to, खुलना khulnā (intr.); खोलना kholnā (tr.)

opinion, विचार vicār, m.; ख़याल khayāl, m.

opportunity, अवसर avasar, m.

or, या yā

ordinary, आम ām

other, दूसरा dūsrā

otherwise, नहीं तो nahīm̐ to

outside, के/से बाहर ke/se bāhar

own, one's, अपना apnā

ox, बैल bail, m.

page, पन्ना *pannā*, m.
pain, दर्द *dard*, m.
palace, महल *mahl*, m.
paper, काग़ज़ *kāg̲az*, m.
pare, to, छीलना *chīlnā*
parents, माता-पिता *mātā-pitā*, m.pl.
part, भाग *bhāg*, m.; हिस्सा *hissā*, m.
pass by (time), to, बीतना *bītnā*
passenger, सवारी *savārī*, f.
pedestrian, पैदल चलनेवाला *paidal calnevālā*, m.
pen, क़लम *qalam*, f.m.
pencil, पेंसिल *peṃsil*, f.
people, लोग *log*, m.pl.
pepper, मिर्च *mirc*, f.
perhaps, शायद *śāyad*; कदाचित् *kadācit*
photograph, तस्वीर *tasvīr*, f.; फोटो *foṭo*, f.
pice, पैसा *paisā*, m.
picture, तस्वीर *tasvīr*, f.; चित्र *citr*, m.
piercing, तीखा *tīkhā*
place, जगह *jagah*, f.
place, to, रखना *rakhnā*
plan (scheme), योजना *yojnā*, f.
pleasing, to be, पसंद आना (को) *pasand ānā (ko)*
pleasure, ख़ुशी *k̲huśī*, f.; प्रसन्नता *prasannatā*, f.
plot, षडयंत्र *ṣaḍyantra*, m.; साज़िश *sāziś*, f.
pocket, जेब *jeb*, f.
poem, कविता *kavitā*, f.
poet, कवि *kavi*, m.
pole, बल्ला *ballā*, m.
police, पुलिस *pulis*, f.
poor, ग़रीब *garīb*
population, आबादी *ābādī*, f.
possibly, संभवत: *sambhavataḥ*
post (mail), डाक *ḍāk*, f.; post office, डाकघर *ḍākghar*, m., डाकख़ाना *ḍākk̲hānā*, m.; postman, डाकिया *ḍākiyā*, m.
pot, घड़ा *ghaṛā*, m.
pour, to, डालना *ḍālnā*
practice, अभ्यास *abhyās*, m.; to practise, अभ्यास करना (का) *abhyās karnā (kā)*
praise, to, प्रशंसा करना (की) *praśaṃsā karnā (kī)*
preparations, तैयारियाँ *taiyāriyāṁ*; to prepare (for), तैयारियाँ करना (की) *taiyāriyāṁ karnā (kī)*
prepared, प्रस्तुत *prastut*
print, to, छापना *chāpnā*
printed, to be, छपना *chapnā*
probably, संभवत: *sambhavataḥ*
produce पैदावार *paidāvār*, f.
produce, to, पैदा करना *paidā karnā*
progress, तरक़्क़ी *taraqqī*, f.; प्रगति *pragati*, f.
proportion: in proportion as . . . so, ज्यों-ज्यों . . . त्यों-त्यों *jyoṁ-jyoṁ . . . tyoṁ-tyoṁ*
pull, to, खींचना *khīṁcnā*
punctually, ठीक वक़्त पर *ṭhīk vaqt par*
put, to, रखना *rakhnā*
put on (clothes), to, पहनना *pahnnā*; to have on, to be wearing, पहन रखना *pahn rakhnā*, पहने होना *pahne honā*

quarrel, झगड़ा *jhagṛā*, m.
quarrel, to, झगड़ना *jhagaṛnā*; लड़ना *laṛnā*
quarter, a, चौथाई *cauthāī*, f.
question, सवाल *savāl*, m.; प्रश्न *praśn*, m.
quickly, जल्दी (से) *jaldī (se)*
quite, (absolutely) बिलकुल *bilkul*; (to a large extent) काफ़ी *kāfī*

rain, बारिश *bāriś*, f.; to rain, बारिश होना *bāriś honā*; rainy season, बरसात *barsāt*, f.
raise, to, उठाना *uṭhānā*
rajah, राजा *rājā*, m.
read, to, पढ़ना *paṛhnā*
ready, तैयार *taiyār*; प्रस्तुत *prastut*
recognise, to, पहचानना *pahcānnā*
red, लाल *lāl*
refusal, इनकार *inkār*, m.; to refuse, इनकार करना (से) *inkār karnā (se)*
regret, अफ़सोस *afsos*, m.
relationship, संबंध *sambandh*, m.
remain, to, रहना *rahnā*; (stay) ठहरना *ṭhaharnā*
remaining, बाक़ी *bāqī*
remember, to, याद रखना *yād rakhnā*; etc. (see pp. 118–9)
repeat (a god's name, etc.), to, जपना *japnā*
request, माँग *māṁg*, f.
rescue, to, बचाना *bacānā*
resemble, to, मिलना (से) *milnā (se)*
resident, रहनेवाला *rahnevālā*
resound, to, गूँजना *gūṁjnā*
rest, आराम *ārām*, m.
restaurant, रेस्टरेंट *resṭarenṭ*, m.
return, to, लौटना *lauṭnā* (intr.)
reward, पुरस्कार *puraskār*, m.
rich, अमीर *amīr*
rickshaw, रिक्शा *rikśā*, m.
right (hand), दाहिना *dāhinā*; on the right hand side of, के दाहिनी (दाईं) तरफ़ *ke dāhinī (dāīṁ) taraf*
Rigveda, ऋग्वेद *ṛgved*, m.
ripen, to, पकना *paknā*
rise, to, उठना *uṭhnā*; (advance) बढ़ना *baṛhnā*
river, नदी *nadī*, f.
road, सड़क *saṛak*, f.; रास्ता *rastā*, m.
roof, छत *chat*, f.
room, कमरा *kamrā*, m.
rope, रस्सी *rassī*, f.; रस्सा *rassā*, m.
run, to, दौड़ना *dauṛnā*; to run away, भागना *bhāgnā*
rupee, रुपया *rupayā*, m.

safe, to be, बचना *bacnā*
sari, साड़ी *sāṛī*, f.
satisfied, संतुष्ट *santuṣṭ*
Saturday, शनिवार *śanivār*, m.
save, to, बचाना *bacānā*
saved, to be, बचना *bacnā*
say, to, कहना (से) *kahnā (se)*
scarcely ever, शायद ही *śāyad hī*
school, स्कूल *skūl*, m.; at school, स्कूल में *skūl meṁ*
score, बीसी *bīsī*, f.
scrape, to, छीलना *chīlnā*
sea, समुद्र *samudr*, m.
season, मौसम *mausam*, m.
seat, सीट *sīṭ*, f.; lower seat, नीचे की सीट *nīce kī sīṭ*
seat, to, बिठाना *biṭhānā* (see p. 108)
seated, बैठा *baiṭhā*
second, दूसरा *dūsrā*
secretary (minister), मंत्री *mantrī*, m.
see, to, देखना *dekhnā*; to see off, बिदा करना *bidā karnā*, रवाना करना *ravānā karnā*; to see to (attend to), देखना *dekhnā*
seem, to, मालूम होना *mālūm honā* (p. 51), जान पड़ना *jān paṛnā*
seer (weight), सेर *ser*, m.
seize, to, पकड़ना *pakaṛnā*
sell, to, बेचना *becnā*
send, to भेजना *bhejnā*
sentence, वाक्य *vākya*, m.
service, सेवा *sevā*, f.
seven, सात *sāt*

sharp, तीखा *tīkhā*
shawl, दुपट्टा *dupaṭṭā*, m.; चादर *cādar*, f.
she, वह *vah*
sheet, चादर *cādar*, f.
ship, जहाज़ *jahāz*, m.
shirt, क़मीज़ *qamīz*, f.; collarless shirt, कुरता *kurtā*, m.
shop, दूकान *dūkān*, f.
shopping, to go, बाज़ार जाना *bāzār jānā*
shortage, कमी *kamī*, f.
shout, to, चिल्लाना *cillānā*
show, to, दिखाना *dikhānā*
shyness, संकोच *saṅkoc*, m.
side (direction), तरफ़ *taraf*, f.
sight, नज़र *nazar*, f.; दृष्टि *dṛṣṭi*, f.
silent, चुप *cup*
since, (of time) जब से *jab se*, conj.; से *se*, ppn.; (because) चूंकि *cūṁki*, क्योंकि *kyoṁki*
sing, to, गाना *gānā*
sister, बहन *bahn*, f.
sit, to, बैठना *baiṭhnā*
sitting, बैठा *baiṭhā*
six, छह, छः, छै *chah, chaḥ, chai*
slander, to, बुराई करना (की) *burāī karnā* (*kī*)
sleep, नींद *nīṁd*, f.
sleep, to, सोना *sonā*
slink, to, घुसना *ghusnā*
slowly, आहिस्ता *āhistā*, आहिस्ते *āhiste*; धीरे *dhīre*: often reduplicated
small, छोटा *choṭā*
smile, मुसकराहट *muskarāhaṭ*, f.
smile, to, मुसकराना *muskarānā*; हँसना *haṁsnā*
snow, बर्फ़ *barf*, f.
so that, जिससे *jisse*; ताकि *tāki*
sob, to, सिसकना *sisaknā*
soldier, सिपाही *sipāhī*, m.; जवान *javān*, m. (p. 165)
someone, some (particular thing or person), कोई *koī*
something, some (indefinite), कुछ *kuch*
sometimes, कभी *kabhī* (often reduplicated)
somewhere, कहीं *kahīṁ*
son, बेटा *beṭā*, m.
song, गाना *gānā*, m.
soon, जल्दी (से) *jaldī* (*se*); as soon as, जैसे ही *jaise hī*, ज्योंही *jyoṁhī* (see also pp. 144–5)
south, दक्खिन *dakkhin*, m.; दक्षिण *dakṣiṇ*, m.
speak, to, बोलना (से) *bolnā* (*se*)
speech (lecture), भाषण *bhāṣaṇ*, m.
speed, जल्दी *jaldī*, f.
spend (time), to, बिताना *bitānā*
spite of, in, के बावुजूद *ke bāvujūd*
spoiled, ख़राब *kharāb*
spoon, चम्मच *cammac*, m.
spread, to, बिछाना *bichānā*
squad, छक्का *chakkā*, m.
staff (stave), लाठी *lāṭhī*, f.
stamp (postage), टिकट *ṭikaṭ*, m.f.
standing, खड़ा *khaṛā*
startled, to be, चौंकना *cauṁknā*
state, (condition) हाल *hāl*, m.; (nation) राष्ट्र *rāṣṭra*, m.
station, स्टेशन *sṭeśan*, m.
stay, to, रहना *rahnā*; ठहरना *ṭhaharnā*
stealthily, दबे पाँव *dabe pāṁv*
stick (cane), छड़ी *chaṛī*, f.
stone, पत्थर *patthar*, m.
stop, to, रुकना *ruknā* (intr.); रोकना *roknā* (tr.)
story, कहानी *kahānī*, f.
straight, सीधा *sīdhā*

stream, नाला *nālā*, m.
street, रास्ता *rāstā*, m.; सड़क *saṛck*, f.
string, रस्सी *rassī*, f.
strong (objects), मज़बूत *mazbūt*
student, विद्यार्थी *vidyārthī*, छात्र *chātr*, m.; छात्रा *chātrā*, विद्यार्थिनी *vidyārthinī*, f.
study, अध्ययन *adhyayan*, m.; to study, पढ़ना *paṛhnā*, अध्ययन करना (का) *adhyayan karnā* (*kā*)
stupid, बेवक़ूफ़ *bevaqūf*
stupidity, बेवक़ूफ़ी *bevaqūfī*, f.
subject, विषय *viṣay*, m.
suburb, मुहल्ला *muhallā*, m.
successful, सफल *saphal*
such, (of this sort) ऐसा *aisā*; (of that sort) वैसा *vaisā*
suddenly, अचानक *acānak*; सहसा *sahsā*
suggestion, प्रस्ताव *prastāv*, m.
suitable, उपयुक्त *upayukt*; suitable for, के लायक़ *ke lāyaq*; worth seeing, देखने लायक़ *dekhne lāyaq*
sun, सूरज *sūraj*, m.; sun's heat or light, धूप *dhūp*, f.
Sunday, रविवार *ravivār*, m.; इतवार *itvār*, m.
suppressed, to be, दबना *dabnā*
surround, to, घेरना *ghernā*
sway, to, झूमना *jhūmnā*
sweet, मिठाई *miṭhāī*, f.

table, मेज़ *mez*, f.
tailor, दर्ज़ी *darzī*, m.
take, to, लेना *lenā*; to take away, ले जाना *le jānā*; to take off, take down, उतारना *utārnā*
talk to, बोलना *bolnā* (*se*), बात (बातें) करना (से) *bāt*(*eṁ*) *karnā* (*se*)
tall, लंबा *lambā*
Tamil, तमिल *tamil*, m.
tank (reservoir, etc.), तालाब *tālāb*, m.
tea, चाय *cāy*, f.
teach, to, पढ़ाना *paṛhānā*; सिखाना *sikhānā*
teacher, अध्यापक *adhyāpak*, m.
tear, to, फटना *phaṭnā* (intr.); फाड़ना *phāṛna* (tr.)
telegram, तार *tār*, m.
telephone, फ़ोन *fon*, m.; to telephone, फ़ोन करना (को) *fon karnā* (*ko*); someone telephoned me, मेरा फ़ोन आया *merā fon āyā*
tell, to, कहना (से) *kahnā* (*se*); (relate) सुनाना (को) *sunānā* (*ko*)
temple, मंदिर *mandir*, m.
ten, दस *das*
than, से *se* (p. 92)
that (pron. and adj.) वह *vah*; as many/much as that, उतना *utnā*; of that sort, वैसा *vaisā*; (conj.) कि *ki*
then (= next) फिर *phir*
there, वहाँ *vahāṁ*
they, वे *ve*
thief, चोर *cor*, m.
thing (matter), बात *bāt*, f.
thing, चीज़ *cīz*, f.
think, to, सोचना *socnā*
third, a, तिहाई *tihāī*, f.
thirst, प्यास *pyās*, f.
thirsty, to be, प्यास लगना (को) *pyās lagnā* (*ko*)
this, यह *yah*; as many/as much as this, इतना *itnā*; of this sort, ऐसा *aisā*
thought, विचार *vicār*, m.; ख़याल *khayāl*, m.
three, तीन *tīn*; three-quarters of, पौन *paun*

throw down, to, डालना *ḍālnā*
Thursday, बृहस्पतिवार *bṛhaspativār*, गुरुवार *guruvār*, m.
tie, to, बाँधना *bāṁdhnā*
tied, to be, बँधना *baṁdhnā*
tiger, शेर *śer*, m.
time, समय *samay*, m.; वक़्त *vaqt*, m.; (occasion) बार *bār*, f., दफ़ा *dafā*, f.; at that time, उस समय *us samay*; for a long time, बहुत दिनों से *bahut dinoṁ se*; for some time, कुछ समय *kuch samay*
to, को *ko*; से *se*; की तरफ़ *kī taraf*; के पास *ke pās*
today, आज *āj*
tolerant, सहनशील *sahnśīl*
tomorrow, कल *kal*
tonga, ताँगा *tāṁgā*, m.
topic, विषय *viṣay*, m.; बात *bāt*, f.
towards, की तरफ़ *kī taraf*; की ओर *kī or*
town, शहर *śahr*, m.
trace, पता *patā*, m.
tradition, परंपरा *paramparā*, f.
train, रेल *rel*, f.; by train, रेल से *rel se*
traitor, देशद्रोही *deśdrohī*, m.
tree, पेड़ *peṛ*, m.
troubled, परेशान *pareśān*
trousers (cotton) पाजामा *pājāmā*, m.
truth, सच *sac*, m.
try, to, कोशिश करना (की) *kośiś karnā (kī)* प्रयतन करना
Tuesday, मंगलवार *maṅgalvār*, m.
two, दो *do*; two and a half, ढाई *ḍhāī*
type, प्रकार *prakār*, m.

underneath, के नीचे *ke nīce*
understand, to, समझना *samajhnā*
university, यूनिवर्सिटी *yūnivarsiṭī*; विश्वविद्यालय *viśvavidyālay*
until, जब तक . . . न *jab tak . . . na*
up to, तक *tak*
use, to, इस्तेमाल करना *istemāl karnā* (p. 58); प्रयोग करना (का) *prayog karnā (kā)*
usually, अक्सर *aksar*; प्राय: *prāyaḥ*; ज़्यादातर *zyādātar*; आम तौर पर/से *ām taur par/se*

vacation, छुट्टी *chuṭṭī*, f.
vehicle, गाड़ी *gāṛī*, f.; सवारी *savārī*, f.
very, बहुत *bahut*
via, होकर *hokar*
victory, विजय *vijay*, f.
village, गाँव *gāṁv*, m.
villager, गाँववाला *gāṁvvālā*, m.
visible, to be, दिखाई देना *dikhāī denā*; दीखना *dīkhnā*; दिखना *dikhnā*
voice, आवाज़ *āvāz*, f.

wait, to, ठहरना *ṭhaharnā*; to wait for, इंतज़ार करना (का) *intazār karnā (kā)*; प्रतीक्षा करना (की) *pratīkṣā karnā (kī)*
waken, to, जागना *jāgnā* (intr.); जगाना *jagānā* (tr.)
wall, दीवार *dīvār*, f.
wander, to, घूमना *ghūmnā*
war, लड़ाई *laṛāī*, f.
warm, गरम *garm*
wash, to, धोना *dhonā*
washerman, धोबी *dhobī*, m.
watch, to, की ओर देखना *kī or dekhnā*
watch, घड़ी *ghaṛī*, f.; by my watch, मेरी घड़ी में *merī ghaṛī meṁ*
water, पानी *pānī*, m.
way (manner), तरह *tarah*, f.; प्रकार *prakār*, m.; in every way, सब प्रकार से *sab prakār se*
we, हम *ham*

wear, to, पहने होना *pahne honā*; to give to wear, पहनाना (को) *pahnānā* (*ko*)
weather, मौसम *mausam*, m.
Wednesday, बुधवार *budhvār*, m.
week, हफ़्ता *haftā*, m.
well, कुआँ *kuāṁ*, m.
well, adv. अच्छा *acchā*; अच्छी तरह (से) *acchī tarah* (*se*); (all right) ठीक *ṭhīk*; to be well, तबीयत ठीक होना *tabīyat ṭhīk honā*
west, पश्चिम *paścim*, m.
wet, भीगा *bhīgā*
what? क्या *kyā*; what sort of? कैसा *kaisā*
when? कब *kab*
whenever, जब भी *jab bhī*
where? कहाँ *kahāṁ*
wherever, जहाँ भी *jahāṁ bhī*
whether . . . or, चाहे . . . चाहे *cāhe* . . . *cāhe*
which (particular thing or person)? कौन *kaun*
white, सफ़ेद *safed*
who, (interrogative) कौन *kaun*; the one who, जो *jo*
whoever, जो कोई *jo koī*
why? क्यों *kyoṁ*
wickedness, बुराई *burāī*, f.
wife, पत्नी *patnī*, f.
wind, हवा *havā*, f.
window, खिड़की *khiṛkī*, f.
wire, तार *tār*, m.
wish, to, चाहना *cāhnā*
with (together with), के साथ *ke sāth*
withdraw, to, हटना *haṭnā*
without, के बिना *ke binā*; के बग़ैर *ke bagair*
woman, स्त्री *strī*, f.; औरत *aurat*, f.
wood, लकड़ी *lakṛī*, f.
word, शब्द *śabd*, m.
work, काम *kām*, m.
workman (skilled), मिस्तरी *mistrī*, m.
world, दुनिया *duniyā*, f.; संसार *saṃsār*, m.; the next world, परलोक *parlok*, m.
worse, बदतर *badtar*
wounded, ज़ख़्मी *zakhmī*
wrap, to, ओढ़ना *oṛhnā*
write, to, लिखना *likhnā*

year, बरस *baras*, m.; साल *sāl*, m.; वर्ष *varṣ*, m.
yes, हाँ *hāṁ*
yesterday, कल *kal*
you, आप *āp*; तुम *tum*; तू *tū*
younger, छोटा *choṭā*; younger brother, छोटा भाई *choṭā bhāī*, m.; younger sister, छोटी बहन *choṭī bahn*, f.

zamindar, ज़मीनदार *zamīndār*, m.